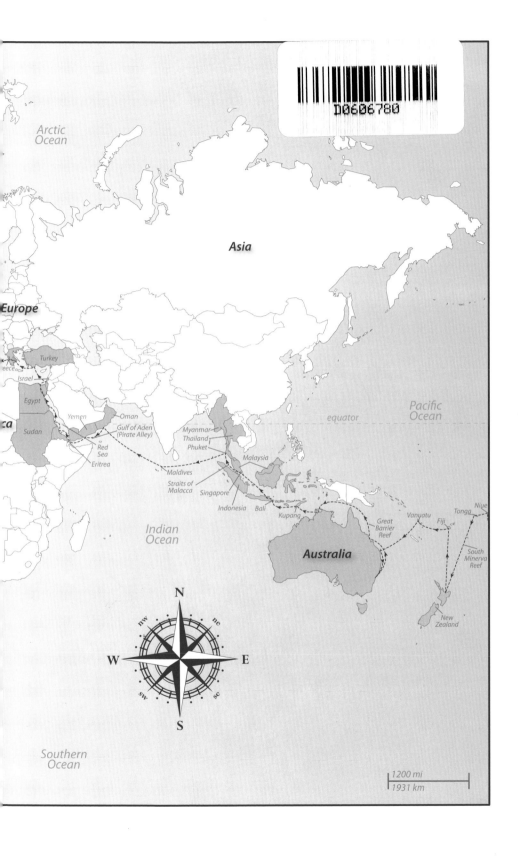

To Roger,

Thank you for
your support. May
all your dreams come
true!

[signature]

The Boy Behind the Gate

*How His Dream of Sailing Around the World
Became a Six-Year Odyssey of Adventure, Fear,
Discovery, and Love*

LARRY JACOBSON

BUOY PRESS / EMERYVILLE

For more photos, products and information about the author and journey:
www.larryjacobsonauthor.com

The author welcomes comments and questions at:
larry@larryjacobsonauthor.com

Published by:

Buoy Press
Emeryville, California
www.buoypress.com
sales@buoypress.com

Ordering information:
Orders by U.S. trade bookstores and wholesalers, please contact:
sales@buoypress.com

ISBN: 978-0-9828-787-9-8
Library of Congress Control Number: 2010913404

Book design and production by Joel Friedlander
www.TheBookDesigner.com

World map by Rachel Arends

Printed in the United States of America

Author's Notes

This book is based on a variety of sources. They include emails to and from friends and family, radio calls, the ship's logs, phone calls, and my personal journal. It's also supplemented with contemporaneous writings that hopefully fill in the gaps left when piecing all of the above together. Specifics include:

 Personal Journal entries, ship's log and emails: You're reading them as they were written, with the addition of some narrative and accurate dialog additions to emphasize certain moments. The grammar has been corrected, and definitions of nautical terms are included for the nautical novice.

New copy, written post-voyage, that fills in the gaps of information, is in italics.

Some names have been changed.

All latitude and longitude positions are accurate from logs. All course directions, wind speeds, wave heights, weather conditions, and other facts and figures are all taken directly from the ship's logs. Radio conversations are taken from radio logs. Many conversations are taken from meticulous journals. Some have even been transcribed from video onboard.

A note on time: All times onboard are based on a 24-hour clock. For those unfamiliar, here's the simple trick: If the time noted is 1259 or less, then you need not calculate anything. For example 1000 is 10 am. If the time noted is higher than 1259, say 1300, simply subtract 12 and you get the time of 1. You know it's pm because it's past 1259. 1 am would be 0100. Once again: If it's 0900, that's 9 am. If it's 2200, subtract 12 and get the answer of 10 pm.

Times used ashore are am and pm.

Unless otherwise indicated, all monetary amounts are in U.S. dollars.

Regarding measurements: Sea heights are commonly measured in meters or feet; I use feet for your ease of recognizing the size of the seas.

Regarding speeds: They are measured in knots, the common nautical language. A knot is approximately .13 percent faster than a mile per hour. Occasionally, I translate this 10 percent difference for you.

Latitude and longitude positions are given at points of interest to sailors and for those wishing to follow our specific route.

Told through email updates sent to friends, ship's log entries, and my personal journal, I reveal my most intimate thoughts and experiences including my hopes, fears, joys, sadness, and, ultimately, changes. *In some places, I have an email and a personal journal entry for the same event or day, which show how sometimes, what we say, is different than what we are thinking.*

Table of Contents

CHAPTER ZERO

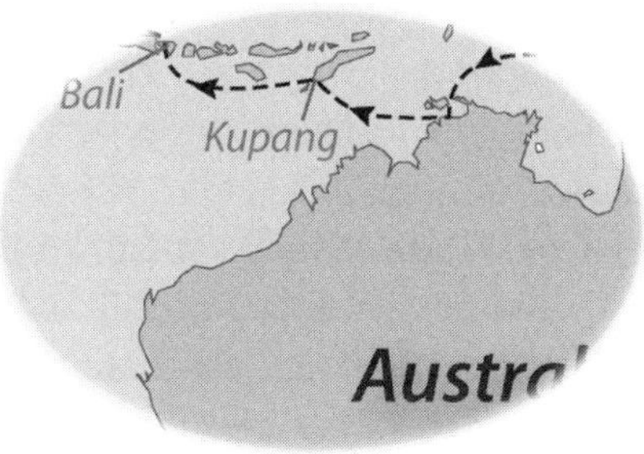

Will I Ever Sleep Through the Night Again?

"Sail Forth—steer for the deep waters only. Reckless O soul, exploring. I with thee and thou with me. For we are bound where mariner has not yet dared go. And we will risk the ship, ourselves, and all."
WALT WHITMAN

I can't help it. It's not my turn to be on watch, and this time, I am so tired I'm almost out before my head hits the pillow. I drift in and out of sleep for a couple of hours, but at 0300 wake up and call out the hatch to Ken, "How's it going up there?" No reply. "Hey, are you sleeping? You're supposed to be watching." Silence. "Ken?" I leap out of the bunk and race naked up the ladder to an empty cockpit. "Ken. Ken! This isn't funny! Where are you?" I sprint back below and search every cabin, then fly back up on deck and look over both sides to see if he is dragging alongside.

Nothing. He has vanished.

I hit the Man Overboard button on the GPS, jump to the wheel, and spin *Julia* around 180 degrees while starting the engine. The sails flap deafeningly, and the boom crashes back and forth over my head. We are only 10 miles from shore. Can he make it? Maybe a fishing boat will find him. "Mayday! Mayday! Mayday!" I shout into the radio. "This is the sailing vessel *Julia*. Man overboard! Man overboard! Position in the Malacca Straits is North 2°5', East 102°12'. Mayday! Mayday! Mayday!" There is no response, just the crackling of radio static. I try again, but there is no answer to my pleas. I scan the dark waters for any break in the waves or a strobe light. How could he have gone overboard? "Ken!" Oh no, I can't lose him. I just can't lose him. I keep searching and searching, but there is only dark, all-consuming sea.

I awake with a start—will I ever sleep through the night again? When will these nightmares stop? I lie awake in our apartment staring at the ceiling while Ken's deep breathing evenly rises and falls. Clearly, he's sailing in calm seas. I reach into my nightstand for the bottle of sleeping pills, pop one into my mouth, and whisper to myself, "Tomorrow, I'll sleep without pills." I grudgingly fall back down on the bed.

Soon, the drowsiness washes over me. As my mind settles into a haze, I think, *so this is what sailing around the world has done to me.* I end up in an apartment that certainly is not going to float away, but I can't sleep because of the dread that when I wake up to take my turn on watch, Ken will not be there—the victim of a rogue wave. I can't shut my mind off from the small noises of the night; they cause me to worry we are having another mechanical breakdown.

Six years is a long time to live and breathe the freedom of roaming the world's oceans at will. It's also a long time to endure foul weather, two-story waves, and ill-intended boats through pirate territory. I guess it's going to take a while longer for my transition back to land.

I try to picture us far away on a warm tropical beach in turquoise waters clearer than any swimming pool. Yet sometimes those images are overshadowed by memories of tools flying across the salon floor as we made engine repairs in 15-foot seas.

It was the same on the boat. I would usually go a couple of days without sleep until sheer exhaustion put me out. Even then, the slightest noise shook me awake, and I would be forced to start the fragile, often futile, process of falling asleep all over again.

While my rest hasn't improved much, lying next to my partner reminds me that if not by rest, at least I'm blessed by companionship. In six years circumnavigating the globe, I didn't lose Ken overboard and I didn't lose his love…. although, like being squeezed between ships in the Panama Canal, that was touch and go for a while. I drape my arm over Ken's shoulder, he moves into my embrace, and I join him on that warm tropical beach. This is my story.

CHAPTER 1

Shattered Dreaming

"Twenty years from now, you will be more disappointed by the things that you didn't do than by the ones you did do. So throw off the bowlines. Sail away from the safe harbor. Catch the trade winds in your sails. Explore. Dream. Discover."
MARK TWAIN

I don't remember having many dreams or wishes as a young boy. I was happy playing baseball in the streets of Long Beach, California, riding my bike, and enjoying every day like most other kids in our middle-class neighborhood. I had visions of someday being a major league baseball player—and being famous for hitting home runs out of nearby Dodger Stadium—but that was about it. Then something happened that changed everything. In an instant, I went from footloose and fancy-free to bedridden, and I had all the time in the world to dream.

When I was 13, I shattered both bones in my right leg while skiing and was laid up at home for more than three months in a hip-to-toe cast. My mother, Julia, who was well educated and trained as a registered nurse, tried every trick in the book to keep me smiling. I still remember her comforting food, her soothing voice of encouragement, loving care, and promises of better days to come. Day after day, I would stare out the window into the brilliant California sunshine and dream about life outside. I wanted to run with my dog in the park, play ball, and roam the streets. As I sunk into a depression, my family brought a variety of magazines and books to read. I searched to find something of interest amidst the periodicals—from *Boys Life* to *Popular Mechanics*—and found myself drawn to those about sea adventures. I asked for more and began to read everything I could get my hands on about boats, small and large; short trips and long ocean voyages. I imagined they could take me away on adventures that weren't yet clearly visible in my mind. They would set me free—and I would never be stuck in one place again.

Shortly after the cast came off, as I was hobbling around just enough to be annoying, my brother, Jeff, brought home an 8-foot Styrofoam Sea Snark dinghy he had scrounged from a garbage pile. While in pretty bad shape, it looked like a super yacht to me. I bought a can of bright yellow paint and began my first boat project, and that was the day I began dreaming of sailing around the world. At 13, of course, I had no clear picture of how that longing would play out; just that I would someday take on the Everest of sailing—circumnavigating. Self-taught, I sailed at every opportunity—it consumed me. In high school, I bought my next boat, a 14-foot twin-hulled Hobie Cat, and began racing. After school, several days a week, when the 3 o'clock school bell rang, I would hop on my bike and ride the 6 miles to Alamitos Bay where I kept my boat *Jake* to practice tacking, jibing, and the art of crossing the start line at just the right time. Sometimes I would sail *Jake* out the channel to open water and imagine what it would be like to keep going.

One Saturday, with two other Hobie Cat sailors, I kept going, and ended up sailing the 26 miles from Long Beach to Catalina Island in just three hours. From there, I called my parents to tell them what I had done; while it didn't seem like a big deal to me, my father was furious. He wanted me to take up his sport—golf—and spend weekends at the club, but not being even remotely interested in pursuing a little ball for miles on land, I continued to spend weekends sailing.

In the late summer afternoons, I would ride over to the marina where the big boats were docked. The gangways were always locked. I stood behind the gate staring at the yachts, imagining what it would be like to stand at the wheel, to back out of the slip, head up the channel, turn south, and keep going. Even then I didn't want to be the boy behind the gate. I wanted to be at the helm calling, "Cast off the bow, we're headed to sea."

Practice paid off as I regularly brought home trophies, including the 1969 California State Hobie Cat Championship. I was eager to get into the open ocean. My first experience sailing on a big boat happened with Mr. Derivas, my high school history teacher. He was a good sailor and instructor, and eventually became a circumnavigator. Around that time, 16-year-old Robin Lee Graham began his five-year circumnavigation, which was chronicled in several issues of *National Geographic* magazine. I didn't see any reason why I couldn't do the same.

As a boy, I didn't even consider that my fantasies were too big or too difficult. Once the dream seized me, my only option was to live it. In hindsight, I'm compelled to caution myself on what I put on my wish list, because now I believe I can make any of my dreams come true.

Fulfilling that vision was not easy. I spent 20 years in business, selling and operating group-incentive travel programs and conferences for corporations, and was fortunate to ride the high-tech wave. Our company chartered luxury ships and trains, arranged cocktail parties on top of glaciers, produced fabulous events in famous palaces, and treated our clients' guests like royalty. Flying first class around the world was glamorous— intercepted by limos at airports, staying in premium suites at the finest hotels, and dining at restaurants most people only read about in the pages of *Bon Appétit*.

It wasn't easy. Somewhere in between the cars and caviar, I worked long hours and surrendered most of my weekends to the business. And while the corporate world had equipped me with bankable planning skills, I still lacked the hands on mechanical proficiency that would be necessary to pilot a boat. I'm a sailor, not a mechanic. I grew up racing sailboats, not rebuilding pumps and engines.

My father wanted me to take auto mechanics in high school, and how I wish I had listened to him. Instead, I became class president and served in student government, and while that may have helped me in business, it didn't do much good when the engine broke down 500 miles from the nearest repair facility. It's funny how things turn out. Now I know more about the nuances of diesel mechanics than I ever would have learned in school—I just had to learn it the hard way.

How do you do it? How do you take that first step to make a vision become reality? While it may have begun with a dream, I believe turning that vision into a goal was critical. Here's how I started...I still have the piece of lined yellow paper on which I wrote my goals in 1991. Among them:

Ten years from now:
- Own a 50-foot boat
- Sail across the Pacific and cruise island to island

Five years from now:
- Honor Mom in a significant way

Three years from now:
- Run a medium-size business

It seems as though putting goals down on paper changes everything; not sure exactly how, but it works.

Everybody has dreams. Some people make plans for them, but the real challenge is actually working the plan. One day, you have to embrace the idea and immerse yourself in everything that will prepare you to let go of the dock lines and sail away. Then comes the hardest part about making it come true: *letting go.*

Imagine my situation. I was running a successful company with Bob Joyce, my life and business partner, living in a custom home in Berkeley, earning a decent income, driving a fast car, and pretty much living the American dream. I had a good life. Bob and I met 20 years earlier in a gay businessman's bar in San Francisco. His youthful good looks, big smile, and defined 6-foot tall muscular body seduced me. Good looks aside, it was his sense of humor; casual, easy manner; and self-confidence without pretense that really struck me. I had wanted to score that night, but he made us wait three months before we made it to the bedroom. Bob wanted to be sure that I was the right one, and that made me respect him. It turned out that we were both just right for each other, and while our years together weren't perfect, they were some of the best of my life.

At a certain point, though—three years before departure—I knew I was burned out. The business had taken its toll on our relationship, and we needed a break. While always in the back of my head, it wasn't until that point I saw the opportunity to make my fantasy of sailing a reality. Bob and I were able to sell the company, but after paying half of the profits in taxes, we were left with just enough money to tease me into thinking I could afford this journey.

I had it in my head that I was going for two to three years, and upon my return, I would still have a savings account. Looking back, that's almost funny. By the time I got home, nearly six years had passed, I no longer owned a house, and almost all the savings was gone. Part of my dream had assured me I wouldn't ever return to work, but life happens, doesn't it? After 40,000 miles and 10 years, sitting at the keyboard, and overlooking San Francisco Bay, the money may be gone, but my dream is fulfilled. And it was well worth the price. What's next? Author, speaker, motivator—these are some of my ideas, but how do I make them a reality? How did I do it before?

CHAPTER 2

Struggle With Identity—
What Happens If I Let Go?

"Once you make a decision,
the universe conspires to make it happen."
RALPH WALDO EMERSON

During my career, when asked what I did for a living, I would explain the incentive and motivation business. Now who am I? A sailor? A writer? An impulsive adventurer who one day gave it all up to see the world with no clear idea how it might turn out? I've encountered many people in my travels, and I ponder how they go through their lives wondering who they are, trying to identify with being "something."

One conclusion seems inescapable: We are much more than just what we do for a living. However, our career seems to be that with which we identify most often, if not most dearly. Join any conversation. When someone asks you about yourself, you almost invariably reply, "I'm a nurse"... or "a lawyer"...or "a plumber," etc. Even out in the cruising world, where it's almost taboo to ask about someone's previous life, many people asked me, "What did you do before you left to go sailing?" and so the identity of what we do to earn a living carries with us.

I was a whitewater rafting guide in California and New Zealand before it was "in." I was a travel agent, a young entrepreneur, and even started a group travel company with my college boyfriend, John van Duyl, soon after graduation. Then I became a business owner, and at last a circumnavigator. Now I can say, "I'm a writer."

While I may be happy with my new identity, I often wonder about those who aren't so pleased with who or what they are. I'm fortunate to have followed my dream to alter my life several times. What about people who are not happy in their current lives or are not fortunate enough, and find it difficult to change directions? Fear of what a change might bring is one of the main reasons many people never let go of an identity, and so they miss the opportunity to become something different—radically and positively—transforming their lives.

It's not necessarily difficulties that prevent us from doing great things. In fact, it's usually the good that prevents us from doing the great. Many people have a good home, partner, family, career, and income—why risk those things for the chance of something else? For me, it was the right thing to do. For you? Only you can answer that.

Circumnavigating the globe teaches you things about life. I've learned goals don't become reality without action. I'm not even sure if I saw the steps I was taking at the time, but looking back, I can see I had to:

- Overcome the fear of leaving the old and familiar;
- Rise above the fear of what the new might be;
- Make a plan;
- Identify and follow through on *the first step* in that plan.

The decision to quit a job to start my own company was one of the most difficult I ever had to face. Once I made that jump, things fell into place because I made them happen. At that point, there was really no choice in the matter: Make it work or there would be no money for the new mortgage. The day we left the Mexican coast and headed across the Pacific Ocean didn't leave us much choice of turning back. We were forced to follow through on our commitment.

It seems there are many days we have ideas, or plans become more formulated, or an opportunity arises. Yet we have to actually *act* to make things happen. Knowing when the time is right comes from listening for the knock on the door and acting consciously.

One day I woke up and a light bulb went off: "I need to go sailing." Action is often a process rather than an event. It was three years from that time until I sailed out the Golden Gate, my doorstep to the world.

You can *dream* about anything: to get into or out of a relationship, to get a new career, to better your present one or, as in my case, throw everything away and go cruising. The point is whether or not you ever make your dreams come true, at least you can try, and you never know where that will lead you next. One thing is certain: It will guide you out of a current situation you may be eager to leave or change. The rest will follow.

CHAPTER 3

Passion Trumps Fear

*"There is a time to take counsel of your fears,
and there is a time to never listen to any fear."*
GENERAL GEORGE S. PATTON

I admit the decision-making process was a mixture of excitement and cold feet. When it came right down to it, I had that Nike moment: *Just do it.* The decision to leave my known life came when there was no more information to help me decide one way or another. Like stepping off the curb to cross the street, or deciding what to have for lunch, the time had arrived to make the decision to go. After all the planning was complete and my crew and I were ready, we just left. No fanfare, no cheering crowds, there is no line you cross that makes it official. You just go, and all of a sudden you realize you have actually done it.

My exodus from a 20-year relationship with Bob was, to say the least, a tough decision. Sailing wasn't Bob's dream; he didn't want to leave everything and venture around the world, and I respected him. I had long been talking about sailing out the Golden Gate and turning left, but still I was torn. Bob was my partner, my best friend, and my rock. He still is the definition of values that are dear to me, including loyalty, dedication, and kindness. Yet we both recognized we were ready for a break. And I needed to at least attempt to make this crazy idea of sailing a reality. It was scary to both of us as we were treading new waters with no real experience how to move on from the safety of our relationship. There were many days I found myself an emotional wreck, unsure if I was doing the right thing, but I remained determined to at least try to do this for me. If I didn't go, I felt I would be letting myself down. Bob was incredibly supportive, but I'm sure he had thoughts of, "All right, go already!"

Then there was the financial situation. I was used to having an income, so I won't kid you, letting go of my future security was truly difficult. While I was busy making the departure happen, there wasn't any thought about a post-sailing plan. I left home with no idea if, or when, I would return, but ignorance is bliss…. I'm not suggesting that one should leave without a plan, but don't let too much planning dissuade you from making your voyage—whatever that may be. Imagine what I would have missed had I allowed the fear of not knowing what would come discourage me from going. I originally left with the intention of sailing south to Mexico, and then crossing the Pacific to New Zealand and Australia. After that, I really wasn't sure what would happen.

Oh, I was definitely scared. Unsure of my return, I left friends and family not knowing when—or if—I would ever see them again. My mother thought I was absolutely crazy and wrote me frequent emails reminding me to "Watch out for sharks," and "Why don't you turn that boat around and sail home so I can cook chicken soup for you?" For the most part, though, friends and family, including Mom, were overwhelmingly supportive to see someone live out his fantasy. Some said they had never seen anybody actually quit their current life, but that was before watching me walk away (or in my case, sail away) and do precisely that. For that matter, I'd never known anyone who had done it either. With no real guidance from others, I was forced to pretty much figure things out along the way, being led only by my own heart and desire.

More than deciding to go, I had to be brave. Or blind and stupid. Maybe inspired passion? I could see what I was doing, and it definitely seemed like an extreme idea. Nevertheless, I kept going, drawn to my vision with a pull I couldn't resist. And though I had been sailing nearly all of my life, I wasn't prepared for the magnitude of challenges involved in sailing around the world.

I learned to face my fears about leaving and went anyway. I learned I had to be the one who makes my dreams come true. They don't just happen on their own and rarely will anyone make them happen for you. So I untied my dock lines and followed my heart. Perhaps by reading and living what I have done, you too will be encouraged to follow your own path.

This is not just the story of me fulfilling a lifelong passion. It is also a story of the lessons I learned from my experiences on this trip, from the sea, and from the people I met along the way. And it's the story of the changes that took place in me. I still find it surprising to read my first emails and journal entries that show how little I knew at the beginning. How ignorant I was of what cruising was really about, how wound up I was about the wrong things, how upset I became when something broke, and how, by the end of the trip, I was a changed man in so many ways. The decisive way I deal with things now, I owe to this journey. The way I appreciate the love I have in my life comes from knowing what it's like to feel alone. Before the trip, I was uncomfortable not knowing what tomorrow would bring, but now I see each new day as another adventure and opportunity to enjoy this wonderful world. I'm older, and I've spent all of my money, but I'm wiser and wealthier than if I had all the riches in the world.

CHAPTER 4

You Can't Leave 'Til It Floats

*"Take a chance! All life is a chance. The person who goes far-
thest is generally the one who is willing to do and dare. The
'sure thing' boat never gets far from shore."*
DALE CARNEGIE

Thinking I had found the perfect cruising boat, I sent the details to
Nick Barraud, my good friend and sailor, to share my excitement. He
quickly emailed back with the typical wit I have grown accustomed to
over the years. Nick was born in England, and even though he moved to
Switzerland as a young boy, that British sense of humor has stuck, and I
can always count on him for a dry and direct retort. We met early in my
travel career while his company was handling operations for one of our
groups. I once commented that I was surprised he was so funny because
I had never met a humorous Swiss before. He said he hadn't either and
then owned up to his British background. So I wasn't taken aback by his
email response:

"You can't buy one of *those*."

"Why not?" I countered, "They have all kinds of great cruising features."

Nick was unmoved and sent another message: "I said, you cannot buy one of those."

I pressed my case: "Once more, why not?"

"Because they're ugly, and life is too short for ugly boats."

I knew Nick was right; it was back to the Internet to continue the search for a better boat. After months and months of looking with Stuart Fox, my tireless and patient yacht broker, seeing dozens of boats, and dragging my friend Bill Claypool to various cities across the country, I finally found her in Fort Lauderdale, Florida.

"Florida?" asked Stuart, his eyebrows raised. "You couldn't find a boat you like on the West Coast?"

"Nope," I reconfirmed, "this is the one I want," and then drifted off into my "This is what I want...." A few minutes later (or an hour, in Stuart's version), I concluded with, "It has the best of all cruising boats combined into one: speed, space, comfort, ruggedness, and beauty." And that was that.

With her raised salon and flat foredeck adorning a sweeping hull that came to a narrow beam in the stern, she was gorgeous, even though in need of some fixing up, about $70,000, worth according to the marine surveyor. I was about to learn my first lesson from the sea: When it comes to boats, things cost about three times what you'd expect. I ended up putting close to $200,000 in improvements into a 1986 Stevens 50 cutter-rigged sloop to bring her up to the standard I deemed acceptable to cross oceans. The list seemed endless, and from the time she was delivered in March 2001 to the boatyard in Alameda—on a very large truck—until we sailed nine months later, I worked on her day and night.

And so did my friends. Bill Claypool is a sailor, but unlike me at the time, he's mechanical. Yet he offered more than mechanics. From the moment Bill and I met a few years earlier, it seemed we had known each other all our lives, our most common bond being a positive view of life. In his youth, Bill was a model, and though 10 years my senior, and standing 6 foot, 2 inches, with striking features and blond hair, he still turns heads everywhere he goes. And he smiles a lot; even while giving advice about the work we were doing onboard. While Bill wasn't eager to see me leave, he encouraged me to follow through and kept me focused on the goal.

About the same time, I met Patrik Hendrickson via the Internet when he answered my ad on a local sailing bulletin board: "Gay skipper looking for crew…" At 32, Patrik was calm as if he had already experienced many things in life. Raised in the Iowa farmlands, looking like the all-American boy, he was young at heart, energetic, and without a career to tie him down, was keen to sail away to a tropical paradise where there were no cornfields. Patrik (no "c") spent countless hours at the boatyard to prove his intentions, and became a loyal friend and valuable crew member.

And then there was Ken Smith. I also met Ken on the Internet, back in 1995 when it was just bulletin board postings. At the time, I was looking for a weekend sailing buddy, and got so much more. See, it pays to advertise. Ken was 30; his slim body and short schoolboy haircut made him look like he hadn't even reached 21 years old yet. His good looks were matched by a boyish, puppy dog way of looking at life—happy and eager. We were attracted to each other right away, and we fast became weekend sailing and bedroom buddies.

For the things we couldn't do ourselves, we hired boat builders Barrett and Rob, Neal the electrician, and Peter the sail maker. I had to rent a storage space for the overflow of gear while we worked on the boat, and the garage at our home was packed end to end. Did I mention that the to-do list was endless? The list had lists! What had I done?

With my assembled crew, we replaced almost all of the existing equipment on board: the main engine, most of the electrical wiring, systems, and electronics panel. We also addressed all plumbing and rigging, bought new sails, installed a new watermaker, and instruments, including radar and chart plotters. We moved on to the installation of new computers, monitors, TV, propeller shaft, steering pedestal and wheel, and even a fresh water misting system in the cockpit to keep us cool in the tropics. We were going so fast and didn't fully know what we were doing, which is why we also removed the Aqua-Drive, a flexible coupling for the propeller shaft—you'll hear about this fateful mistake later.

I determined the need for most of the equipment replacements based on the fact that I didn't want to spend my time with breakdowns on my cruise. I wanted new equipment, and I wanted nothing but the best. We'll revisit almost all of this equipment during the next six years.

One thing I learned in the course of preparing for sea was to filter advice. Everyone in the marina knew we were leaving, and it was common for people to stop by and ask questions or offer recommendations. One lanky, grey-haired, armchair sailor who kept offering ideas, yet never took his boat out of the slip, was too much to take. He told us we didn't need all chain for anchoring, that we could use mostly line (a rope becomes a line aboard a boat) in order to save weight. We knew he was wrong, and proved it when our chain wrapped itself around a coral head in the Tuamotus, something that would have cut through line in a few minutes. My reply to him may have been a bit harsh: "Sorry, but I don't take advice from people who never leave the dock." That was the end of him.

With counsel coming from all directions and mounting refit issues, there were times that the whole idea of going just seemed too daunting. I thought we would never make a fall departure, and I considered putting it off for another year. That's when I started writing my personal journal, which allowed me to blow off steam.

Personal Journal / June 13, 2001

Plenty of people are telling me there are more reasons to stay than to go. "You don't have enough money." "You aren't ready." "You don't have the knowledge you need." "You don't have enough crew." "You can't leave this fall; you'll never make the weather window in time." "Forget it, wait 'til next year." I slump into my chair and wonder if they're right about these things, and then I get mad. Mad at them for doubting me, but mostly mad at myself for even considering their doubts. So the story about the chicken and the eagle is true? It's easy to stay where it's safe, but I'm doing this. I'm going to soar like the eagle and experience my full potential. I will dig deep inside to find what I need and make the voyage. I'm going.

Is this easy? Not even close. Scary? Very. Exciting? Yes, but there certainly are more surprises along the way I was not expecting. The knowledge? Not being ready? Nonsense. If I had let those things stand in my way before, I wouldn't have made it this far. As I learned in business, I am the one who must filter the noise and listen closely for the words. How do I know what to do and how to make the decisions I'm making regarding money, crew, and equipment? I don't, but I'm the captain, so I guess I better start acting like one.

Personal Journal / July 28, 2001

There I stood staring at the pipes and fittings in the hardware store. How many ways are there to plumb new drains in a sink? There are many; and I have to choose one. Based on what? I have no idea what I'm doing. It took me two hours and almost all of the next two days with lots of help from Bill. This kind of project makes it seem like business was easy.

I'm trying to use something I know well: organization. I delegate a priority to every project that goes on the list:

A = Must do before going to sea

B = Should do before going to sea

C = Would be nice to have (usually doesn't happen)

D = Someday we'll get to that (Don't count on it)

Too many things in the "A" category. How are we going to make it by fall?

Personal Journal / August 16, 2001

I feel like I'm on a freight train careening down the track at high speed to a destination unknown. Where will I be in a year? Two years?

We started the new engine today for the first time, and the sound perked my spirits up like a bright sun does after a rainstorm. That engine is going to take me on adventures and places I can't imagine. Sounded steady and solid…I hope it's a good sign.

Personal Journal / August 25, 2001 / The Naming Party

The tension building up to this day has been unnerving. We've all been working like dogs. Last night, Ken, Patrik and I stayed onboard until 0300, cleaning and polishing. We continued today until noon when I finally blew the "It's time to go shower" whistle.

More than 50 people showed up at Emery Cove Marina for the party; we went through two cases of champagne, including a magnum that was used to christen the boat. *Julia* is now official, and Mom was so happy the boat was named after her. *Julia* looked sharp: Freshly polished, she shined from stem to stern, and everyone who had worked on her was beaming. I barely made it through the ceremony without tears. It began with the captain's speech, something I had been working on for days:

"The boat you are looking at is what happens when dreams are combined with hard work. In this case, though, it may be *my dream*, but it most certainly is *not only my hard work*. I'm proud to say [I fibbed] there's nobody in this crowd who ever said, 'You'll never make it.' I thank everyone here, but special thanks are in order to a few who have gone above and beyond.

"First of all, to someone who has put more hours into this project for less money than ever should be allowed. A yacht broker should sell boats to buyers quickly and efficiently, but sorry for that gent who landed me as an account. Stuart Fox, thank you for your tireless patience, and interest in me." Ever-humble Stuart still couldn't manage to take credit when it was due but did manage a smile and raised his glass.

"To someone who has always encouraged me to follow my heart. My partner who for years lived with me rambling on about this whacky dream, choosing a boat, naming the boat, then endured a garage and house full of smelly gear, and never uttered a whimper of complaint. And how else am I going to be able to leave without somebody paying my bills and doing my taxes? Bob, thank you for the days and years, past and future." As he raised his glass in response, our eyes met and in that instant, we reconnected, professed our everlasting love, and said goodbye....

"Tradition is for the mast to be stepped on a gold coin, and this mast is stepped on a custom gold and sterling silver coin made by Brooke Battles and designed and brainstormed by Brooke and Bob. Thank you both for giving us good luck with this coin." Standing arm in arm, they tipped their glasses, and I knew that coin was made with love.

"Imagine what it would be like working on the boat, rebuilding systems, whether they are electrical, plumbing, or just cleaning out lockers, always having to do it 'Larry's way.' These guys worked day and night, from the dirtiest jobs to computerizing the boat, and they still want to go on the trip. A special thank you to my crew, Ken and Patrik." Dressed in new blue shorts and bright white shirts, Patrik and Ken stood so proudly I almost lost control of myself.

"The last special thank you goes to my friend Bill. He has unquestionable faith in me and has put huge amounts of energy and work into my boat, even though he has his own. When I would sit down and cry, 'What have I done?' while covered head to toe in oil and paint, it was Bill who would pick me back up. When I was tempted to compromise on anything less than the best, it was Bill who would remind me that wasn't acceptable. Without you Bill, we would not be here today." We stared at each other, saying everything that needed to be said…without uttering a word.

"How many of you were involved in the naming process? I considered: 'It's My Next Adventure,' 'I've Come Full Circle,' and the runner-up, 'I Told You I Was Going.' Ultimately, I wanted this boat to honor someone most special, someone who has endured the roughest that life could throw at you. I wanted this boat named after the person who has inspired me the most to keep going when things are tough, and from whom I can draw strength when my crew is looking to me to be strong. It was an easy choice—there is only one name for this boat that will carry my friends and me safely across oceans. With great pride and joy, I present: *JULIA.*"

On that, Ken and Patrik lifted a blue canvas, revealing the name for all to see. When the cheers and applause and oohs and aahs died down, it was only then Mom really 'got it.' Smiling, 80, and still going strong, Mommy Julia was sitting in the front row wearing her favorite color purple and looking a decade younger than her age. She stood up, pointed, and said, "Hey, that's *my* name!" As the light bulb went on, we could see her 'get it,' and she started to cry… the crowd cheered again. It was a beautiful moment and happened exactly as I imagined.

Following tradition, I asked Poseidon to take back the previous boat name, and poured expensive bubbly from East to West across the boat and into the water.

Then I asked Poseidon to bless the new name, *Julia.* More champagne from East to West.

And finally I appealed to the four wind gods. More champagne while addressing Boreas, ruler of the North Wind; Zephyrus, ruler of the West Wind; Eurus, ruler of the East Wind; and then Notus, ruler of the South Wind. "Please don't hit us with a hurricane."

A few days later I received this:

Larry,

Had a great time on Saturday. I already miss you. Someone asked me what I thought about you leaving for so long. I said that I feel sad in a selfish sort of way but very, very happy for you. This is YOUR LIFE; did anyone expect anything else of you? I always knew you would be on a boat, and you knew it too. It's where you belong.

Love,

Your Sister

Darlene

I replied:

My Dearest Darlene,

Seeing you on Saturday made my spirits soar, but the thought of leaving for a long time doesn't sit well with me because I'll be missing you and others in my life. To tell you the truth, in many ways, I don't really want to go. I'm over the travel thing you know, and I can do without the "festival of the natives" in whatever land I go to... However, it's always easy to default to the stable, the known, and the familiar. You're right, I do belong on a boat ... at least for a while, and I owe it to myself to see how much I like the lifestyle...

We go through our lives searching: for who we are, for our purpose here, and for what makes us happy. While we're supposed to be content on a daily basis, I believe it is this searching that makes some people always strive for more and better. I am one of those people, and therefore I shall cast off the lines and head out to sea.

I, too, miss you already but feel you in my heart always. I'll look for you in the moon every time it's full.

Love you always,

Your Brother

Larry

My emotions rose and fell like the blip on a heart rate monitor. After being really low from the idea of actually leaving, my joy came back when we took the boat out for a test sail. It wasn't the last time my emotions were to soar and plunge....

Personal Journal / August 30, 2001

We actually sailed today! Just six months after buying the boat and virtually nonstop work, we took *Julia* on a test sail. She sails like a dream. Heavier than I'm used to, but that means she's stable. The new sails are beautiful and have fantastic shape. I couldn't have asked for anything more. Maybe we'll make a departure this year after all.

Ken and I are really falling for each other, and it's confirmed he's going on the trip. Still, he keeps saying he only wants to go for half a year and then come back to build his career as a computer engineer. Does that mean he's my boyfriend or not? The ups and downs of our budding relationship are one more frustration. He's young, passionate, needy, and smart. And he sure makes me laugh.

CHAPTER 5

Tears, Fears, Excitement, and Good-bye!

*"Keep your fears to yourself,
but share your courage with others."*
ROBERT LOUIS STEVENSON

Personal Journal / September 23, 2001

Ka-Boom. In one instant, the world changed forever: September 11, 2001, and the destruction of the World Trade Center is an event that will change everything. I won't let it. Many questions arise: Is it safe to go? As Americans, surely we are a potential target. I have to reconsider the idea of going all the way around the world because it means crossing the Indian Ocean and most likely transiting the Suez Canal...not exactly the most American-friendly place in the world. Should I let 9/11 influence this adventure and me?

If, as the Dalai Lama says, the purpose in life is to be happy, then *no*, it shouldn't affect me, and I must pursue my goal. However, 9/11 *will* affect me. Our business, even though we sold it, is still paying us a small percentage of the revenues, which will now be reduced dramatically because groups will not want to travel as much. We saw this happen after the Gulf War and that was not nearly as frightening as 9/11.

Selfishly, I am angry at the situation because it is changing so many things for me. Yet how can I be concerned about myself when so many perished, were injured, or lost loved ones? I have my life, my health, love, and the perfect boat almost ready to go. Now I want to stay at home where it's safe, cozy, easy and familiar. I'm not really caring about seeing foreign lands and experiencing other cultures. I *do* want to sail and hope that desire will propel me to re-energize for the trip. I know I'm going, I just want all of me to be behind it, and instead, I'm suddenly depressed. I could keep the boat and sail to San Diego, maybe Mexico, and just hang around there for awhile….

No. I want to do this. Many things have stood in my way, and I have gone over, under, around, and through them. I better say goodbye to the world as I've known it. I'm going for it, but I really have the jitters.

Personal Journal / December 5, 2001
Tears. Bob and I hug and cry and hug some more and cry some more. We are both struggling to let go; yet we both know it's the right thing to do. I sure do love him.

It was time to go. We at least had to leave the dock. Emotions surrounding the departure were getting in the way of being captain; I asked Bob to drive me to the marina to meet up with the rest of the crew who were already waiting onboard. In addition to Ken and Patrik, Rajat Dutta, would accompany us down the coast to Long Beach. Bill was there too. Bill said he figured the only way he could really get us to leave, other than cutting the lines personally, was to be aboard. And if he had to put the engine in reverse himself, then so be it! Even though he would only sail to our first port of Santa Barbara, having him along for the first leg injected confidence. After that, it was going to be just Ken, Patrik, and me.

As I walked down the gangway in the late afternoon, I turned around one more time to see Bob standing there, more handsome than ever. He was smiling, but he was rubbing his eyes…and I swear I almost ran back up the gangway. Something very strong inside me was saying, "Stay, don't go. Don't be a fool;

nobody does this. Are you crazy?" Yes, I was. I gave one last wave, then turned around and headed for Julia. *I wiped my eyes, stepped aboard, and said, "Who wants to go sailing?" As four pairs of hands shot up, I added, "Well then, what are we waiting for? Let's go!"*

Personal Journal / December 6, 2001

A day filled with emotion and balancing acts, trying to run last minute errands, and squeeze our departure through a tight weather window. Storms are stacked up across the Pacific, and we're late in trying to get down the coast without encountering them. We'll go when the weather window opens…which looks like tomorrow. Butterflies.

Feelings of relief, excitement, but also missing some of the joy. Melancholy still prevails as I leave Bob and my life as I know it behind me. Am I doing the right thing? I need to do this, want to do this, and have worked so hard to make it happen; I have to go. I shared this with Bob at the dock.

"I'm going to miss you. Heck, I miss you already," I said through tears.

"Me too. I'm torn," he responded.

"I have to go. This is it for me. This is what I need to do, and you have to find yourself, in your music, and in your art, and you'll only do that if I'm gone. Still, I'm worried about you," I said.

"Me? Ha! I'm not the one going out *there*! Don't worry, I'll be fine. You need to do this, and it'll be good for us. It's what we need now," Bob said, with his usual wisdom.

"I know, I know. I love you Bob. I will always love you," I babbled.

"I love you too, Larry. Always will. Come back safe. Now, go." And that was it.

I had been watching the weather forecast for days, and it wasn't looking all that pretty. There appeared to be a 48-hour window of fairly decent weather coming on the 7ᵗʰ, just enough time to get us south as far as Santa Barbara, but it was still cold. So cold that we lay out our long underwear and foul-weather gear for an early morning departure from the Sausalito anchorage.

I could tell that everyone was nervous. Ken and Patrik didn't say much because they didn't really know what to expect. They too were leaving their lives behind. Patrik was the most excited as I think he saw the grandeur of the adventure.

Ken repeated what he had been saying all along, that he was only going until *June and then wanted to return to San Francisco to be near his family. While this bothered me to no end, I really didn't believe it. I figured he would be so excited by the adventure he would end up staying for the duration of the trip. At any rate, I didn't have time to dwell on that. I had a boat and four crew to manage.*

Personal Journal / December 7, 2001

We're going. Up at 0500, and we are alone as we pass under the Golden Gate at 0700 to catch the tail end of the outgoing tide. It's cold, and the wind is light so we are motoring. I cry, I sing, laugh, and jump for joy. I can't believe it…what a flood of emotions. I am truly lucky to have such a great team aboard: Bill, Ken, Patrik and Rajat. Everybody is excited, but I am the only one watching the dream of my life unfold before me…oh my God, *I have to pee.*

A mixed day of motoring, sailing, and motor sailing (motoring with the mainsail up, which keeps the boat stable, and because it creates our own apparent wind when we move under power, actually boosting speed). Weather is light in the afternoon but then comes up to 33 knots with 10-foot seas at night with Rajat and myself on watch. I finally figure out how to secure the dinghy tightly and safely on the davits, and *Julia* rides smoothly under the watchful steerage of our autopilot, which manages the helm better than I can in heavy seas.

First whale sighting: two large blue whales less than 100 yards off the starboard bow, a breathtaking sight. In the afternoon, dolphins everywhere, as if they were welcoming us to their world, or at least that's how I saw it.

Bidding farewell to San Francisco was difficult. I didn't realize I was such an emotional person (*Oh, c'mon Larry, who are you trying to kid?*). Memories of sailing away some 24 years earlier when I crewed on another yacht across the Pacific came flooding back. Then I was just one of a crew of six, had no control of where we were going, or anything onboard except what I produced in the galley. I just knew I wanted to go sailing and bum around for a while. There was one similarity with that departure and this one. At the time, in 1977, I was madly in love with my college boyfriend John van Duyl. Yet, when offered the chance to go sailing across the Pacific, I left him too. Is sailing more important to me than love? Can't I have both?

That experience really whet my appetite for this, the real thing, as captain. I swore if I were to go again, I would be nice to my crew, unlike the skipper I sailed under in '77. This time, though, it's all a bit calmer, as if I've been somewhere before and I'm totally in control. Yet it still seems like a half-baked scheme with no recipe to follow.

A special thought for Bob whom I leave behind, wishing it wasn't so, but knowing it's right. I feel a renewal and wonderful love and respect for him, hoping he too will enjoy his new freedom and time. So long, San Francisco. See ya, but not goodbye forever. Or is it? What if I *am* leaving forever? I don't remember being sad in my dreams. Is it supposed to be like this? Come on, Captain, get it together!

Personal Journal / December 8, 2001
Motoring all day as we race to stay ahead of a coming storm. Hard to sleep with the engine droning, but it's nice to be moving. Hoping for some wind.

I struggled with the sudden unforeseen engine problems we were having, and I didn't yet know it "comes with the territory." Funny how I couldn't sleep then because of the engine noise, but by the end of the trip, the purr of the motor was music to my ears.

Personal Journal / December 21, 2001
We made the run to Santa Barbara in 48 hours but along the way, the water pump failed, and we lost power. It was late at night when Ken heard the exhaust emitting an unfamiliar sound. Instead of its usual dry, throaty note, and then the "whoosh" of water, he only heard a dry sound— no water. If no water is coming *out*, then no water is going *in* to cool the engine, and that's bad. Good thing he was attentive. No sooner did he say, "Hey Larry, I don't hear any exhaust water coming out," I flew up to the cockpit and shut the engine down before certain mechanical disaster.

I was nervous as I radioed the Santa Barbara Harbor Patrol, requesting a tow as we approached the port. Within an hour, we were in the marina, and then spent four days in Santa Barbara awaiting a new pump and repairs. To me, it was both worrying and distressing. Here we were less than two days into our maiden voyage, already broken down. And the engine is brand new. This isn't an omen, is it?

It was hard to see Bill leave us here. His time aboard was short, but he was encouraging and gave me strength. "Can't you stay another week?" I pleaded.

"You don't need me. You're doing just fine. It's time for you to get your confidence level up to your skill level, and that'll take longer with me aboard," Bill said.

"This engine problem has really got me on edge," I said.

"It's just another day at the office for you now," Bill countered. "You can do this. I know you can, and most importantly, *you* know you can."

"Okay, then I'll see you down the road somewhere," I said as I hugged him.

"Down the road then, somewhere," Bill agreed, as he walked up the dock and waved.

Sailed to Santa Cruz Island for a one-night anchorage at Smuggler's Cove. Dolphins for as far as we can see, hundreds of them leaping out of the water. Just like when we sailed out of San Francisco, they are giving their official "Welcome to the world of cruising." Maybe I'm already starting to go a little cuckoo because I think of the dolphins as my friends.

Had trouble starting the engine again but finally got it to kick, and we headed for Long Beach. What's wrong with it? Got caught up by a fast moving storm with gale-force winds and seas. Wake up time. I shared the helm for 10 hours with the autopilot, which works amazingly well. I'm pleased how well the boat sails…she's everything I wanted and more. Spent five nights in Long Beach at the Long Beach Yacht Club. More engine repairs. A broken wire kept the engine from starting this time, and we had to be towed in again. My dream yacht *Julia* towed into Long Beach where I learned to sail? This is embarrassing and frustrating. A broken wire? I know there's not going to be a towboat most of the places we're going, so we better get this fixed, and more importantly, learn to troubleshoot problems ourselves.

We docked in Alamitos Bay, Long Beach, where I sailed a Styrofoam dinghy as a boy and raced my Hobie Cat as a teenager. I traveled down memory lane many times, paddling my kayak around the bay where I used to practice sailing after school 30 years ago. I felt an incredible sense of pride and accomplishment. I wanted to shout out loud, "Hey! Remember me? The kid who wouldn't stop sailing? Yeah, that's me, and I'm on my way to go cruising, so what do you think about that?!" Then it dawned on me: We were docked exactly where I used to stand behind the locked gates looking at the big boats. Only now, the boy behind the gate is standing at the helm.

There were warm and fuzzy feelings all around; Jake, Jeff, Dan, Dolly, and of course, my mother, Julia, visited the boat for a holiday get-together. Long-time and loyal friend Bill McDonald was there to see me off, just like he had done when I sailed into the Pacific as a crew years earlier. Mom is still as wonderful as always but getting a bit frail; I hope she'll be okay. I'm glad my siblings are there to take care of her while I pursue my dream. Mom was clearly worried about my leaving: "You be careful out there, and don't go sailing in storms."

"Mom, I'll be fine," I said.

"Well, why do you have to go across the ocean? Why don't you sail around here, maybe a little trip to Mexico if you want so much adventure," she added. "If you stay here, I'll cook for you and make cookies."

"C'mon, Mom, you know I'll be just fine. You have confidence in me, don't you?"

"Of course I do, my little *shoshee* (Yiddish for cutie), don't take chances then. And come back to me, okay?" She cried as she grabbed my cheeks in her hand and squeezed as tight as a vise.

"I promise I'll come back to you, Mom. I promise."

Then it was my brother Dan's turn. "You're not still going—are you? I mean in light of everything."

"You mean the 9/11?" I asked. "Well, I have had second thoughts."

"In case you haven't noticed, Americans are not too popular in certain parts of the world these days," Dan said.

"Don't forget that I'm gay and Jewish," I added, trying not to take too seriously where the discussion was headed. "That reminds me, I need to get another rainbow flag."

"You're nuts," Dan said.

I knew he meant well, but I couldn't allow myself to go there, so I ended the conversation with, "What's wrong with being a little crazy?"

Rajat left us today to return to his career.

Still having problems getting the engine started and none of the mechanics can figure out why. Oh great, if they can't figure it out, then who can?

First Email / December 31, 2001 / To the *Julia* Group

Instead of planning the trip, I'm now living the trip; now that's a New Year! It's New Year's Eve, and we just dropped the anchor in Bahia de San Quintin, 160 miles south of San Diego on the West Coast of Baja. We're anchored in a huge open bay with swells that make *Julia* roll side to side as each one passes under our keel. We departed San Diego yesterday…yes, we actually left the United States, and that feels like a really big accomplishment to us. We're excited about our first foreign port and getting here on our own—the feeling of accomplishment and pride is gushing all over this boat. We have exceeded our self-expectations and those of each other and are truly working closely as a team.

Patrik said, "Hey, Skipper, we made it."

"Holy crap, we did. We left the U.S.," Ken said.

"I couldn't have done it without you guys. You're the best," I said.

"No, *you're* the best," Patrik and Ken said in unison.

"No, you are," I added.

"No…you," they both repeated while laughing.

"Get over here," I said, as we all had a big laugh and group hug. It was an amazing moment in our lives I'm sure none of us will ever forget.

Email / January 3, 2002

We're anchored in Turtle Bay, an enormous yet calm inlet halfway down the coast of Baja, California. There are only two other boats in the bay and a nearby, sleepy fishing village, but so far there are no turtles. It's getting warmer and, for the first time, the thermometer hit 80 degrees, which means nothing more than T-shirts and shorts. We await Ernesto's arrival with the diesel supply to pump from his *panga* (a brightly painted small open motorboat) into our tanks. Ernesto also provides water, food, takes our garbage, and helps cruisers any way he can…for a fee of course. I guess he's the first of many agents we'll use on our trip.

Everyone is healthy, eating well (too well I'm afraid) and happy. For me, I'm working on my "slow down" skills, and Mexico is a good place to practice. I don't think I ever realized how wound up I was until I saw how wound down others are.

Personal Journal / January 18, 2002
Received a disturbing email from our weather router Bob Cook about a recent pirate attack not far from us.

"Larry, FYI: About 4 miles off the coast, a motorboat pulled up alongside a sailboat. Two men asked for water, so the owner went below to get them a drink. At that point one of the men hopped onboard and accosted him with a knife, asking for dinero. The pirate then attacked and slashed the owner with an 8-inch serrated knife, and the other pirate hit him with a heavy object, knocking him unconscious. He's in the hospital and is going to make it, but keep your eyes open out there, boys."

Oh no, do we have to be worried about pirates already?

It's been a lot of work to get to this point. Even yesterday, we had the task of finding a coolant leak on the main engine. We have maintenance schedules to make and live by, always cleaning or fixing something—where's all the time for reading and writing that was advertised in the brochure?

Baja is beautiful—the contrast of brownish red desert and blue water is stunning, our first encounter with truly clear seas. There's abundant marine life, and we already have caught mahi-mahi—they're such good eating. We see dozens of rays as they sport out of the water, dancing and playing (or so it seems to me). Evidently they jump as part of a courtship display, or to get rid of parasites on their skin, or to escape predators, but it looks like play to me.

Funny thing happened at Mag Bay. The port captain, Gregorio, offered to take us to the vegetable market in San Carlos. This is the same gentleman who, when we checked in and paid the $48 fee, proceeded to open his wallet and without hesitation, deposited the money inside with no shame. He is also the one driving a new Chevy pickup truck. Innocently, or blindly, we enlisted his services, not thinking it would be very expensive for a 20-minute ride each way in his *panga*. We spent $8 on vegetables—great. He then presented us with our $70 fee for the *panga* ride. It's not as if I don't know, especially when traveling outside of the U.S., that I should ask the price before getting into a taxi, even if it is a boat. Perhaps I should learn to be more aware of the signals I see, such as the pickup and the size of Gregorio's wallet.

The air is warm and soft on my skin, and so clear I can see the mountains and hills ashore as if they were painted on a canvas within arms' reach. I'm getting used to the constant movement of the boat as it rolls gently to the seas. I'm beginning to like it.

I was naïve to think a strong wind would get us quickly to our destination. In this case, it meant a trough, which usually means very strong winds. We had no business setting sail in those conditions.

Ken and Patrik had total faith in me, and I think I was trying to impress them with my ability to read weather charts. Unfortunately, I didn't really know what I was doing but didn't know that I didn't know… ignorance was bliss.

I had intense lower back pain; however, I had not yet discovered the relief offered by prescription pills…something I depended upon later in the journey.

Personal Journal / January 19, 2002

It's time to go now; it's too windy and the swell coming from a different direction than the wind makes it too rolly as an anchorage. The upside: We'll make the 150-mile crossing over to mainland Mexico and Mazatlan in no time.

I felt so responsible for Ken and Patrik. Here I was taking two beginner sailors to sea, and while I had plenty of years of sailing experience, and good instincts, I certainly didn't have the kind of ocean experience I would now ask for in a captain. They looked up to me as if I did have that experience. Maybe it was my sales and marketing skills at work.

Personal Journal / January 22, 2002

Now I know what a "trough" is when reading the weather, and it's not something we should have sailed into on purpose. We had 30-knot winds and 12-foot seas, and although *Julia* performed brilliantly, we should not have put ourselves in it. I really need to learn to read the weather better and stop believing I know things I don't. We all bumble our way through certain things in life, but something tells me the weather is not one of those things that allows for errors.

For the first time, we are starting to feel part of a sailing community. There are probably 10 boats here from San Francisco, and it's easy to make friends. Now I'm preparing Alka-Seltzer for the crew as both Patrik and Ken are paying for playing.

Been thinking about Bob. I could never be doing what I'm doing without his support at home, as he continues to deal with the annoying bits and pieces of our company that still exists on paper. I just hope he is getting to experience his sabbatical time without too much work and other distractions from our previous life because, for me, the pressure is easing, and I almost feel like I'm cruising. Oh wait, I am!

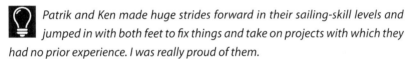 *Patrik and Ken made huge strides forward in their sailing-skill levels and jumped in with both feet to fix things and take on projects with which they had no prior experience. I was really proud of them.*

As I began to relax, I found myself falling more deeply for Ken. He was the one that enabled me to sail away with my arm around someone who I love…he was part of the dream. Yet when I would try to get closer to him, he would pull away saying, "Remember, I'm leaving in June." To which I would reply, "No you're not, you love this." He would counter, "Yes, I am." And I would turn away….

Personal Journal / January 23, 2002
Yesterday, Klaus the middle-aged, blond German fix-it man living in Mazatlan (we think he was running from someone or something in Germany), came over to assess the electrical system problems. Great guy and he ended up staying all afternoon, troubleshooting with Ken, and shooting the breeze.

I look at Ken and am delighted at the changes I see. He is responsible onboard for just about everything I am not. He has truly become my right hand and someone I can rely on when anything needs doing. I look at him with wonder and lust as his hair is turning gold, and his body becomes tan from the sun. When I think of him leaving the boat to go back to California, I start to well up. That's what he says he wants to do, though, go back after six months of sailing. I don't know what I'll do when he leaves and how to continue this journey without him, but I guess that's something I can worry about later.

Personal Journal / January 29, 2002

We're at the island of Isla Isabella, a mini-Galapagos bird sanctuary. Dinghied ashore to explore this incredible island full of birds: frigates, blue, and yellow-footed boobies, pelicans, bird nests and their eggs, and even the rare sight of baby boobies in the nest. While climbing to the top of the brush-covered island, iguanas of all sizes crossed our path, and literally thousands of birds circled overhead. We didn't see one bird collision. Then again, we didn't spend too much time looking up for fear of what was dropping from the sky. Great views of the boat and lots of interaction with the birds as we stood at the peak, high above the sea, among hundreds of nests and many different species... always keeping one eye on us. They don't seem to object to our presence though. The blue-footed boobies are extremely proud of their beautiful blue feet. They put one foot out in front of you, look down at it, then look up at you, down at the foot, then up at you again, as if to say, "Look at my beautiful blue feet." It's prehistoric and Cousteau-like, all in one place.

It was becoming painfully obvious I didn't know everything about boats. In fact, I barely knew anything about the mechanics and workings of a yacht the size of Julia. We had many systems aboard that were fairly complicated including systems for making power, making water; refrigeration, computers, navigation, weather fax, a main diesel engine, a diesel generator, and solar panels. One of the biggest challenges throughout any boat's journey is the production and management of electrical power, and we finally got it nailed down sometime around 2006....

Personal Journal / March 1, 2002

We are always fixing things, studying manuals, preparing food, reorganizing, etc. When I look for a tool or a spare part, it's buried. As Patrik says, "Everything can't be on top." When stowing things, a typical conversation goes something like this:

Ken: "Where should this go?"

Larry: "Oh, that can go anywhere."

Patrik: "Sorry, anywhere is full."

I'm impressed we're actually in Zihuatanejo, this far down the coast. I was struck again by the realization that cruising is a lot more than just sailing. We all serve as mechanic, electrician, plumber, and general tradesmen of repairs. I'm so glad Ken and Patrik are onboard; each makes his own contributions with Ken leaning towards the electrical, and Patrik showing a flair for plumbing and carpentry.

Puerto Vallarta, our current location, is the gathering point of the group called the Pacific Puddle Jumpers who are all headed across the Pacific at the same time. We're meeting fellow cruisers and making some good friends, including Chuck and Amy from Emeryville, California, onboard *Kiyomi*. Chuck and I have become fast friends. He's older and towers over me with his large frame but is gentle as a puppy. He and his pretty, small-framed wife, Amy, are quite the odd couple, but they're fun and Chuck is a confident sailor, so we've invited them to join us aboard *Julia* for the Pacific crossing. We'll have more experience and manpower onboard, and that makes me a little less nervous.

I left *Julia* and my crew for New Zealand to fulfill a commitment made two years earlier to a client. With tears and some trepidation, I gave my crew permission to take the boat sailing without me and to follow Chuck and Amy down the coast towards Manzanillo. It didn't feel right to ask them to wait for two weeks, and I'm going to have to learn to trust these guys at some point. I also hoped by my not being there, they would rise to the occasion, and they did. Both have progressed dramatically from where they were in their sailing skills, but maneuvering a 50-foot, 25-ton boat in and out of tight places is always a challenge. The morning of my departure, I gave some last minute lessons on maneuvering in the marina; both did beautifully, yet they were still nervous about commanding the boat by themselves. I was comfortable leaving them, though, as I knew how much they both care.

Turns out they had quite an exciting time in my absence, including weathering an intense lightning storm and 50-knot winds rounding Cabo Corientes (similar to Pt. Conception in California where the winds are notoriously strong) and some difficult anchorages. Upon my return, I noticed two big differences onboard: First, both Ken and Patrik grew by leaps and bounds, and both stood a little taller with their newfound confidence and skills. They had been anchored at Careyes when a fast moving storm from the south caught them by surprise in the late afternoon.

At the end of the day, they made the right decision to stay where they were, and I could tell when I got back that they were beaming with the pride that can only come from challenge and achievement.

The second change I noticed was that Ken and Patrik seem to have a newfound respect for the captain's position and all of the responsibilities that go along with the title.

Thus, my welcome back from New Zealand was warmer, more loving, and appreciative than I could have ever imagined.

"How was your sail down the coast, guys?" I asked.

"Scary, exciting, hard," the response echoed. Patrik added, "We like it better with you here." Ken chimed in, "I don't want to be captain anymore—*you* be the captain."

Zihuatanejo is a charming little fishing village set on a wide-open but calm and protected bay, where we've counted between 50 and 100 cruising boats at anchor depending on the day. Z-town, as they call it here, has become a tourist destination but has retained much of its original character. The small shops sell colorful blankets and woodcarvings along quaint walking streets, there's easy Internet access, a beautiful beach, and plenty of delicious, inexpensive restaurants with fresh seafood. I jump in the clean bay every day for my morning swim, and it's a good place for kayaking. Between the swimming and paddling, I'm getting stronger, losing weight, and for the first time, am truly beginning to relax. From here, it's back up north to Puerto Vallarta to get ready for the Pacific crossing, where the real adventure will begin.

In the meantime, we have met some new friends: Brad Hillebrandt and Laura Mooney on *Pura Vida*, and there's talk of them sailing across the Pacific, too, on their boat. They're young and also from the San Francisco Bay Area. Laura is tall, blond, and Nordic good looking. She always seems to be laughing about something; a trait I find admirable. Brad is smaller framed, wiry, and has six-pack abs that make us all jealous. Countless hours playing Yahtzee and talking late into the night over margaritas have bonded us rather quickly.

We met them on the morning radio net when they asked if there were any boats that could spare some fresh water. Onboard *Julia* we run our watermaker every day and had plenty to spare, so we offered; they came over, and we became fast friends. It's always good to give. When you give, not expecting anything in return, something always comes back to you bigger than what you gave. We found new friends—priceless—just for a few gallons of water.

Personal Journal / March 6, 2002

This morning, I stumbled and fell down the companionway stairs, tumbling into a heap on the salon floor. I stood up thinking all was fine until I noticed my left arm had two bleeding slices about 4 inches long. I heard Super Glue was developed for the military to close wounds in the field, so I figured I'd try it. Guess what, it worked. With my newly glued arm, I went back up on deck, and with an inviting warm ocean before me, jumped in, had a wonderful 100-yard swim to shore, did yoga on the beach, and then sat at the shoreline building a sand castle. I had a nice easy swim back to the boat, where I ran into Ken. "I see you're starting to relax," he said, smiling.

"What makes you say that?" I asked.

Without hesitating, Ken said, "Because I know you, and you only build sand castles when you're relaxed." He was right. I hadn't built a sand castle in a long, long time.

I'm nervous about being the captain responsible for five lives crossing almost 3,000 miles of open ocean but hope I don't reveal it to the crew. I wonder how they would feel if they knew their skipper was anxious? Nervousness, like fear, can be contagious, so I keep my composure.

Further on in the trip, I learned my anxiety about ocean crossings was useful; it heightened my senses and made me check and double check things. It was normal. Heck, who wouldn't be a little nervous about crossing an ocean in a small boat? By the end of the trip, I used the word "excited" instead of "nervous," but that was to be years away.

It's amusing how I saw Mexico's slower pace as annoying at the beginning of the journey, and how, by the voyage's end, I appreciated the cultural differences that represented a more peaceful lifestyle.

CHAPTER 6

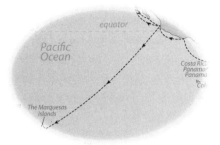

Crossing the Pacific:
It's Only Water, Right?

"Man cannot discover new oceans unless he has
the courage to lose sight of the shore."
ANDRE GIDE

Personal Journal / April 1, 2002

Without fanfare, we departed Punta Mita, today at noon, and head-ed across the Pacific. The boat felt heavy, full of fuel, water, people, and enough food for five of us to last at least 45 days. I have to say, it was kind of strange to be sailing *away* from land and heading out into such a vast body of water. We watched in silence as the last bit of terra firma disap-peared behind us; we heard the "whoosh" of the water going by—we were sailing. We were going!

For so long, I have dreamed of crossing the Pacific again, but this time as skipper of my own boat. Now here I am. I feel proud and happy yet have great trepidation about leaving home. At the same time, I'm keyed up at the prospects of new adventure. That's a lot of feelings for one day.

Mexico was a challenge; finding spare parts for the outboard motor, buying oil, or the food we wanted seems more difficult than in the States. However, I have a feeling much of that fault was due to our own misunderstanding of the local way of doing things. I'm sure we'll get better at adjusting as this is only our first country out of many more to come. It's our responsibility to adapt to different cultures, not the other way around. Still, after less than three months, we were all ready to leave Mexico. While we enjoyed the relaxed and easygoing atmosphere, the frustrations drove us crazy:

"*Hola*, we would like to buy these rivets, *por favor*," I said to the shopkeeper.

"*Uno momento, señor*. The cashier must count them," said the small man behind the weathered wooden table.

"Count them? They're already in sealed bags, and there must be over 200 here," I countered.

"*Sí señor*. She will count them for you, *no problemo*," he said with a smile.

"Why? It says right here on each bag there are 10 rivets inside," I said.

"*Sí, no problemo*. She will do it for you," the shopkeeper repeated, still smiling.

"That could take a very long time," I said.

"What is the hurry, *señor*?" The shopkeeper really meant it.

"*Sí, no problemo*," I gave in. What *was* the hurry?

We have more new friends with John and Lynette Flynn aboard *White Hawk*. As with Brad and Laura, we gravitated toward both of these upbeat and energetic young couples. From Southern California, John and Lynette are blond, tan, have toned physiques, and certainly know how to keep a party lively. Over many pitchers of margaritas, we found comfort in sharing our fears and excitement as we all prepared to cross the Pacific at the same time.

While anchored at Punta Mita alongside *Pura Vida* and having our farewell dinner, there was nervous laughter aboard and everybody was busying themselves with little tasks. By now, while everyone on both boats had some cruising experience, I was the only one who had actually crossed an ocean. Laura asked, "What's it like out there?"

I replied, "My strongest memory is there's nothing out there, absolutely nothing. It's just you and the boat. I remember liking that part."

Laura raised her eyebrows, "Gee, I don't know if we should be doing this."

"I'm sure we shouldn't be doing this," added Brad. "Are we nuts?"

"Yeah, we're all nuts. If you really think about it, nobody should be doing this, but we're going to love it. Besides, what could happen out there…?" Oops, that was the wrong thing to say. A chill quiet settled over us, as each person was alone with thoughts of what actually might happen. I was trying to lighten up the conversation, but it didn't really work. After a couple of minutes, I had to break the silence and get the conversation going again. "Come on Brad, let's look over the ITCZ again. I'm thinking we should shoot for crossing the equator about here, somewhere between 125° and 130° West." It snapped us back to the moment.

"I was thinking the same and it's what everyone says to do. We're going to wait one more day and then we'll be right behind you," Brad said. "You know, we were originally only sailing down here to Mexico. And now because of you guys, we're going to cross the Pacific Ocean."

"So it's our fault?" I asked.

"Yep, sure is," Brad said as he smiled.

"I'll take full credit then. Guilty as charged."

"Come on guys, one more cocktail together. The next one will be in the Marquesas Islands," Patrik said.

Glasses full, everybody chimed in: "To the Marquesas!"

Email / April 8, 2002 / One Week at Sea

While we are in radio contact with our friends on other boats, we realize we are truly alone and all we have is our boat and ourselves. At times we're all rendered speechless by heavy doses of fear and exhilaration.

It's 2230, clear, lots of stars, and balmy enough for just a T-shirt. I am on watch but have taken a short break to pee and write a quick email. There is a strict "no peeing overboard" rule on *Julia* because it's a common cause of people falling overboard; plenty of people have been plucked out of the water with their flies open. The wind is blowing a gentle 12 knots, and *Julia* is leaping along at 6 knots south and west toward the Marquesas Islands. We are making about 135-150 miles a day and that should steadily

increase as we pick up the trade winds over the next couple of days.
N 18°51'W 107°46.6'

Email / April 14, 2002 / Fourteen Days at Sea

This morning, while on watch in the early hours, I heard the familiar breathing sound of my dolphin friends. I stealthily made my way forward to the bow, and there they were, a pod of them, playing and surfing in our bow wave. As they streaked back and forth, their trails glowed green and white in the dark waters. Some places in the ocean have a high concentration of phosphorescence in the water, caused by dense pockets of plankton. When stirred up by our boat, dolphins, schools of tuna, or other sea life, that disturbance lights up the plankton. It's magical, almost alien, and the dolphin trails make it dazzling because of their speed.

We've been at sea for two weeks and as we are clocking more than 150 miles per day, one contemplates how immense the ocean really is. We have seen waves the size of two-story houses rolling along under us. They're not very steep, just big rollers that remind me of the low foothills of the Sierra Nevada. While more steady now, the winds have increased in strength, and there have been plenty of rainsqualls. From first light until sunset, we see schools of flying fish leaping out of the water trying to escape the predators.

I spend my days routing and navigating according to weather forecasts we receive via the SSB radio. I make my best attempt at interpreting the information and am becoming a student of weather forecasting. I'm also busy fixing rigging in need of attention, attaching leather chafe gear to protect lines from wearing as they rub against any hard surface, assisting on other people's watches, standing my own watches, and, of course, sleeping. With five people onboard, we have the luxury of three-hour watches, followed by nine hours off. The crew, except me, rotates as cook every fourth day. I stand the extra watches and am always available to assist with anything, anytime. Seems like I'm never caught up with all of the tasks needing attention. And while I take my turn in the sack, I really don't sleep much, constantly aware of the goings-on aboard.

While the seas aren't rough, the boat is in a relentless motion and we awake from sleep feeling as though we have had an isometric workout. We have almost lost track of time except now we're all fairly ready to be somewhere, anywhere that the boat's movements will be calmer. We're two days away from the equator where the crew will be inducted into the Society of Shellbacks, a small, elite group of sailors who have crossed the equator while at sea. Having been inducted on my previous Pacific crossing, I am exempt from the wrath of Neptune at the upcoming event. There will be a big party with champagne and even a surprise visit by Neptune himself. *(Shhh*, don't tell the crew.)

We have traveled 1,540 nautical miles and have another 1,200 to go before we make landfall on the island of Fatu Hiva in the Marquesas Islands, the first island chain on our route across the Pacific.

Spinnakers (the big round colorful sail in front you see in the pretty pictures) are quite finicky about staying in place and require a lot more attention than other sails. We probably shouldn't have it up in this darkness, but it's a thrill. It's a jet-black night, and we are charging into the dark at 7.5 knots leaving a trail of phosphorescence behind, making a loud whooshing sound while pushing tons of water out of the way…it's both beautiful and edgy.

Personal Journal / April 15, 2002

At sea for 15 days and I love this crossing. I don't want it to end, but I watch the miles click by day after day and realize that like everything, this too will eventually be over. I can't think of anything else I would rather be doing—I belong at sea.

And I love this boat. I'm rapidly learning everything I can about her, from sail configurations to engine maintenance, down to where every wire and hose leads. I'm also becoming in tune with the sounds she makes underway—those which are normal, and those which are not. She has quickly become a part of me.

We have had great weather. Light winds for a few days, then 20 knots for several days, plenty of chance to fly the spinnakers and improve our skills. At 10° north and again at 4° north, we hit the ITCZ and its rain-squalls with winds to 35 knots, rain that came down sideways and in buckets. Exhilarating. Gave the boat a good dousing too, as all of the dust and dirt from Mexico drained into the sea. I went up on the foredeck with a bar of soap and enjoyed getting pounded by the refreshing cool rain, a welcome relief from the humid, 85° tropical heat. "Whoo-hoo!" I shouted, as I stood up there naked to the world, washing my cares away.

Being captain is a challenge but I like it, and I hope I'm doing a good job of managing the boat and each person's contributions. Every crew member is responsible for a system or two. For Ken, it's power production, either through the main engine, the generator, or the solar panels. That means everybody has to go through Ken to get something done. Patrik is in charge of making fresh water, and he needs power to do so. Amy oversees refrigeration and needs power to keep the food cold. Chuck manages the propane gas, limiting how much the chef can use, and I hold the key to diesel fuel consumption, which limits Ken's ability to produce power, and that trickles down the grid, and so it goes—each system tied to the next.

The negotiations are funny:

"Oh, please Ken, can't I run the refrigerator just another hour to get the temp down a little more?" Amy whines.

"Nope, sorry. You'll have to wait 'til we run the generator this evening when Patrik will be making water…then you can run the fridge at the same time," Ken, our power czar, declares.

Later that night, I saw an entry in the log from Amy disclosing she had hand steered her entire three-hour watch so she wouldn't use power for the autopilot, "in the hopes it will buy me favors with the power department."

In addition to perusing the log, it's surprising how people don't think I overhear the conversations, and therefore don't know all that is going on…but oh, how wrong they are. I hear everything because I don't sleep much, and I don't sleep much because I hear everything. *Julia* speaks to me in the night and tells me all that is going on. I wonder if I'm losing it out here?

Ken and I are getting along wonderfully, but I'm still devastated by his declaration to leave the boat and go back to the States in May or June from French Polynesia. He's become a new person out here, reaching new heights in responsibility, and we're having lots of fun and laughing a lot. I will miss him terribly and already feel like I'll be alone in this venture. Sometimes, I just stare at him, and the other day, I took his picture through the porthole into our cabin from the cockpit while he slept. What am I thinking, that I'll paste the picture onto the window in his place? I've left Bob for this crazy adventure, and now my new boyfriend is going to leave me. I'm screwed, so to speak....

We were having real difficulties with our autopilot slipping, and I was becoming concerned. Even so, with five of us aboard we had plenty of manpower for hand steering. I would find out later, when there were just two of us aboard, just how significant it was to lose the autopilot....

Email / April 16, 2002 / Across the Equator
We've crossed the equator. Having traveled more than 2,000 miles, it was now my duty to induct the others into the Shellback Society, a sailing custom. With the crew assembled in the cockpit, I appeared on deck dressed as King Neptune: wearing a bright silver crown and carrying a shiny trident (both of which I had been secretly working on for days using foil and cardboard), earrings made from rubber fishing lures that looked like squids, and a bottle of Absolut vodka in my hand. I could barely keep a straight face while reading the "Welcome to the Society of Shellbacks" certificate I had prepared for each crew member before departing Mexico.

The idea is for King Neptune to provide a welcome by sharing various sea creatures with the pledges. With that in mind, I dumped warm, gooey pasta; relish; mayonnaise; apple sauce; and powdered sugar, all representing the squiggly, yucky creatures of the sea, onto the naked bodies of Ken, Patrik, Chuck, and Amy while they sat obediently in the cockpit. King Neptune also provided warm saltwater showers along with plenty of fine champagne I had been hiding just for this day. It really was an afternoon of hilarity, and we all laughed until our sides hurt.

Topping off the day, and in spite of how rough it was, everyone went swimming so we could honestly say we'd swum across the equator. Only one person jumped in at a time tethered to the boat with a 15-foot safety line. Two others were on shark watch while each swimmer frolicked and enjoyed this special treat. We were humbled by how small our boat looked in comparison to the ocean. We were reminded once again what Bill Claypool always said: Out here, the boat is the most important thing... in fact, the boat is everything.

What an amazing experience crossing the Pacific Ocean. The southeast trade winds are steady enough to set our sails and not change them for days on end. While desolate, because there are no other boats around us, it is a remarkable place to be, and I am clearheaded. The sea is full of surprises too—today we were hit by another round of wind squalls with heavy rain. Thinking the squalls would be similar to most of the others of about 20 knots, we kept the spinnaker flying. Big mistake. As if Neptune were trying to remind us who's boss, the wind piped up to over 40 knots and triggered a fire drill to get the spinnaker down. With *Julia* heeled over way too far, we were finally able to release the sheet, and with the sail flapping wildly, drop the halyard and recover the spinnaker damage free. It was thrilling and we're better sailors for it. Stay alert; you never know what the wind will blow your way.

S 02°00′W 129°51.2

Personal Journal / April 19, 2002

More dolphins torpedoing across the bow at night. We see nothing but ocean, long rolling hills of blue liquid that go on forever.

Recently, there's been some stress among the crew, but we all recognized it existed and dealt with the issues. The tension was a buildup from being at sea more than 18 days. The undulating seas are big and nobody is sleeping very well; thus, little things to one person, like leaving a dirty dish around, or not tidying up the cockpit at the end of a watch, become big things to others. Put five people in a small space in these conditions, and I'm impressed we've only had these problems now.

More rainsqualls at night and more fire drills getting the spinnaker down before the winds blast us. It's great having a five-member crew, especially performing spinnaker work. Two nights ago, a 40+ knot squall hit while Ken and I were on the pitching and heaving foredeck, trying to get a spinnaker down after it had wrapped itself around the forestay. What an adrenalin rush it is working on the foredeck in these dark conditions! Afterwards, still naked and soaking wet, we yammered on excitedly about how hard it was to get the sail back down, laughing to avoid talking about how dangerous and scary it really was in those conditions. Drying off, we jumped into bed, giggling like schoolboys.

The feel of the rain stinging in your face, the wind howling through the rigging, the seas trying their best to throw you off balance or overboard, wearing nothing because you ran up there with nothing on…dangerous or not, I feel *alive*.

I'm enjoying the challenges that arise onboard: physical strength, sail setting, navigating, and reading the weather. Although the emotional challenges loom even larger as I deal with the fear of the unknown. Who will be onboard to crew? Should I stay in Auckland or Sydney? Sail back home like most cruisers do? Or continue around the world?

A feeling of enormous accomplishment best describes what was going through my head after completing the first ocean passage as captain of my boat. I knew it was the first of many ocean crossings to come, and now that this one was over, I felt as if I could achieve anything. I could manage the boat, the systems, repairs, and the crew. However, I did begin to realize how little I knew about fixing things, and how important my crew was to those repairs.

The closer we got to Tahiti, the more Ken talked about his departure. I was still in denial and thought after he saw how beautiful the South Pacific was, he would change his mind….

Email / April 22, 2002/ *Julia* Safe At Anchor

After 21 days at sea and more than 2,750 nautical miles, *Julia* is anchored safe and sound in Hanaveve Bay on the island of Fatu Hiva in the Marquesas Islands. Our days ranged from a short 90 miles to a very respectable 170 miles in 24-hour periods. *Julia* never even flinched the entire way. I've discovered the boat can take the conditions a lot better than we can…we just have to learn to give her what she needs.

After three weeks at sea, all hands were on deck scanning the horizon for terra firma. We had already noticed an increase in the number of birds circling overhead. However, the first indicators weren't the birds or the land but rather stationary cumulus clouds 30 miles in the distance with bright green undersides reflecting the island below. Soon came the smell of wet soil, lush vegetation, and the faintest perfume of unusual wildflowers. At last the shout came from the bow at mid-morning, "Land, ho!"

When we were close enough to see the actual mountainous terrain, I was so emotional I had tears in my eyes. This was much sweeter than my previous arrival in the Marquesas. The sheer beauty of these islands is more stunning than I remember, and the sense of satisfaction at having navigated successfully to this tiny speck of land in the world's biggest ocean is truly a once-in-a-lifetime thrill.

At the moment, everyone is headed to bed to get the first full night's sleep without moving in almost a month, and even though there's a swell in the anchorage, it feels like we're on solid ground. What a stunning sight this is—how can the scenery anywhere else ever match the striking contrast of color and beauty surrounding us? This bay and island are known as the most beautiful in the Marquesas, and they live up to their reputation. Thriving vegetation clings to black lava cliffs and tall spires, which jut up hundreds of feet like overgrown stalactites covered in varying shades of green, all surrounded by palm trees, mango trees, and bright pink hibiscus flowers. This scene is exactly what you picture when you think of the South Pacific. Millions of years ago, volcanic activity produced these islands; they are rugged, rough, and seem to jump straight up from the ocean. There are only 8,000 people on the island chain, maybe because, as cannibals, they used to eat the brains of their enemies in order to gain their knowledge. The books say the cannibal days are over; I hope we can believe what we read.

Speaking of delicacies, we've already been ashore to buy French bread; it tasted like manna from heaven. The French government still provides the starter culture for the bread that is baked, with consistent expertise, in all of her territories. We bought three loaves and they were consumed in no time, so we put in our order to pick up more tomorrow morning. We'll see if we can get the legs moving again when we hike to a 600-foot waterfall. We experienced our first case of land sickness while trying to walk on shore. I had thought it to be a rumor—but it's real—as we all were dizzy and had trouble making a straight line.

The locals are very friendly, and a little bit of my high school French is coming back, although not fast enough, just sufficient to get me into trouble because the locals start out thinking I understand them. I can ask a question like, "Where is some fruit?" or state, "We would like some bread," but the answers come so fast I can't understand what they're saying. I end up using hands, pointing, speaking a few words of each language, and then we finally understand each other. It's all very entertaining to the locals and to us.

We brought gifts to give to the inhabitants of small villages like this one. We have pens and paper and candies for the kids, and rope, fish-hooks, perfume, combs—all luxuries—for the older islanders. They showed their appreciation by rewarding us with banana-leaf baskets full of fruit. The giant green-skin grapefruits called *pamplemousse* are not bit-ter like we're used to back in the States, and they're the size of coconuts. Deliciously sweet red and yellow mangoes, breadfruit, guava, limes, and avocados fill our galley, and a fresh bunch of green bananas is now hang-ing from the davits while they ripen in the warm tropical sun.

We met our first international cruising friends, Harvey and Jean Cooper, an English couple in their late 60s who have just arrived from the Galapagos Islands on their boat, *Guitar*. Moments after we dropped anchor, Harvey dinghied over to greet us and while exchanging pleas-antries, we asked if they sold ice-cold beer ashore. That generated a real laugh as he pointed out we were basically in the middle of nowhere, and there wasn't even refrigeration on this island. To our great surprise and delight, two hours later, he dinghied back and knocked on the side of the hull.

"Welcome to the anchorage," Harvey said as he handed us a dozen ice-cold beers and some very chilly cans of vodka fresh from his freezer. As he climbed aboard I thought, "Here's a guy we're going to be friends with for a long time." Their liquor supply had been replenished on a small Venezuelan island in the Caribbean called Isla Margarita where alcohol is incredibly cheap—and evidently comes in cans. I made a mental note of the name. Over drinks, we learned Harvey and Jean had been living in Florida when Harvey was diagnosed with cancer. He told the doctors, "The heck with you, I'm going sailing," and he is doing just fine. His red hair, freckles, and wiry body distinguished him, and I liked him right away. His elegant wife, Jean, was tall and slender with long blond and grey hair, her body clearly reflecting a career as a dancer with the Royal Ballet of London. We sat for hours listening to stories from them both, but I was particularly interested in Harvey's career with Reuters, and the colorful work he did for the Central Intelligence Agency while reporting the news.

We are beaming with the reality of where we are. After 25 years and lots of dreams, this is the real thing: the scenery, the welcoming locals, and meeting new friends from around the world. Does it get any better? S 10°27.852′ W 138°40.085′

Personal Journal / April 24, 2002

The light pitter-patter of rain woke me this morning; it's the kind that, along with the tropical heat, makes the vegetation so intensely verdant in the Marquesas. On land, I would just roll over and enjoy the sounds, but on a boat, things are different. Someone needs to get up, run around closing hatches and portholes, and wipe up water that has already come inboard.

The locals seem genuinely glad we have chosen to visit their island and are eager to stop and talk as we stroll through the tiny village. I am struck with how neat and spotless they keep their idyllic villages. The thatched huts are swept clean, the cement buildings are freshly painted, and vegetable, fruit, and flower gardens adorn most of the houses' front or backyards. Walking along the roadside, it's common to come across a patch of land being used just to grow multi-colored flowers for decoration and lei making. Everything seems oversized: Ferns stand taller than us, and some palm leaves are large enough to use as blankets.

We were hoping to go diving today; however, yesterday, we saw nettles in the water (stringy jellyfish-like things) that sting with a vengeance. Now that the rain is stopping, I'll head up and have a look at the water… Nope, no swimming here. Too late. Amy jumped in without looking. The screams followed, "Aaaah! Help! Help!" We ran up to look over the side, thinking she was being eaten by a shark, but she was already scrambling up the boarding ladder. Amy's body was covered with a mosaic of red stings. Growing up on the beaches of Southern California was not all wasted, as every kid knew vinegar is what is needed on jellyfish stings (or you can pee on them, but I think in this case, vinegar was a more appropriate call). The vinegar offered some relief, but it was still difficult to watch one of my crew in pain, especially knowing it would be a day or two before she felt better.

Our last port in the Marquesas was Nuku Hiva, the same place I made landfall a quarter century ago. It felt good to enter that same bay, this time on my own boat, in charge of my own destiny. This is the bustling center of commerce for these islands; one morning, we got together with some other cruisers to shop at the 0430 market for vegetables and freshly caught tuna. Our new friends that morning included Gay from *Mobisle*. When Gay introduced herself to me, she said, "Hi, I'm Gay." I replied, "So am I." We had a good laugh.

I have always loved and respected the sea and the creatures that inhabit this most incredible frontier. However, I was still a bit ignorant and can't truthfully tell you I knew an octopus was different from a squid. It was interesting to see the difference in people's attitudes towards an octopus. Chuck and Mercury were both hunters and felt it was below us in the food chain, and therefore ours for the taking. Others, like Carly and Ken, were adamantly opposed to killing it. They both knew the octopus was a relatively intelligent sea creature,and felt bad once we killed one and it was in the frying pan. However, no matter whose view you might ascribe to, once it was sautéing in olive oil and garlic, all were eager for the feast and nobody boycotted.

I was struck by the diversity of people we were meeting: Rixene was a doctor in her early 50s from Canada, who left her husband behind to go sailing; Mercury was a studly 20-something crab fisherman from Alaska with biceps he loved to show off; his girlfriend Carly was a sweet blond college student; and Phantom was a Rastafarian from Jamaica with braided hair.

We had been "buddy boating" with John and Lynette from White Hawk *and Brad and Laura from* Pura Vida. *This grouping became our little fleet of boats that continued across the Pacific together. We sailed with* Pura Vida *until they turned back to the States from Tahiti,* White Hawk *continued on to New Zealand and New Guinea, and we sailed with Harvey and Jean on* Guitar *all the way to Turkey in 2005, where they settled in a condo on the water. Ages ranged from 30s to late 60s, but our attraction to most of the people we met was their adventurous spirit, and desire to enjoy more of life than what they had found at home. The people we met along the way were the source of much continued inspiration throughout the trip, and we have remained friends with most of them.*

Email / May 7, 2002 / A Seafood Feast

We snorkeled for scallops along the edge of the bay with Rixene, Mercury, Carly, and Phantom from *Karma Laden*. To our delight, we discovered there were plenty for the taking, and we learned which ones to leave behind from Mercury's knowledge of the sea. We must have looked like a feeding frenzy, all nine of us snorkeling in 15-20 feet of water, pulling up scallop after scallop, filling two bags—but not more than we could eat—for our eventual feast.

Then the controversy began. Patrik discovered a good-sized octopus, and Chuck's well-placed shot with the spear gun ensured this was truly going to be a meal to remember. After hauling the dead creature into the dinghy, Mercury encouraged Ken to cut off its head in preparation for the fry pan. Ken complied, but then just after the not-so-delicate surgery, he regretted what he had done and fell into depression over his part in the killing.

What's done is done; we boiled the scallops and the octopus, chopped them up well, fried with garlic and onion, and served hot. What a succulent feast! We had enough octopus left over to make a mouth-watering soup that lasted two more days. Ken is right, though. That's the first and last octopus we'll kill; they are too smart and beautiful to kill—and we're not that hungry. From now on, we'll just enjoy their beauty.

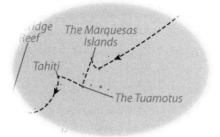

CHAPTER 7

Just Another Beautiful White Sand Beach in Paradise

"Love doesn't make the world go 'round. Love is what makes the ride worthwhile."

FRANKLIN P. JONES

Email / May 17, 2002 / The Tuamotus

We entered the Manihi Lagoon—to a hard-won anchorage—through a narrow pass no wider than two boat lengths, running the engine full power against a 5-knot current and 2-foot waves. Our entrance was purposefully timed to the ebbing tide, as the boat is easier to handle when going against the current. Still, the strength of the river of water exiting to the sea was surprising—maybe we were off in our tidal predictions. We also consider the time of day; the colors of the water are intensified by the bright sun, making the hours of 1000 to 1400 the best time for entering a pass between dangerous reefs. At that time, the daylight allows us to read the depth of the water ahead by color: White is very shallow, reflecting the sand below; light blue is getting deeper; and as the blue deepens, so does the water. Unless, of course, you're looking at a black spot, which is often a coral head waiting to bite.

Manihi is comprised completely of white coral rising only a few feet above sea level, but it's enough to protect the 50 square miles of sapphire blue lagoon, making it an almost perfect anchorage. Once through the narrow pass and inside the lagoon, you've arrived in paradise. Because the land is actually coral, there's no dirt runoff to cloud the water. After dark, I turn on the spreader lights and watch them illuminate our own backyard swimming pool, and even though I know it's not safe to swim at night (sharks like to feed then), I can't help myself. Tomorrow, we're going scuba diving with a company that says we should expect to see lots of sharks outside the pass. Not quite sure how I feel about that yet.

Personal Journal / May 19, 2002

Slow down. Another lesson recently learned the hard way. We tried to make it here to Manihi in three days because, upon leaving Nuku Hiva, we discovered we could motor sail at almost 9 knots with the light spinnaker. We were flying along beautifully for almost 48 hours, excited about our record-setting speed, when at 0400, just when the morning is darkest—*BAM!* A 25-knot rainsquall came out of nowhere, heeled us over, and before we knew what was happening, we heard the spinnaker *rrrrrrrrip* right up its belly and across the sail's width. It flapped wildly in the wind, while the sheets (lines) snapped back and forth until we were able to lower it fully to the foredeck. We had been stupidly pushing the boat hard, trying to make the passage in three days rather than four. The trip ended up taking three and a half days, which meant we had to stand off and wait for morning light on the fourth day anyway. What was I thinking? I was using my old, fast, city-life principles. Don't push it; as the shopkeeper in Mexico said, "What's the hurry?" Slow down.

In the meantime, tension aboard had increased, and it was getting to me. Hey, this was supposed to be fun. At times, I felt like I was back in the office, trying to manage a team on a business project, and when I saw that happening, I knew it was time to make some changes. I felt I had lost control of my space and time, and instead was catering to the busy goals and adventures of everyone else. Ken and I discussed the subject and concluded it was time for the additional crew to leave. Chuck also felt the tension. He and Amy had served their purpose well, enjoyed our time together, but the boat was too crowded…and they had to be the first ones to go.

One morning as I was lying in bed, Chuck jumped in next to me, and being his direct self, popped the question, "Do you want us to leave?" I was surprised by his straightforward attitude, impressed by his sensitivity to the situation, and relieved he asked before I did. I knew it was time for them to leave but was chicken to play the bad guy. I gave him a big hug and said, "Yes, it's time," and the next day, Chuck and Amy departed Julia.

Manihi is home to over 60 black pearl farms, and the locals aren't shy about peddling their wares. While I appreciate their beauty, owning a string of these gems has never been a priority. We cheerfully watch our friends haggle for them; yesterday, Harvey and Jean traded two bottles of scotch for a bag containing nearly 100 of the shiny treasures.

The cruising community has discovered Ken's computer expertise. Several times a day, our VHF radio comes to life: "*Julia*, this is *So and So*." After the usual pleasantries comes the reason for the call. "Hi Larry, how are you, how is Patrik, and oh, by the way, is Ken there?" A few minutes later, a dinghy pulls up to our boarding ladder and Ken is whisked away to fix somebody's computer problems. He loves the attention and the challenge, and it sure makes us popular.

I'm re-connecting with my kayak. On a two-hour paddle today, I began to appreciate how the alone time is good therapy and clears my head. Away from the boat, the water was perfectly still and the colors so vivid it seemed as though I was gliding on a sheet of glass above an aquarium. In fact, I would have been able to read a newspaper if it had been sitting on the bottom, but I was content to watch the fish and look at the brilliant coral just a few feet below the surface.

The weather can change fast in the tropics, and only an hour later, my paddle back to the mother ship was through 2-foot chop, 20-knot winds on the nose, and rainsqualls. I've always said I like to feel the weather—rather than be insulated from the elements—and I sure experienced it today. As I strained for each yard gained back to *Julia*, I felt the cold rain pounding down on my bare shoulders, the air temperature falling, the salt burning my eyes, and my muscles aching as I struggled upwind. This is what I have been looking for—this is why I sailed out the Golden Gate, and turned south.

 Email / May 22, 2002 / Tropical Paradise Found

Underwater visibility is spectacular at well over 100 feet, making it easy to see the exotic tropical fish, large schools of tuna, barracuda, and enough sharks to last a lifetime. At an irresistible temperature of 90 degrees, we spend most of our days in the water, snorkeling for hours on end. Reading a plastic fish-identifier card below the surface is no problem until I become giddy—when I have to surface, choking from laughter over the water clarity.

In the afternoon, the rich blue sky is disrupted by clouds that always seem to remain low on the distant horizon—white, puffy, and billowy— with dark grey undersides revealing the rain they are about to dump on our heads. The air temperature matches the water at 90°, but the trade winds blow steadily and just enough to cool things down perfectly. I sit watching tall palm trees on the beaches—not for how pretty they are as they sway in the wind—but looking for the rare occurrence of witnessing a coconut fall from the tree. Like kids at the pool, we jump from the boat into the water, climb back up, and jump off again and again. In this calm protected haven, *Julia* rests rock steady, and at last I feel a sense of ease. Can it get any better?

Some days seemed too good to be true. When the weather was perfect, when everything mechanical was doing what it should be without breaking down, when we all stared in amazement at the sunset or the stars, when I was alone on watch, feeling the balmy air on my naked body, a warm feeling would wash over me like a drug. The natural beauty was important to me, and I tried to soak up all I could. At these times, I wanted the moment to last forever, and I knew this is what I had been searching for; this is what I had promised myself....

I loved crawling into the berth in the aft captain's cabin, which Ken and I shared. We would push and shove each other out of the way, laughing and teasing until we fell asleep in each other's arms. We were having a blast together.

 Email / May 25, 2002 / From Manihi to Ahe and Moving Again

After three days anchored inside the well-protected lagoon at

Ahe, we are on the move again. The Tuamotus are comprised of 78 coral islands, which could take years to explore. We don't have that kind of time but feel fortunate to be on the way to visit the third of these magnificent, protected lagoons. At 1430, we weighed anchor and motored into open ocean, headed to Rangiroa, the most populated of the coral islands. We exited the narrow pass at slack water to avoid strong currents, and once outside the lagoon, in the company of five other boats in our little flotilla, turned toward our next landfall, just 80 miles to the southwest.

At sunset, we set up our fishing gear—and bingo! Within minutes, we caught a beautiful yellowtail tuna, put the line back in the water, and soon, caught another one. After cleaning the fish, Patrik made sushi. Talk about fresh! We even tried a piece right off of the fish as it was being cleaned… Ewww, but yumm. What a perfect day.

Email / June 2, 2002 / Fun Island
While in Rangiroa, we met Mimi, a lovely young lady crewing on another boat who surprised us one day with her presentation of a poem. Who knew she was a closet poet? For the most part, we tend not to ask about previous lives, which means everybody gets a fresh start. We have become "party central," and a day doesn't go by without some sort of event onboard.

Fun Island

Entry to Fun Island is two beers

and you've got to pay the fee

Or you won't get in to *Julia's* flotilla

of inflatable armchairs and air mattresses

The pool toys glisten in the South Pacific sun

trailing in a line behind Larry's 50' yacht

If you're a listener, you know VHF doesn't lie

Julia has fun monopolized in this lagoon

Roger this and Shirley that

Garcon! Garcon! more wine and cheese

Over here God, oh God where have

all the gay sailors gone?

Where has the zest gone?

If only all joy in life and love and oil changes

were this simple for all to achieve
Aboard *Julia*, fair *Julia*, where even a spent solenoid
comes to life with plans
To scrap the main salon and put in a dance hall
a hideaway bar, so go ahead and put on RuPaul
We'll be lounging in the cockpit
we'll be under the mister
spinning around the anchorage
dinghy surfing, mixing drinks on a mooring ball
While Ken shouts over the Yamaha
Here you are sailing into the sunset
You never thought it'd be like this
with priorities like brie and beer
There's only one demand
and that's your social schedule
We've each got something to learn in this life
And we can learn it here on Fun Island

Email / June 4, 2002

It's the middle of the night and we're motoring in calm seas, no wind at all, under a black canopy of sky dotted with an unimaginable number of stars surrounding us all the way down to the horizon—like the inside of a planetarium. While stark and desolate, it's strangely peaceful at sea tonight.

Our plans were to stay in Rangiroa just a few days, but there's no other way to say this: We were simply having too much fun to leave. *Julia* rested in the calm waters for eight days, smack dab in front of the magnificent Kia Ora Hotel, known for its luxurious bungalows scattered on the white coral beach and jutting out into the lagoon on stilts. We spent countless hours floating on the surface of the water face down staring at a coral and fish-filled area called, appropriately, The Aquarium. From 2-inch blue and pink neon damsels and gobies, to 5-foot white-tip sharks, blue coral to black spiny sea urchins, it seemed like the flagship demo store of all the sea has to offer.

Tonight, we're on our way to world-famous Moorea, which sits only 12 miles from the main island of Tahiti. By tomorrow afternoon, we'll be anchored in Cook's Bay.

It was easy to fall into a trance under such dream-like conditions, but like an alarm clock buzzer early on Monday morning, something would happen to wake us up. You have to pay attention out there, and if you're silly enough to stay in a hazy state, the ocean will snap you out of it in an instant. It wasn't the last surprise from the ocean floor we were to encounter. As the saying goes, "It's not the ocean that gets you, it's the hard bits around the edges."

Personal Journal / June 11, 2002

At Moorea, inside Viare Pass in the late morning. Right turn towards Sofitel Hotel. Grey skies meant limited visibility. Slowed to 3 knots, and then, just as we saw brown-colored water, put it in reverse but *too late—THUD*, and we're aground, jammed between a coral head and a pile of sand. Lowered the dinghy and motor, hung it over starboard side on spinnaker halyards with Ken as added ballast, heeled *Julia* over enough to change the keel's angle. Then full reverse to spin us off. Pivoted around a coral head and we're free with little more than a few scratches. Humbled, luckily, at a very cheap price.

The more people we met, the bigger our social calendar seemed to get. Because Julia *was one of the larger yachts among the group now sailing the Milk Run together, she became home to many endless parties. We were looked upon as the young boat with the gay guys, which may have meant we were hip and cool. We were referred to as the "Most colorful boat in the anchorage" more than once, and gladly accepted our new nickname, "Fun Island." I was glad to host so many people aboard* Julia. *There was always someone coming or going, parents dropping their kids off at our boat for movies and popcorn, dinghy surfing, diving, and sharing of our fresh water with those who didn't have watermakers. We were a hit I and loved it.*

The physical beauty was spectacular, but no matter where we were, the conversation always came back to the weather, which was discussed endlessly. Along with the captains of other boats, we often shared cocktails and weather forecasting, or coffee and weather forecasting, or, "C'mon over for chips and olives, and we'll look at the latest downloads of the weather maps." While tiring, we all knew the importance of this task.

In spite of all the fun we were having, Ken remained adamant about his plan to go home. We were now arguing about it, but no matter what I said, he remained firm in his decision. While outwardly cheery, I was becoming inwardly despondent and could think of nothing else. I remained in a state of denial, not believing he would actually follow through on it….

Email / June 20, 2002

Moorea. Just the name conjures up images of tall mountain peaks, exquisitely deep blue and pale aquamarine waters, Tahitian dancing, excellent sailing in warm trade winds, and just hanging out, enjoying life. Moorea has been all of that and more. We are secure in Cook's Bay (named for the famed Captain James Cook), which has to be one of the world's most beautiful anchorages and making everybody wonder how future islands and harbors might be any better. The other day, while kayaking inside the reef, a white tropicbird flew overhead; I noticed the undersides of its wings were reflecting the water color...imagine that, turquoise-colored wings. It's been raining a fair amount and as a cold front is passing through, we slept under a sheet last night to stay warm. As this unsettled weather hovers around French Polynesia, we are staying put in Cook's Bay. Our friends Brad and Laura sailed to the island of Huahine a few days ago and got slammed by 60-knot winds on their passage. We were supposed to go with them but at the last minute decided to stay—I just had a feeling—and we're glad we did. I'm learning to trust my gut. Alas, the larger it gets, the more I trust it.

Personal Journal / June 25, 2002

The calm passage from Rangiroa to Tahiti required we motor the entire 24 hours. As a result, we had emptied our main fuel tanks by not paying attention to the number of engine hours and fuel consumed. I'm the captain and I have to pay attention to everything—haven't I learned that yet? The tanks went dry at 0300 (why do things like this always happen in the wee hours of the morning?), and we had to bleed the air out of the engine, a job new to me. I did it though. How about that: me with a wrench in hand bleeding a diesel engine. That's one for the books. If only my father, Abe, could see me now.

In Moorea, we went on a shark-feeding dive...scary. The dive master seemed fearless. He is a very cute, tall and slim French blond man in his late 20s and had an accent that melted ice with his first word. All of the paying divers gathered together on the ocean floor 40 feet down and waited. Jean-Claude, or Jean-Luc, or Jean Val Jean, or whatever his sexy French name was, pulled out a hunk of raw meat and waved it around to get the scent of blood in the water. Sounds a bit crazy, doesn't it? I mean, who would actually do this on purpose, and moreover, who would pay to be nearby? There's something rather seductive about watching a shark feeding frenzy; there was a waiting list to get onto one of these dives.

As the first shark hit the meat, it took all the balls any of us could muster to do as we'd been told: "Stay rock solid still." Another shark arrived and another, until there were at least a dozen of the frenzied hunters going after the meat Jean-Claude threw into the water. While he and the sharks had clearly done this dance for the few and fearless before, there didn't seem to be much room for error, and I think most of us warmed up the inside of our wetsuits during that dive.

I couldn't believe it: Upon arrival in Papeete, Ken's first desire was to go to a travel agency and buy his ticket home. I really thought we had become a couple. Everybody thought the same...except Ken. He reminded me, "I was always planning to leave in May and it's already June." I would desperately reply, "Yes, but that was before you knew how great this was, before you knew how great we were together."

Personal Journal / June 28, 2002

The dreaded day has come. I'm devastated, can hardly move. I'm numb. I never thought he would do it, but he did; Ken left yesterday for San Francisco. We piled his luggage into the dinghy, and Patrik, Ken and I crawled in on top. Ken was silent, and I was catatonic; Patrik started the motor and piloted us ashore trying to at least keep Ken dry for his flight. It was a little funny taking a dinghy to the airport, but there wasn't much levity at the time. After a short taxi ride from the dock, we made our way to the Air France counter in absolute silence.

"Please don't go," I begged.

"Don't do this, please don't do this," Ken said.

I threw my arms around him and held on tight. Tears streamed down my cheeks mixing with the sweat already covering my body. I looked up and saw Ken was crying, too. I kissed him one last time and whispered, "I love you." As he turned, I tried to smile for him but my lips just quivered, and the lump in my throat prevented me from saying anything else.

It was a good thing Patrik was there because I could barely walk. "I have to sit down," I said. We sat in silence for quite a while until I spoke: "Why did he have to go? Why did he leave me?" I asked in a shaky voice. My eyes were bloodshot and we attracted lots of stares, but I didn't care.

"He had to go. He had to do it for himself," Patrik said. "He needs to find himself and be independent, and he can't do that with you around. Maybe he's not ready for the relationship you want."

"Or maybe I didn't show him how much I really cared," I said. "Perhaps it's my fault."

Patrik put his arm around my shoulder and held me while I poured out my tears.

"Come on, let's get you back to the boat," Patrik said after we watched Ken's plane lift off and climb until it disappeared high in the bright sky.

Back at *Julia*, I sat alone on the foredeck and stared at the horizon. The boat was empty and quiet, and the laughter was gone. In the evening Patrik said, "Hey, Skipper, come on, get in the water and go paddling," as he was untying and getting my fast red ocean kayak ready. I went paddling but had no strength and before long, returned to the boat.

I already miss Ken's smile, his laugh, goofiness, energy, snuggling in bed, and waking up next to him in the morning. I'm scared of continuing this voyage without him; he was, after all, part of the dream. Even though Patrik is onboard and we get along well, I feel alone. And that's what I have feared the most.

I'm trying to tell myself this is what I came for—to discover who I am and what I'm all about, and I can only do that by myself. Is Ken any different? Isn't that what he's going home to do, to find himself? I have to respect his choice, and I know I have to let go. Sometimes it's just bad timing; our relationship has definitely grown in the last seven months, but maybe I was putting too much pressure on him.

We're leaving Papeete because the airport is here and it reminds me of Ken's departure. Tonight, we'll sail for Huahine, our first passage without him. I hope Ken will return but in the meantime, I'm lost, my heart aches, and I can't stop welling up when I think about him.

In my lonely hours and days after Ken's departure, I didn't have to turn very far to find support. Patrik truly rose to the occasion as best he could without moving into the aft cabin. He repaired things, cooked, cleaned, and hugged me with plenty of "C'mon Skipper, you're gonna be okay" type encouragements. Patrik was there for me when I needed him most. While the passage of time supposedly heals all, this took longer than I had expected. I've never enjoyed being depressed, sullen, or upset. Some people do, but not me. Yet this time I just couldn't seem to pull myself out of this slump....

Email / July 11, 2002 / Raiatea and Tahaa

From our anchorage at the island of Tahaa, the view is of the sun setting over Bora Bora in a golden light that rises to a pale sky, and then the first crescent of a new moon appears, followed by Venus, bright as a lighthouse. We spent the last five days at Raiatea surrounded by spectacular scenery, great snorkeling, and good friends anchored nearby, including Peter from *Torea* and Rob from *Surfer Girl*, both young and fun San Franciscans.

One afternoon, I kayaked into the middle of the pass and suddenly was surrounded by a large pod of dolphins. The short, sharp breathing puffs of their breathing; the backdrop of a 1,000-foot green lava mountain; the crystal clear water; and the view of *Julia* from afar with Bora Bora in the background was thrilling.

While Raiatea and Tahaa are stunning, when you see pictures promoting French Polynesia, they're almost always of Bora Bora. If someone is describing an island in the South Pacific, it's the one most people picture with its tall mountain peaks, perfect thatched-roof hut hotels that extend out into the lagoon, manta rays easily seen while snorkeling, and honeymoon couples walking hand in hand on the beaches. It must be the prettiest island in the world...except for Moorea...and Fatu Hiva...and....

Personal Journal / July 19, 2002

Patrik and I sailed back to Moorea to pick up our guests for the next two weeks: Bob is here! He's visiting with our friend Alan from Seattle and is providing a much-needed lift.

Bob and I are getting along better than we have in years and spending some quality time together. I'm so glad he's here! His enthusiasm for me to keep going is important. I'm encouraging him to follow his creative passion and discover himself through his art. Having such a good time playing Rummikub on the foredeck, paddling, swimming, and driving around the island, I wish it would never end. We're both loving this time together and are working on clarifying our relationship as best friends.

Keeping a boat operating at optimum is a challenge. When using wind power rather than diesel, it's more difficult to adjust the amount of horse-power the sails are producing, which greatly affects how the boat handles. If the wind is blowing 15 knots, we would put all of our sail up to generate as much power as possible, but if the wind is blowing 25 to 30 knots, that much sail provides excessive power and would make Julia unmanageable. Therefore, sailors know how to "reef," which simply means to reduce the amount of sail. It's not a hard process and we became very good at it, but it involves one person going to the mast and adjusting the halyards and reef lines, while the other person manages the additional jobs, including steering from the cockpit. One reef is usually put in at 20 knots of wind, two reefs at 25, and three reefs, which shrinks the main-sail down to bed-sheet size in higher winds and rough seas. Basically, the rule of thumb is, "If you are thinking about reefing, it's probably too late."

And there's more to do than just adjust the sails. The batteries are essential for maintaining power for the autopilot, radar, and other instruments, including GPS, wind speed, boat speed, and, of course, the ship's computers. They require constant vigilance and charging, usually using the generator. There is a plethora of other issues that present a challenge to keeping everything running smoothly.

I suppose it was partly because Ken wasn't there to bounce around ideas with, that I was forced to learn the intricacies of every system onboard. I was in tune with the boat and more aware of noises out of the norm. I was starting to hear more sounds like grinding metal from the autopilot and knew something was wrong.

Email / August 14, 2002 / Rarotonga
After a windy and rough four-day passage, we have made it to Rarotonga, a small densely vegetated island, which is the center and capital of the Cook Islands—and to us, it's heaven. Rarotonga is administered by New Zealand, which means proper English is spoken, the U.S. dollar is two-to-one over the NZ dollar, and a beer is $1.50 rather than the inflated

$8 in French Polynesia. The island boasts markets with fresh vegetables and fruit, and a hardware store. Ahh, the little things that excite me; I used to take them for granted.

Avatiu harbor is tiny, and after a two-day wait anchored out in the "cheap seats," our turn finally came to be stern tied to the wharf with 15 other boats, where mooring space is so tight we can literally step boat to boat—this leads to many spontaneous cocktail parties.

The boating community really comes together and helps each boat drop anchor out in the harbor and then back into the wharf "Med style," using dinghies as mini tugboats to guide each boat to its space. It's a challenge because most sailboats have only one propeller and don't back very straight, but it's fun.

Personal Journal / August 15, 2002

We have met some wonderful people on this island-hopping leg of the journey. As each boat leaves, their crews shout, "See you in Tonga!" and we realize these are the people with whom we will cruise the rest of the Pacific, and with some we'll continue to who knows where? We have made friends from all over the world. We're enjoying the company of *Final Straw, L'eau Life, C'est la Vie, Avventura, White Hawk,* and *Gitana* from California; *Scott Free, Guitar,* and *Duet* from England; *L'il Gem, Cardinal Sin, North Road,* and *By Chance* from British Columbia; *Mobisle, Harmony, Raven,* and *Windarra* from Washington State; *Pegasus* from Connecticut, and plenty of others. *Pura Vida* has turned back to the States, and we'll miss Brad and Laura. It's the nature of cruising, a revolving door of friends who come and go into and out of our lives. I guess Ken now falls into that category.

Email / August 17, 2002

With a cold front came an unusual north wind, which is blowing right into the north-facing entrance to the harbor. *Julia* is handling it well though and pitching much less than most other boats because of her weight. Everyone is waiting to move on to Tonga but not 'til the bad weather eases up. We're expecting more wind tomorrow along with rain and thunderstorms, so I'm guessing we're in for quite a ride.

Between rolls, while cozily nestled in the aft cabin, I've been reflecting on the adventures we've had on this island to date. The most memorable is the long, very steep, half-day hike through tropical rainforests across the island. Dressed in shorts, T-shirts, and sandals, our group of 20 from various boats set out in somewhat cool but still very humid weather in the morning. At first, we walked up paved roads, then gravel, dirt, and finally a mud track steep enough to require holding onto the trees to pull yourself up. The steep trail turned everyone's feet reddish-brown; our bodies became hot and sticky, and we were dripping with sweat. I panted out, "I think I'm going to die if we have to go any further." Patrik replied, "Oh, c'mon Skipper, don't die yet, we're not to the top and you haven't seen the view. Then you can kick the bucket!" At last we made it to the crest over 1,200 feet above sea level and stopped for lunch at the base of the famous needle, a black lava spire jutting hundreds of feet straight up from the mountaintop. The views were well worth the effort, but the hike was a real challenge and especially difficult on the knees after spending so much time at sea with little exercise.

The entire island is only 6 miles long by 4 miles wide and begs to be explored. A few days after recovering from our hike, and again with many of our cruising family, we rented mopeds and rode village to village on the coastal road all the way around the island. First, we were required to visit the police station and take a moped test in order to obtain a Rarotonga driver's license. We shopped for souvenirs, stopped for lunch, checked out the various beaches, and had a swim. On the way back to the harbor, the skies opened up and dumped everything they had, soaking our whole biker gang of yachties to the skin. We loved it and happily rode our open scooters back to the boats laughing like kids do when they are playing in the rain.

The open-air market is a colorful place to buy fresh vegetables and fruits, and you can also see many of us wandering the aisles of the hardware store. When the small cargo ship arrives from New Zealand, it seems the entire island population turns out to watch as it enters the tiny harbor, drops anchor, spins around and lands right at the dock. While the locals are more interested in the cargo, we are in admiration of how the captain handles his vessel. We have the best seats in the house, and the ship's arrival is good cause for a spur-of-the-moment cocktail party. Then again, cruisers don't require much to have cocktails.

Email / August 23, 2002

This doesn't seem like the balmy South Pacific; we're dressed in foul-weather gear, and it's as cold as a summer day in San Francisco. We're on our way west for the 400-mile passage to Beveridge Reef, a submerged coral atoll between Rarotonga and Tonga. We're looking forward to a calm anchorage because everyone is feeling rather sick. We haven't been at sea in over 12 days and have just downed seasickness pills because, as the saying goes: "There are only two stages of seasickness." Stage One is, "Oh, my God, I think I'm going to die." Stage Two is, "Oh, God, I wish I were dead."

S 21° 06.8′W 160° 24.5′

Personal Journal / August 26, 2002

Engine won't start. Tried reset button and nothing. Pushed the starter repeatedly about ten times and then it kicked over. It's getting worse, I'm sick of this problem, but more importantly, I need a reliable engine. It's a new engine. What the heck is going on? Also getting an error message on the power inverter. And the batteries aren't holding their charge like they should. I don't know much about these things and don't see how I can manage!

Email / August 26, 2002 / No Rain, No Rainbow

They say, "No Rain, No Rainbow," and I agree. All bad weather comes to an end, and after two days of hard work, we were rewarded with beautiful sunshine, glorious spinnaker sailing, small seas, and double rainbows as the last of the squalls dissipated.

Our big prize is a quite extraordinary anchorage at a most remote place called Beveridge Reef. The charts show only the name followed by the word "obstruction," which indeed it is if you were going to sail through it. This is firmly established by the shipwreck on the reef not far from us. What makes this place such a unique atoll is there is no land anywhere, and in many places, the coral only breaks the surface at low tide. There are no markers or buoys to show the entrance on the west side, just word of mouth, and a photocopy of a hand-drawn map from the Rarotonga Harbor Master.

It's rather adventurous searching for the uncharted entrance to a reef, and we're happy as clams having found and entered the pass safely. *Julia* is anchored in 30 feet of water so clear we can check the anchor by simply standing on the bow and looking down as if it were air. To make it even more exciting, we are the only boat in this desolate mid-ocean marvel.

It wasn't only Julia that needed constant maintenance. It's every boat that goes cruising for an extended period of time. The equipment just isn't built for these tough conditions and rigorous use. I was beginning to wonder if I had done something wrong because of the ongoing repairs.

I discovered the most important skill needed for cruising was tenacity, and I knew I had plenty of that. More than one client told me in my business career I was the most tenacious salesman they had ever seen. "Ah, so it's just a matter of slowing down, being patient and tenacious" I told myself. "Okay, I can do that." Or could I?

Email / August 27, 2002 / Sharks

Beveridge Reef is a great place for discovery where we watched the grey-tip sharks fight for our food scraps. It occurred to me they were here because we provided the opportunity for them to prey. It seems you have to watch out for sharks anytime or place in life—from business to Beveridge Reef—but if you don't present yourself as a target, you won't attract sharks. Needless to say, we didn't go swimming.

Email / September 3, 2002 / Incredible Niue

We are in Niue, one of the world's smallest countries. It's independent but under the umbrella of New Zealand. Niue has a population of only 1,600, and aside from a few tourists who fly in each week, us yachties are pretty much the only visitors. Upon arrival, we radioed the Niue Yacht Club (which we joined for $10). Mary, who *is* the Niue Yacht Club, said we would have to wait for a mooring ball as all 12 were occupied. Normally, we wouldn't care about a mooring ball, but the only semi-protected anchorage is in the lee of the island and the depth is a deep 90 feet, where we anchored and waited.

Ashore, we rented a car from Mary who appears to wear many hats. No credit card deposit required…it's a small island and there's nowhere to run off with a car if you were to steal it. The island of Niue is all coral and limestone, which has created a stunning array of caves, caverns, and natural pools along the entire coastline, and we stopped to snorkel in a few. Some of the caves are huge and boast beautifully eerie pink and white stalactites and stalagmites.

The waves crashing into the caves and the wind howling through them have made for some fantastic hikes over the jagged, grey terrain. One such trek was to Togo Chasm: It requires a half hour walk along a jungle trail completely covered in a green canopy of vines, ferns, palms, and fruit trees. Where the jungle opens up, it's another half hour across a steep coral path, which winds its way through a field of 15- to 20-feet tall black sharp coral pinnacles resembling huge razor blades—definitely not a place to walk barefoot. The track ends at a nearly vertical homemade wooden ladder that drops more than 50 feet onto a white-sand paradise filled with palms and surrounded by steep grey rocks. After a picnic lunch in the enclosed oasis, we climbed up the ladder, took in the vast panorama of the sea, and made our way back to the road. This island is fascinating.

There's hardly a store on the island. Patrik and John (our new temporary crew member), set out to get vegetables, and after asking around among the locals, they were directed to the prison where there were two—you read that right, two—prisoners who grew a garden. We don't know what they're in for because when asked they simply replied, "Doesn't matter, does it?" They've been here long enough to grow an awesome vegetable garden, and we agree with the locals: They're the best gardeners on the island. They seemed happy enough with their home; it consisted of a house and a semi-specific area within which they were supposed to stay. They gave the vegetables free for the taking. These guys sure have turned a tough sentence into something approaching a happy lifestyle.

We went on a most edgy dive in 150-foot visibility water today. I have become obsessed with this visibility thing, but this has got to be as good as it gets. However, much to my chagrin, Niue has a significant poisonous sea snake population; I'm not keen on even the gentle garden variety, let alone these serpents. Even so, I had to deal with rattlesnakes while working as a river rafting guide back in the 1970s. The rattlers would slither their way into camp and tuck into a warm spot near a rock, and invariably one of the guests would discover it and scream: "Aaaaaaaah! S…

Sn...Sna...Snak...SNAKE!" We'd rig a long stick with a loop on the end, capture the angry snake, and carry it flailing and squirming down to the river knowing it would find a new home further downstream. I hated that job but couldn't very well show my fear, at least not outwardly. Now I'm older and admit my dislike of snakes.

Sitting at anchor, we could see the sea snakes' heads break the surface long enough to breathe before heading down to the ocean floor where they prefer to shelter until needing more air. They're 2- to 3-feet long, an inch in diameter, and are quite pretty with silver and black stripes. Okay, they're not pretty; there's nothing really pretty about any snake in my mind, and these are so poisonous, one bite is likely to kill you. They have small mouths, though, and it would be difficult for them to bite. Still, you wouldn't want any extra appendages hanging down; no nude swimming here.

The diving is so good here, there's a waiting list—you go when you're called. The morning of our first dive, I asked the dive master where we were headed and he casually replied, "Snake Gully." With a hint of desperation, I turned to ask Ian, the company owner, "Isn't there any other place we can explore?" to which he replied with smart New Zealand wit, "Sure is, mate, lots of places, but today is Tuesday, and we always dive Snake Gully on Tuesdays." For a moment, my thoughts raced: I could feign illness right now, I could break some of my equipment, I could come up with an earache in an instant, and yet I chose to dive. I wasn't going to let a few hundred deadly poisonous snakes ruin my day.

There were so many snakes we had to watch where we were swimming. They lay at the bottom in piles like a scene out of *Indiana Jones,* and I got the shivers taking in the scene. At any given time, a dozen or so were swimming around us, up to or down from the surface. You had to push the water in front of them to ensure they didn't run into you. This took all the bravery I could muster. I faced my fear and thank you very much, I have no desire to do it again. I was reminded that I could face my fears and overcome them by jumping in and going for it.

Because Niue is limestone and coral, there is very little runoff of mud or dirt, and thus the water clarity is some of the best in the world. We dove to coral gardens 100 feet down, where even at that depth the bright purples, blues, greens, reds, pinks and yellows showed vividly on the many types of coral: fans, tubes, brain, antler, plate, and fire tip that causes an intense sting and burn if touched. The abundant marine life included ribbon eels, lionfish, parrotfish, white tip sharks, barracuda, and turtles. We swam into dark caverns and caves with dark nooks and crannies requiring flashlights and frequent looks over our shoulders to make sure we knew the way out.

This edgy diving reminded me of the scarier scenes from the classic T.V. drama, *Sea Hunt*. Back on the surface, I blurted out: "Did you see that pile of snakes? Did you see the size of that eel? Holy crap! Did you see…" and the other divers too couldn't stop stammering about what they had just experienced.

Once back on the dive boat, we saw a pod of spinner dolphins and motored over to see how close we could get to them. We jumped into the clear warm water and swam with the group. Much friendlier than snakes, I might add. While most of them were not interested in a bunch of humans flailing about, two of the sleek mammals were so playful they kept swimming under and around us in circles and frolicking like young puppies— that is, if puppies weighed 200 pounds. This was a dream come true: We were actually swimming with dolphins in the wild. Unbelievable.

To complete another Cousteau-like day, while sipping cocktails, a radio call came in over the VHF: "Whale, ho!"

"Where, where, where?" I asked.

Clark Straw from *Final Straw* replied, "280 degrees on the compass!" Sure enough, there was an entire pod of humpback whales. Sitting inside *Julia's* hull, we could actually hear them clicking and squeaking as they communicated with each other. It was truly a magical and memorable day on the water. I feel very connected to the sea today.

Anchoring a boat properly is such an important skill but is often over-looked by many. Sailing courses teach how to make a boat go and often emphasize how to make it go faster. However, when cruising, the ability to slow the boat down with control and then to anchor securely in any and all conditions is the real challenge. It's like the gas pedal vs. the brake pedal in a car. When the proverbial shit hits the fan, which one is really most important?

While I always insisted we set the anchor hard by backing down on it, I still slept uneasily. If any one piece of equipment used for anchoring—including the chain and shackles—were to fail, the boat could wind up on the reef or onshore. We always had the GPS anchor alarm set to go off if we moved only two boat lengths, and I woke up every couple of hours even in the calmest of anchorages to check our position.

We put out as much scope as possible (the ratio of chain to the water's depth). Three-to-one is bare minimum, six-to-one is markedly better, but in deep anchorages, that can be more chain than most boats carry. Niue was an anchoring challenge because of the depth, which is why they had mooring balls installed for the visiting yachts.

The accident happened while waiting for ours....

Personal Journal / September 4, 2002

Niue was unique: one rugged island with no fringing reefs. The anchorage is in the lee of the island and only protected from the southeast trade winds. One night, the wind shifted around to the west which made for a very uneven ride putting us against a lee shore with only three-to-one scope, not a safe position to be in. Thus we became very alert to anchoring safely here.

While waiting for our mooring ball, we had quite the fire drill. It was mid-afternoon; *Julia* was anchored in 90 feet of water with 300 of our 400-foot chain in the water holding nicely. Remembering, "chain doesn't do any good sitting on the boat," Patrik admirably wanted to let out more. Before going to the foredeck, he asked me how much chain I thought was already deployed.

"Three hundred feet," I answered.

"I think we only have 200 out," he replied.

"No, more like 300," I emphatically repeated. The next thing I heard was the windlass opening and the chain running out. I thought, "That chain sure is running out fast considering we only have 100 feet left aboard." Patrik opened the windlass brake wide, and still sure we had plenty left onboard, he let it fly, and fly it did...out of the locker much faster than expected—and in seconds, it was gone.

"Larry! Larry!" Patrik shouted below to where I was reading at the chart table. "I let it all go! I let it all go!"

"You what?" I replied in disbelief. This frantic but brief dialogue went back and forth until I had determined yes, indeed, all of the chain was gone. "Are you telling me we are no longer attached to the bottom of the ocean?"

"Yes!" he said with a look of fear and surprise, "That's what I've been trying to tell you. It's all gone from the boat!" Convinced by Patrik's pleas, I leapt out of my chair and flew up to the cockpit to find Patrik already at the engine controls.

The last 100 feet of chain ran out so quickly Patrik couldn't stop it, and the weight of the anchor and chain jerked hard enough to rip loose the safety rope knot between the chain and boat. Just like that, the chain was gone. Patrik hit the engine starter button repeatedly until we finally felt the comforting vibration of the purring motor under our feet. I moved to the controls, slipped the gearshift into forward and held our position, while John and Patrik got the second anchor ready. I hit the MOB (Man Overboard) button on the GPS to mark the place and hopefully retrieve the anchor later, and we proceeded to set our secondary anchor and chain. Once secure, we had a moment to think. Because of the depth, there was no way we were going to try and find the chain on our own, so we radioed Niue Divers and set an appointment for the next morning with one of their professional divers. I was pretty angry with Patrik but knew we needed a solution first, and he needed a lecture later. I barely slept that night.

The diver wasn't able to reach the end of the chain because it had sunk in over 120 feet of water, but he managed to attach a line to the anchor, which was still resting at 90 feet. We were handed a bill, and the end of a line tied directly to a 120-pound anchor and 400 feet, or 700 pounds of $^3/_8$" chain, making a total weight of 820 pounds hanging straight down in 90 feet of water. You want to talk heavy?

I tried to keep calm as John, Patrik and I, using a winch on the mast, spent the next three hours hauling up the anchor, followed by all 400 feet of chain onto the deck. At mid-day it started to rain heavily and my calm turned to the utterance of small angry curses under my breath while putting the chain back in the locker, fixing it around the windlass, re-tying the safety line, and getting the anchor ready to reset.

It was a back-asswards fiasco, which would have been a real comedy if it hadn't been so difficult, and I hadn't been fuming. I knew we had to get the job done and my talk with Patrik had to wait. He wanted to defend his actions right then: "I didn't let it slip too fast," and "I was sure there was only 200 feet out." I held my tongue and simply said, "We'll talk about it later."

We hauled up the second anchor, stowed it away, and reset the primary anchor. Our hands were cut and scraped from handling the chain; we were soaking wet from rain and sweat, and at 1300, we crumpled onto the deck exhausted after completing the arduous task.

For the first time onboard, I really lost my temper. I felt justified because what Patrik did was a dangerous thing, caused by carelessness. In a voice surely heard on nearby boats in the anchorage, I made my point very clear: "You didn't check how much chain was out by looking for the markings, you didn't listen when I told you how much chain was out, and you let it fly much too fast! Do you think this is a toy we're playing with? When you're in charge of the anchor, be in charge!"

Patrik was silent but clearly angry, surely at himself because he is indeed a very responsible person. He knew he had been too cavalier. He was also angry with me for my reaction, which neither of us anticipated, and he saw a side of me rarely displayed: real anger. I told him he was confined to the boat for anchor watch, while John and I went to the bar, and that threw more fuel on the fire. He stormed off to his cabin while we got ready to go ashore.

It was a nasty moment, and I felt bad because I swore I would never yell at my crew like I had been yelled at when I was crewing for Captain Bligh's twin in 1977. This was serious, though, and I don't think it would have sunk in had I pussy-footed around saying, "Oh, that's okay, just do a better job next time." At sea, the repercussions of one's actions are escalated simply because of where we are, and Patrik needed to learn that.

In the end, though, I am the captain, and the lesson was driven home; everything that happens out here is my responsibility. Even though Patrik tied the safety-line knot, I should have checked it and, if it wasn't correct, I should have re-tied it to my satisfaction. Even though he was in charge of the anchor, I should have been there looking over his shoulder because the responsibility was still ultimately mine. It took us two days to get over it, but we made our way through, and I'm sure we both came out stronger people. This also reconfirmed how important it is to have a second anchor ready to go anytime. Which simply translates to "Always have a backup plan." Not just in anchoring; it goes for many things in life.

Out of 600 log pages for Julia's trip around the world, a lot of the pages are wet, torn, and blurry, but only one page is missing—the one that records this anchoring incident—and nobody can account for its disappearance. I guess we'll never know what happened to that page....

That was the first and last time in six years I ever yelled at a crew member for any mistake made aboard. Patrik, please accept my apologies.

Ship's Log / September 5, 2002
0900: En route to Tonga. Autopilot acting up badly. Heading alignment keeps changing. Set screw not holding. Can hear it slipping. *%#$@&. Hand steering all 240 miles to Tonga.

Email / September 11, 2002 / Remember and Reflect...
We have crossed the International Dateline and by default, we are now a day ahead: We crossed on a Friday, so the next day became Sunday, and thus we missed an entire day, Saturday, September 7, 2002. Hmmm, another Saturday I can't remember. The significance of this transition is not lost on us. Magellan's crew first discovered the lost day on September 7, 1522, exactly 480 years ago. There's not much we can do about certain things in life we have no control over; you just have to learn to let go. It's a slow process for me, but I'm working on it, and letting go of that lost day is a good start.

It is September 11, one year since the world stopped cold, and this morning, there are American flags flying at half-mast on many boats. The entire anchorage (some 35 boats) is eerily quiet as we all had a minute of silence to honor those who perished on this day last year (although there was some discussion as to which day we should be doing this because while it's the 11th here in Tonga, it's really the 10th in the U.S.). The more technical people agreed with the more practical among us who said, "Oh, c'mon, why complicate things, the calendar says it's the 11th, then it is."

It's a time to remember and reflect. And it makes us think: Don't waste another day doing nothing. Make each day count for we never know when it will be our turn. "Well, Patrik, here's to life," and I raised my coffee cup in salute.

"And to each and every moment," he replied.

Email / September 16, 2002 / El Niño

It's official: The weather gurus have declared this an El Niño year, which means changes in the temperature of certain ocean currents are affecting the weather. For once, the weather people are right. The last six weeks have been much cooler than normal, and there have been more rainsqualls, troughs and cold fronts than usual. I'm worried about what else will come our way because of the changing patterns.

Here in Tonga, we're really feeling it. Pleasant cool temperatures rule the day, and the rain can be intense at times. Two days ago, an all-day rainstorm filled our dinghy twice and the downpour was so thick we couldn't see the boat next to us in the anchorage. It blew through in a day and we made the best of it. On the VHF radio we announced: "Rainy-day movies aboard *Julia*" and dinghies soon began arriving until the main salon was full of friends and their children. The kids ate popcorn, the adults got hammered, and we opened and filled our water tanks with sweet, fresh rainwater.

Scuba diving today through dark caves and caverns, we saw more vividly colored coral, and the famous black fan coral prevalent in Tonga. Lots of whales here; two were within 100 feet of the dive boat. They are impressively graceful animals considering their immense size.

So many things went wrong for us mechanically in Tonga I thought, "This is never going to work. How can I continue?" For example, I didn't know where to even begin to look for a problem in the water pressure system. Now, I could probably troubleshoot that issue over the phone. It was about this time I realized it wasn't good enough to wait until something broke. We had to address things proactively and set up a regular schedule of maintenance for virtually every system onboard, from changing water filters to routine examinations of engines, sails, and rigging. If you will bear with me through the mechanical failures, you will understand how they truly did direct much of my cruising life. The magnitude of the problems was overwhelming, or so I thought at the time because later on the problems got bigger than this. Much bigger… but it was through managing the repairs I found I could handle anything.

I discovered what significant friends we were making with our cruising bud-dies and what good people they were. It wasn't too much to ask other boats for their spare parts or help. Our friends, including Lindsay, John, Adrien, Clark, Kevin, Harvey and Biagio, thought nothing of coming over to Julia and spend-ing day after day working on a problem. We were like a family that didn't want to let anyone down. And Patrik really stepped up to the plate. He jumped in and became my right hand working tirelessly to repair anything in need of attention. At this point, he was beginning to feel like he had truly moved up to the number-two spot onboard. It made me smile to see all of this camaraderie among friends and crew.

I also discovered the repercussions of how one thing leads to another on a boat. This is why I and most other skippers are so strict about systems and proce-dures. Who would have thought simply heeling the boat over would lead to fire onboard...?

Personal Journal / September 25, 2002

We had forgotten to close off the forward sink intake while sailing heeled over and water had rushed into the sink, overflowing and flooding the nearby electrical plug. We removed that plug off of the grid to dry it out—no big deal. Two days later, Patrik and John were ashore one night when I decided to restore power to the plug. After tripping the breaker twice and seeing no power, I gave up. Then I turned to look forward and noticed a flickering light coming from the head. I didn't remember leaving a light on up there...and why would it be flickering? It took a few seconds for my brain to process the information and realize what it was: Flames were reflecting on the white interior walls! "Fire. *FIRE!*" Who was listen-ing? The guys were gone ashore and I was alone.

Obviously, fire is extremely dangerous on a boat. Knowing this, we have a fire extinguisher in every cabin and almost within arms' reach from anywhere onboard—and boy, did that ever pay off.

I jumped forward. Sure enough: Flames were shooting from the elec-trical outlet and black smoke was filling the air. Now my brain was in overdrive: I'm alone! The boat is burning! Soon we'll be sinking and I'll be drowning! Survival instinct kicked in and only half a heartbeat later, I grabbed the extinguisher from the Pullman cabin, yanked the pin, and blasted the area with a cloud of talcum-like chemical large enough to douse a forest fire. My heart was pumping like there was no tomorrow, but the fire was out.

As I tried to calm myself, I opened the hatches and aired out the boat while keeping my eyes on the electrical plug. For good measure, I shot more chemical into the outlet and turned off the power to the entire forward area. I was shaking so much I could barely hit the glass while pouring the vodka.

The two smoke alarms in that area of the boat didn't sound because someone had turned them off, a common practice while cooking, as they sound every time we fry bacon. The rule is to turn them back on afterward. The next day, although the smoke had cleared, someone was going to get fried. Knowing I hadn't cooked in a couple of days, I asked, "Who turned off the alarms?"

"I don't know."

"And, who didn't turn them back on?"

"I don't know."

"I don't know either."

"Well, if it wasn't any of us, then who was it?" I pressed. "There are only three of us aboard."

"Must have been the bitch."

"Yeah, I'm sure it was that bitch."

"Same one who sneaks aboard and scratches our non-stick pans?"

"Yeah, it was her, all right."

Since no one 'fessed up, I let it go. We had a spare outlet onboard and Patrik, the new fix-it man who had stepped in for Ken, replaced it. Powered up and *voila*! It worked. We clearly needed some method of plugging the outlet and to remember to close off the sink plumbing when we sail.

I'm getting better at fixing things and, more importantly, I'm learning to be less panicked about them as they break. I have to start recognizing these things are bound to happen, and the only difference I can make is in my attitude. I suppose that goes for a lot of things in life. Some people will come out of a rainstorm smiling and soapy clean having had a good shower, while others will be wet and miserable. Pass me the soap.

Today, I was determined to fix the fan in my cabin, which had stopped working. I checked the wiring; there was voltage through the wire but it still didn't work. I searched and searched for the problem but couldn't find it. I closed the door to my cabin, sat down, and let my emotions get the better of me. These things were easy for Ken and he would have had this fixed in two minutes. I was jolted into a reminder of how much I miss him.

"There is nothing—absolutely nothing—half so much worth doing as simply messing about in boats." That's what Ratty said to Mole in Kenneth Grahame's classic, *The Wind In the Willows*. I agree with Ratty. In spite of the mechanical breakdowns, at least I'm still messing about in boats.

The sailing around Vavau is nothing short of excellent. The calm waters enclosed by the reef and 30 islands makes for dozens of great anchorages. At last count there were over 120 boats sailing in the area and many of us have bonded into a community—with activities, including Friday-night races. We have raced twice aboard Keith's boat, *Bonkers*, and have won two first places. I'm impressed by the amount of sailing experience here. The racing brought back lots of memories from my childhood and I was reminded that if you put eight sailors on a boat, you'll get at least eight opinions. Yet when it came to teamwork, everyone aboard pitched in and made the boat fly. We all knew what it took to make a boat go fast and we had plenty of beers at the Mermaid bar afterwards to celebrate.

It was about this time I noticed a guy who frequented the Bar. He was easy to recognize as he always wore a sun visor, had a beer in hand, and was often sailing remote-control sailboats off the dock. I was briefly introduced to Pete, his controller still firmly in hand, but it was rumored by some that he was conservative, an ex-marine, and probably homophobic, so I stayed away....

It's one of the reasons I don't listen to other people's opinions about people anymore. I prefer to make my own judgments to avoid this mistake again in life. How many people stayed away from me because I am gay?

I'm still haunted by the loneliness I feel for a soul mate with whom to share it all. I am trying to come to grips with the fact that Ken is gone, so I'm open to meeting new people. Sometimes, though, I realize it's nice to be alone. After all, it's not like I'm miserable; how can I be miserable surrounded by so much natural beauty? My loneliness frequently leads to depression. I wonder; is my desperation showing?

Lynette told me the other day, half joking (or was she?), "Now you stay away from John, he's mine," and we laughed. I had my eyes on Keith Sedwick, owner of *Bonkers* from San Francisco. He's tall, slim, has a full head of thick, dark hair; is quiet but always smiling with a nice confidence. I peppered him with questions. "I hear you're from San Francisco, and you're single? No girlfriend, and you're good looking, and dress nicely. Are you sure you're not gay and available?" Very comfortable in his own skin, Keith said, "Sorry, if I were, you'd be the first to know, but I'm afraid I'm as straight as they come." That's okay, I'm happy to have another good friend.

I send emails to Ken almost every day but don't get as many replies as I would like. The ones I'm getting are short and typically only address fixing things on the boat. He doesn't usually respond to questions about returning or our relationship. Even though I'm getting used to his not being here, I'm not giving up on him.

The saga continued with the mechanical problems. The good part was how those problems brought out the best in our friends and brought us all closer together. I got to know Biagio Maddaloni, a short but powerfully built Canadian who always sees the bright side of things. And Lindsay Stewart, a quiet silver-haired boat builder from New Zealand with a heart of gold and a soul to match, and his lovely wife, Olive. He gave me the confidence to start taking things apart and to keep going until we found the solution.

I continued my kayak paddling and that helped keep me sane in what seemed to me like a world that was one big mechanical breakdown.

Personal Journal / September 29, 2002

We first heard about it from Holly, manager of the Moorings Charter Company in Tonga, while having a cocktail at the Mermaid Bar. "They're missing, just gone," she said.

"Who's missing?" asked a whole group in unison.

"The German couple and our boat. A Beneteau 38 named *Guinevere* has been missing for a few days now. We've just put it out on the radio."

"Any idea of where they might have gone?" I asked.

"They weren't supposed to be going anywhere," Holly said. "They have no experience and they were told to stay in the area. They were using the boat kind of as a hotel…but the weird part is…"

"Yeah?" All ears were aimed at Holly.

"Well, it's weird that people in town saw them buying things."

"Like what?" we all asked in near unison again.

"They bought two pigs, two chickens, two dogs, and a bunch of farming equipment...and one of the locals saw them load it all onto the boat one night. They had bags of wheat, seeds, and fertilizer too. Very strange."

Personal Journal / October 3, 2002

I've been kayaking every day we're anchored here and it's working to slow me down; it keeps me sane, feels good, and is fun. I paddled far around the point of Neiafu to the other side and the Back Bay. It was quiet and peaceful, and I stopped for a little while for a senses check.

Heard: Birds of all kinds underscored by a light wind blowing around my head.

Saw: Birds; white ones, black ones, some hunting, some just flying around, some sitting in the marshes on the water's edge, petrels, frigates, herons, egrets, terns, kingfishers, and ducks. Blue and orange butterflies following me, a sea snake 3 feet long, a large brown and beige turtle; got to within 10 feet of it before he dove for the bottom. Dense green jungle covering the hills, blue sky with a few white puffy clouds, wonderfully clear slightly rippling water in shades of aquamarine.

Felt: Warm air on my body, penetrating sunshine on my shoulders, aching muscles from paddling, and sweat dripping down my stomach.

Smelled: The sweet and sour scent of burning coconut husks.

Tasted: Salt from the sea and my sweat.

And a chance to think about what I'm doing out here and what I'm searching for. No answers yet, but I'm beginning to be more comfortable with the questions. It's a beautiful day, and I'm going up on deck for a favorite activity: skinny-dipping.

Ship's Log / October 8, 2002

1400: Depart Tonga. Wind SE 20-25, squalls, rain, blustery, 100% cloud cover but forecast for clearing. En route to Fiji.

1900: Wind 35 knots, seas 10-12 ft, very rough. Autopilot slipping.

2000: Wind 45 knots, seas 12-15 ft, triple reef main, staysail, very, very rough. Autopilot fails. Crew seasick. Can't turn rudder more than 20 degrees starboard.

2010: Turning back to Tonga. Need engine to tack. Motor sailing at 4 knots.

2400: Arrive at coast, motor through narrow passage by radar in heavy rain, little visibility.

0130: On mooring ball at Neiafu.

0200: Exhausted, sleep after twelve hours of hell.

My plan was to include Fiji in this year's crossing of the Pacific Islands, and even though I was enjoying Tonga immensely, I felt the need to push on to Fiji, I suppose because it was part of my plan. I knew it was getting late. We had to get out of the Pacific hurricane season in the islands, which meant arriving in New Zealand sometime in November. Almost every cruising boat was headed to New Zealand in the south or the Marshall Islands in the north. Either way, everyone was leaving the hurricane zone. I thought about just staying in Tonga and relaxing more before sailing to New Zealand but was rather neutral on the subject. When I asked Patrik and John for their preference, they both said they wanted to get to Fiji this year, so we continued with our plans. It's odd how, when you're making a decision, you don't always know what the consequences will be, but this surely was the wrong decision, and I learned my lessons....

With all of my dedicated studying of the weather maps and learning how to interpret them and their forecasts, I felt pretty good in my ability to see what was coming our way. Sometimes that worked, and sometimes it didn't....

Now I never leave on a rainy day.

Personal Journal / October 13, 2002 / What a Week

Five days ago we finished provisioning, cleared customs, which allowed us to fuel the boat with duty-free fuel, filled our water tanks, and said many farewells as we headed out into the cloudy and rainy day toward Fiji, 420 miles to the west. We expected the weather would be foul at first, but the forecast was for lighter winds. Rather than easing, the wind began to pick up to 30, 35, then 40 knots and held steady there with gusts over 45. The seas were 10-15 feet and we were screaming down them at more than 10 knots with our sails reefed down to virtual handkerchiefs. Unfortunately, and stupidly I might add, this would be the sea trial for the autopilot fix a few weeks ago; alas, it didn't hold. Who uses a passage as sea trials for repairs? Not us anymore.

As is often the case on boats, problems were compounding. The set-screw we put into the rudderpost sheered off, so we were back to hand steering. Patrik and John were horribly seasick, both lying on the main salon floor as we were encountering rough conditions with that perfectly awful roll caused by seas on the beam. In my gut, I knew we should turn around but at the same time didn't want to give up. Honestly, though, I was starting to get a little scared. This was too rough, the crew was sick, and it just *didn't feel right*. I had more questions and was handling more problems than I had answers.

I was faced with the decision of hand steering more than 400 miles to Suva, or turning around and pounding 16 miles back into the wind and seas to Tonga—and accepting failure. While it now seems like an easy decision, old tapes played in my head about not giving up, not being weak, standing strong, and that sort of horse-hooey. The SSB radio was crackling with activity as I initiated contact with our friends:

"*White Hawk*, this is *Julia*, how copy?"

"*Julia*, this is *White Hawk*, good copy, what the hell are you doing?" Even through the static, it was clear there was not an ounce of humor in Lynette's tone. She was deadly serious.

"*White Hawk*, what do you see on your forecast? We've run into 45 knots and 15-foot seas, we've lost our autopilot, and I'm having problems turning my rudder to starboard. I thought this weather was supposed to clear up, but I missed the last weather fax."

"*Julia*, what we see isn't good. That trough looks like it's not going to clear; it's only going to get worse…you need to turn around. NOW."

Other boats were monitoring our transmission. "*Julia*, this is *Pegasus*, we agree."

"*Julia*, this is *L'eau Life*, get your butts back here, turn around!" Adrien said in his typical no-nonsense style.

How could I have misread the weather so badly? Was I just allowing myself to be rushed to get to Fiji? Did I ignore reality, missing some important details in the forecast? Probably. Plus, the prediction had changed and I didn't follow it as we left that afternoon.

"*Julia*, come in *Julia*…*Julia*, come in *Julia*…*Julia*, COME IN *Julia*!" Lynette shouted through the radio from *White Hawk*. I stood at the chart table assessing our situation in the dark. I looked at my crew lying on the floor, heard the autopilot struggling to grip the rudderpost, and felt the boat shudder as waves slammed us from the beam. The rain came pelting down in sheets, and for a brief moment I was paralyzed. Just then, a dinner plate flew across the galley, crashed onto the floor, and I snapped out of it.

"This is *Julia*. We are coming about. Our ETA is five hours, will you guys please stand by on this frequency?" I could hear the partial relief in the voices of our friends as they responded, "Roger *Julia,* we'll be standing by."

"Get up, get up, now!" I shouted to Patrik and John, "we're coming about!" I ran forward to where the medical kit was housed, threw it open and grabbed a Scopolamine patch, the strongest of all seasick cures. Patrik was already stumbling his way to the cockpit and while John was still on the floor, I slapped the patch on him behind the ear and said, "You'll be fine. Let's go!"

I raced back into the cockpit, started the engine, and reluctantly, but with new determination, turned the boat around, which wasn't easy, even using the engine, and we motor sailed at a snail's pace back to Tonga.

Because it was dark and raining heavily, we navigated our way into the narrow entrance and up the channel toward Neiafu using radar as our guide. Occasionally we could see the silhouette of the dark hills through the rain only a quarter mile away on either side. In our sleepy state, those hills looked like they were too close, but the radar doesn't lie—if you read it correctly. Then we heard the VHF come to life: "*Julia*, look for my light, can you see me? I have a mooring ball for you."

"It's Adrien!" shouted Patrik. Sure enough, as my jaw dropped and then a smile returned to my face, we motored toward Adrien, who was lovingly sitting out in the rain in his dinghy to guide us to a mooring ball. Seeing him and his blinking flashlight was like getting a distant glimpse of light while crawling around in a dark cave. Adrien Fondiller is slim and wiry, and I couldn't help but wonder how he could see through his wet glasses in the rain. His bright red and white foul-weather jacket dwarfed his small body but appeared to be keeping him dry enough, at least his upper half. A bathing suit completed his outfit.

"Adrien! What are you doing out here in the rain?" I shouted as I nosed *Julia's* bow up to the ball. He handed the line up to Patrik and said, "What am I doing out here? What the hell are *you* doing out here? You guys okay?"

"Yeah, we're okay. Thank you, thank you," I said, as he waved and motored back to his wife, Paula, and their boat *L'eau Life*, also from San Francisco. I had been on the helm most of the way back and was feeling beat up and exhausted, but the protected waters had already calmed our stomachs, and Patrik soon handed me a drink.

Being captain means knowing the best course of action is not always what you had planned. I wasn't used to giving up, but I decided it's okay to turn around and start again. It's not giving up—it's simply good seamanship.

The next day, after the weather had calmed, we found Lindsay from *Cruiseaway* and Biagio from *L'il Gem* to get their advice about the autopilot. They came aboard and promptly went to work analyzing the situation. I handed out beers and saluted them.

Biagio was a metal-works engineer in his previous life and, along with Lindsay the boat builder, the two of them attacked the problem with zeal while I looked helplessly on and played nurse by handing them tools. Together, these two guys were an incredible team and within a couple of hours had designed a new way to attach the autopilot arm to the steering quadrant.

Skeptical, but not wanting to rain on their two-man parade, I asked, "Where are we going to get aluminum channel for the job?" Biagio calmly replied, "On my boat; don't worry about it, I have everything we need." I watched in amazement (and served drinks) as Biagio, Lindsay, and Patrik spent that afternoon, evening, and almost all of the next day fabricating from scratch an entirely new system using materials they brought over from Biagio's boat.

Personal Journal / October 20, 2002

Tonga is known for a high concentration of humpback whales, which migrate from their feeding grounds in the Antarctic to the warm waters of Tonga every year to mate and give birth. We had seen the whales from afar but wanted to get closer; along with many other cruisers, we chartered a whale watching boat with professionals who knew just where to go. We were amazed at how close the boat was to these incredible animals, and they didn't seem to mind our presence. Some of the group even got in the water and swam with the whales. The humpbacks slapped their flukes on the water, breached high into the air, and we could almost feel the breath from their blowholes.

No visit to the Vava'u Group of Tonga would be complete without visiting two famous caves. Swallows Cave is only accessible by dinghy or kayak and over a few days time, I visited it more than once by both modes of transport. You can paddle right into the 50-foot tall entrance to an enormous cavern, lined with sharp limestone stalactites pointing down to the perfectly clear waters, which make for some pretty eerie snorkeling. Swallows nests cover the walls and ceiling of the cave, and you can feel hundreds of eyes watching as you frolic in their home.

While that cave may be easy to visit, Mariner's Cave is another story. This entrance is marked at the water's edge by "the green branch next to the black rock" on the side of a cliff. The next instructions were to "swim submerged for 20 feet under the cliff toward a faint blue light." Since we visited without a local guide, we couldn't be sure we were going to find the cave until we tried it. You want to talk about nervous? John from *White Hawk* was first, and after he had been gone for a minute, it was time to follow suit. I was shaking, but with mask and fins on securely, I took one last gulp of air, dove straight down 10 feet, and then swam frantically for the longest 20 feet underwater in history. After it seemed like my lungs would burst, I looked up, and could see a muted light, but still wasn't sure if I was going to be surfacing into air. I risked it—broke the surface—and found myself in a vast limestone chamber lit only from the bottom up. It was only the glow from the outside funneling through the underwater tunnel that gave the room its faint turquoise hue, which reminded me of a fairy tale.

Limestone stalactites clung to the moonlike ceiling, and the air was damp and heavy. Then without notice, the water lifted slightly, my ears popped, and the cavern filled with mist, like a dense fog, caused by the air being compressed with the rising water. As the water receded, the air cleared again to its mystical blue. This happens one or two times a minute as the swells rise and fall outside the cave. The others had to assume I had either drowned or made it into the cave, and assuming the latter, soon joined me. Our voices echoed around the room as we each exclaimed how incredible this experience was. It's an eerie place, though, one where you aren't really sure what's going to happen next, and after a few minutes of this discomfort, one by one, we all swam back out to the warm sunshine and fresh air.

Email / October 21, 2002

I just witnessed the most spectacular color display in the sky. In the west, the sun set through thin, wispy clouds as they turned various shades of grey; then the sky at the horizon changed from a pale blue to yellow, gold, and finally to bright burnt orange. As the clouds deepened to charcoal, their undersides lit up bright red as if on fire, and the entire western sky faded to black.

In awe, I watched as the eastern clouds changed from shades of pink to purple, and then bright blue. As the colors deepened, I wondered what was causing such intense light. Just then, the enormous full moon popped out from behind the clouds and the sky turned a brilliant pink and white.

The coloring has faded; the rippling water is reflecting the biggest, brightest, silvery white, most romantic luminary disk imaginable. If you look at the moon tonight, know I'll be looking, too…especially you, Dolly. While I may be on the other side of the world, it's still the same moon and I hope you get the same color show we did. Maybe I'm a softie, but moments like these choke me up. The beauty of nature in its full splendor makes me smile wide and tear up at the same time. It's so overwhelming, it almost hurts.

Personal Journal / October 22, 2002

We were once again having cocktails at the Mermaid Bar, and Holly was sipping eagerly on her third drink. "We found 'em," she said. "We found *Guinevere*. She was smashed up on the island of Late."

"The volcanic island 30 miles from here?" I asked. "Is there a place to anchor over there?"

"No anchorages, no people, nothing, but this couple had to get to Late." Holly ordered another drink. "They thought Late was the place the aliens were going to meet them, pick them up, and take them away. Because their rendezvous was a month off, they needed the animals and food to survive until their spaceship arrived."

"You're making this up," shot a comment from the end of the bar.

"Nope, it's all true. They belong to a religious cult. They believe the world is coming to an end and the alien spaceship would save only those on Late. So they wrecked the boat on the island and were homesteading when our spotter plane found it. And there was the happy couple working in their new garden."

"You mean *Guinevere* was up on the rocks?" I asked.

"She sure was," Holly confirmed.

"Then I propose a round of drinks. We'll all have a Guinevere on the Rocks, please."

The entire bar, including Holly, burst into laughter as we made the drink up on the spot.

My friend Nick loves adventure, and we had been talking for some time about his coming to join *Julia* for the notoriously rough passage from Tonga to New Zealand. He's an avid sailor and was one of my most enthusiastic followers of the journey. His loyalty meant flying all the way from Switzerland to Tonga, and I never doubted for a minute he would be there.

On the other hand, John had been looking to leave, either from boredom, fear, or just because he was done working on engines. One day, following the false start to Fiji, he announced, "I'll be leaving next week; I've taken a new job back home." It didn't bother me because, while he did his share of work, we hadn't really bonded. Nick could have the forward cabin, and I was more interested in his well-being.

Patrik and I sailed together for 10 days south through the remote Ha'apai group of islands to Nukualofa, the capital of Tonga, where we met Nick and prepared for the trip to New Zealand. There was excitement aboard, and we were all looking forward to putting to sea. We fueled *Julia*, shopped and provisioned, and checked in with Bob McDavitt, the weather guru in New Zealand, to find a good departure window. We also consulted with Bob Cook, our own weatherman, studied the weather charts, and talked to others who had done the passage.

It's common knowledge that, between Tonga and New Zealand, the weather pattern cycles every five to seven days. The only choice is whether you want the bad weather at the beginning or the end of your passage. Unless you're really lucky, you're going to see some heavy weather. While there were a few other boats leaving for New Zealand, we chose to sail by ourselves and not buddy-boat with anybody else.

We took our lickings in the form of a full-blown gale and had our share of breakdowns. We dealt with the problems the best we could, and Nick's overwhelming gusto helped boost my courage to face any obstacle. He wasn't yet sick of the mechanical breakdowns because he hadn't been living it day to day, so his view of simply "Let's fix it!" was just the infusion of enthusiasm I needed.

I was excited at the prospect of getting to New Zealand and spending the next six months there. Almost everybody who does this route stays at least until May, while awaiting the passing of the Pacific hurricane season, before heading back to the tropics.

This was the roughest weather I had seen in all of my years of sailing, but it wasn't the roughest I was to encounter before making it all the way around the world. In fact, it was only a warm-up….

CHAPTER 8

Open Ocean, Open Heart

"Accept or reject, but don't tolerate."
JULIA JACOBSON

Email / November 1, 2002 / Heading Down Under

I can't believe we're on the final passage to New Zealand. We left Tonga today, delicately working our way out of the complicated reefs in the harbor, and by early afternoon we were heading south into open ocean. It's 1,050 miles and based on our projections, we're expecting it to take eight days.

Our landfall is planned for Opua, on the North Island of New Zealand. From there, we'll sail to Auckland where we have reserved a slip in Bayswater Marina and plan to spend the entire summer and fall Down Under. It's thrilling to be on this milestone passage, but it's starting to get cold. Not sure if that means we're going to get our butts kicked by the weather early or later on; keep your fingers crossed for only a light spanking.

Personal Journal / November 5, 2002

We set course for North Minerva Reef, giving us the option of stopping there should the weather take a turn for the worse. With good wind and weather, we sailed an "S" curve right between North and South Minerva Reefs and kept going. We are on high alert sailing between the two reefs; mindful of the couple on *Pnuema* who recently became legend in these waters after falling asleep on the same route. They ended up on the reef, abandoning their boat as a total loss, and our friends on *White Hawk*, *Scott Free*, and *Infidien* had to go to their rescue.

So far, we've had long periods of glassy calm and motoring, then "noserlies" (when the wind comes right at you on the nose), forcing us to beat our way into it, making a rough ride. This morning, I called for a change to a much smaller headsail; not a popular call at 0730, but the wind was building and it turned out to be the right decision. An hour later, the wind had increased to 20, and by noon, it was a steady 25, gusting to 30. In spite of a 2-knot current against us, we were screaming along at 8 knots.

Personal Journal / November 6, 2002

When we lost the SSB radio, for a brief moment I turned to ask Ken to have a look...and it struck me: The electronics wizard was no longer aboard. There was no time for pity, and since my troubleshooting skills were as good as anyone's aboard, I opened the manual and started reading. I found the blown fuse and replaced it, turned the radio on, and it blew again. I repeated the process three times until I was out of fuses. Losing the SSB also meant no weather forecasts via email, weather faxes, or voice traffic. I announced, "Well, gentlemen, that's it for weather forecasts, the radio is dead."

To which Nick replied, "Why don't we call Bob Cook for the forecast?"

"Yeah, right," Patrik said, trailing a laugh. "Do you see a phone booth nearby?"

Were we ever surprised when Nick returned from his cabin holding a new Iridium satellite phone, saying, "As a matter of fact, yes, I do." Talk about a morale booster! We were able to call and get our weather forecast...and I discovered a new toy I must have. Have also lost the generator; can't get it restarted and are having to charge the batteries with main engine.

Personal Journal / November 7, 2002

Having Nick aboard is a blast; he's an excellent sailor and friend, and we've talked long into the night about business, family, friends, and life in general. Nick is a weather enthusiast, and together we plan our route according to the forecasts—now via his phone.

More calms and more motor sailing. Getting a little nervous about fuel, aware that we have a long way to go, and are monitoring it very carefully. Still can't start the generator.

Today's cold, fresh wind slapping my face reminded me of San Francisco where the wind bites and stings the skin and then penetrates into your bones. I looked around and saw nothing but grey, heavy skies, and was very much alone.

Personal Journal / November 8, 2002

I missed Ken again when we saw nothing but "error" on our navigation equipment. I'm sure he would have taken more serious measures, but I have managed to reset the instruments and solve the problem—at least for now. Saltwater leaking in through the windows probably doesn't agree with the electrical panel.

This passage hasn't allowed much time for reflection, and this morning the wind built again to a steady 20-25, handing us a wild ride on rough seas. Then, eerily, just as quickly as they had grown into something short of a mild fury, the seas calmed. I don't like the looks of it.

Personal Journal / November 10, 2002

Yesterday afternoon the wind came back, and this time, with reinforcements. For the next 18 hours, we had a continuous full-blown gale with winds steady at 30-35, then increasing to 40-45 and gusting over 50 knots. The seas were surprisingly violent, and *Julia* was flying over and through huge 15-20-foot waves; spray flying everywhere, green-water waves (all water, not just spray) crashing regularly over the boat, and plenty of water found its way into our normally dry areas.

Whoever happened to be on watch would just sit in the companionway, harnessed in, holding on, humbled by the ride. The autopilot fortunately held and performed admirably, but I still hear grinding noises coming from what I think are the gears. I know we haven't seen the end of our autopilot troubles.

The strong wind was from the SW, so we were close reaching and beating all through the night, and because the batteries needed charging, the engine ran all night helping to speed us along. With only the dim light of the compass and the green glow from the radar screen, we were otherwise blind, unable to see anything ahead in the blackness. We were dressed in foulies, boots, and harnesses, and the ride was so bumpy you didn't dare venture into the cockpit without being clipped in for fear of being thrown overboard.

At one point, feeling rather beat up, wet, and tired, I looked out to the cockpit and saw Nick at the wheel smiling, then grimacing, then smiling again. I shouted up to him, "Pretty crappy, isn't it?" He smiled and answered in his ever so calming but exciting way, "No, this is what we came for! Ya-hoo!" I paused for a moment and realized he was right. This is the adventure I wanted. Okay then, "Ya-hoo!" I shouted back.

This afternoon, the wind dropped to 20 knots but still on the nose, preventing us from making landfall at Opua. We changed our plans and headed directly for Whangerei, and by 1600 were all smiles as we reached the entrance to the Whangerei River Channel.

Finally seeing the intensely green New Zealand coastline appear over the horizon made my heart skip a beat. All of my memories of good times there and the kinship I have with the people and lifestyle, made me smile. I felt ecstatic having pulled it all together to make it back here, and I was slightly proud of my seamanship, too. The weather is cool and crisp—a welcome change from the tropics—and we're even wearing shoes, socks, underwear, and long pants.

We wound our way up river to the commercial wharf where a genuinely nice customs agent met and politely cleared us into the country. *Thump, thump, stamp. Thump, thump, stamp. Thump, thump, stamp.* We were in. "Welcome to New Zealand, mates. I'm only supposed to give you a year visa, but you seem like nice blokes, so I'll put you down for two years. Enjoy your stay."

"What's the matter, Skipper?" asked Patrik, as he saw me wiping my eye.

"Oh jeez, now what?" Nick said, rolling his eyes.

"Nothing. I'm just happy," I said.

"Well, hallelujah," Nick said. "Pass me the bottle opener, will ya?"

Making it to New Zealand was indeed like coming home. I already had a few friends there, including Andre whom I had met on another trip while in the incentive business. While Nick had to leave and go back to Switzerland, Patrik and I sailed down to Auckland by ourselves. When we arrived at Bayswater Marina, Andre promptly came by the dock to welcome us to Auckland, invite us to dinner, and bring us into his inner circle of friends, including Tom, John, and others.

Email / November 14, 2002 / At Dock in Auckland

G'day mates, we're here! *Julia* is made fast in her new berth in Auckland's Bayswater Marina. According to our log, we have sailed 12,997 miles to get here—that's enough miles to go halfway around the world—and we're only in New Zealand.

Personal Journal / November 24, 2002

It's clear we've been at sea for a long stretch; Patrik and I are in awe of being in the big city, and Auckland's not that big (just over a million). Whenever we have gone ashore, for the last year, we've been in small towns and villages, with streets of dirt and sand, shopping in stores the size of walk-in closets, wearing no more than shorts, T-shirts, and flip-flops. Last night we were in a wild gay bar with hundreds of men, dancing till dawn, and living the city life again.

Meeting new friends and getting closer to old ones is making me feel like I belong here. I remember meeting Andre Hodgskin at the Hero Parade, Auckland's gay festival, when I was visiting a couple of years ago. I haven't seen him since then, but rather than growing apart over time and distance, it seems the years have brought us closer together. We're about the same age and share similar views about people and life, and he has taken me under his wing to make me feel welcome. As one of New Zealand's most famous architects, he seems to know nearly everybody in Auckland and my social calendar is already booked.

I am continually drawn to the supermarket aptly named Food Town.

It's just like any other oversized supermarket back home, but with an overwhelming selection of fresh, healthy foods. I stand in the vegetable and fruit section laughing with awe at the abundance compared to what we had in the Pacific Islands. In the islands, we used to be excited at the thought of going to the store and finding bread. As I stand drooling in front of the bakery, I'm asked by the baker, "What kind of bread, mate?" as he waves his hand across a vast array of fresh baked goods I haven't seen since San Diego. "Do you want rye, wheat, white, soy, buttermilk, potato, cake, cupcakes, scones, croissants, biscuits…?"

The contrasts between the Pacific Islands and this Western nation are an important reminder about what an amazing abundance we live with at home. It's more than the wealth we have; it's the contrast. I'm afraid without people seeing the contrast as I just have, there's no way to know the difference. Curiously, those wonderful people whom we met on the islands with fewer choices certainly seem happy. In fact, they seem happier with their one loaf of bread than most people I know who can choose from many different types of baked goods. It's not what we have—it's how we look at what we have.

It's windy every day and while *Julia* is not exempt from rocking and rolling in her berth, it's comfortable and cozy aboard. Bayswater Marina, nicknamed "Blowswater," reminds me of Emery Cove in Emeryville; it's right across the bay from the city, fairly small, and has a comfortable atmosphere. Free Internet allows me access to my friends and the rest of the world again. For now, the adventurous rough part seems to be over; I'm back in the civilized world and very much a part of it again.

Yet, as I'm trying to get settled here, it seems strange not really having anything I *must* do. Traveling through the Pacific Islands, there was always the next anchorage to study about, something to fix, someplace else to go, but here I have all the time of the day and I can choose to do nothing at all.

It's lonely though; all of this time to myself, not having to put any energy towards anything or anyone else. Honestly, not sure if I like it. The independence is liberating, but I miss having someone to share it with— there I go again with the lonesome thing. I need to get over it. Not to paint the wrong picture; my days are happy, I smile and laugh a lot, and am building a life with the people I meet and the things I do, but at the end of the day, when all is quiet and it comes time to crawl into bed, I'm reminded of how alone I really am in this whole adventure. It's more than just the absence of Ken. It seems everybody except me has some sort of purpose. I really did check out and leave it all behind, didn't I? I'm no longer a part of "it" anymore.

I am reminded of *Julia's* namesake and the advice she gave me in the past: "Accept or reject, but don't tolerate." Can I accept my situation of being alone? I know I have been tolerating for too long, and it's time to make a choice. I choose to accept my life as it is, and I know that somehow happiness is coming my way. Enough loneliness; it's time to move on.

Since I'm going to be here at least until May when the hurricanes clear out of the Pacific, I've really moved into my temporary home. I bought a car, a 1988 Honda Accord for a mere $2,000 NZ, which is about $1,000 US. Because of the extremely favorable exchange rate, shopping for anything is like a half-price sale. I now have a cell phone, bicycle, and bank account with an ATM card. I've joined a gym and hired a personal trainer—I'm in real need of getting my body back into shape after sitting on the boat for so long.

It feels good to be here in New Zealand, and I think it will feel even better as time goes on and I meet more people and get more entrenched into the local scene. Lots of people going home for the holidays, but I don't think I will. I like it here. I like the people, the easy way of life, and for a big city, it's kind of slow, which is refreshing. I think I'll stay right here and just be where I'm at rather than wishing I were somewhere else. Well now, how's that for attitude improvement? I'm learning.

 It was only after truly letting go of Ken that I opened up my eyes and heart, allowing David into my life. And then Ken reappeared....

Email / December 7, 2002 / One Year Ago
It's hard to believe, but today marks the one-year anniversary of *Julia's* departure out the Golden Gate. Where has the time gone?

- Three months in Mexico
- Three months in French Polynesia
- Two months in Tonga
- Three weeks in the Cook Islands

- Two weeks in Niue
- Almost a month in New Zealand already
- 760 hours on the new engine
- Ripped four sails
- Caught six mahi-mahi, four tuna, and two wahoo

The year of cruising has been rewarding, fulfilling, and both mentally and physically challenging. On the other hand, it's been more difficult than I ever anticipated, and far more expensive than I imagined. I have met wonderful people along the way, especially fellow cruisers, and have experienced their overwhelming generosity and kindness. I have been welcomed into the cruising community with open arms, and while maybe the camaraderie is because we are all "in the same boat," I still feel the people I've made friends with will be in my life long after the voyage ends.

As far as adventure is concerned, I have never felt more alive than on this most recent passage to New Zealand, with the winds gusting to 50 knots, waves crashing onto the boat, and *Julia* racing along under sail, climbing up and down 15-foot seas; it's a guaranteed adrenaline rush.

Personal Journal / January 8, 2003
I'm being pretty lazy and don't do much of anything stressful or difficult. It's lonely, but easy. I eat well. Got a nice comment from fellow cruiser Linda who said, "Hey Larry, you're looking good. The gym is really agreeing with you," as I walked down the dock. "What a pity you're gay," she sighed. I laughed and we chatted a bit—she made me feel good. I think my friends see me as always happy, and for the most part, I would have to agree with them. What they don't see is my loneliness—maybe because it's dwindling?

Personal Journal / January 14, 2003
It happened late at night in a popular Auckland gay bar that Patrik and I frequented. There he was playing pool, drinking a beer, dressed in a T-shirt, jeans, and cowboy boots. Cowboy boots? In New Zealand? Always willing to make a fool of myself, I went up to this most beautiful man and said something stupid like, "Are you from Texas?" Groan. David Robertson, being the cool, calm, collected one, replied easily in a very Kiwi (New Zealand) accent, "No, but my boyfriend is. Who wants to

know?" I dug my hole even deeper and crawled inside by saying, "Just me wanting to know, and I was hoping to take you to lunch. Here's my number, I hope you call." We chatted for a couple of minutes, and then I turned and walked away thinking I had most certainly screwed that one up.

David called the next day, we met for lunch, and instantly fell for one another. I can't believe my good fortune. David is tall and slender, and very handsome. His mix of Japanese and Kiwi heritage gave him black hair, sensuously smooth skin, and deep, dark eyes. Once again, I fell for a big smile and great sense of humor. I even met David's partner, and he's fine with me coming into their lives. It's one of the cool things about my experience in gay society. Because we don't for the most part create a family by having children, we know the family we create with our friends is the family we choose and keep. David is definitely going to be family.

However, David has a partner and probably isn't going to be leaving him to sail away with me, although we talked about the idea. I told him about Ken because, while growing fainter, still gnawing away in the back of my head are far away thoughts of Ken's hopeful return.

Personal Journal / January 20, 2003

Ken casually mentioned on the phone that he would like to come and visit. I couldn't believe what I was hearing. "What do you mean by visit?" I asked.

"Just visit, and you have to promise you won't pitch me on why I should stay," he said emphatically. He's arriving Feb. 9 and is planning to stay for five weeks, maybe longer. I promised not to "pitch" him for the first four weeks of his stay.

We're flying to Sydney for the Mardi Gras party, and I'm really looking forward to being together again. I think he is too, but I'm not going to get my hopes up too high.

And now it's more complicated because David and I are having a great time. We spend days together at the beach in Takapuna, go out for meals, attend parties, and I have the beginnings of a life without Ken.

 Email / February 2, 2003 / Life in the Slow Lane

Some of you have asked what life is like in New Zealand; here are a few highlights. It's definitely slower here; life is relaxed, casual, and not frantic.

There are lots of celebrations and with the America's Cup in full gear, Auckland is buzzing. There are symphonies in the park, lots of people on holiday, and fireworks to celebrate summer and all the beauty it brings. Christmas isn't spent pining away for Frosty the Snowman, but rather a day at the beach in search of sun and tan lines.

The people are kind, happy, generous, and very willing to help. When shopping in a store for boat parts, it's not uncommon for the salesperson to point out a better buy than what I've selected, or even point to another store. When searching for a new water pump, the clerk at Sailor's Corner pulled me aside and whispered, "Hey, mate, go over to Foster's Chandlery; they have these pumps on sale today."

One day, I was parking my car in the city and could only find a 30-minute space. There were two meter maids standing right there, so I asked in my sweetest, most innocent tourist voice possible, "How can I stay for an hour and a half in a 30-minute space if the meter won't let me accumulate coins?" Their reply was: "You can't, mate, but if you pay for 30 minutes, we'll give you the extra hour for free." Now, I ask you, where else in the world can you negotiate with the meter maid?

Life is good here. I feel rested, relaxed, and am in a nice, easy routine entirely different than running through airports, chasing clients, and searching for new business. The contrast is great, and I have learned there is more to life than business. The best part is I feel as though I'm living the dream.

Personal Journal / February 4, 2003
Tuesday evenings are reserved for dinners with Andre. We meet at his apartment in Auckland and then walk to Tony's Steak House, or the truly authentic Chinese restaurant up the stairs, in the back of an old building, where we are usually the only non-Asian patrons. We're both enjoying the company as we get to know each other. On weekends, there are often dinner parties at Andre and Tom's apartment, and I'm meeting new people every week.

Most other nights, I'm with David, either on the boat or at his house on the beach, cooking, watching movies, laughing, and playing long into the night. At 32, his youthful energy is both inspiring and exhausting, but we sure do have fun together—in and out of bed. So far, it's a wild, passionate ride. As I meet David's friends, these new acquaintances make me feel almost like a local.

Personal Journal / February 9, 2003

I've settled into a happy routine, with the gym, some work on the boat, weekly dinners with Andre, and most of the rest of my time with David. Nevertheless it's all somewhat confusing as last night we bid an emotional farewell to what has become a budding new relationship.

Ken arrives today. It's not yet dawn, and he doesn't land until late this morning, but I'm up, dressed, ready to go to the airport, and my heart is doing back flips. I'm an emotional wreck; I don't know what Ken is thinking; is he coming just for his five-week visit as planned? Will he fall back in love with me and stay permanently? Will he at least stay for another season? All I know is what he told me, he wants to see me for a visit. Except for having to say goodbye to David because of Ken's arrival, everything else about Ken coming back feels great. David is so kind and understanding, he even took me on a test run to show me the way to the airport yesterday.

I told Ken on the phone yesterday, "My stomach is full of butterflies."

"Me too, but no pitching, remember? I'm only coming to visit," he reminded me.

"Yeah, yeah, I know," I said.

I'm ecstatic, but don't know what seeing Ken for the first time in almost nine months is going to be like. All I know is my life is about to change dramatically—again.

It was liberating having the freedom to decide where we would go next. We could choose to stay in New Zealand for the winter, or we could sail to Tonga, Fiji, Vanuatu, and New Caledonia. I did lots of reading of cruising guides, talked with other sailors, and did extensive research on the Internet to determine the next destination. While sometimes I was only one anchorage ahead of us, for the most part I had a basic plan—go west! Thus, the world was mine, and I was master of it all.

Except for the engine troubles. At first I really was able to take the engine overhaul in stride, but then it began to eat away at me. Years after the incident, I have chosen to forgive and forget; at the time I was really ticked off. Besides, it couldn't have happened in a better place because for boat work, New Zealand is the best place in the world.

Email / March 12, 2003 / Summer in Auckland

There's no joy in Mudville, and lately it's been a little sad Down Under as our favored New Zealand lost the America's Cup to the Swiss team. Many of us, including most of the locals, are in shock at losing what is clearly a New Zealand-dominated sport. Countless restaurants are empty, the shops are offering their wares on sale, and it's just a little too quiet when compared to the frenzy this city has seen for the last couple of months. It feels like the party's over and it's time to leave. We would go sailing around this beautiful area, except for one thing—*Julia* is not well.

When servicing the engine, we found water in the pistons, and then removed the head to find the engine was rusting and corroding beyond serviceability, especially considering it was brand new when we left San Francisco. Not sure what caused it, but I'm lining up the experts to bring aboard. We have removed the engine from the boat, no simple feat, and it is currently being completely rebuilt; it will set me back about $10,000 when all is said and done. Ouch.

We are hoping to depart Auckland sometime in May, and there is talk of sailing north to Fiji and Vanuatu before heading over to Australia. Our departure will depend on the engine. As they say Down Under, "No worries, mate: cheers!"

I remember it as though it were yesterday: the warm summer night's air on my skin, the vibrant colors, the electronic-trance music, and the beautiful bodies all in a perfect rhythm.

It was 1 in the morning and Ken and I were standing at the Queen's Steps (no pun intended) in Sydney, attending the famous Harbour Party—prelude to Mardi Gras. In the glow of the bright moon stood the Harbour Bridge and the illuminated Sydney Opera House. It was a balmy summer night, and our elevated view overlooked 2,500 shirtless men dancing while pulsing purple and green laser beams flashed a mesmerizing light over the crowd. I even remember the words to the song playing at that moment—"Forever," by Dee Dee :

"Day by day, heart to heart, I hope that we will ever be together
Will it be, me and you, a dream that our love will last forever?
Hold me tight in your arms; I know we have the strength to stay together
Walk with me, hand in hand. I promise to be there...forever...forever."

Ken turned to me, his eyes reflecting the colored lights, and said, "You've done
a good job of not trying to make me stay, and I appreciate that. I've made my
decision, though—I'd like to stay anyway."

"What do you mean 'stay'"? I asked, my heart skipping a beat. "Stay on the
boat? For how long...? Stay with me?"

He smiled and simply said, "I want to stay with you forever."

Maybe it was the Ecstasy coursing through our veins, or the warm air on my
skin, or the music, or the setting, or all of it combined, but I melted like ice in the
desert. And that was that. My dream of Ken coming back to the boat, coming
back to me, coming back to us...had come true.

Personal Journal / March 12, 2003
What a month! Ken arrived, we're together, and having fun with David as well. I'm laughing again as we snuggle our way to sleep in the aft cabin. My life has gone from being alone to being surrounded by friends and love. What more could I ever want?

It was quite something to fly more than 1,200 miles of ocean in three hours rather than sail the same distance in 10 days. David and Andre joined us and we all had the most wonderful time together in Sydney for Mardi Gras, celebrating along with the rest of the city.

The people of Sydney are happy, friendly, and embrace the gay community much like San Francisco; it's easy and safe to be gay there. Before and after the festivities, we toured the city by foot and ferry boat, saw the maritime museum, Bondi Beach, Manly Beach, the zoo, wandered Oxford Street, went out for every meal, and even took the train to go hiking in the Blue Mountains. We were just being tourists and had a blast together. The Mardi Gras party itself was incredible, with 19,000 people dancing the night away into the early morning. We had a good laugh as we saw ourselves on the next day's local news. There happened to be a TV crew taping people exiting the party at 6 in the morning—not anybody's finest hour after a night of decadence.

I have a renewed spring in my step; I smile a lot and always seem to be in a pretty darn good mood these days. There is nothing more important or exciting as love. Again, it seems to be all about the contrasts. Had I not known the true meaning of loneliness, or want for love, I wouldn't be able to appreciate the abundance in my life now.

Personal Journal / March 13, 2003

While nursing a hangover as big as Australia, we're back onboard *Julia* facing engine issues again. I should have listened to Bill after the new engine was first installed. "There's a problem. You shouldn't have exhaust shooting 20 feet out behind the boat," he said.

"The guys who installed the engine said it's fine, and the dealer's mechanic who approved the installation said it was normal. Don't you think they should know what they're talking about?" I replied, determined not to find yet another problem.

"Yep, they should know," said Bill, "but they don't. I'm telling you something's wrong with the exhaust pressure, and it's going to come back to haunt you."

"Nah, it'll be fine. Besides, how many experts am I supposed to ask?" I said.

"As many as it takes until you find one who knows what he's doing," Bill retorted, with less patience.

I did keep asking. The mechanic in Santa Barbara said it was okay. Then the mechanic in Long Beach gave his approval. Yet Bill Cunnington, the owner of Motor and Marine Services, the first New Zealand mechanic to look at it said, "How long have you had the back-flow pressure problem? That's not normal, you know…."

I stared at him and blurted out the most intelligent thing I could come up with: "But, but, but…how do you…how did you…are you sure?"

"Geez, you Americans crack me up," said Bill, the mechanic. "So smart about everything, but you miss the simple things. This engine has to come out, and I'll bet you a beer your exhaust is too small. You're probably going to have to rebuild the engine."

I thought about it. He was right; we do miss the simple things. From enjoying an afternoon in the park to a larger exhaust hose, we're often too busy to see how the elementary things in life matter more than we recognize.

Even though I'm frustrated about the engine, my attitude remains good and that's a real improvement for me. After all, here we are in New Zealand where the boating people really know what they're doing, and I'm quite enjoying being stuck at the dock in Auckland. We have become friends with Bill, as well as Mark Thetford our electrician, and feel we're in good hands. Plus, it allows more time with David and Andre.

Email / April 13, 2003 / Getting Busy in New Zealand
It's a warm, sunny Sunday evening in Auckland; and while our lives have been slow and calm, there's lots brewing, and the feeling is, "It's time." Time to get going again, time to get all of our boat projects done, and time to sail *north* to warmer weather because fall is in the air Down Under.

Everything changed for the better with Ken back aboard. Problems that seemed too daunting before were now approachable. Not necessarily because of Ken's expertise in a particular area but rather his presence gave me a newfound eagerness I had been lacking since his departure. Even while the engine fiasco was happening, we found time to go out at night, take mini vacations by car, and of course, to shop for new boat parts. I'm sure I spent more money because Ken was there. When shopping for a boat part, he never allowed me to buy the cheapest, only the best. And while this has always been my philosophy, he ensured I adhered to that way of thinking. In addition, what a relief and joy it was to have the original team together again.

Personal Journal / April 20, 2003
Between boat projects, Ken and I have been exploring the countryside. It's such a beautiful road trip north to the Bay of Islands, where we stayed in a lovely, charming (old) B & B with a tourism-board view. I had always wanted to go to Arihopa Beach where one goes "Blow Karting"— land sailing—on the beach. We laughed a lot, even about missing out on our chance at racing three-wheeled sailing vehicles at top speeds down the beach because there was no wind that day. Standing at the rental shop, I looked at Ken and he looked at me, and we started cracking up as if to say, "Well, what are you gonna do? We prayed for calm conditions; we just got them on the wrong day!" So we went on a long walk along the beach,

skimming rocks into the water and chasing seagulls. I think we're in love.

Since we couldn't take *Julia* anywhere, we visited Waiheke Island by ferry to stay at Andre and Tom's summer house while the engine guys worked on the boat. The other night, I was reminded what a funny guy Tom Maguire is as I read a card from him:

"You boys are so brave. I think of losing sight of land, of darkness at sea. I can't even think of a storm, rain and turbulence; really I can't. I think of something breaking down, and I just want to know, what do you mean we're out of sun-dried tomatoes?

You should be on the cover of Time *magazine. I shake my head with admiration that you guys actually took on such an adventure. Seriously, it's something everyone would love to do but would never have the courage to take on. It's getting dark and the wind is picking up—and all I want is a glass of pinot noir and, oh, maybe some crudités and a dip, a little goat cheese, but you're not to go to any trouble—and we're in the frigging middle of the ocean. Hats off to you both."*

Ken and I have discussed what it would be like for just the two of us to sail the boat, and we consider it a real possibility in the future. The dynamics onboard have definitely changed. Before, we were a party of three, and now we are a couple with a third crew member onboard. I don't think we could ever find a better fit than Patrik, though, and we all get along very well. That being said, as we see other couples sail away, we're wondering if it would be better with just the two of us onboard for some of the journey.

Email / May 3, 2003

*Drip, drip, drip, tip, tap, tip, slosh, slosh, drip, tip, tap, slosh...*the sounds of the rain splattering on the deck above. I'm all warm and cozy in my berth down below, but there's a big storm moving in to Auckland and the rain is really starting to pour.

Ken and I have just returned from running errands, and we are rapidly crossing things off of our three-page to-do list.

We did make a big new installation...an electric toilet in the aft head. It's really for Ken. When I asked him what he wanted for his birthday, he replied, "An electric toilet."

"Why electric?" I asked.

Ken said in his usual direct manner: "Because I signed up to go sailing, not camping."

Now we have a fabulous new electric head with push-button flushing, and I have to admit it's pretty cool. No more hand pumping for skipper and mate!

The best way to prevent boat breakdowns is simple: Keep it out of the harsh marine environment. Obviously, using a boat hard for over a year every day takes its toll; it's not like weekend sailing in the Bay Area.

I really enjoyed New Zealand. I opened my heart and found love again. I got fit and healthy, and re-energized to go sailing again with a fresh new outlook on this journey. I was truly living the dream as I had imagined it: In charge of my own destiny and as a couple. Sailing back into the South Pacific seemed like the logical thing to do. Many other cruisers were going back to the Pacific, since like us, most only got as far west as Tonga. While that officially ended the Milk Run, some of the best of the Pacific was still ahead of us. We decided to sail to Fiji, then Vanuatu, and then down to Australia, all good decisions.

Patrik decided not to continue on with us. He was running out of money and wanted to stay in New Zealand to work for a while. Moreover, I can see how he felt like the third wheel. Ken and I were such a happy couple; perhaps we excluded him so he no longer felt like part of the core group. And Patrik is an adventurer and needed to pursue what felt right for him. In a way, I wonder if I encouraged it so Ken and I could be alone together....

Personal Journal / June 1, 2003

It's June already and I've been in Auckland over seven months. When I left San Francisco, my goal was New Zealand and having achieved that, I'm feeling nostalgic. Now it's time to move, so it's north to the Pacific and then to Australia. It's all dictated by the seasons anyway. Now is the time to be in the South Pacific, not sailing across to Australia; we go where the seasons allow us to go, and that means north.

I'll miss New Zealand and my friends here. David and I have become very close so quickly, it took me by surprise. When I arrived here, I imagined meeting someone special, and David was that person; he really helped make my stay in Auckland meaningful.

While we'll miss Patrik, he is in charge of his own adventure. I hope he rejoins us somewhere down the road. Patrik was as much a part of *Julia* as any of us. He cared for her, fixed and cleaned her, and his spirit will live onboard long after his departure. I wish him well and the best of luck. And Ken and I are kind of excited (and a bit nervous) that it's going to be just the two of us. After finding out Patrik was leaving, our trepidation threw us into a frenzy trying to find another crew. The ones we have interviewed turned out to be flakes. Besides, I'm confident we'll be fine.

The potential crew we interviewed seemed to be mostly looking for a free ride to Fiji and didn't seem willing to do their share of the work. We decided just the two of us would sail the boat. That is, until we met Femke. We were on-board interviewing a cute guy, who was nice to look at but seemed useless as a can of peas, when there was a "knock, knock!" on the hull. I came up on deck to see a tall, beautiful, blond woman with a smile as wide as the Mississippi.

"Hello, I hear you are maybe looking for crew? My name is Femke, from the Netherlands."

"I, uh, was just interviewing someone actually...." I looked at the beautiful, blond, young man below, who couldn't seem to form a complete sentence, and then looked back at Femke who clearly had more education in her baby finger than the lad did in his entire brain, and the captain in me answered: "He was just leaving...."

Femke Noordzij came aboard and melted us with her charm, wit, nearly perfect English, happy demeanor, desire to work, and eagerness to sail to Fiji. Only problem was she had a boyfriend, and they were a party of two. I didn't think we wanted two crew members; I hemmed and hawed...

"Why don't you come back tomorrow with your boyfriend and we'll see." Sure enough, the next day Femke showed up with Ralph Thoen, who was equally engaging, and we were sold. He towered over us, had curly, blond hair, and a smile to match Femke's. They made a beautiful couple, and we always knew they would someday marry, which they did in 2009.

Sometimes you just get lucky as they were the perfect addition to Julia. They moved aboard and jumped right in with cooking, cleaning, stowing, and had a zest for life and eagerness to learn that matched our mood perfectly. And this wasn't to be their only passage with us....

CHAPTER 9

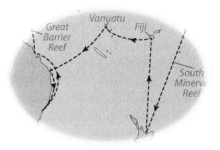

The Perfect Boat Day Sails Eight, Dines Four, Sleeps Two

"To be yourself in a world that is constantly trying to make you something else is the greatest accomplishment."
RALPH WALDO EMERSON

Email / June 10, 2003 / On the Eve of Departure
A storm has just passed through Auckland, and I can tell it's time to go north. It's been dreary, rainy and cold as winter approaches. It reminds me of San Francisco in December, more than a year and a half ago, when *Julia* was getting ready to sail south to warmer weather.

First, we'll sail to Kawau Island, a short 20 miles away to get our feet wet again. Then, it'll be an overnight sail to Opua in the Bay of Islands, a good place to wait for a fair south wind that will push us north 1,100 miles to Fiji, and warmth. Supplies onboard include enough oil and filters to last six months, food for two months, a freezer full of pre-cooked meals (thank you, David), and clean fuel in freshly scrubbed tanks. The rebuilt engine is running smoothly, starts at the first press of the button, and the host of other systems, which have been fixed, repaired, or improved upon, should keep us going happily for the sailing season. It does seem odd, though, to be sailing *north* into the South Pacific.

I've handed over my car keys to Patrik and my bicycle to Biagio; I'm free of land once again. Farewell New Zealand, and to all of our mates. It's been a magnificent dream come true.

Email / June 13, 2003 / Close Call

It was a beautiful moonlight sail up the sparsely populated, and therefore dark, rugged coast. Except for lighthouses, the silhouette of cliffs could barely be distinguished from the waterline. While we missed this place upon our initial landfall in New Zealand, we have finally made it to the Bay of Islands and the small town called Paihia. With a population of 1,700, this is the home of the pharmacy that makes the famous Paihia Bombs, one of the best seasick pills in the world. We ordered two bottles and the good-natured pharmacist will have them ready within days. What a country.

On our way here, as the moon lit up the night like a stage set, I watched a nearby boat on the radar as it made some very erratic movements. Figuring it was a fishing boat, and knowing they have a reputation for not watching where they're going, I altered course by 30 degrees to give it a wide berth. Then it too changed course and was clearly going to intercept us. I changed course back 60 degrees the other way, and sure enough, it followed, putting us on a collision course. I called on the radio: "Fishing boat, fishing boat, fishing boat!" No answer. Typical; they're too busy with their nets, buoys and lines to be bothered with a little sailboat like us, and they do have the right of way. After two more course changes on both our parts, Ken had sensed our erratic movements and was scrambling up the ladder.

"Take a look at this boat on the radar," I said. "Either it's pirates determined to get us, or a fishing boat. What do you think?"

After a minute of watching the radar screen, Ken said, "Definitely a fishing boat. Look at his track; he's probably dragging a net." I grabbed the high beam, but even after shining a million-candle watt light at the boat, there was still no response, even though we were probably no more than 100 yards away. I gave five blasts on the air horn, the international signal for immediate danger—nothing.

"Let's get the hell away from this guy. Ken, give me a course."

Out of 8,000 photos taken, these are some of the best. For more photos, go to www.larryjacobsonauthor.com.

Hobie Cat sailing after school in Long Beach and dreaming of crossing oceans.

Working as a river guide on the Tuolumne River, California, 1975. Tough guy still hates snakes.

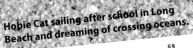

Julia, 50 feet long and weighing 25 tons, arrives at the boatyard in Alameda, California, from Florida.

Rebuilding Julia *was a bigger job than expected.*

The mast-step coin
designed by Brooke
and Bob.

Larry and the
always upbeat
Bill Claypool.

Mommy Julia so happy at the naming ceremony.

A calm day of sailing in the South Pacific, still 2,000 miles to landfall.

Ken preparing for the Shellback Society initiation ceremony at the equator.

Spinnaker trimming requires constant attention.

All around the world, dolphins provided endless fascination as they rode our bow wave.

Rainsquall headed our way in the South Pacific.

Cozy in his bunk, Patrik kept a journal.

After 21 days at sea, Ken, Patrik, and Chuck welcome landfall in the Marquesas Islands.

Patrik, Larry, and Ken beaming after our arrival in Tahiti.

Ken's superb underwater photography captured this diagonal-banded sweetlips against a backdrop of beautiful plate coral.

Cook's Bay, Moorea, with the Goddess Leli in the background (tilt your head right to see her looking skyward).

The skipper kayaking up the Faaroa River in Raiatea, French Polynesia.

Bob kayaking in water as clear as a swimming pool in Bora Bora.

Larry *skurfing* (water skiing on a surfboard) in Huahine, French Polynesia.

Alone on watch at sea during sunrise is a great moment to reflect.

Bob visited us in Moorea, 2002.

Patrik in Huahine, French Polynesia.

Unexpectedly removing the engine for its rebuild in New Zealand.

Julia, after receiving fresh bottom paint in New Zealand.

Femke and Ralph, from the Netherlands, joined us for the New Zealand to Fiji passage.

Mahi-mahi caught during the hilarious fish circus en route to Fiji.

Happy times motoring between islands in Fiji.

Sunset in the Whitsunday Islands, Australia.

L to R: Andre, Ken, Larry, and David celebrating Ken's 40th birthday in the Whitsunday Islands.

The Yasur Volcano in Vanuatu. The caldron
is over half a mile across!

The villagers of Tana
watch another cruiser
and I patch their
valued dinghy.

Village children pumping water in Tana.

The tribal circumcision dance performed in Banam Bay, Vanuatu.

Ten-foot Komodo dragon on the island of Rinca, Indonesia. They may look cumbersome, but they're fast!

Sydney, Australia, was a great place to fall back in love.

Twilight on the beach at Kupang, Indonesia, as seen from Teddy's Bar.

A typical long tail taxi boat in Thailand.

James Bond Island in Phuket, Thailand, where *The Man With the Golden Gun* was filmed.

A tourist sailing junk in Phuket, Thailand.

Kayaking through narrow passages in Phuket, Thailand.

We were the only private dinghy at Ko Phi Phi Island, Thailand.

One of the many incredible anchorages to choose from in Phuket.

Boatyard worker
in Phuket,
Thailand, before
the 2004 tsunami.

We frequented this dive shop on Phi Phi Island many
times before the tsunami hit on December 26, 2004.

"Okay, then turn starboard, 45°, no, 90°, and let's see what that does." While Ken was playing "pong" on the radar screen, I was following the colored lights of the other boat. Mr. Fisherman matched our turn and was now following us. It was like sailing a match race where our adversary followed every move we made.

"Ken, let's get away from this guy. I'm turning starboard—how far?" I asked.

"I don't like this one bit; he is way too close. Oh, hell, just turn starboard 180 degrees," Ken yelled, as he was now becoming one with the radar screen.

With the engine running, I swung the wheel hard over to starboard and headed in the opposite direction. The boom came flying over as we tacked through the wind. Everybody was awake as the engine was revving high and the flapping sails badly needed trimming.

After about 10 minutes, Ken, still staring at the radar screen finally said, "Okay, we're clear. Come to port, back to course 315."

"315, roger. Damn fishing boats; it's always a fishing boat." After a few minutes of nervous laughter about the incident, I urged everyone to go back to bed and get some rest, but this had been a little too much excitement for the new crew.

"I vill stay and watch for more boats," Femke said in perfect English and a distinct Dutch accent.

"Yeah, I'm going to make some sandviches," Ralph added, also in perfect English but with that slight "v" in his voice.

"Well, if you're all going to stay up, then you don't need me. I'm going back to bed," Ken said.

This was Femke's first real scare at sea, and I think she'll be the best watch person ever due to her paranoia of hitting other boats. And it reminded all of us that we can never let our guard down out here.

Email / June 20, 2003 / En Route to Fiji

Julia is sailing beautifully under spinnaker and mainsail, and we're starting to get our rhythm back of how to fine-tune her. Ralph and Femke are as happy and upbeat as we had hoped, and are proving to be good sailors. Their good cooking, however, is adding back a few of those hard-lost pounds.

Each day Femke tries to teach us a new Dutch saying, and we all have a good laugh at what a difficult language it is.

"Geen paniek" is the saying for today, Femke said.

"Say it again?" Ken asked. "Hind yick?"

Femke was cracking up. *"Geen paniek.* Like this, Hine panick," Femke repeated slowly.

"Hinsch panic," Ken said again. Then, amid the laughter, Ken suddenly blurted out, "Hine paneek!"

"Yeah, yeah! That's it!" Femke said, beaming proudly about her quick students.

"What does it mean?" I asked.

"It means don't panic!" said Femke, now holding her side from laughing so hard.

We used that one a lot. The only other Dutch phrase that stuck with me is, *"Stank voor dank,"* or "stink for thank you," which really means, "That's all I get for doing this for you?"

It wouldn't be a sailing trip without something breaking, and we're hoping that losing the autopilot last night is the extent of it for this trip. We had some sort of a power surge causing the autopilot to go haywire not knowing which direction it was headed. Fortunately (or unfortunately), this had happened to me last year in Tonga and I knew how to fix it. It was a series of button pushing that reset the whole system and we're back in business. This same power surge may have something to do with the blown solar panel regulator, which we'll have a look at when it turns daylight. Ken said, "As long as we're going to break things, I'd rather be fixing them while at sea and enjoying some sailing. Beats fixing them at the dock." We're very cozy inside the new dodger and Bimini with clear top and sides, and sitting on the new waterproof cushions, which easily dry off after the daily rainsqualls. We can see horizon 360° around us, so there was nothing to get in the way of the double rainbows that arched fully across the sky from one horizon to the next. What a sight.
S 31°19′ E 176°04′

Email / June 22, 2003 / Fishing for Laughter

You should have seen it! We should have sold tickets to it. It was the "Fishing Circus" onboard *Julia* this beautiful early Sunday morning, about halfway between New Zealand and Fiji. The air was already warming up so no foul weather jackets were needed, just T-shirts and shorts.

Then it began. "Fish on!" I shouted to a sleeping Ralph and Femke. No sooner than you can say mahi-mahi, when strike two. "Fish on the line! Two fish on the line!" I shouted. Both of our lines were now trailing fish about 100 yards back and we were sailing at 7 knots; we were caught by surprise. We needed to slow the boat down to reel in the fish, and we needed our fish-capturing gear.

"Where's all of the fishing stuff?" I asked Ken.

"I have no bloody idea," panted Ken as he struggled to wind in the fishing line on the starboard side. Ralph ran up the ladder to get in on the action. Together, we rolled up the giant jib and slowed *Julia* down to about half our speed.

"Femke, can you pass some things up to me?" I asked.

"Oh, the sweet dear fish, poor fish," she was mumbling.

"Yeah, poor fish, but anyway…can you pass the filet knife, and a plastic bag to put the filets in? Femke? Hello?"

"Ya, ya, okay, but I will stay down here," she replied sadly.

Ralph was head down in the lazarette storage space searching for gloves, spray alcohol to kill the fish, the gaff, wash-down hose, and a bucket. After a couple of minutes of digging, grunting, and groaning, Ralph shouted, "Found it! Here's everything."

Ken continued to wind in the first fish, not an easy task. I leaned over the lifelines with the gaff trying to hook the flapping creature behind the gills. "Yumm! Mahi-mahi! This one doesn't want to come aboard," I said, leaning over further.

As I struggled to gaff the 4-foot green and yellow beauty, suddenly the "Jerk to Inflate" emergency pull-tab on my safety harness got caught on the lifelines and—*Wham!*—my harness automatically inflated and scared the living daylights out of me. In a flash, the life jacket had inflated to its full size and bulk, and I could barely move. I had the fish hooked; he was thrashing around like crazy and I was caught in the lifelines. "Help, help, help!" I was screaming with laughter, "Get me out of this harness! No, wait, hand me the spray bottle with the alcohol!" The fish slammed into the hull splattering blood everywhere, and now everybody was laughing so hard at me, they were frozen in place.

"Murder, it's murder!" screamed Femke, and then in the same breath she said, "Smile, say *fromage*," and snapped a picture. I finally subdued the poor thing and began the filet and release process. It's an ancient art that was passed on to me from Bill Claypool and his partner, Larry Fusch: Cut one big filet off each side of the fish and release the skeleton back into the sea.

"Hey, can I get a little help over here?" pleaded Ken. Ralph, Femke, and I had forgotten about the other fish, and there was Ken, now fighting to reel in the prize on the port side. Ralph grabbed the gaff, hooked another 3-foot mahi-mahi, and hauled it up onto the deck, but the fish was fighting furiously. Ken stood on it to hold it down while he sprayed the alcohol into the gills. "I'm out of alcohol and now he's really pissed! Pass me a winch handle."

"It's Freddie Kruger, look at him go," I said as Ken whacked the poor fish on the head over and over again until there was blood everywhere.

"Murder! Murder! It's murder," Femke said, now laughing. "Smile for the camera."

As I deftly used my knife to filet the second fish, Femke took more pictures, Ken grabbed the wash-down hose and started spraying everything and everyone with warm saltwater, and we all fell to our sides howling. The blood and fish guts washed overboard and our bloody clothes can be cleaned; it's a small sacrifice for the good of the hunt, mahi-mahi meals for days, and a morning of hilarity.

What a great way to start the morning—with laughter. Laughing is the best medicine for anything: seasickness, boredom, or for no reason at all. It just makes my insides smile.

S 27°29 E 176°52'

✉ **Email** / June 28, 2003 / Safe Haven
We're still en route to Fiji but have pulled over at a kind of "roadside rest stop."

On our sixth day at sea, we got a call from *White Hawk* on the SSB radio. "*Julia, Julia, Julia,* this is *White Hawk.*"

I answered, "Where are you guys? After Lynette gave me their position and I plotted where they were, I radioed back, "Have a look 3 miles off your port bow."

A minute later Lynette came back to me, "*Julia!* I can't believe you're this close. This entire big ocean and we're nearly on top of each other. Small world, isn't it?"

"The wind is really supposed to be piping up; we're thinking about heading into South Minerva Reef. Care to join us?" I asked.

"Affirmative," Lynette said. "John wants to do some lobstering, and we just caught a 5-foot wahoo, so we'll have a fish feast."

South Minerva Reef is an incredible place only a few people ever have the opportunity to visit. Similar to Beveridge Reef, it's an enclosed reef with only one entrance wide enough for use and is the perfect safe haven for boats going to and from New Zealand. John and Lynette are quite the hunter-gatherers, and the second day here, John caught seven lobsters, each over 18 inches long.

"They're too big to fit in the pot," Ralph said.

"Oh, the poor lobster, do we have to kill it?" Femke pleaded.

"Only if you want to eat it," John said.

The anchorage is calm compared to the 10-foot seas we see crashing on the outside of the reef, not able to get through the protective coral safety barrier. The colors are sapphire and aquamarine again, the wind is blowing 25 knots and howling in the rigging, and the trade winds actually have a cool bite to them. Still, Femke was struggling with how *Julia* was bouncing around in the turbulent sea.

"It's so rough, and the wind is so loud! How long do we stay here?" asked Femke.

"Hine paneek!" Ken said using his new Dutch language skills. "Have you seen how rough it is out there?" Ralph and John were cooking the lobster, and Lynette, Ken and I were opening champagne.

"We're not leaving inside here until it calms down out *there*," I said. You're much better off in here. Have a glass of champagne and hold on." And so went the night. Our lobster and champagne festival lasted from 1600 in the afternoon until, well, um, actually, I'm not sure...but I do know it was a highlight of the passage.

S 23°56.6'W 179°07'

Personal Journal / June 30, 2003

"Larry, Larry, sorry to wake you, can you come up please?" Femke whispered.

Some captains don't want to be bothered when they're not on watch. I'm the opposite and I always want to be wakened if there's *anything* a crew member is unsure of. I had instructed Ralph and Femke, "You will never get in trouble for waking me, only if you don't wake me."

"What's going on?" I said rubbing the sleep from my eyes and stumbling up the ladder.

"I see a ship. A big ship, and it's coming straight for us," she said anxiously.

"Hine paneek, hine paneek," I said. "Show me the ship."

"Right there," she pointed toward the bow. "See the light?"

"I sure do. Show it to me on the radar," I said. We looked at the radar screen and saw nothing. I looked back at the horizon, saw the bright light, took another look at the radar, and again saw nothing. One last look at the light on the horizon, and I started quietly laughing. "Femke, now look at the light."

"Oh!" Femke was laughing too, as we both realized the light was now higher in the sky; it was a brilliant star. That's how clear it is out here.

Email / July 3, 2003 / Safe Arrival in Fiji

There's nothing quite like making landfall after a long passage. The smell of the land, the calmer seas, entrance into the reef in the morning, and finally dropping anchor in 88° crystal clear, light blue water, signaling we have entered the shallows. It's a sense of accomplishment, pride, and joy knowing we made it safely across 1,100 miles of ocean. We're anchored at Musket Cove Yacht Club on Malolo Island along with 80 other boats. The yacht club's $1 lifetime membership fee includes use of the swimming pool, bar, laundry, showers, and we're getting our dollar's worth. Ah, the highs in cruising are so high.

Personal Journal / July 24, 2003

I usually write when there's some sort of crisis or something big going on in my life. Having great days of sailing and sunshine—and love— isn't all that big enough news? Yes, these are indeed days to remember.

While we always knew they would leave soon after our arrival in Fiji, we were sad to see Ralph and Femke go. Like most other people who haven't completely lost their senses (like me), and checked out of their lives at home, they had obligations in the Netherlands. So Ken and I are alone on *Julia*, and we're enjoying our time alone. We're spreading our things throughout different closets, and reorganizing clothes and personal effects the way we want them. Now that it's just the two of us, we can truly be ourselves; we spend more time without clothes, we spend more *personal time*, and I have to say, it's just as I imagined.

In a conversation with other cruisers, the subject came up of what it's like being gay and cruising the oceans of the world. My hunch is that we are the only gay *blue water sailors* (sailors who cross oceans) out here this season—and we have "gaydar"—we would know. If we go around the world, then I'm sure that will make us the first gay couple to circumnavigate. Until somebody else steps up to the plate, the title is ours. And that's too bad, because we would really like to spend some time with other sailors like us. Not that we would all run around naked together, but it's a matter of having things in common like our coming out stories, family issues, or just plain old insider jokes.

What other things have hit my radar about being gay at sea? For one thing, we're labeled. *Julia* is the "gay boat with the guys from San Francisco." As far as other sailors are concerned, just about everybody we meet knows we're gay because we don't hide it. While we're not flamboyant, I'm not really one to mince words, and I never lie about my sexuality. Most of the people we come across are kind and accepting and don't care, and the ones that do seem to keep their distance. The rainbow flag flying from our spreaders surely answers the question: "Do you think they are?" When we interviewed Ralph and Femke to be crew, I said, "You know we're gay, right? Are you okay with that? To which Ralph replied, "So? And I like to eat pasta."

"Huh? What does that have to do with it?" I asked.

Femke chimed in, "Exactly...who cares? It's not important if you're gay or straight. It's only an issue if you make it one." Too bad all of the world can't think like the Dutch.

We tend to attract the younger crowd anyway, and they're usually quite accepting. I think it may be kind of hip for them to have gay friends. For example, our friend Dick Hunterson, who is as straight and conservative as they come, says he doesn't care. There are times though we definitely sense antagonism. When we were hauled out at Gulf Harbor boat yard and sitting at the café having breakfast, we couldn't help overhearing another table filled with locals making gay jokes and limp wrist gestures. They were the big, burly yard-worker type with a bark worse than their bite and we didn't pay them any mind. We hear from our "sources" about some cruisers who talk behind our backs, but these same people are nice face to face. Everybody sends their kids over to hang out on *Julia,* so we are clearly trusted.

For the most part, we are treated no differently by just about everybody we meet in the cruising world, and we seem to be well-known, as *Julia* tends to be party central in a lot of anchorages. That being said, we don't tell the local Fijians we're gay, as we know that wouldn't sit well with their culture and we have no interest in challenging their customs.

Well, that about does it for today; I need to go for a kayak paddle.

Email / August 8, 2003
We're sharpening our navigation skills in probably the most challenging waters we've seen to date. This isn't Sailing 101. Doing a 20-mile passage in a day, it's hard enough looking for reefs that are on the chart and dodging them. In Fiji, though, where the charts are unreliable, we are forced to scan the water for reefs not on the charts. It's exhausting, kind of like sailing through a minefield. And it's not all paradise, as we've had more mechanical problems with the autopilot, generator, and main engine alternator.

Personal Journal / August 28, 2003
"Our friend Dick." It makes me laugh when I reread the recent entry about what it's like to be gay and cruising. You never really know someone's true colors, do you? Unfortunately, we found out Dick's aren't those of the rainbow. One day, while at Musket Cove in Fiji, Dick came over to our boat after being at the bar with some of his super yacht crew friends. It seems that because Dick was hanging out with us, they thought he was gay too and this upset him to no end.

He's wasn't on our boat two minutes before he started in with, "You guys are acting so, so…so gay." I became quiet: I was shocked and seriously disappointed. Didn't he get the memo? We *are* gay. He pressed on: "My friends are giving me a hard time and calling me gay, and it's all your fault. What are you going to do about it?"

At first, I thought he was joking, and I stared at him in disbelief. When I realized he was serious, in fact, furious, my reaction was fairly simple. With a non-understanding frown, I responded, "It's not my problem; it's yours." If he was comfortable with who he was, then why should it matter what people thought, or why would he even care? After telling people he was straight, didn't they believe him? What exactly did he mean by "acting so gay?" Had I put my arm around Ken's shoulder? Was my T-shirt too tight? Did I wear a shirt and shorts one day that looked good together?

Ken piped in: "Let's see, Dick… I went through the struggle of coming out to friends and family to be who I am and decided I wouldn't change who I was for them. And you want me to change for you? *I don't think so."* Ken's face was turning red as his blood began to boil.

Dick's anger seemed directed at me, though, and this led to a barrage of vulgar language pouring out of him: "You're a jerk, you're unsympathetic, you're being selfish, and now all my friends think I'm gay!" He even threatened to beat me up. Beat me up? When was the last time that happened, sixth grade? I stared blankly at him for 20 seconds, more agonizing for him, I'm sure. He was big, about 6 foot 4 inches and towered over me with clenched fists and a most intimidating look, but I didn't care. I had been here before in my life.

I knew first-hand what it was like to be bullied for being a fat kid, for being Jewish, and then for being gay. I wasn't about to take this from anybody as an adult. Matter of factly, I said, "Okay, two things could happen: One, I could change, but…hmm, like Ken said, 'I don't think so.' Or two, you could simply not hang around us anymore," and I pointed to the companionway.

He chose the latter, stormed off the boat, and jumped into his dinghy. As he struggled to get his old outboard motor started, we could hear him cursing; he finally zoomed away to his own boat. And just like that, it was "Good bye…Dick, and good riddance!" That ends our buddy boating with

him, and is our first—and hopefully last—encounter out here with big-
otry. The next day, we put up a new brightly colored rainbow flag and I
swear it seems as though boats anchor further away from us now...or is
it my imagination?

Personal Journal / September 10, 2003
My impressions of Fiji were not as favorable as I had imagined. I
found the locals to be a bit surly, even while attempting to be friendly. It
seems as though the financial opportunities associated with tourism has
lit their individual fires, but they don't really want to do all the work necessary to handle the tourists who bring in that money. The guys at the fuel
docks are slow and not too eager to help, and the restaurant staff is doing
you a favor by serving ketchup with your fries.

Even so, there were many highlights to Fiji. One in particular was
swimming underwater into the caves at Blue Lagoon in the Yasawa Islands
(where the movie of the same name was made). Not everybody gets to go
into the caves...just those who are willing to make the acceptable bribe, or
rather, gift. The typical *gift* given to a village chief is a kilo of kava, the root
used to make a dishwater-tasting brew that numbs the mouth and gives
a slight cocaine-type buzz. Aware of this tradition, we eagerly purchased
several kilos at the open market before heading into these more remote
islands. Upon anchoring in Blue Lagoon, we sought out the village chief's
hut and were invited in for the kava ceremony. This consists of the chief
and a few other stoned elders sitting around a circle passing cup after cup
of the daily concoction to celebrate your gift. The chief half-heartedly accepted our present and then tossed it into the corner where there was a
floor-to-ceiling stack of the root brought by previous cruisers. We sat on
the floor mats in the damp, musty hut, drank a potion you wouldn't even
wash your socks in (which is what it tasted like), clapped our hands as
instructed, and passed the bowl back for refills. Then the next person
took his turn. While not quite as jaded as a Waikiki Beach luau, we could
certainly tell they had done this before...about a thousand times.

As we were leaving the chief's hut, he pulled me aside and said,
"Captain, would you like to see the caves?"

"We would love to see them," I replied.

"The caves are very important and sacred. Not everybody gets to see them…there is a small donation." Being an entrepreneur myself, how could I fault him? There he was sitting on top of a great asset. Why should he be any different than other people around the world and not make a fast buck? "For a small donation, my son will lead you there," he offered.

Kava drunk, cash paid, and led by the village chief's teenage son wearing Adidas shorts and Nike shoes, we squeezed through a narrow crack in the rock wall to find ourselves inside a huge cavern the size of a small church, with stalactites on the ceiling and a beautiful pool of glittering green water below. "Follow me," said our trusty guide, and we all jumped into the water after him. "It's easy, go down, swim 10 feet that way under the rocks, and then come up." Just like at Mariners Cave in Tonga, and with great trepidation, one by one we dove down and swam under the rocks for what seemed an eternity and then popped up in the inner sanctum, even more amazing than the outer cave. An opening to the sky filled the cavern with light. The only way in or out was the way in which we entered. We were giddy with tension, because it was spooky being inside this truly remote place. It was dazzling and certainly worth the donation.

Email / September 12, 2003 / At Sea Again
Our farewell to Fiji was provided courtesy of a pod of dolphins crossing *Julia's* bow just outside of the pass. Some were very big, more than 10 feet.

We're sailing along nicely under a mesmerizing silver moon. Dinner is finished, Ken is asleep, and I have the first night watch. It's lonely, peaceful, exciting, fulfilling, and there is plenty of time to think about how perfect this day has been; from the love I have in my life to the stunning natural beauty around us. It hasn't always been nor will it always be like this, so I'm getting better at appreciating things when they are this good. S 18°16.5′ E 176°26′

Email / September 13, 2003
We were looking for the true South Pacific where we could pass days lazily under a coconut tree. We found it in the same place James Michener did: Vanuatu. Our first views were impressive: Tall volcanic islands covered in lush greenery, steam escaping from vents around the edges of the anchorage, and a huge plume of smoke rising from the

center of the island, inspiring a sense that we had entered *Jurassic Park*. We are anchored along with seven other boats, and this morning it is so quiet, peaceful and beautiful, even I am moving around on the boat quietly not wanting to disturb the serene atmosphere.

Tourism has not tarnished this place. The people are friendly, sweet, kind, but very shy about meeting us. Upon our arrival, three outrigger canoes—the real ones dug out from a solid tree trunk—each holding two young men, approached our boat. The skinny children, with very black skin and curly hair, sit in their canoe 20 feet away staring and absorbing us, and our beautiful *Julia*. The first boat held a couple of boys, probably about 11 to 12 years old, who just wanted to say, "Hi and welcome to Vanuatu." While chatting with them, making allowances for their broken English, we discovered they are in school and in need of pens. We rummaged through our supplies and gave them enough Bic ballpoints to set them up for a year; they were most appreciative.

In the second boat, a young man held up a single flashlight given to them by a previous cruiser: "Excuse me, do you have batteries?" Of course we had batteries; *Julia* is a virtual battery warehouse, and we were glad to pass on a good supply to him. Then, blushing a little, the other boy in the canoe points to his shirt that had enough holes in it to be mistaken for Swiss cheese and says, "Excuse me sir, do you have T-shirts?" We shared T-shirts, rope, candy, fishhooks, and swim goggles with these kids, and they were genuinely appreciative of it all. They have very English-sounding names: Peter, Jimmy, Nelson, Richard....

The third canoe was selling lobster. We bought three for $10 total but since we don't have a pot big enough in which to boil them, the boys offered to do this for us. How? They took them over to one of the steam vents right down at the water's edge and put them in the hot water pool, and brought them back perfectly cooked. Talk about working with what you've got....

While I'm still reserving judgment, I can't help saying to myself this is what the real South Pacific is supposed to be. The children's smiles are big and they laugh a lot. These are happy people and I wonder what makes them so. What do they have that the Fijians don't have? If anything, they have less. It's certainly not about how much you have, how many things you have, or even what you think you may get in the future. It's about living in the here and now, and appreciating life just for life's sake. S 19°31.5′ E 169°29.6′

Personal Journal / September 15, 2003

Last night, following a nice dinner, we were watching a movie, when suddenly the VHF radio came to life: *"Julia, Julia, Julia,* Help! Help! Help!" For sure, it was Helga's German accent, which told us it was *Explorer* anchored only a few hundred yards away. Bob and Helga were in some kind of trouble. We tried to raise them in a return hail but got no response. We jumped into our dinghy and raced over to see what was happening. About 5 yards astern, certainly close enough for anyone onboard to hear us, I called out: "Bob?! Helga? Hey...*Bob!"* Nothing. Just the winding down of our outboard as Ken cut the engine and drifted up to their stern. As we were tying the dinghy to the swim step, we got the first glimpse of a trail of blood leading to the cockpit. Ken shot me an anxious look while we quietly climbed aboard.

Moving closely together, we found Bob sitting in the cockpit, swaying back and forth, holding his hands up to his lip, and blood everywhere. Helga was down below, beside herself. She was pacing around, not knowing what to do, so Ken went to calm her.

"Bob, what happened to you? Is Helga okay? Is there anyone else onboard?" Either he couldn't understand me or he was in too much shock to respond. I had a look at Bob's lip as I searched around the cockpit to spot a rag or paper towel or anything I could use to arrest the bleeding. I pressed forward with my interrogation. "Bob, look at me. How did this happen?" Through a slurred delivery of nouns and verbs, he told me how he had fallen on the swim step and split his lower lip wide open into a T-shaped cut, which was now hanging on by a small bit of skin. It went without saying he was pretty smashed.

It was a really, really bad cut. Bob, who is a dentist, was drunk calm about it all and proceeded to ask me if I knew how to suture. "Uh, well, um, I've practiced on a towel in my onboard first-aid class, and I've sewn ripped sails but have never done it before on a person."

"Thash okay," he slurred. "I'll guide you shrew it. Or, if you can jush hole zha mirror, I'll shew it up myshelf."

"Yeah, Bob, and tomorrow you'll find your lip is sewn to your nose. No way, you're too drunk," I replied. Either I was going to be stitching, guided by a patient three sheets to the wind, or we were going to get help.

"Wait a minute; wait just a minute…what about taking you to the hospital?" I asked, aware that my question was delivered more like a captain's order. We soon agreed this wasn't a good option as the only clinic was on the other side of the island, and there were no cars at Port Resolution Bay. Someone would have to somehow travel 20 miles by foot, by hitchhiking or donkey, on a one-lane dirt road over the mountains to the other side of the island and bring back the doctor, something that could take all night and half the next day, and that's *if* we found a doctor. No, we were on our own and had to handle it ourselves, one way or another.

After calming Helga down, Ken came up to the cockpit. He looked at me, "How's Bob?" I shrugged and nodded toward my patient. Ken took one look at Bob's lip and nearly tossed his cookies right there. When I told him I was going to sew it up and he would have to hold the light and be my assistant, he started thinking hard about alternatives. I needed a solution fast and I needed to break Ken's attention before he totally lost it. Before I could say anything, Ken was down the swim steps leaping into our dinghy. "I'm going to the other boats to get help!" he shouted over his shoulder as he zoomed off into the ink-black night.

In the meantime, I got on the radio: "Pan-pan, pan-pan, pan-pan" (the international call signal for a state of urgency but not imminent loss of life). "Any boat, any boat, any boat in Port Resolution Bay, this is *Explorer*." I released the switch. Nothing. Dead air. I clicked on again: "Pan-pan, pan-pan, pan-pan. Any boat, any boat, any boat in Port Resolution Bay, this is *Explorer* with a medical emergency. Does anybody copy?" When I released the switch, the silence was frightening and only intensified my worry. We were nowhere near any emergency services and evidently all boats in the anchorage had switched off their radios.

I snapped back to the attention of my patient while directing Helga with restrained calm: "Helga, do me a favor and get some more ice, will you?" She left, and moments later returned with a bucket that probably recently contained the same vodka now coursing through Bob's veins like the I.V. they would have given him if we ever found a clinic. Grabbing a fistful of ice and wrapping it in a fresh washcloth, I kept pressure on the bleeding, and we waited. "Well, you really did it this time Bob," I joked to lighten the moment.

"Shure did," he mumbled struggling a crooked smile.

You want to talk about good luck? The first boat Ken pulled up to was a chartered catamaran from French-speaking New Caledonia. Of course, everyone onboard spoke French, but two people in particular also spoke excellent English. Why? As luck would have it, they were both very well-educated doctors. In fact, they were surgeons.

Ken came roaring back to *Explorer* shouting the good news and within minutes, the two surgeons arrived, full medical kits in hand. It wasn't long before they had begun sewing Bob up and an hour later we were all having a celebratory cocktail (though Bob elected to stick with just plain water). The doctors had done an amazing job, and while Bob's lip resembled Frankenstein's forehead, they assured us he would heal just fine.

Lessons learned? Keep the VHF radio on all the time…stay connected. Be careful. We're on our own out here, and by out here, I mean anywhere. It's good to be lucky. And most importantly, it's okay to ask for help.

Email / September 16, 2003 / The Volcano

Greetings from magical Vanuatu. The local kids stare at us as we walk through the village, and they smile and giggle and wave and practice their English with "hello" and "bye-bye." Since they rarely see westerners, they become very excited to meet anyone with whom they can practice the English they study in school. Vegetable stands manned by entire families sell fresh produce, live chickens and pigs, and wait for prospective buyers on the side of the dusty roads. Many of these daily markets are situated under huge banyan trees, considered special meeting places because they're sacred. On a more practical note, the shade offers relief from the intense heat and provides shelter from the heavy rain showers.

We're in Tanna, home of one of the few active volcanoes in the world. From our anchorage, we can see the dark ash and smoke spewing into the sky as steam vents hiss in the black lava rocks on the shore a hundred yards away. These openings and underground springs bubble to the surface right at the water's edge and form perfect natural hot water pools. While sitting in one yesterday, I discovered I had found the original; this must be the place every hotel spa has emulated. Boiling water mixes with cool saltwater surging into the pool every few seconds to keep the temperature just perfect. Ten-foot tall ferns and colorful jungle vines surround it all. I'll never be able to look at any man-made spa the same way again without judging their results while attempting to copy this one.

Our trip to the Tanna Yasur Volcano was nothing short of spectacular. Along with three other couples, we piled into a Land Rover with the village chief's son as guide. (It seems as though village chiefs are often pawning their sons off as guides in this part of the world.) We drove along a dirt road that is literally slashed through the jungle. Uphill we went and over a dale, then up another hill, another dale, through small villages, past the pigs grazing on the left, taking a right at the school, a left at the banyan tree, and about an hour later, we're driving on the moon—nothing but grey ash. Cresting the final hill, we arrived on a mile-wide plain at the base of the volcano. We tumbled out of the vehicle, and as I made our first footprint in the ash, I recited, "One small step for man…"

As we started the trek up the steep side of the volcano, we could see steam and smoke coming out of the top; we heard a hissing like escaping gas, and then a more throaty sound like a blowtorch or a flamethrower. Our anticipation mounted. The trail was filled with pieces of lava strewn about, which had recently been flung from inside the caldron. We suddenly realized that there were no barriers to keep us away and no park ranger to tell us to get back behind the fence—it was the real thing with simply no restrictions.

At the top of the trail, we were rewarded with a view to remember: the edge of a real, live, active volcano, easily a half-mile across. Speechless, we gawked at the huge sunken crater, exactly like you imagine a volcano to be: covered in volcanic rock except in the center where steam and smoke spewed from a red molten pit hundreds of yards wide. Out of this redness flew huge bits of lava, so red hot they still glowed and smoked after landing on the ground, some not more than a hundred yards from where we were perched.

Halfway down into the volcano's pit, a ring of smoke hovered all the way around the inside perimeter. As the steam rose, dangerously close to where we stood on the edge, it collided with the cooler air and curled back down, reminding us of the thick fog banks that pour over the Sausalito hills back home.

When the sun dropped behind the giant pit to the west, a smoky, pale yellow sky surrendered to darkness. Within minutes, the night show began as a pink and red glow growing from the lava pit, revealing just how much lava rock the volcano was spitting out. We soon realized some of the pieces were the size of cows and small cars and were being shot hundreds of feet through the air. We sat and watched the eruptions, which then went quiet for a few minutes, ending with a faint hissing from steam tainted with toxic gas. Soon our feet and legs trembled as the ground began a deep low rumble, and then a roar, followed by another, even bigger eruption shooting more enormous rocks high into the air. As the darkness deepened, the show transformed from magical to devil-like with bright reds and oranges, filling the caldron with a mystical glow. The lava fireworks, which had been hidden by daylight, were now at their brightest.

It was easy to see how the islanders see magic and spirits in the depths of the volcano. After watching the show for another hour, we made our way in silence down the ashen slopes, each of us touched and mesmerized by the spirits from within the earth. There was simply nothing left to say.

Personal Journal / September 19, 2003

We are in a slice of absolute South Pacific heaven. However, others before us met a different fate. A yacht recently went aground at the point of Resolution Bay, and its owners gave the villagers everything that could be stripped from the boat as a gift, including an inflatable dinghy. Unfortunately, someone from another village was jealous about all of these things, snuck over one night and slashed a 4-inch long hole in one of the tubes. Other cruisers had attempted to fix the hole but none of the patches held. The locals have been waiting for someone to come along who really knew how to fix dinghies, and having patched quite a few in my days as a river rafting guide, I felt qualified. As I worked to prepare the surfaces and the patch material, a crowd gathered and one among them nicknamed me, "boat doctor."

Eight adults and 10 kids crowded around as I cleaned, sanded and stuck the surfaces together, clamping them tight to wait a good 24 hours. I used inside and outside patches knowing, because of the size of the hole, that was my only chance. The villagers made a day of it, laughing and talking among themselves, and to us. They were so polite and sweet and very happy their dinghy would soon float again. Talk about pressure! Not even sure if the patch would work, but appreciative of our help, some of the elder women from the village handed Ken and me five beautiful hand-woven baskets filled with fruits and vegetables as a thank you. We were truly touched. There was something tribal in all this; something akin to one of those King Kong movies or Errol Flynn pictures when the Europeans break bread with the natives. Only this was real. These were genuine people with huge hearts.

We returned the next day to remove the clamps and pump up the dinghy to see if the patch held. Now there was a big crowd, and you could feel the tension in the air: Would the repair hold? Would the village have a dinghy again? In my heart, I knew I had done my best to fix it properly, and it held.

The next day, everybody waved at us as we walked through the village; we had become their friends, and "insiders." We stayed in that bay a full week more because we felt so welcome. I was sad as we sailed out the other day. We were fortunate to be able to help the villagers with their dinghy repair, and I have all the reward I need: It feels good to help, and give to others. I don't want or expect anything else—it just feels good.

Personal Journal / September 23, 2003

I'm becoming concerned about how much alcohol Ken and I consume (as I sip a vodka on ice). I think we and other cruisers drink out here basically because it's boring. Yes, it's boring; it really is. It's lonely, too, terribly lonely. One beautiful island after another, and then what? Another beautiful island. Which is why I like my pattern of staying in the islands a while and then getting back to a First World country like Australia. I'm learning too much of a good thing can be boring; it's the contrasts that make life interesting.

Just as I was lamenting the lack of good friends, Mike Scouse came into our lives. We first met Mike when, aboard his boat Indulgence II, *he was headed for the same anchorage, Lamen Bay. He didn't have the proper charts and radioed to ask if he could follow us into the bay at night. It was the beginning of a good friendship with its assorted share of ups and downs. Mike and I have lots in common; particularly how we see life as something that should be enjoyed to its maximum. Being a New Zealander, Mike is strong willed and has the can-do attitude I strive for in my life.*

Like me, he was in business and decided to chuck it all and go sailing. He didn't know exactly where he was going or for how long—just that he was going. Being a well-respected ocean racer, though, puts him in a category of sailing expertise far beyond mine. We learned lots about sail trim and how to make a boat go faster from Mike. Traveling with his 10-year-old son, Ben, and partner, Elke, made for some fun times and we all got along famously.

Email / October 3, 2003 / Our Turn to Be Lucky

Yesterday, we were drowning our sorrows, lamenting the future prospects of losing all of our food because we couldn't start the generator. This morning, we opened the generator box, looked closely, looked at each other, tried a couple of fixes we know, all to no avail. We looked at each other again and shook our heads in despair.

What to do? I tuned in the radio to the morning cruisers net, a place for all those sailors in the Vanuatu area to share information… "Does anybody know where the closest diesel mechanic would be to Lamen Bay on the island of Epi?" Given the odds, I may as well have been asking for a Royal Navy ship full of mechanics to pop up over the horizon. Sure enough, I received: "See if there's a boat named *Nikita* in that anchorage with a New Zealand diesel mechanic named Tomo onboard. He usually hangs out there and can fix anything," the anonymous voice advised. Ken raced to the cockpit grabbing the high-powered binoculars to scan the anchorage and see if such a boat was around. Lo and behold, *Nikita* was a quarter mile away. The generator is now running like a top, the freezer is cold, and the batteries are charging beautifully. I ask you, how lucky is that?

We could have fixed it ourselves…we just needed a bit more courage to keep bleeding the engine further and try things only an expert mechanic would try. Next time, we'll have that courage. The learning never stops.

Email / October 11, 2003

Today, we swam with a dugong. A what? You're wondering what a dugong is…and why we decided to swim with one? It's a marine mammal, similar to a manatee. Fourteen feet long, big as an elephant seal, with the tail of a whale, and a face of a uh, um, well, a cow, no, a shar-pei dog, or something like that, but a face only a mother could love. We swam down, looked it in the eye, watched it feeding on the grassy bottom, circled around it, rubbed its belly, and when it surfaced for air, we were able to see and touch its rough skin up close. What a treat! Oh, and why did we do it? Until you've had the opportunity to swim with one of these creatures, there are simply no words to relate the experience. Still, if you get the chance...do it!

In the same bay were dozens of big turtles. After many tries, and certainly influenced by those Hollywood movies suggesting this was even possible, I finally got close enough to one of these beautiful creatures to reach out and try to grab it by the back of its shell. I touched it and held on for what I hoped would be a great ride, and *whoosh,* like a rocket, it slipped through my hands leaving me wondering where it had gone. No free rides today! They may look slow but they have incredible power when they need it, and there was no way I was going to get a ride from that turtle.

After a couple of fun days in Lamen Bay, while lifting our anchor, we heard a loud bang. We are sensitive to noises on the boat because unusual noises usually mean something is very wrong. Upon closer inspection, we discovered our windlass (the electric winch that pulls up our 110-pound anchor and 400 feet of chain) had sheered all six bolts holding it in place.

Wouldn't you know we didn't have six spare bolts 7 inches long and $3/8$ inches thick? In fact, we didn't even have one, and neither did any other boats in the anchorage. One boat, however, had some threaded steel rod, and our friends on *Rampart* offered assistance. Jim, the captain, his son Aaron, and Estelle, their always-smiling Australian crew member, came aboard and again demonstrated the camaraderie of cruisers. Jim was a mechanical engineer in New Zealand and showed us how to fashion the rod into new bolts by attaching nuts to the top of the rod, grinding them down, locking the threads, and cutting screwdriver grooves. Presto! We had four new bolts. We think they'll hold until Australia.

We're certainly learning how to make something out of nothing and how to improvise. Out here you don't have any choice; you have to find a solution.

Email / October 12, 2003 / Wreck Diving and Custom Dances
During World War II, more than 100,000 American troops were stationed on the island of Santo and they left their mark in many ways. This is the island Michener wrote about in his famed *Tales of the South Pacific,* and I was glad to have reread his book recently. There are Quonset huts (the round top aluminum buildings) everywhere, which have since been converted into stores, storage sheds and workshops. On the abandoned airfields, we run around like kids pretending to be airplanes and pick up Coca-Cola bottles from the 1940s that are still intact and say "Bottled In Oakland." The soldiers also left a couple of things underwater for us to see....

We have made three fantastic scuba dives here in Santo thus far, the first one on Million Dollar Point, which, according to the historical record, got its name this way: After World War II, the French were in control of Vanuatu (then known as New Hebrides). The Americans didn't want to cart back to the states all of the Corps of Engineer equipment, so they offered it to the French government at bargain basement prices, but the French turned them down. They were hoping the Americans would give in and leave it for free.

One day, the American commander invited the French officials to the seashore for a picnic and to watch a "demonstration." The Americans offered one last time, for 10 cents on the dollar, all of this nearly new equipment...but the answer was still *"Non."* While lunch was being served, a large rumbling sound proceeded down the road and through the bush. The stunned French watched the "crazy" Americans drive everything over the edge of the cliff into the sea. Bulldozers pushed jeeps, trucks headed for the water with soldiers flooring the gas pedals and then leaping out at the last minute, forklifts somersaulted into the ocean, tankers, and then finally the bulldozers themselves pushed each other to their watery graves. (I presume the drivers bailed out at the last second.) The American commander turned to his French counterpart and said, "You should've taken the deal...."

And so we have Million Dollar Point, a great scuba diving site where we went underwater window-shopping among all of the old, rusted, historical equipment. In what must be one of the most crowded salvage yards underwater, we sat in jeeps, pretended to drive the bulldozers, and searched the bottom for anything of value—I will admit it sounds way better than it is. The reality is you're swimming through a garbage dump, and there is nothing of value. I mean, seriously, ever tried starting a jeep that's been underwater for more than 60 years?

Million Dollar Point was just a warm-up for the big daddy of wreck dives. On October 26, 1942, the *SS President Coolidge*, a five-star luxury liner that had been converted to a U.S. troop carrier, arrived in Santo with more than 5,000 soldiers and struck two of our own mines in the harbor. Within 90 minutes, she was listing heavily; all aboard except two safely abandoned ship before she sank onto the reef. The captain tried to beach the ship, but it struck a reef just short of the shoreline. Disastrous for the ship, but fortunate for us as she now lies within walking distance of the beach. The bow rests in about 90 feet and the stern in 180 feet; the two dives we've enjoyed were to 120 feet.

We had never even heard of the *Coolidge* before arriving in Vanuatu. While walking through town, we popped into the local scuba shop on a whim. It was packed with tourists who had flown in from all over the world just to see the *Coolidge*, which is evidently the best wreck dive in the world because the ship is intact, accessible, and she's a luxury liner, not a freighter. Lucky us who just happened to be here. If you remember the opening scenes in the movie *Titanic,* that will give you a good picture of what it's like descending into the depths, and then seeing the ship looming in front of you. The *Coolidge* is 650-feet long, 81-feet wide, and underwater she looks gigantic. We toured the promenade deck, the bridge, the ballroom, saw the big guns that had been mounted on the foredeck, found helmets, rifles, gas masks, mess trays from the galley, and even the captain's china. In the cargo holds, we saw stacks of jeeps as well as an upside-down tank. Because only two soldiers were unfortunate enough to die onboard, we weren't worried about encountering too many ghosts. However, heading into the darkened holds was eerie, and I couldn't help but imagine what it was like on that day so many years ago when this great ship disappeared. At one point, we turned off our flashlights to see the tiny glowing shrimp that live there. Oh, my God, that was scary. In retrospect, maybe we *did* see ghosts.

In contrast to the modern sport of scuba diving, we attended a "custom dance" in the village at Banam Bay, a place renowned for its traditional ceremonies. It was so tribal…so primitive, almost scarier than the darkness of a sunken ship. We knew we were watching something very special and rare as the afternoon light reflected on the dancers' black skin, decorated in white paint. Some 60 natives, representing the entire village, participated. The men wore nothing but the paint on their bodies and leaves wrapped around their privates to form what is known as a penis sheath. Believe me, it sounds better than it looks.

While supposedly peaceful, the ritual appeared as though they were setting up for a cannibalistic dinner. The circumcision dance is a tradition performed just before cutting—on a boy's 12th birthday. The rhythms kept building, and the dust clouds kicked up enough to look like a mist shrouding us from seeing the actual circumcision, and it was just like being in a live issue of *National Geographic*. (Though boys will be boys no matter where you are on earth: Some of these kids didn't look very happy.) The people are quite friendly, though, and since the last incident of cannibalism was reported in the 1960s, we felt safe.

Email / October 19, 2003 / Search for the Perfect Anchorage
Along with *Indulgence II* and *Charlotte*, we headed towards Oyster Island and what sailors call the outer anchorage. We had no problem getting in behind the reef with 6 feet to spare under the keel. However, this anchorage was still pretty rough and while rocking and rolling in the chop, we enviously eyed the two boats anchored in the calm waters of the inner anchorage. On the charts, the pass reads 5 feet, 11 inches, less than our 7-foot draft, but we were feeling bold, lucky, and we have a new handheld depth sounder we were eager to use.

Armed with a radio and the depth sounder, Ken hopped in the dinghy and zoomed off to scout the very narrow pass (only 20 feet wide) and locate a route through the coral heads. He soon came roaring back signaling I should follow him.

"It's tight so don't get crossed up, and there are coral heads everywhere," Ken said, "but I think you can make it." I checked the wind; 25 knots pushing us sideways meant I would have to keep our speed up—not a good thing when dodging underwater coral heads the size of trucks—affectionately known by sailors as "bommies." Sure enough, we made it inside with a foot to spare under the keel. A bit close for my comfort, but we're now inside the most beautiful tropical paradise lagoon you can imagine. The water is midnight blue, flat as a tabletop, and stretches for over a mile. We're surrounded by dense jungle filled with birds singing an orchestra of calls. Thick mangroves grow at the water's edge and are covered with oysters for the taking. Not more than 100 yards away is our next dive: an American warplane that didn't quite make it to the runway 60 years ago. And to top it off, ashore is a tiny lodge and French restaurant we plan to patronize as long as we don't have to wear shoes. This entire scene is so dramatic it seems as though a Hollywood studio created it. Except this is the real thing.

S 15°22.7′ E 167°10.9′

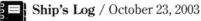 **Personal Journal** / October 21, 2003

It seems the islands keep getting better and better in Vanuatu. We've been to Epi, Efate, Malakula, and now are in Santo where the considerable amount of World War II history interests me to no end. Ken and I are getting along great and enjoying our time together.

We seem to have found friends again. For my birthday, we invited four other boats and within an hour, there were 14 people onboard. Ken spent all day baking carrot cake, my favorite. Mike decorated *Julia* with palm fronds and leaves, creating our very own tropical paradise. What a great gift to be with good friends.

In spite of getting older, I'm feeling younger than I have for some time. When a rainstorm filled the dinghy to the gunnels with sweet fresh rainwater, I took an *alfresco* bath. With soap and shampoo—all biodegradable of course—and in the pouring rain, I splashed around and let the kid inside me come out and play again.

Ship's Log / October 23, 2003

1430: Raising anchor for short sail to Champagne Beach.

1440: Anchor back down, Ben has fallen. Bleeding badly, head cut wide open, trouble breathing. Lungs? Ribs? Trying to find hospital. We're so far away.

Personal Journal / October 26, 2003

We're still anchored in Peterson Bay on Oyster Island. We had planned to leave three days ago for Champagne Beach and then to the island of Maewo, which we heard was a great place to visit for its hiking and waterfalls. We had said our good byes to *Indulgence II* and *Charlotte,* and were actually pulling up the anchor when it happened. Mike's 10-year-old, Ben, and Brian, the 12-year-old son of *Charlotte's* Tomas and Jill, were jumping from the spreaders—15 feet above the deck into the water—laughing and having a good time like kids do.

Ben stood ready for his next leap. "Look guys!" he hollered to us. Right before our eyes, as Ben moved to jump, he lost his footing and fell. We watched in horror as he tried to hold on to the shroud, which slowed his fall slightly, but down he tumbled head over heels 15 feet to the steel lifeline where he hit his side, then again over the side of the lifeline, and slammed his head into the steel toe rail of the boat, finally splashing into the water. He popped up screaming in pain, "Aaaa, Aaaa, Aaaa, Help! Dad!" Blood gushed out of his forehead.

There was only one decision to make: Take the dinghy or swim? They were anchored 25 yards from us. I shouted to Ken, "Get the anchor chain back out...and bring ice!" I made a shallow dive and sprinted like I was going for the gold. Tomas witnessed the accident from the cockpit of *Charlotte* and together, we managed to haul Ben out and lay him in their dinghy.

"Ice, here's the ice!" Ken said, as he wrapped it in a thin towel. We applied the towel to Ben's head to stop the bleeding while checking for breathing, broken bones, and any other injuries.

"I can't breathe, I can't breathe," Ben was crying, while gripping his side tight with both hands. "Hold on Ben, hold on, you're going to be okay," I assured him, wondering if my voice carried any confidence. We took him to Mike's boat and carried him below. Considering the fall he took, his little 100 pound body survived pretty well, although we didn't know just how well yet.

His forehead was cut wide open 4 to 5 inches long, in a semi-circle all the way down to the scalp. After we calmed Ben down, he kept complaining he couldn't breathe, and we worried about a punctured lung from a broken rib. His ribs were bruised, swelling fast and turning purple, so we kept applying ice to his ribcage. We treated him for shock. In spite of the stifling heat, he was shivering, so we covered him in blankets, put his feet up, checked his vision, his comprehension, and his pulse, which was 120; not too bad considering how panicked he was. Mike kept up the encouragement: "Hey big guy, you're going to be all right." I could see the look in Mike's eyes that made me wonder if he believed what he was saying.

In the meantime, Ken and Tomas departed in the dinghy to the nearby resort to call for an ambulance. Finally, after about two hours, we heard the VHF:

"*Indulgence II*, this is Ken, get Ben ready to move, we're on our way with a stretcher." In his rush to get to the phone earlier, Ken hadn't pulled the dinghy up the beach far enough and the tide had come in while he was waiting for the ambulance. He returned just in time to discover the dinghy floating away and had to go for a long swim to retrieve it; he showed up at the boat drenched and exhausted.

We carried Ben up on deck, strapped him to the buckboard, and gently lowered him into the dinghy and headed for shore. Mike and I hopped in the ambulance with Ben for the hour ride over very rough dirt roads. The poor boy was in a lot of pain bouncing along over the bumpy surface, and there was plenty of "Oh, Ow, Aaah, Stop, Pleeeeeese, Dad…." coming from the back where he lay holding his father's hand. An hour later, we arrived at the Luganville Hospital. Hospital? Well, let's just say it isn't Cedars-Sinai. The complex consisted of a couple World War II Quonset huts and a few dilapidated buildings with fading paint and chipped plaster walls.

"May I help you?" asked the tired-looking woman who appeared out of nowhere as we wheeled Ben into the "emergency room," a small chamber dimly lit by one fluorescent fixture, with two beds, and some cupboards of medicines, cleansers, and a few Band-Aids. The staff, which occasionally walked by were friendly, but the whole scene appeared to us to be a rerun of a *M.A.S.H.* episode, as disorganized as if we were under fire.

I asked, "Which room do we go to? Where do we wait?"

"Wait here, they're coming," the older nurse with the grey hair said.

"Who is coming? When will the doctor be here? *Is* there a doctor…?"

Mike, one of the bravest men I know, was trying his best to be stoic but I could tell it was difficult for him to see his little boy in such pain, and he and his son were both scared. Mike held Ben's hand, and I held Mike's while a nurse cleaned the wound. We looked at each other for support and knew that somehow we would make it through this.

We wheeled Ben to another room for an X-ray, and although the equipment was fairly old, it worked. Then we returned to the E.R., where after another hour, Chris, the doctor, arrived directly from the soccer field in his shorts, tank top, and tennis shoes. He was a local guy, about 35, trained in Fiji, and had a soothing bedside manner: "Don't worry, I see this kind of thing all the time here. We'll have you fixed up in no time, young man."

Chris was a professional who had clearly seen his share of fieldwork. While Mike held Ben's hand, and I held the flashlight so the doctor could see the wound, he began the stitching procedure. Good thing we had that flashlight with us because, with darkness coming on, and only a single flickering overhead fluorescent light, I don't know how Chris otherwise could have seen well enough to do his work. The cut was all the way down to the scalp, and he did plenty of sewing inside and out because of its length and depth. I watched closely, all the while wondering if I really could have done this for Bob's lip without sewing it to his nose a few weeks earlier.

Ben was a brave boy but in great pain, so he cried often. After finishing the stitches, Chris gave the final prognosis. While the X-ray showed a cracked rib and bruises, Ben was going to be all right.

Since we had no cell phones, I felt I had to get back to the boats to report on the situation. I left Mike and Ben in their hospital room. It was now late in the evening and the return trip to the boat was so far that no cabbie wanted to make the journey on the unlit dirt road. I finally ended up offering a driver an unheard of amount of money to enlist his services and made my way to the beach at Oyster Island. My VHF finally had a clear signal, and I was able to raise Ken who came to retrieve me by dinghy.

Here we are, three days later, staying in Peterson Bay with our friends Mike and Ben, with whom we've now bonded. A crisis can do that faster than time. I don't care about missing the other anchorages because there is nothing more important to me than friendship. What a lesson today: how important and valuable life is, and how important to treat it as such.

Personal Journal / November 5, 2003

It's a rainy morning and we're securely tied to a mooring in Port Vila, Vanuatu. Andre and Tom have been with us for the past five days. They were happy and appreciative to be here and have put us in wonderful moods. The down side was they brought five bottles of vodka and lots of chocolates, which we've entirely consumed. Tom, who is an extraordinary chef, cooked all of the meals, giving us a great break. We ate like royalty.

The other day, I had just hopped into the dinghy and as I reached over to start the outboard motor, my eye caught a glint of bright silver right near the motor swivel. I moved in for a closer inspection, the silver moved, then the black stripes moved, and then I saw its head—SEA SNAKE. "Oh no," I groaned. "Didn't I see this movie in Niue? Ahhhhhhh!"

Even after facing them down in Niue, I still have no lost love for deadly poisonous snakes, particularly those sitting on the motor in my dinghy. I jumped about 3 feet into the air, shouting, "Snake! Snake!" and while I got lots of attention in the anchorage, I was still on my own. The crowbar was conveniently in the dinghy; I picked it up as my first line of defense. With sweat dripping down my face and body from the blazing sun, and fear running through me like a madman, I banged it onto the dinghy floor and then on the motor. The snake remained dormant. I banged again. Nothing. I finally had to prod the lazy sunbathing reptile to wake up. Once he started to move, I started jumping again, shouting, and pushing it towards the water with the crowbar. Only when it finally slithered over the side did I see how huge it was—2-feet long by 1 inch in diameter. Hey, it was still poisonous. Sometimes size *doesn't* matter.

Personal Journal / November 8, 2003

I am continually amazed at how long it takes to actually leave someplace and how many things there are to do before departure on a long passage. Here's our checklist just for departing Vanuatu:
- Check out with customs
- Check out with immigration
- Apply for Australian visas
- Come back to get the customs receipt because they had run out of receipts

- Come back to pick up visas five days later
- Fill propane tanks
- Fill fuel tanks
- Fill water tanks
- Shop for provisions at the grocery store
- Shop at the open-air market for fresh vegetables and fruits
- Purchase duty-free liquor at one store
- Purchase duty-free wine at another store
- Change headsails; replace the genoa with the smaller yankee
- Clean the cockpit
- Change the generator engine oil
- Change the main engine oil
- Make a route; check it again the next day when sober
- Stow all of the food and provisions
- Bring food from the deep storage areas up to the surface
- Pre-cook meals
- Stow the foredeck
- Stow and reorganize the lazarette, the enormous locker in the cockpit
- Put the dinghy on deck or up on davits
- Check the weather forecasts
- Check the weather forecasts again, and again, and maybe yet again

Weather changes. Right now, we're comfortably tied to a mooring, and looking outside, we sure don't see the same clear, calm weather of the forecast. It's cloudy, drizzly, and it's blowing 20-25 knots. I don't think we'll go today....

Email / November 8, 2003 / Holding Pattern, Vanuatu

Not one of my best traits in the past, I have learned patience is a virtue and has clear benefits. It's especially important when considering the right weather before a passage. We have been waiting in Port Vila, Vanuatu, for a weather window to open for our sail to Australia...and so we wait. We were all set to go today but woke up to clouds and rain, which didn't feel right. Ah, the luxury of staying in place; not going anywhere, not having deadlines. Imagine if I had that comfort in my past life: "Sorry, Mr./Ms. Client, today doesn't feel right for me to come to a meeting, perhaps tomorrow."

It was that past life, which made this one possible. It wasn't too long ago, while sitting in the back of a pickup truck bouncing along with dust flying, baking in the sun, I couldn't help but laugh out loud at "I used to be an executive." Yes, while driving one's own car is more comfortable than a hitched ride, sometimes the price one pays for those comforts is an awfully high stress level.

 Reading and understanding weather maps is tricky business. While not bad at the art of forecasting by this time, I certainly wasn't a professional. There were enough boats gathered in Port Vila waiting to head Down Under to Australia, that by the time we decided to leave, we felt confident the weather window was a good one. Wrong again as the wind gods toyed with us all the way to Australia.

Many people wonder if you can stop a boat while at sea to rest. The answer is yes, but it is an art that is tricky to get right and best practiced in calm weather. Fortunately, I had insisted we practice "heaving to" back at home in San Francisco Bay, and once in a while at sea to keep the skills fresh in our minds. The idea is to round the boat up into the wind and backfill the jib while locking the rudder in the opposite direction the boat wants to go. The jib tries to push the boat one way and the rudder counteracts that force. The result is the boat stalls, facing fairly close to the wind with the seas hitting just off the bow, making for a fairly comfortable ride while only moving about 1–2 knots. We were fairly accomplished at heaving to and it sure paid off this time.

You never know what is going to happen on a passage. You hope for the best and prepare for what you think could be the worst. However, some things take you by surprise, and all you can do is deal with the situation when it happens using whatever skills you have. What could have prepared us for the impending nightmare…?

CHAPTER 10

The Yellow Brick Road
Is Very Bumpy

*"Adversity has ever been considered the state in which a man
most easily becomes acquainted with himself."*
SAMUEL JOHNSON

Ship's Log / November 9, 2003
1440: Spinnaker rips and we bring it down in pieces. Bad way to
start a passage.

Email / November 9, 2003
What a wonderful feeling it is to head offshore, knowing that the
land will soon disappear and it will be just us and the sea. Your senses
become keener, and your heart is lifted with each rise and fall of the rolling swell.

The SSB radio was buzzing, as a half dozen boats left Vanuatu, all
headed on the same route to Australia. Every cruiser reports their boat's
position and weather so a boat in the back of the group will know what to

expect. Cyclone season is fast approaching and everyone is a bit nervous about getting out of the area in time before the first one hits. I'm starting to feel like a migratory animal following the seasons as we sail north and south to avoid them.

S 17°46.951' E 167°32.904'

 Ship's Log / November 10, 2003

0300: Surrounded by dark clouds and rainsqualls.

0310: Heavy rain, seas calm.

1100: Wind shifts to south. Main furler drum wrapped in overrides, we clear it. Remote autopilot wire broken, Ken fixes it. Very confused seas to be repairing anything.

1700: Wind 15-20 SSE swells building to 6 feet.

2200: Surfing to 10 knots.

 Ship's Log / November 11, 2003

1800: Sea birds use solar panels as landing strip; we let them stay.

 Ship's Log / November 12, 2003

0700: Bird poop all over solar panels. Yuck. Like cement.

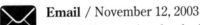 **Email** / November 12, 2003

We left Vanuatu in what looked like a perfect weather window; in the last four days we've sailed through two troughs with 30-knot winds, very rough and confused 10-foot seas, and endured upset stomachs…so much for forecasts. Both spinnakers have ripped. We also had to fix a problem with our propane stove. In a big wave, just like on the passage to New Zealand, a pan flew out of its place and fell behind the stove knocking off the propane hose. Imagine how the smell of propane added to our discomfort in these big seas, not to mention the potential for explosion. We have it holding with a hose clamp and a wish and a prayer.

Ship's Log / November 13, 2003

0700: Have turned south around Chesterfield Reef. 10-foot seas, wind 25-30 knots, speed 8.5 knots, rough ride.

2245: Huge seas and building, wind 30 knots sustained, breaking waves into cockpit, constant spray, everything wet, lines floating in 6 inches of water at our feet.

2330: Autopilot making loud groaning noises.

2345: Autopilot quits. Heave to. Heavy seas, wind 30 knots.

S 20° 42' E 155° 44.5'

Ship's Log / November 14, 2003

0300: Autopilot broken again—this time for good. Hand steering. Tired.

1430: Very hard steering in rough conditions, gusting 35 knots.

2200: Genoa car blows out of track. What's next?

Ship's Log / November 15, 2003

0001: Forestay lets loose and yankee is hanging by the halyard. Can't figure out what broke, but we have no forestay... Turned downwind, lowered main to baby-stay height.

Heavy rain, gale force winds over 40 knots, huge seas over 20 feet.

Ship's Log / November 16, 2003

0130: Australia still 150 miles away. Jury-rig halyards in place of forestay. Heck of a night to have to work on foredeck. Both completely exhausted. Very rough going. So tired and cold.

Personal Journal / November 20, 2003

The passage from Vanuatu to Australia was more like a rodeo than a sailing passage. It was easy going for the first day, and then the winds picked up and stayed at 25-30 knots for most of the way. Frequent squalls to 40 knots with relentless rain and nauseating seas.

First the spinnakers ripped, then the autopilot failed. The clutch stopped working 500 miles from the Australian coast, so we hove to. Ken took the autopilot out in the dark and opened it up to find the metal gears had worn against another set of plastic ones. We were able to use the bottom portion of the plastic gear by cutting it in half with the dremmel tool.

The joy and pride of that repair didn't last long; with 330 miles to go, it stopped working yet again. We hove to—again. Ken removed the autopilot—again, and discovered the metal gears had stripped the outer plastic ring. After two hours of exhausting work, we put the unit back together and crossed our fingers. It was quite a task working below in 15-foot seas, with tools flying across the salon floor, trying to keep track of all of the little parts, all the while attempting to keep our dinner in our stomachs. However, all the wishing and praying were for naught. That fix lasted only an hour, and when it failed this time, it failed for good. We were all out of creative solutions. Why would anybody build an autopilot with metal gears grinding against plastic ones? Had the engineers never been to sea? I'd like to get my hands on those people!

"I'll take the first watch," I said matter of factly taking the wheel. Ken went below to get some rest, and my heart rate increased when I realized what we were in for: 36 hours of hand steering. I would go for as long as I could, up to six hours, but then needed relief. I ended up on the wheel for about 26 of those hours because I was comfortable at the helm in big seas. At first, Ken was hesitant to steer in such conditions. Not having much choice, he jumped right in to learn and by landfall was steering like a pro.

There we were sleepily steering at midnight, with only 150 miles to go, and—*BAM!*—we heard what sounded like a gunshot. Loud noises in the darkness are especially scary in a drowsy state. We tried to pinpoint the source but failed so we sailed on hoping it was nothing, knowing full well that no matter how hard you wish, unusual noises are never "nothing." Later in port, we discovered the explosion was a stainless steel fitting that blew right out of the genoa track, something that took a heck of a lot of lot of force.

We continued looking around with the bright spotlight, venturing just a short ways out of the cockpit, when the situation got even worse—much worse. *BOOM!* This time it sounded like a canon had fired. Frantically scouring the boat, and struggling to see through the darkness, heavy driving rain and 40-knot squalls, we discovered the forestay (the forward wire cable that holds the mast in position) had separated from the mast. The jib was flapping wildly in the wind, held up by just the halyard (the line used to raise and lower a sail), and its roller furling foil was banging around 5 feet off the bow, also hanging on by just the jib halyard.

What's up with the gods? Dark night, huge rough seas, heavy rain, heavy winds, no autopilot and loud blasts…. Didn't I use expensive enough champagne at the naming ceremony? My anger was ousted by the need for action. I knew that without the forestay to hold it up, the mast had to be secured from falling.

At this point, I glanced over at Ken and saw fear in his eyes, which were as big as saucers. I asked him, "Are you scared?"

He hesitated and then blurted out, "Yes! We could lose our mast; it could rip the house off the deck, then we could take on seas and sink." It's strange where the mind can take you when you're sleep deprived.

I moved closer to him, kept one hand on the wheel, threw my other arm around his shoulder and held him tight while shouting through the driving rain: "Look at me! Listen! We are not going to lose the mast! We're going to do what it takes to secure it, and not let things get any worse. Do you understand?" Ken nodded. I reminded him how we already had turned downwind to ease the pressure from the forestay. I explained how we were going to secure the mast from falling, by jury-rigging a new forestay. Ken snapped out of his fear and accepted my explanation and strategy. We went to work.

With Ken steering, I crawled forward along the slippery deck to the mast, where I found and unclipped the spare jib halyard. While holding the halyard in one hand, I crept forward and clipped it to the bow plate. I inched my way back to the mast, wound the halyard around its winch, stood up hugging the mast to keep me in place, and cranked the winch with all the strength I could find. It took about 20 minutes, but our first pseudo-halyard was in place.

We were soaked, and it was only the taste of salt that distinguished the drenching waves and spray from the heavy rain. *Julia* seemed so small in the big seas and that compounded our fear. The only good thing about the blinding darkness was we couldn't see the enormity of some of the waves coming at us. I was very aware of what Bill always told me: It's all about the boat. "Take care of the boat," I repeated to myself. It didn't matter that it was tough moving around on the foredeck. Right then, it was all about the boat.

Exhausted from hand steering for so long, and because it was rough, we crawled at a snail's pace, taking turns going to the foredeck to secure the mast with all the spare halyards available. There you are, crawling on your hands and knees, halyard in one hand, holding on with the other. The boat takes off the top of a 15-foot wave and slams down into a trough, making it nearly impossible to work. It was a dangerous and violent experience. There were times it was so brutal I remained frozen, holding on, drenched, waiting for a calmer moment to move again. The wind was screaming through the rigging, making verbal communication impossible, and while the bright spreader lights helped illuminate the deck, they also made the scene surreal, as if it were a movie set.

All we could do was focus on the job and try to block out the elements. Being tossed around on the bow, we both felt the loneliness, the almost helplessness and the fear of being flung overboard. One of us always remained tethered in the cockpit trying to steer as soft a course as possible, while dreading the thought of losing the other. In those conditions that certainly would have meant death.

We ended up with four halyards working as our temporary forestay: two spinnaker halyards, the spare jib halyard, and the main jib halyard. I felt it was enough to safely hold up the mast. Besides, it was all we had; it had to work. We secured the roller furler and were able to wind in the jib, got the mainsail reduced to a triple reef, unfurled the staysail to balance the pressure on the mast, crossed our fingers, and rounded up toward Bundaberg.

I literally fell asleep at the wheel. At other times, I hallucinated. In my sleep-deprived state, the rain seemed to form shapes of mountains and land, and I heard voices. At one point, we came within a quarter mile of a ship because we were half asleep. Ken said he smelled popcorn they were cooking onboard; we were that close...or was he hallucinating too?

Even though we were making landfall on our first continent since North America, all we cared about was that it was land—any land. Because of the low terrain, we didn't see it until after sunset when we were 10 miles from shore. Ken just pointed and whispered, "Land!"

We were cold, wet, exhausted and drained, but looked at each other and smiled. In no uncertain terms, we had dug deep for strength and succeeded in meeting the challenges head-on.

The silver lining? The experience brought Ken and I closer, showed we can make a great team in the face of adversity, increased our boat handling skills, and gave us a deep feeling of accomplishment. I also learned it's okay to be afraid. Yes, I was afraid—you would have to be dim not to be—but I noticed my senses were sharper, my brain more alert, I was stronger, and I could master what was needed. Some people have said this passage was a disaster. I say to them, just the contrary—it was our finest hour. No one died, no one was hurt, we saved the boat, we persevered, and we grew.

What happened? We lost the forestay because a simple cotter ring broke, allowing a steel pin to work its way out. From now on, all cotter rings and pins will be silicone-sealed into place. And, I've since given in and ordered a new hydraulic autopilot. I wanted adventure…I sure got it now!

How important is the ability to handle a boat in rough weather? At this point, we thought we had passed the test. We wouldn't truly find out until the Red Sea, some 28 months hence….

Email / December 13, 2003 / Two Years
Richard Henry Dana did it and wrote *Two Years Before the Mast*. Now I have done it as well. It's been two years (last week) since leaving San Francisco and the time has blurred by; I have experienced many different events and personal changes in the last two years. Sometimes I find it hard to believe it all actually happened. I'm better at problem solving, jury rigging things, and, out of necessity, have become more mechanical than I ever wanted to be.

We made it to Bundaberg, a small city of 50,000 on the Queensland coast, not far north of Brisbane. At this time of year, it's about as far south as you can get without beating into the wind and is a common place for other cruisers. The customs agents are used to inspecting several boats a day this time of year and even provide kangaroo-skin boat "shoes" for their dogs to come aboard. The land is low and filled with sugarcane fields as far as the eye can see. And it's hot—very hot—over 100° every day. When we're not working on *Julia*, we head to the beach with Mike and Elke to do some body surfing. Or we head to town, which is kind of a hick place with billiard halls and cheap restaurants, but there's a K-Mart, so imagine our joy.

Personal Journal / December 23, 2003

What else can I do but laugh? I'm laughing my head off. Not really from humor but more for how amazingly hard all of this is. We were set and ready to go. We had cast off all dock lines. Ken shifted to reverse, gave it the gas and *nothing*. No prop wash, no propeller spinning, nothing except a high revving engine followed by the sound of grinding metal. A quick inspection in the engine room revealed all: The coupling that connects the shaft to the engine transmission was—let's just keep it simple—trashed.

I wonder how much I could get for *Julia* here in Australia?

Email / December 26, 2003

The Australians we've met are sure eager to offer their help any way they can. After two days of failed repairs on our propeller shaft coupling, we were getting pretty frustrated. It was Christmas Eve and we did *not* want to stay in Bundaberg through the holidays until the machinists' shops reopened. We were depressed; it was one of those times when I really questioned how fun this world tour really is.

Then Santa Claus dropped in (strangely disguised as Brad the mechanic). He swooped down on the boat, said, "Don't worry, kids," and called a mate of his who agreed to come in that night to machine a new solid stainless steel piece. We couldn't believe our eyes. The next day, we departed the dock at 0900. Thanks, Brad...or rather, *Santa*. We bolted down to Fraser Island where we shared the holidays with Mike and Elke lying by the pool at the Kingfisher Bay Resort. My present will last a lifetime: I learned to laugh it all off.

If we only knew the enormity of the mistake we were making by putting in a solid stainless steel coupling...a mistake that would become painfully clear in Indonesia...and again in Turkey....

Personal Journal / January 2, 2004

We've arrived at our southernmost destination, Mooloolaba, Australia, a sleepy surfer town turned chic. It's about 50 miles north of Brisbane and it's *the* place to be if you're a visiting yacht to Australia. There are miles of beaches with good surf, shark nets to protect the swimmers, a multitude of beach restaurants, and a young, hip crowd mixed with cruisers from all over the world. Getting this far south meant three days of beating into a 25-knot southeaster, and although the weather was tolerable, I was again reminded that man was not made to go upwind. I have a new boogie board and flippers I'm eager to try in the surf, which is across the street from our marina. Could this be heaven?

On our way here, we stopped for New Year's Eve at Noosa, a very fashionable beach community with more surf shops and clothing stores per square mile than I thought possible. Our New Year's Day wakeup call came from steep waves hitting the anchorage. Just as we were wondering about the abrupt change in conditions, the local lifesavers—dressed only in their small red Speedos and matching caps—looking so tan, healthy, happy and so…Australian, zoomed up in their inflatable dinghy. Staring at their tan bodies, I struggled to concentrate on what they were saying, until they snapped me out of my dreamy state with a warning that the swell would increase to twice the size by the afternoon. They urged we move much farther out or down the coast. Even while we were discussing our options, the waves began breaking bigger, closer to shore, and were starting to get awfully close to breaking over our bow. It was a race against time but we managed to pull up both anchors. A very peaceful anchorage one evening can become a very dangerous place only hours later. You have to anticipate what the conditions can become, not just see what they are. Goes for most things in life.

Email / April 6, 2003

It's official; *we are going all the way around the world.* It's a monumental decision I don't take lightly, because from this point on, there's no turning back. I sure do hope the world is round.

We've scheduled the rest of the journey and our plans call for returning to San Francisco in the summer of 2006. Of course, it is subject to modification because as my friend Joyce Clark says, "With a plan, at least you have something to change."

Rather than sailing around South Africa, we have decided to go through the Suez Canal and the Mediterranean. There's only one reason *not* to go through the Mediterranean: that route takes us through the Gulf of Aden, commonly known as "Pirate Alley," en route to the Red Sea. Either way, we'll still be going through the Malacca Straits in Southeast

Asia, currently the most notoriously pirated area in the world. We're starting to think more and more about possible attacks, and no, *Julia* is not armed.

Personal Journal / April 17, 2004

We've actually reacquainted ourselves with Dick, whom we last saw storming away from *Julia* in Vanuatu following our dispute over being gay. A funny thing happened to the three of us the other day at the chandlery in Mooloolaba. We were chatting with the guys who work there and something came up about the Queen of England. One of them said, "We have our own queens at the marina."

"Really, where?" I inquired, actually wanting to know if there were other gay people we could meet.

"Oh, down at the yacht club, there's a couple of them living on a boat," he said. It dawned on us who he was talking about.... Ken, Dick, and I started howling with laughter. The more I learn to laugh at myself, the easier it is to live with myself.

Yes, Dick has redeemed himself and has chosen to be our friend again. He even admitted he had been wrong to judge our being "so gay," and we were his friends whether others liked it or not. Good for him. We have forgiven Dick for his temporary lack of tolerance because forgiveness is important. People make mistakes and deserve another chance.

Personal Journal / April 28, 2004

In the face of all of the work that needs doing, we are getting along great; the projects bring us closer together. Went to the doctor for malaria pills in anticipation of being in Indonesia and Southeast Asia. Hope we don't need them or anything else in the medical kit, which is starting to look like its own E.R. supply.

Email / May 3, 2004 / Autopilot Woes: Not Again

While sailing north toward the Whitsunday Islands, *Julia* suddenly rounded up into the wind, the autopilot motor whining at top speed—but no response. A quick inspection revealed the arm was broken clean through. We're back in Bundaberg and the arm is being repaired as we speak. Yes, I'm laughing.

Personal Journal / May 23, 2004

We spent Ken's birthday, May 15, anchored off beautiful Whitehaven Beach, one of many in this spectacular island chain, known as The Whitsundays. These striking green islands are dotted with huge granite boulders and countless bays and coves lined with pristine beaches.

And the best of them all is Whitehaven, a strip of pure white silica sand stretching for over 3 miles and is so soft your feet sink several inches deep with every step. Andre and David were here helping celebrate, and our time frolicking on the beach was so much fun, you'd think we were kids. We went dinghy surfing, tumbled down sand dunes, and skinny-dipped to our hearts content with other similarly unclad beach-goers. The four of us are a good group, and these have been happy days together.

On a sad note, I received an email from Olive, the wife of Lindsay who fixed our autopilot in Tonga last year. I was shocked to hear Lindsay recently died in a sailing accident in the Mediterranean. While working at the top of the mast to clear a halyard, he was thrown into the water, and the crew lost sight of him in very rough weather. When the coast guard helicopter finally found him, he was hypothermic and didn't survive. It would have been typical of Lindsay to climb up there without a harness. He was a great guy who gave and gave, and finally gave it all. Lindsay was the one who taught me everything can be fixed. I learned much about how to relax and how to work problems from him. Lindsay's death hit me hard; the fragility of life and how valuable loved ones are to us. Here's to you Lindsay, a man who lived life to the fullest.

I love being with Ken these days and it makes me realize how precious love is. There are a thousand ways to die out here, and now that it's just the two of us sailing I'll admit to a heightened fear of losing Ken overboard while I'm asleep. Lindsay's death hasn't helped this. It's one more thing that prevents me from falling and staying asleep.

Until now, I've been at least vaguely familiar with the territory through which we've traveled. From here on, the geography is entirely new to me. I'm about to get out the charts and begin the research of where to go on our way north through the inside of the Great Barrier Reef. Is there a common route? Which islands are the best to visit? Are there any hidden dangers? Are the charts accurate? We have 1,500 miles to go to Darwin

157

and six weeks to do it in, which seems like enough time—if I do my homework and know where we're going, and if we don't have any major mechanical breakdowns. That's a lot of "ifs."

Email / May 27, 2004

For those of you who have seen the movie "Finding Nemo," you're familiar with the East Australian Current (EAC), which runs north to south along the coast. Like little Nemo's dad, we are now too familiar with the EAC, fighting it all the way up to the Whitsundays, reducing our speed by up to 2 knots. Fortunately, the current should turn in our favor as we proceed north up the coasts toward the top of Australia.

Personal Journal / June 2, 2004

We were sad to leave the Whitsundays, but if we want to be in Darwin by mid-July, we have to keep moving. As we journey north, with long day sails of 50-80 miles, we pass one place after another we would like to stop. What's the point, though? We can no longer swim or kayak, as there are saltwater crocodiles (called salties) from here on that could take all the fun out of an afternoon dip or paddle. The salties are huge, aggressive, territorial and plentiful in this northern region of Australia, and known to kill one or two people every year. They live in marshes, up freshwater rivers, and venture well offshore. They've even been known to jump out of the water, grab a person sitting on the side of a dinghy, and take their fresh meal underwater for the famous death roll. Just the same, I have to admit I would at least like to see one…from a distance.

Email / June 7, 2004

The rainforest-covered mountains, which rise from the ocean, are in striking contrast to the city built at their base. The tourist-packed boats parade in and out of the marina carting passengers to the reef and resort islands with grand efficiency. Yet the birds are oblivious to the entire scene, unaffected by the influx of tourism. The quantity and different species of birds in Australia continues to amaze me and nowhere have I noticed this more than here in Cairns (pronounced "cans"). Nightly, the setting sun is the nocturnal alarm for millions of bats to take flight from the mountains and head for the low swamplands. As they begin their forage for food, the sky turns black with their numbers.

The sounds from the birds and the bats, each crying for its share of the sky, usher in the colors of the sunset. The pinks, oranges and reds radiating from the west are absolutely fluorescent. As the sun drops behind the hills, muted grays and blues soften the approaching night in the east.

Personal Journal / June 20, 2004

In the Coral Sea, normal wind conditions are 20 knots, which makes it difficult to find a calm anchorage for diving. Yesterday, though, was breathless and the water was like glass. With *Julia* loaded with friends, we stealthily motored several miles behind the Lizard Island dive boat to the Great Barrier Reef, the world's largest living organism. Without local knowledge, it's not easy to find the best scuba locations on a reef that stretches over 1,600 miles. Even so, we pinpointed the boat's exact position with radar, and after they left the site, we swooped in and picked up *the* public mooring, putting us smack dab on top of the world-famous Cod Hole.

In just 40 feet of calm, clear water, we dove with magnificent, enormous spotted potato codfish weighing over 200 pounds each. They have mouths a foot wide and were longer than I am tall. These fish are quite accustomed to humans, completely tame, and allowed us to pet and feed them. After we ran our tanks out of air, the remaining afternoon was spent snorkeling and exploring this most incredible reef.

S 14°39.6′ E 145°27′

Personal Journal / June 26, 2004

As we move north along the Queensland coast, I am struck by the desolation of the northern part of Australia. If it weren't for the crocs and snakes, I'd almost like it here.

Put a case of beer, a few bottles of wine and a group of friends on a deserted island beach, and what do you get? Coconut Bacci Ball, the new hit sensation game (which we invented on the spot). Teams are made up of Will and Fiona from *Brandamagio*; Dan, Sara, George, and Conner, the college kids from *IL Granchio*, and us.

The trick to this game is finding the right coconut. Some roll, some don't. Some are filled with fluid constantly shifting the center of gravity as your "ball" rolls, and some are just rotted out old husks. It takes skill in choosing your coconut and even more precision to knock your opponent's out of the game. It's an afternoon of guaranteed hilarity. Meeting new people is one of the best parts of cruising and rolling coconuts with them is pretty high on my favorites list. Note: This does not work as well with mangos.

Email / June 27, 2004 / Escape Up the River
Cape Upstart, Cape Melville and Cape Grenville—all romantic sounding names, which make me think I should know them from school. We're moving too fast to stop and explore every place, but today was different as our 75-mile sail put us at the entrance to the Escape River.

Now that we are 3 miles up river, we've found shelter from the howling winds and we have another purpose here: crocodile watching. Dense, green mangroves line the muddy shores of the murky water, and rumor has it this is a good place to see lots of salties. We'll head out tomorrow in the dinghy and I'm already practicing my tour guide speech: "No swimming, or even leaning outside the dinghy. Please keep your hands and legs inside the boat until it comes to a complete stop and you're safely back onboard the mother ship."

Email / July 1, 2004 / Headed West
We did it. We finally rounded Cape York at the very top of Australia. The directions to Darwin from the locals in Mooloolaba were simple: "You go straight up north about 1,500 miles to the white lighthouse, then turn left at the first island, go straight ahead again for about 600 miles and you'll see it on your port side." This turn clinches it. There's no turning back now—we're headed west.

Personal Journal / July 10, 2004
Darwin still has the feel of a pioneer outpost, and many of its inhabitants are in transit on their way in or out of Australia. The bartenders are either rough-and-tumble locals or college-age backpackers seeking adventure. Many of the yachts here are also in transit. Darwin is a major milestone for sailors as it's the jumping off point to Southeast Asia and the Indian Ocean.

We have sailed 1,900 beautiful and difficult miles from Mooloolaba to get here. I wonder if we'll remember the long, hard sails, or after the trip is over, will we only remember the good parts?

Turns out I remember both the good and the not so good about cruising. The long, hard sails up the coast of Australia are etched into my brain and I can still become exhausted just thinking about the amount of work that was involved for two of us to sail a boat the size of Julia every day for such a long time.

And I also remember the good times. Easy afternoons just hanging out on the boat reading, cocktail in hand, talking about the weather and planning our next meal. Not only do I remember it all...I miss it, too.

CHAPTER 11

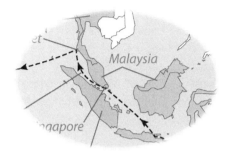

Gee Toto, Looks Like
We're Not in Oz Anymore

"What you leave behind is not what is engraved in stone monuments, but what is woven into the lives of others."
PERICLES

Personal Journal / July 23, 2004

Mike, with whom we bonded in Vanuatu, was going to join us for the sail from Darwin to Kupang—but he never appeared. To this day we haven't heard from him. It's a tough lesson, but I've learned not to count on anybody joining us. If they show up, great: if they don't, then I'm not going to worry about it. Looks like Ken and I are in this by ourselves.

Before leaving Darwin, I received emails from two of my brothers and multiple friends back home, all smart people who were being influenced by media sensationalism. The emails were all similar to this one:

Dear Larry,

I hear you are going to Indonesia. Don't do it! They are attacking and killing Americans and putting many others in jail. The State Department has issued a

"No go" for there. Please don't go to Indonesia!

Love,

Dan

And sure enough, the State Department had put Indonesia on the list of places Americans should definitely not visit. Those people at State really need to get out more.

Email / July 24, 2004

We're off. Along with 40 other boats in a rally, we're on our way to Kupang, Indonesia. I usually run the opposite direction when there's a group involved. Spending 20 years at conferences will do that to you. I almost couldn't take it at the rally group BBQ, wearing a name badge that said, "Hello my name is…." Joining the rally saved us time and hassle getting our cruising permit for Indonesia, and we've met new friends while bonding with old ones.

We are now looking back at Australia as we sail west into the sunset. We have been in "Oz" almost nine months—no more waltzing with Matilda. Good-bye, Australia, and hello again, Third World. This will be the first time no one onboard can speak the language of where we are. We bought an Indonesian phrase book and are practicing each day—but it seems more difficult than the romance languages we're accustomed to muddling through previously. We're uneasy, as we are about to enter a part of the world entirely unknown to us.

S 12°09.9 E 129°59.8

Email / July 25, 2004 / Halfway to Indonesia

We are currently 200 miles from Kupang and off to our starboard, I can see the bright lights and flames of an oil platform 30 miles away. One of the boats in the rally thought it was a ship on fire and kept calling them to see if they needed help. Soon, several others radioed back explaining the source of the flames. Still unconvinced, the "rescuers" repeatedly asked the oil derrick crew if they should bring over their fire extinguishers. Oh, brother.

The 40 boats in the group are now so spread out we can only see the lights of a few. We're down to 3 knots and that means starting the engine. Just for fun, try driving to your next destination at 3.4 mph.

Email / July 26, 2004 / Ocean Oxygen

There's something I've noticed on this passage more than before; the scent of the air at sea. Actually, it's not the aroma of the air; it's what one doesn't smell out here. There are no hints of dirt, green trees, fresh cut grass, burning leaves, wet cement, smog, animals, people, cars, buildings, or any other land-based odors. The only thing I inhale now is pure, fresh ocean O_2 and it really doesn't smell like anything at all—it's what air should smell like.

S 11°07.5′ E 125°20.4′

Email / July 27, 2004

Ten miles from Kupang, we suddenly heard a new whining noise and the propeller stopped turning. We're wondering what hellish problem we're facing now....

Email / July 29, 2004

What a wonderful warm welcome we have received in Indonesia. The people in West Timor (Kupang) are happy, smiling, peaceful and kind. The physical beauty of the land is impressive; unfortunately, we're anchored in dirty water. We haven't yet explored our surroundings, because half of yesterday was spent checking in with customs, which was a long, slow process, yet one filled with plenty of smiles.

"Captain, please show us the liquor you have onboard," said the agent. He was middle-aged, short, and had jet-black hair, but stood tall in his khaki-colored uniform, adorned with epaulets bearing enough stripes to show his seniority. While serious, he was quite friendly and we returned the kindliness with snacks and soft drinks.

"Certainly. Ken is the first mate, and he'll show you to the liquor cabinet," I said while pointing to the cabinet in the galley where we kept a dozen bottles handy. This cabinet was conveniently located far away from the deep bilge storage, which contained 250 more bottles of wine and liquor bought duty-free in Australia.

"Ohhhh, you are exceeding the amount to bring in," the customs agent said (we knew he was lying), as he counted the 12 bottles in the cabinet.

"I didn't know that was too much," I said while struggling not to break a smile. I continued finessing the impending deal. "You see, that's not all ours. Two bottles are for you and also two six-packs of beer are for you. We bring this in appreciation of your hospitality. Now are the numbers correct?" I asked.

Without missing a beat, Ken added, "Do you prefer white or red wine?" as he pulled out the bottles and started bagging them up.

"Oh yes, very good, Captain. Welcome to Indonesia." It was time for the official stamping of the papers. The customs agent brought out his stamp, and we heard the familiar, *"Thump, thump, stamp. Thump, thump, stamp."* A little voice inside of me said, "You've gotta get one of those stamps...."

If two bottles of wine and a dozen beers could make customs go that easy in every country, I'd gladly pay the offerings. With 40 of us arriving at the same time, the customs, health and immigration officials made their rounds from boat to boat, extracting these minor bribes, so by the end of the day, we presume they were quite happy.

The other half of the day was spent in the engine room with a local mechanic where we uncovered bad news. It doesn't do any good to shift the weak point from one place to another, which is what was done in Australia by installing that big, strong stainless steel coupling. The transmission tail shaft sheared off completely, right at its new weak point—the gearbox.

Domi, our local mechanic, tells us "no problem" through Ben, our translator. In a land where there is no local shop to fix your transmission and install new parts the same day, it appears they have learned how to make their own. Domi is confident he can fix the problem and sure seemed to know what he was doing after taking the transmission apart.

At the rally welcome banquet, we justly received an award for the "unluckiest sailors" in the group. It's an award I don't plan to keep.

This is a land where patience, kindness, smiles and more patience are needed; as we slow down from our fast-paced Australian life, we're reminded once again, these are the important things. Our engine will be fixed one way or the other; it's just a matter of time and, fortunately, that's something we have a lot of out here.

Email / August 4, 2004

We were able to find new bearings, seals, and rings in Kupang, and with our mechanics Domi and Ben, we've been working our butts off for five days. After installing the repaired transmission, and going for a test motor, all seemed to be working fine. Boy, oh boy, are you getting the abbreviated version on this one.

After five days of repairs and many farewells, we departed Kupang yesterday morning. Sixteen hours later, a squealing noise pierced our ears. We were almost afraid to open the floors to look at the engine but knew we better face the music (which wasn't *Happy Days Are Here Again*).

Mustering our courage, we opened the floors. Sure enough, the transmission was leaking oil, spewing smoke into the engine room, and there were metal shavings scattered everywhere. Oh, if you could have seen the look of disappointment on our faces! There's no choice but to head back to Kupang, which we are trying to do as I write this. It's 0800 and with almost no wind, we've only covered 10 miles in six hours. The sea is flat calm; it's hot, very hot; there's no wind; and the engine is useless. As I sit at the helm trying to squeeze every bit of speed out of *Julia*, the sweat is dripping off me. My hair is soaked and the only breath of wind comes from the sails slapping back and forth. I must have looked depressed as Ken glanced at me and said, "Hey! C'mon, we'll make it. The wind has to come up sometime."

I gave him a half smile: "You're right, but when we get back, the transmission has to be removed again, taken apart, and who knows what we'll find." I know I said this is the land of smiles, happiness, and patience, but I'm beginning to lose a little of each.

Email / August 6, 2004

When we got back to Kupang, it was night and we again dropped the anchor in blackness under sail, and promptly fell into an exhausted sleep. This morning, we went to Teddy's Bar to look for *the* taxi driver who knows *the* mechanic. The bar is where everybody from local guides to Australian ex-pats hang out, and luckily, we found the driver within an hour. He soon delivered Domi, our trusty mechanic. Then, an Australian who had heard of our woes said, "Hey, there's a mate of mine here who's a marine engineer. If I can get him up after his hangover, I bet he'd have a look." So we waited for "Animal" from Darwin. After buying him a couple of beers, he, Domi, Ben, Ken and I all piled into the dinghy and motored out to where *Julia* lay at anchor. We opened the floorboards to discover the output flange was falling off of the output shaft. (I don't know much about this stuff, but I do know that wasn't good. Heck, that doesn't even sound good.)

We've located a new transmission and flexible coupling in Australia. Tomorrow, we'll see if they can send them up on a bi-weekly Darwin to Kupang flight. The phone calls from Kupang to Australia are made from a tiny, dirty, dingy, lightless cubicle in the Telecom office—a far cry from my office, wearing a headset, and speed dialing anywhere in the world. Not that I'm complaining, but each day is a new challenge, whether it's making a phone call that could take hours to get through, or finding the mechanic through the taxi driver, or waiting for a reply fax. For some reason, faxes take an eternity. I'm still trying to use my Christmas present though: the ability to laugh it off.

I try to share my desperation with the person on the other end of the line. "No, I'm sorry, there is no place you can call me back. Could you please check now if you have the transmission we're looking for? We really are in a bind here, ma'am. I'm calling you from a cubicle in the post office." The clarity of the call is like two tin cans and a string, but with static. Lots of static.

"Where did you say you're calling from?" asks the woman on the line.

"Indonesia. We're in Kupang, Indonesia," I repeat with urgency.

"Can you hold on a minute, please?" I hear her saying to a colleague that she has a guy on the phone calling from Rhodesia. "He says it's urgent."

"G'day, can I help you?" says Frank, my new contact at the engineering company in Darwin. "You're calling from Rhodesia? I thought they called that Zimbabwe now."

"Yes, hello? No, I'm calling you from Indonesia. I-N-D-O-N-E-S-I-A. There's been an accident. There's a boat here in urgent need of a transmission I think you may have. You do carry ZF transmissions, right?"

"Twenty dollars," says Ken, signaling that the call has reached that amount. He pats me on the back with encouragement. Sweat has caused the ink on my notes to run, so I rewrite model numbers and names while holding for Frank to get back to me.

"Hello. Yeah, listen mate, we don't have that transmission you want, but I know someone who does. It's in Brisbane. Can you pick it up in Brisbane?" Frank asks.

"Brisbane? No, we're in Indonesia. Can you please help me to get it here?" I plea. "Hello. Hello? Hello!" Nothing, the line was dead. I grab my head with both hands as I lean over in the chair telling myself to "breathe, breathe…" After another 20 minutes, we are reconnected with the engineering company in Darwin. "Hello, may I please speak with Frank?"

"I'm sorry, but Frank left for lunch," says the secretary. "He should be back in about an hour if you'd like to call back."

"Yes, I'll call back," I say dejectedly. "C'mon, let's go," I say to Ken.

"Where are we going?" he asks.

"To Teddy's Bar for a drink," I reply.

"We have to get it fixed eventually. I mean, we're not going to be here forever," Ken says, as he looks at me for reassurance.

"No, we're not," I said. "We'll figure it out. We just have to work the problem. I only wish everybody else knew how urgent this was."

"It's not," Ken said. "It'll never be urgent for them. Maybe instead of trying to speed them up, we just need to slow down."

I looked at him and smiled. "Two more beers, please," I said to our bartender buddy.

Personal Journal / August 6, 2004
It seems that Mechanic A says, "Do this." Mechanic B says, "Do that." Mechanic C comes along and says, "What? You did this…and that? All wrong." And that's where we find ourselves: Listening now to Mechanic C. There's so much clutter that needs filtering. I just feel depressed; it's all very frustrating…and it's still damned hot.

Email / August 7, 2004 / The Transmission Saga Continues
We finally found a new transmission and coupling in Sydney, not Brisbane, but we can't get the parts here until Tuesday, another four days away. In the meantime, we sit at anchor on a lee shore in dirty Kupang harbor, sweating. No swimming due to the foul water. We're just waiting for Tuesday's airplane to arrive. We smell burning leaves and coconut husks onshore, and the other smells of a Third World city…entirely different from ocean oxygen. On the other hand, the people are very friendly,

the fruit and vegetable market has plenty to offer, we had a great tour of the waterfalls, and we're healthy. We're trying to make the best of it and look at the upside.

 Personal Journal / August 8, 2004
Email today from Darwin Marine Engineers:
Dear Larry,
Your gearbox has arrived at our workshop and is ready to be picked up.
Regards,
Sheila
I don't know whether to laugh or cry.

Personal Journal / August 11, 2004
I threw my back out today carrying the dinghy up the beach. After raiding the first aid kit, I have discovered how easily I can relieve the pain with prescription pills but am not sure that's a good thing.

Email / August 11, 2004
I went for a massage in a little village up in the hills today. The houses were all made with palm leaves with floors of dirt covered with straw mats. In the street, chickens were roaming free, dogs were barking, and kids played stickball. I could feel the curious eyes staring as I exited the taxi and was directed towards a small, thatched hut. There was one set of eyes that didn't see me but sensed my presence: the masseur, a blind 65-year-old man whose aura began to relax me the moment I stood before him. He didn't speak but rather motioned for me to lie down on a thin floor mat and then proceeded to give me one of the most relaxing hours of my life. It was just the thing to ease the stress of waiting for boat parts from Australia.

What do we do with the rest of our time? Yesterday, we shopped for fresh fruits and vegetables at the market: watermelons for a quarter, oranges for pennies each, and two fresh tuna cleaned and ready for sushi for a few dollars. For a buck each, we bought a bunch of pirated movies for our afternoons and evenings. These are the kind of movies made by someone filming a widescreen from their seat in the theater. When they cough, the camera shakes. When the person in front of them shifts, then there's a head in the view until they move again. It's more entertaining than the movies themselves.

Today, while preparing for the big parts arrival, I bought seven small squids from a fisherman who was catching them in the shadows made by our boat. He rowed his little wooden dinghy over and offered them for next to nothing. Sautéed in olive oil with garlic and onion, they were terrific.

I hoped it wasn't an omen. I had a dream last night in which the parts missed the plane in Darwin. Maybe that's why I soon found myself waiting around all morning, drinking beer at Teddy's Bar. Finally, at 1 pm, the taxi showed up with our package, which only cost us another 500,000 Rupiah ($60) to get it out of customs.

We ripped open the box to find exactly the transmission we ordered, but the smiles soon turned sour as we dug deeper into the box. "Are you sure it's not in there?" No matter how many times we dug through the box of packing material, we still didn't find a flexible coupling. Was that ever depressing. We felt defeated.

Without the coupling, the transmission does us no good. The rest of the day was spent trying to sort out what had happened. It seems the secretary in Darwin didn't know the difference between a drive coupling and a flexible output coupling (okay, I admit to not knowing the difference, either). Now, after many more phone calls, we have found the correct coupling in Sydney and will have it sent via DHL with a hopeful arrival of Friday or Saturday. In the meantime, we have renegotiated with Animal to continue his stay as long as we pay his lodging, bar tab, and "entertainment."

Personal Journal / August 12, 2004
In my past life, I would have exploded long before now; maybe because I actually do have time, that trigger-point pressure is gone. What a lesson in patience. In fact, other than getting to Phuket for my birthday, I really don't feel any pressure at all now.

Personal Journal / August 16, 2004
The transmission coupling was sent to Jakarta by mistake. In order to get it, we flew Ben to Jakarta with a wad of cash to buy it out of customs.

The tally was $250 for the duty; another $150 for bribes; $400 for Ben's ticket, hotel, food and taxis; the $1,000 coupling and $240 in shipping, plus $3,000 for the transmission. This is getting very expensive. When does it end? Or does it?

Email / August 19, 2004 / End of the Three-Week Saga

I'm hoping this is the end of the saga and I don't want to jinx it, but it appears we have the engine transmission and coupling fixed. Nobody ever told me it was going to be this hard to sail a boat around the world.

Personal Journal / August 23, 2004

I'm starting to enjoy cruising again, and to think, it only took four days to snap out of "transmission hell."

We're on Rinca, a green, hilly island covered in grass and tall palm trees. Coral heads, rocks, and false entrances surround the land, as if this prehistoric, desolate place doesn't want visitors. Still we persisted, and by very carefully paying attention to the charts and watching the water color, we found our way to the one bay that makes it feasible to anchor and stay here. This remote place is home to the famous Komodo dragons. Additionally, there are many poisonous snakes, including cobras and vipers, wild pigs, water buffalo, monkeys, wild horses, goats, deer, wild boar, as well as dozens of bird species.

While relaxing before venturing ashore to this *Jurassic Park,* an outrigger canoe, filled to the gunnels with a family, paddled out to us selling locally made souvenir woodcarvings of dragons and masks. When they knock on the boat, you can't very well hide because they see the dinghy and know we're onboard. "Hello mister, where you from?" "We're from Ameri…No. Wait, no! You cannot come aboard, no, we don't need any crafts, no, no, well, only two of you then, okay, fine, you're already aboard, would you like a Coke?" and the next thing we know, we're serving sodas and snacks to a family of five.

"Hey mister, where you from?" the little one asks again because that's the only English he knows. The family elder motions for the younger boys to display their work neatly in the cockpit. Ken forgets he's supposed to say no to everything. With too much enthusiasm, he says, "Oooh, I like that mask," and "Look at those dragons!" And we are sunk. We negotiate to buy four masks, four dragons, and two bracelets, but still there is the youngest one looking at me with sad puppy dog eyes. "What's the matter," I ask?

The elder explains, "You bought something from each of us except the boy. What about the boy?" I look at Ken and he's laughing and shrugs his shoulders as if to say, "Well, he's got you there." He knows I'm a sucker for this tactic, so we add another dragon and ankle bracelet to our purchases and now everybody is laughing and smiling. My smile remains with me all day as I swim in the clear warm water.

Email / August 25, 2004 / Chased by Dragons

I have always been fascinated with Komodo dragons and was excited about the prospect of seeing them up close and in the wild. While Ken agreed they would be interesting to see, he thought viewing their habits from a distance would be just fine. Turns out—he was right. We were finishing our hike and had reached the narrowest part of the trail when we encountered our very own sci-fi moment: face-to-face with scaly dark green creatures 10 feet in length, 2 feet in girth, mouths hanging open exposing their razor sharp teeth, and yellow-forked tongues darting in and out with each claw-footed step. One was drooling with what appeared to be part of a chicken hanging out of its mouth. Our hearts skipped a couple of beats. The only available choices came naturally—fight or flight. Not wanting to face off with, or be lunch for the dragons, we turned and started walking briskly back toward the park headquarters. Where was the brave ranger now who had just conducted our tour?

After a few seconds of speed walking and taking brief looks over our shoulders, the dragons suddenly broke into a run up the trail, straight for us. Don't be fooled. Like cumbersome-looking crocodiles, Komodo dragons can accelerate to 15 miles an hour from a dead rest—much faster than our sea legs could carry us. What to do? Throw rocks? Shout? Wave our arms? Are you kidding? These things are huge and take down horses and water buffalo with ease. Besides, they probably already thought we looked like overgrown chickens. The park ranger told us that Komodo dragons have razor sharp teeth, but actually it's their poisonous venom that kills the prey. With this fresh knowledge, we ran back up the trail, yet they picked up speed. I shouted to Ken: "Go, go, *go!*" I have never seen Ken run so fast before.

A steep ravine abutted one side of the narrow trail with a 100-foot drop so that was out, but the uphill side had just enough of a break in the vertical rock wall, on a 70-degree angle, to give us a reasonable fighting chance. The dragons were gaining on us and with only 50 feet left between them and what they saw as take-out, we turned to the rock wall and scrambled, climbing, grasping for any rock, root or clump of grass that would hold us. With only bare hands and sandals, we clawed our way 10 feet up the cliff just as the dragons arrived beneath us. While we were clinging to the cliff side, one of the reptiles stopped, looked up, and stared at us, as if to say, "Yeah, and stay off of my trail." Breathing heavily, we encouraged each other to hang on for a couple more minutes.

Those two minutes felt like hours. The trail clear, we clambered down, ran back to the dock, jumped into the dinghy, and raced off to the safety of *Julia* anchored right where we left her. In spite of recent onboard disasters, including all those engine problems, clogged toilets, and a failed autopilot, we felt safe—like a kangaroo climbing into its mother's pouch—only once we were back onboard. This boat *is* home.

Only then did we take deep breaths punctuated by nervous laughs, the type that come from recent close calls. In a world filled with dragons, strange (to us) cultures, and little-understood languages, *Julia* is our one constant, our secure haven wherever we travel. Between "Did you see how it looked at us?" and "I thought we were goners!" Ken looked me square in the eye and asked, "Now, have you seen enough dragons?"

While in Darwin, during the rally to Kupang, and now in Bali, we got to know Pete and Julie Kranker from Sojourner *very well. In Tonga, I had dismissed Pete as a potential friend based on what others said: He probably wouldn't like us. Oh, my God, were they ever wrong. Oh, my God twice, was I ever wrong to listen to them. We became good friends with Pete and his lovely wife, Julie.*

While he may be more conservative than me (who isn't?), Pete is smart as a whip, witty and loyal to the core. We have had many a deep conversation exchanging our political views, and what I see is somebody who is accepting of others, listens intently, and to this day remains a good friend.

I would trust Pete to be the one to come to our rescue should we ever need it, and I would do the same for him. I don't listen to others anymore when they talk about anybody—I wait to find out for myself.

Email / August 29, 2004

We are now members in good standing of the Royal Bali Yacht Club, so a cold beer will be the order of the day. Speaking of yacht clubs, we are also members of the Niue Yacht Club, and the Musket Cove Yacht Club in Fiji. It all sounds impressive, but in reality they're simply paper clubs designed to make fun of the "real" clubs. No jacket or tie required, and shoes and shirts are discouraged—my kind of place.

We are in Bali Marina, a place we wanted to be weeks ago, but better late than never. We were thrilled to see 20 friends from other boats, who had docked days and weeks ago, holding a berth for us. Everyone knew about our transmission fiasco and we received an outpouring of sympathy, especially from Pete of *Sojourner*. He had already found John, a Canadian aircraft mechanic, and scheduled him to come to *Julia* within an hour of docking. The mechanic took one look at the engine and told us it was out of alignment. This is the fifth mechanic to look at the problem since our arrival in Australia, but the first one who has actually used a feeler gauge to check its positioning. We've been covered in grease, grime, coolant, oil, and diesel for days now. At the same time, we have the "boat boys" from the marina polishing the stainless steel and the topsides. They each work eight hours for 100,000 Rupiah per day, which is only $12.

Bali's Hindu population is so friendly and peaceful, it almost catches you off guard. The restaurant at the marina serves great food; breakfast is $2, lunch $3, and dinner $5. No wonder people never want to leave here. We haven't loved every place we have visited, but we sure do love Bali. Is it the cheap movies or the inexpensive breakfast? There's no high-speed Internet in the marina, the roads are lousy, and good quality boat parts are hard to locate. However, when the boat boys show up smiling and early for their jobs, and the taxi driver really does want to help, and the person sweeping the leaves from the street stops, looks you in the eye, and with meaning says, "Good morning," that's what makes this place so incredible. It's the people.

Email / September 4, 2004

The locals are trying hard to recover their tourism business following the nightclub bombing of October 12, 2002. As there are so few visitors, and especially Americans, we are something of a novelty.

Personal Journal / September 7, 2004

At the Bali marina, an explicit sign warns yachties that pot trafficking is punishable by death. On the other hand, magic mushrooms are completely cool, so we figured we should try out the legal stuff. We drank a magic fruit smoothie that, within half an hour, got us so high we were laughing our heads off for over three hours. After *Mr. Toad's Wild Ride* in the back of a taxi, we went nightclubbing, dancing, and experiencing the nightlife of Bali...one more reason to love this place.

Email / September 9, 2004 / Dodging Fishing Boats

Second night at sea, and we have finished sailing through an Indonesian fishing fleet, one consisting of hundreds of boats from small canoes to larger trawlers. We're 20 miles offshore and they're out here bobbing around in the big waves, going all directions with no more than a lantern to light their boats—those are the ones that have lights at all. For those not lit, we just have to hope they see us. With so many targets, the radar screen looked like a video game, making it nearly impossible to track which boat was headed where. At one point, I counted more than 50 targets on the screen, all within a 1-mile radius.

I turned on all of the deck and floodlights since tonight is blacker than the inside of a cave, and went for it. A few boats moved for us but, during the hour and a half it took to get through the fleet, I was forced to make multiple course alterations. I was amazed at the nonchalant attitude of a fisherman in a 12-foot dinghy we nearly cut in half; he looked at us as if to say, "What? You want *me* to move?" Fortunately, this fleet wasn't using nets, but the SSB radio was crackling with "*Julia*, we're 50 miles ahead of you, 30 miles offshore, and there are nets 5 miles long. Suggest you stay where you are at only 20 miles offshore." And so we did. Not much rest on this passage.

At one point, to double-check the bearing of a ship I saw on the radar, I grabbed the hand-bearing compass. I brought it up to my eye and, expecting to take a reading similar to that on the radar, was shocked to see a 30-degree difference. I checked the radar again, then the hand compass, radar, compass, radar, compass, trying to figure out why there was such a huge discrepancy. Were there two ships confusing the issue? No, nothing else out there. I took off my glasses and rubbed my eyes, then took another compass bearing. This time, it was the same as the radar. I checked it again and, sure enough, the bearings matched perfectly.

Then I started cracking up. The glasses I was wearing have a solid band around the head and are held together at the nose by a magnet so they don't fall off while looking down into the engine room. That magnet threw my compass off by 30 degrees. Ha! The joke's on me.

Our first day of this passage, we went through a huge area of fish traps, which were marked by a palm tree branch sticking up about 3 feet out of the water. Yes, a palm frond.

This voyage is a continuous challenge: from fixing a transmission to avoiding ships, from squalls to clogged toilets, from lack of sleep to boredom—to avoiding palm trees at sea. These daily events present an opportunity to face adversity and succeed in accomplishing what at first seems impossible and sometimes even inconceivable. Yet after each incident, I emerge with an enormous sense of satisfaction. Without challenge there is no sense of achievement.

S 6°41.6′ E 114°17.5′

 Ship's Log / September 10, 2004
0300: Close call.
Ship kept coming at us.
Military ship.
Not sure which country.
Way too close.
Incessant lightning.
S 05°43.8 E 112°40'

Email / September 14, 2004
We're 180 miles from Batam where we'll stop for the night and complete our formal checkout paperwork from Indonesia. A yacht must check out of a country as well as in, and Batam is the last opportunity to clear Indonesian customs and immigration. The next day, we'll cross the busy Singapore Straits shipping channel in broad daylight. Should be on our way to Phuket, Thailand, in time to arrive by early October.

We are about to mark another milestone in our round-the-world journey; we are 60 miles from crossing back over the Equator into the

Northern Hemisphere. We have been in the Southern Hemisphere since April 2002. Here, we have been seeing the Southern Cross in the skies, Santa Claus getting a suntan on the beach, and north as the sunny side of the street. We have a bottle of bubbly chilling for the occasion this afternoon; it's as good a reason as any to open a bottle of champagne. In our journey around the rest of the world, we won't return to the southern hemisphere, making it an emotional farewell.

S 00°37.3′ E 107°01.9′

Email / September 15, 2004 / Safe Arrival in Batam
This afternoon we arrived safely at the Nongsa Point Marina on the island of Batam, the last bit of Indonesia directly across the straits from Singapore. Tomorrow, we'll clear out of the country. The trivia question of the day is: "How do you cross one of the busiest shipping lanes in the world?" The answer is: "Very quickly."

We're at the Equator, meaning the weather is hot, muggy, and very heavy. The sweat pours down our bodies, and no amount of showering is enough to cool down. Our cold water in the tanks onboard is 90°, and our refrigerator is working overtime. The air is thick and heavy with humidity, and I find it difficult to breathe. Every afternoon there's a downpour of epic proportions, which sure does keep this part of the world green. A carpet of rich, thriving flora covers the hills, which disappear into the base of the misty clouds.

N 1°11.8′ E 104°05.8′

Email / September 19, 2004
What an exciting way to arrive! It's 35 miles from the marina in Batam to Singapore, the shipping lane is 1.5 to 5 miles in width—and it sure is busy. There is an endless parade of enormous ships: supertankers, tankers, container ships piled 10 stories high, propane carriers that look like nuclear reactors, car carriers, and you-name-it carriers. This is all followed by a Singapore warship about every 20 vessels, sort of like the highway patrol of the water.

To cross the straits, we traveled well down to the west end where there was less merging traffic and the lane was only 1.5 miles wide. We turned at a right angle to the lane, put the pedal to the metal, and went for it. We felt like a squirrel crossing the freeway but we made it without incident.

A minute after we reached the other side of the shipping lanes, the clouds opened up and so began the downpour and thunder and lightning storm of all time. For half an hour, we couldn't see more than 100 yards in front of us and, at times, couldn't even see our own bow. We had to rely on the radar and electronic chart plotter to get us to the next turn to cross the next shipping lane. Even with the rain filter turned up all the way, which helps to differentiate rain from a solid target such as ship, the radar was incredibly hard to decipher. Even though we lost visual of *Guitar* and *Sojourner*, we were in constant radio contact with them, and we all worked together to ensure we arrived at the marina without incident. We're about to head over to the MRT (Mass Rapid Transit) because today we're doing what one does in Singapore: shop.

Personal Journal / September 20, 2004
What a relief. We made it to Raffles Marina. Tough sailing to get here. It's beautiful though: nice swimming pool, bowling alley, great chandlery, good shopping, friendly people, and what a Western world destination. Everything works, the water is drinkable, and the electronics are cheap; it's a hyper clean and modern city. The MRT takes you anywhere you want to go for a couple of dollars, and we're using it to our full advantage to shop for electronics. The bad thing about Singapore is how unbelievably hot it is; so hot you sleep in a puddle of your own sweat. Sometimes I can't stand the tropics—the heat really gets to me. Get out of the kitchen already, and quit whining!

Email / September 28, 2004 / See Ya, Singapore
At present, we're being as careful as we can because we are motoring on the edge of the shipping lanes going up the famous Malacca Straits. Their fame derives from the enormous amount of ship traffic, and we get it; we are seeing ships as close as five minutes apart. One ship just passed 100 yards away. The Malacca Straits are also famous because of the historic frequency of piracy attacks, more than any other area in the world. That was until a couple of years ago when the Singapore, Malaysia, and Indonesian navies cooperatively started patrolling the area. The attacks were mostly on big ships and, according to the locals, there hasn't

been a pirate attack on a yacht here in years. Evidently, all of the attacks have moved to the Gulf of Aden, now known as "Pirate Alley," a place we're dreading, but is still five or six months away. It was comforting to see an Australian warship steam by us this afternoon.

Email / September 30, 2004 / Lightning Show and Sea Monsters
We left Port Dixon yesterday and motored northwest towards Langkawi. It was an uneventful afternoon but as dark settled that evening, the clouds started closing in. We were so busy dodging fishing boats, ships, tugs towing barges, and fishing nets that we actually went right over one net in the darkness. We heard a thump, but it didn't catch our prop.

That night, blinding bolts and rig-shaking thunder pounded us at sea. By midnight, the wind turned right on the nose; 25 knots produced 6-foot seas and a 2-knot current came up against us reducing our speed to a 3-knot crawl. Don't blink. In the time it takes to say, "Close the hatches!" we were *slammed* with 40 knots from the beam with rain that hit horizontally in sheets. It was as though we were on a soundstage filming *The Perfect Storm*, and the director said, "Action!" Except we didn't have the option of shouting, "Cut!" These local storms are called *sumatras* and are common this time of year. It's rough going, but we're learning to live with it.

We stayed up together until the wee hours to monitor boat traffic. Good thing—within 20 minutes, we had a much too close encounter with a tug and barge. We also saw a strange sight: something resembling a huge, lighted sea monster headed our way. As it drew closer, we could make out it was a VLC (Very Large Container) ship, too large to fit in the Panama Canal, spraying water cannons down its topsides to prevent pirates from boarding with grappling hooks. Using this defensive measure, they shine huge floodlights and shoot enormous amounts of water and when the lights illuminate the water's spray, it creates the most amazing mirage of a sea monster. Creepy, but incredible.

As I stared out over the dark water, dodging the occasional ship, I casually mention, "I can't imagine how scary it would be to see that eerie *Star Wars* monster if I were alone."

"Me either," Ken says, never taking his eyes off of the horizon. "You always clip in with your harness…right?"

"Me? Of course I do. It's you I worry about. I can't go to sleep without hearing the click of your harness first."

Laughing, Ken says, "You can't sleep either way, but don't worry, I clip in every time. I don't want to be the one left out there in the dark water as *Julia* sails away."

I shudder, shaking my shoulders to banish the bad thoughts. "I'm not sure what would be worse, to fall overboard knowing I'm a goner or to wake up to find you gone." Ken says nothing, opting instead to reflect.

The silence is too long. I break it with "I suppose it would depend upon if I had insurance taken out on you…which I don't, so no falling overboard." There are only those slight "ha-ha" chuckles from both of us, which don't really count as laughter. We stare at each other for another awkwardly long moment and without saying a word, both recognize how important we are to each other.

Personal Journal / October 1, 2004

Lots of hard work and attention required as we dodge fishing fleets, more ships, and try to stay out of trouble. At 1400, while on watch alone, a craft resembling a fishing boat headed straight for us from the beam. I saw them a couple of miles away and certainly didn't think much of it. They altered course to intercept our track, and since we were in the Malacca Straits, I began to sweat. "It couldn't be pirates at this time of day, could it?" I muttered to myself, not wanting to wake Ken from his sleep, while suddenly considering that pirates probably don't stick too closely to a particular schedule. They're more like "on call." Through the stabilized binoculars I counted seven people aboard the old rust bucket as it increased its speed, evidenced also by the growing cloud of black diesel smoke spewing from the stern. Too many people aboard for a fishing boat, I thought. I altered course to give us a broad reach, our fastest point of sail and started the engine to give a boost. I was about to awaken Ken but didn't want to scare him if it wasn't necessary. For a few minutes, it was looking like they might catch us, but with the strong winds and engine, we finally began to pull away from them; they couldn't keep up with our 9 knots. After 15 minutes, they broke off their intercept, and I breathed a big sigh of relief.

I don't know if they wanted to sell us fish, wanted cigarettes, water, liquor, or if they really were pirates. I didn't want to stick around to find out. Anyway, it was nice to know *Julia* had it in her, and it felt good to leave the whole situation behind us. I hope this is my first and last entry about possible pirates.

Personal Journal / October 2, 2004
We are now safely anchored at Pulau Dayang Bunting. First time I've relaxed in days.
N 6°10.57′ E 99°47.5′

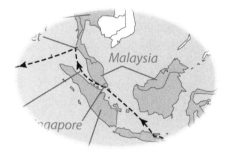

CHAPTER 12

Thai One On for Midlife
and Disaster

"Life is either a daring adventure, or nothing."
HELEN KELLER

Email / October 7, 2004

While on the island of Pulau Dayang Bunting, we wanted to bring one of the tiny Gibbon monkeys onboard as crew—they were so animated and lively. The momma sits with her two babies and they all stretch out their tiny human-like hands, looking up at us with round brown eyes as if to say, "Please, a few nuts, a banana, or that Snickers bar in your hand? We might be monkeys, but we still need to eat lunch!"

It's a short walk from the sea over a rise to Tasik Dayang Bunting, the fresh water "Lake of the Pregnant Maiden" in the middle of the island. We make it a quick visit, as it's over-run with tourists. Quite the contrast to the desolate anchorages of Koh Lipe, Koh Rak Nai, and Ko Ha Yai, all stunningly beautiful places where we stopped along our route.

We have made it to Ao Chalong Bay in Phuket, Thailand. We measure the trip in goals, and since leaving Mooloolaba, Thailand has been our biggest. It's been well over 4,500 miles of sailing and we're glad to be here. Man, are we tired though. An early dinner and a long sleep—not a marching band and fireworks—marked our arrival.

Personal Journal / October 12, 2004

I'm 50. The thing I value most in my life is love and friendship, and here at the villa, I'm surrounded by both. Bob, Andre and David flew in to help with the celebration. I'm lucky to have such loving friends in my life!

Personal Journal / November 1, 2004

Didn't email the group how bad off I was, but a few days into the second week of my birthday celebration, I came down with a terrible flu. While sitting on the deck, all of a sudden, it hit me like a wave and I nearly passed out. My temperature shot up to 104° and the air temperature was so damn hot and humid the fever was almost intolerable. I was miserable. We stayed anchored at Phi Phi Island while Ken, Bob and David patiently cared for me day and night, as my fever slowly subsided. Ken placed a phone call to Mom and she said, "Sponge bathe him in rubbing alcohol!" The fever dropped immediately by two points. Good ol' Mom. We're learning from her while halfway around the world.

Still worried, we went to the hospital while on Phi Phi Island where the doctor tested me for, and ruled out, both malaria and dengue fever. "No mararia, only fru," he said tenderly with a Thai spin to his words. At 5 foot 4 inches, slightly built, the doctor had shiny black hair that contrasted with his white smock. His face was soft, tender, and carried a sweet, sympathetic smile that made me feel better just by looking at him.

"Excuse me?" I asked.

"Only fru," he echoed the reply. As I must have still looked perplexed, he put his hand to his forehead as if checking for a fever and repeated, "Fru, fru, only fru."

"Ohhhhh, flu," I exclaimed.

"Yes, that what I say, fru!" We had a good laugh over our minor language disconnect. The fever broke by Day 7.

I remember the doctor and nurses very well. They were all sweet and concerned for my well-being, and they were such happy people. As we walked into the hospital, we interrupted the receptionist and nurse as they were doing disco aerobics. The room was filled with smiles and laughter.

It certainly never occurred to me while walking through the back streets of Phi Phi Island, shopping for a new thermometer, and maybe a T-shirt or two, that in a matter of weeks the entire island, including the hospital, nearly every shop, hotel, and thousands of people, would be wiped out within minutes. The very streets we were walking on would soon be buried under a wall of water that came crashing down on this most beautiful island, devastating everything in its path. The doctor who optimistically told me I would be okay, the aerobics nurses, the shopkeeper who smiled so graciously even when selling the most jaded tourist three T-shirts for only $10, and the warm smiling young women who gave us all foot massages quite possibly are all gone. Many boats anchored right where we had safely spent our days were severely damaged or disappeared.

Email / November 3, 2004 / Kayaker's Paradise

Spectacular limestone islands leap out of the green water, steep towering cliffs cascade from low, forested mountains, and the white sand beaches are begging for exploration. To get a glimpse of what we're seeing, watch the James Bond movie *Man with the Golden Gun* and *The Beach* with Leonardo DeCaprio. Both movies show off the Phuket area islands well, but it's far more dramatic in person than on the big screen.

Between *Julia*, our new dinghy (nicknamed *Julia's Child)*, and the kayaks, we have access to isolated islands with hidden beaches and stunning vertical rock formations. Some of the islands have "hongs," collapsed cave systems in the middle of the granite and limestone island, connected to the sea only by narrow entrances just big enough for a kayak. After paddling through a dark, mysterious cave, you find yourself in a huge pool that is wide open to the blue sky. Here you know you are in a place seldom seen by most tourists, let alone movie crews.

We spent the night at anchor in Maya Bay on the island of Phi Phi Le, where they filmed *The Beach*. It was easy to see why they chose this place for the movie: crystal clear green-tinted water, thousands of fish eager for our week-old bread, and a protected bay surrounded by giant walls of red and grey limestone jut hundreds of feet high straight up from the sea.

At the head of Maya Bay beckons the shimmering sands of the picture-perfect beach.

At dusk, CJ (our new visiting crew member from California whom we had met in Indonesia), and I succumbed to temptation and went for a kayak paddle. We sat on the pure white sand listening to the sounds of the approaching night: birds of all varieties in the jungle, fish jumping, birds plucking them from the water for their dinner, and a light breeze rustling the lush green vegetation climbing up the cliff faces.

As light faded to dark, we suddenly felt a cold breeze and then saw the first flashes of lightning. A couple of minutes later, the clouds opened up with everything they had. We stretched out in the warm shallow seawater at the beach's edge while the fresh water poured down on us in sheets from the skies, and we watched as a calm evening grew into a torrent of rain and wind.

We had hoped to wait it out, but the rain kept on coming. We jumped back into our kayaks and paddled to *Julia* half a mile across the bay. The rain was so heavy all we could see were our paddles dipping into the bright phosphorescent water, and a fine mist rising up from the sea as the cold rain collided with the warm ocean. We were shouting with joy at how close we felt to nature at the moment.

"Woo-hoo! This is living!" I shouted to CJ.

"Yee-haa! I love it!" he replied through the rain. We followed our noses to the Star of *Julia,* our bright anchor light, and arrived soaking wet but safe and sound, filled with laughter, exhilaration, and the thrill of being one with the weather.

Email / November 8, 2004 / Third World Bureaucracy
The last few days have been a fiasco of paperwork and Third World bureaucracy we thought would never end. We laughed it off as we have already learned from these kinds of experiences.

A Thai visa is only good for 30 days and ours were due for renewal. We answered one of the flyers posted around town that advertises:

"RENEW YOUR VISA! IN ONE DAY! Only $25!"
Ask for 'Mike!'

We called "Mike's Visas" and booked our places for the visa run to Burma (the Union of Myanmar). However, because we had arrived by private yacht there were a few more hurdles to jump. First step was a trip to immigration where we discovered that, before being allowed to leave the country, I had to post a $500 bond because I was captain of a yacht. Off we went in a three-wheeler *tuk-tuk* taxi through the crowded streets of Phuket City to open a bank account and apply for the bond. The bankers were as friendly as everyone else is in Thailand, and cheerfully started the process of taking our money. "Come back tomorrow to pick up your completed bond," the customer service rep, donning a very professional blue blazer, short skirt and high heels, told us while chilling the sweat on her face with a half-moon fan made of dried palm.

The next day, bond in hand, we taxied back to the immigration office. "Oh, no," Sumi informed us, "because Ken is crew rather than a passenger, he too must have a bond. See, look here, says on your check-in papers he is crew."

"Why didn't you tell us this yesterday?" I asked innocently.

"You didn't ask!"

She had a point.

Back into the hot streets and on to the bank with our trusty *tuk-tuk* driver, whom we had now hired on a temporary basis, to apply for Ken's bond.

"Too late today, come back tomorrow," the teller informed us. Next stop, the bar.

The next day, we got Ken's bond and with both in hand, returned to immigration where we found four office workers intently watching a repeat of *Days of Our Lives* on a vintage black and white T.V. As the sand poured through the hourglass, we almost felt guilty for interrupting, but once they resumed working, the four immigration people went at it with gusto. These smiling, happy people then proceeded to engage in almost an hour's worth of paperwork. I'm not kidding—it took 55 minutes to issue our papers to exit the country. One person would rubber stamp a paper, pass it along to another person who had more little rubber stamps to stamp inside the first stamp and complete the box. That paper then moved to a third person who stamped approval, and finally it went to the big boss who looked down at the paper, looked up at us, back down at the paper, and with a grunt, nodded his final approval and sent that paper into a file.

I have never seen so many rubber stamps in my life. There were stamps for date, time, department, and stamps engraved with only one word such as "yacht," and all were hanging neatly on a rotating rack. And the ink...a collection of black, blue, red, purple, and even green stamp pads evidently all had a purpose, still unknown to me. The file of papers they compiled for the two of us was half an inch thick and added to the multiple stacks of already existing files cluttering their desks and the tops of four-drawer vertical filing cabinets crammed into the room. How they would ever find our file, if necessary, at some future date I couldn't fathom. Once completed, we were officially signed OFF the boat, awarding us the distinction of "regular tourists," not those "sneaky yachties." We could finally exit the country so we could re-enter and get a fresh 30-day visa.

We called "Mike's" and told them we were ready for our run the next day. This meant arising in very early morning darkness to dinghy ashore and arrive at the departure point by 6 a.m. for the four-hour drive to the border.

The stunning scenery along the way was little consolation for the inconvenience of driving with eight people crammed into a Toyota minivan, but the group of internationals had lots to talk about, and we passed the time chatting the entire trip. Two hours into our excursion, we stopped for a Thai breakfast of rice and eggs where multiple families were selling their woodcarvings, jewelry, and other assorted souvenirs. I couldn't help myself and bought a bracelet from a smiling young man who greatly appreciated my seeming lack of interest in *over-negotiating*. That's when it started. "Buy from me! Please buy from me. What about *me?*" I was done for when a young boy with sad, big brown puppy dog eyes held out his hand bearing a carving, for which I had no desire, and said in his best, broken English, "Please mister, you buy from him, please...from me?" I knew I was sunk as I had recently seen this same act in Indonesia. It didn't matter; I fell for it again. Before I could say, "Sorry, but the van is leaving," I was the proud owner of three wood carvings, four bracelets, a mask, and a hat. And you know something? The smiles we left behind as we drove away were worth every Thai baht spent.

We boarded the traditional long-tail boat and noticed the poor condition of the vessel. Fortunately, as the brochure had promised, this boat (unlike those of "other visa companies") had life jackets for every person.

Being veteran sailors, we were alert to recognize the significance of this and promptly laid claim to the two nearest us. The smiling captain motored us past squalid villages, dodging ferries, cargo and fishing boats along the way. We soon were docking in Burma, where the guides, who had collected our passports, ran to immigration while we waited on the boat fending off vendors selling cheap cigarettes and liquor.

Ten minutes later, the guides returned to the boat and we motored back to Thailand where we were given back our passports. At last, we had stamps for going into and out of the Union of Myanmar.

We returned to the van, drove back to Thai Immigration and presented our passports to the very same people who had checked us out of the country just two hours earlier. Again, more paperwork and more rubber stamps; we stared in disbelief at the whole process as we were processed back into Thailand. "Welcome to Thailand!" the agents said as if they had never seen any of us before. We crammed into the van for the very long drive back to Phuket City in the rain and by nightfall our visa run was complete.

That night, as I rested in my bunk with the water lapping at *Julia's* hull, I dreamed of sounds from the bureaucratic Third World...the sounds of rubber stamps. Two ink thumps for each paper stamp.

"Thump, thump, stamp. Thump, thump, stamp. Thump, thump, stamp."

And since this seems to be the place, we're going to have a lovely *"JULIA"* rubber stamp made for the boat...

One day in early November, while having a cocktail on deck, we began discussing plans for the Christmas holidays. We planned to anchor at Patong beach because it's such a beautiful shallow anchorage where you can anchor very close to the beach and swim back and forth to shore. It also happens to be the gay beach, and there's always a big Christmas bash the night of the 25th. I could see something was bothering Ken. He looked sad. "What's the matter?" I asked. With a hint of a tear rolling down his cheek he said, "I want to go home. I want to be with my family for Christmas. I know it's last minute, and it's just a whim, but can we go home?"

Because we had already scheduled Julia to be hauled out of the water for interior woodwork, all we had to do was change the schedule a little. Instead of staying in a hotel in Phuket and supervising the work, we could just as easily go home, and find someone in Phuket to supervise for us. And by leaving Julia out of the water longer, we could have more work done on her. It was a change of travel plans that was unusual for us. In fact, it was the only time we changed our plans on a whim during the entire trip. Was it mere coincidence? Luck? Fate?

The next day we walked into the first travel agency we could find and plunked down the money for two round-trip tickets to San Francisco. Ken's impulse was the difference between life and death for us.

The tsunami hit Patong beach the morning of December 26 square on, and so hard the town practically became a modern day Atlantis. Thousands were killed and the wall of water would surely have hit us, too.

All of those beautiful friendly people are gone…vanished. I wonder what happened to the beautiful boy who gave me a massage on my birthday? Christmas will always remind me of how fragile life is.

Personal Journal / November 14, 2004

For the first time in a while, we are actually relaxing. Neither of us have the desire to stay out late at the bars with the boys. We're simply not that attracted to the young gay scene here…I guess I'm feeling too old for this crowd. Is there a switch that is triggered once you turn 50 allowing you to move on from the nightclub and sex scene? It seems as though mine has been flipped.

Tomorrow, we haul the boat out of the water at Ratanachai slipway; we have contracted to have the hull painted and to have the sole and all of the woodwork inside *Julia* redone. The estimates, which I know will double by the time we're through, are a lot cheaper than anywhere else we've been, so I decided to go for it. Thailand is the place to do woodwork and we're saving a large fortune by spending a small one here. This is my home now and, well, I want it to look nice.

We're both excited to be going home—wait a minute, I just said the boat was my home…which is it?

Personal Journal / November 21, 2004

It's a short 10-minute *tuk-tuk* ride from the slipway to our hotel in Phuket City where we have been for a week already after hauling *Julia* out of the water in the dirtiest boat yard we've seen yet.

And we did more shopping for engine parts today, having been directed to a hole in the wall store by our taxi driver. As we stepped gingerly through the front door, we found ourselves in a room no larger than the average bedroom, about 15' x 15'. We were greeted with a great big smile. No words, but a big smile that lacked a few teeth.

Ken pulled two sample oil filters out of his pack and handed them over to the old man asking, "We need 12 each of these. Do you have them?" Nodding affirmatively, he took them into the back and within a minute returned with a few of what we needed. "We need 12 of each," Ken repeated slowly. Again, more nodding and then the loud snap of his fingers and, instantly, the man's son, as did his wife, appeared out of nowhere. Handing both of our samples to the lad, and giving some strongly worded instructions in Thai, he took off like a bolt of lightning. Just as I was about to say, "Hey, where are you taking those?" the man's wife beckoned us to two portable chairs she was opening up and a pot of brewing tea. We smiled and waited, drinking our tea while trying to make small talk with our few Thai words and the couple's few English words. We laughed, breathed in the smell of car parts, rubber, and oil, and had a lovely cup of tea.

The old man had one phrase down pretty well: "Please to wait." We did.

It took about half an hour, but sure enough, the boy came bounding in through the back door with several bags of filters in his arms and handed them to his father. Then, wiping his brow, he gave us a slight bow, a big smile, and was gone. While I stood smiling, Ken checked every filter for the right threads and size, and confirmed they were all correct. Now, that's service.

Personal Journal / November 28, 2004

We have completed our third day of advanced scuba courses. Two days for the advanced course, and a one-day Emergency First Responder course to give us First Aid, CPR, and Rescue Breathing certifications. Since we recently bought a compressor and will be diving on our own in more remote places, we felt it was good to boost our skills and confidence. Our instructor, Patrick (another Patrick, this one spelled with a "C"), is full of smiles, university educated, speaks perfect English, and says he can handle supervising the work on *Julia* while we are in the States. "You have to be strong!" Patrick said. "You have to make the workers do it your way, not theirs!" That was enough for us and we promptly hired him as our supervisor.

Julia is on the hard at the slipway and is quite a mess…there are about ten guys onboard doing all of the sanding we could and would never do. I've upped the budget…I knew the original estimate wouldn't last long once we started work and saw what else needed doing.

We leave in three days for California; we're eager to see family and friends.

In disbelief, and feeling completely helpless, we watched the television news coverage from Ken's parents house in Reno, Nevada. The phone rang continuously with friends and family checking on our well-being. Still, only Ken and I knew our original plans and how one simple decision to fly back to the States, rather than party at Patong Beach, made the difference between life and death.

Our first instinct was to get on the first plane back to Phuket to help our friends, check on Julia, and to pitch in with community help. The news dampened our eagerness with reports of impending disease outbreaks and total devastation. Friends and family encouraged us to wait until things had settled down, but it seemed the longer we waited, the more our fear intensified. We postponed our flight two times before finally mustering the courage to return to Phuket and face what we surely thought was a war zone.

Email / December 26, 2004

In shock. Like you, we awoke today to the horrible news of the tsunami. Thank you all for your concern over our well-being and for concern about *Julia*. We've struggled to contact people in Phuket, finally reaching Harvey and Jean, and from what they tell us, all of our friends and their boats are safe, including *Julia*. The tsunami evidently did enormous damage to all of Phuket, and in particular the Patong Beach area. Fortunately, *Julia* is out of the water in the boatyard still having work done.

"All circuits are busy" was the standard line of the day as we tried Patrick, our boatyard supervisor, Pete and Julie, and several other friends. When we finally reached Harvey on his cell phone, we could barely hear him. "We're all right!" he shouted.

"What about Pete and Julie, and everyone, and what about *Guitar*, and what about *Julia*?" I peppered him with questions.

"All okay, water in the boatyard and it's a mess," Harvey replied.

"What's the situation with food? Water? Services?" I asked.

"Pretty bad at the moment, give us a shout in a few days for an update…" and then the line went dead.

I put the phone down, looked up at Ken, and still in shock, somewhat mechanically said, "Our friends are fine." Almost as an afterthought, I added, "*Julia* too."

Our original plan was to be anchored in 15 feet right at Patong Beach for the Christmas party, and who knows what would have happened to us if we had stuck to that plan. Actually, we do know what would have happened to us; we just don't like to think about it.

The news about Phuket is devastating: The pictures we're seeing are a mess of twisted debris, cars thrown on top of houses, school busses buried in mud and sand, and boats destroyed as they were shoved ashore and into storefront windows.

We are grateful we survived, that *Julia* is unharmed, and for the good fortune of our friends. We are heartbroken for the misfortune of others and are reminded again how important it is to make each and every day count. You never know when it will be your last.

 Email / January 4, 2005 (Ten Days Since the Tsunami) / Delayed Return to Phuket

Today, we were scheduled to return to Phuket but are postponing our flights to a later date. We're obviously concerned about disease, food and water supplies, and vital services, which may still be out of commission. However, our friends in Phuket tell us all is strangely calm. The food and water are holding up, help has arrived from around the world, and the anticipated disease hasn't materialized. The locals are trying hard to get back to a nearly normal life (as normal as can be expected) after the devastation of Patong, Khao Lak, and Phi Phi produced a death toll exceeding 5,000.

Two of the men doing woodwork on *Julia* lost their wives and another's was injured, so we are not expecting to go back and find a lot of happy people. In fact, we're doing a lot of self-reflection and preparing how to greet these people with our heartfelt compassion. We'll start by providing a relief fund to our acquaintances and workers. We're nervous and scared about going back and the news media certainly isn't helping to ease our fears. We're just going to have to see for ourselves and will report back. I still can't seem to shake the nervousness of knowing how close a call this was. With a snap decision—wanting to return home and sit around the Christmas tree with family—we avoided the horrible experience at Patong and are free to continue sailing around the world. Was it really just a lucky fluke that saved our lives? Something seems amiss.

 Email / January 14, 2005 (Twenty Days Since the Tsunami) / Report from Phuket

We're in Phuket safe and sound but torn between many emotions. The mood here is obviously somber; but being such wonderful, friendly people, the Thais still return our smiles, although it is clearly with more effort than before. Nevertheless, I'm taken aback. How can these people smile at all? Shouldn't the courtesies and formalities have long since gone out the window? For most of the people here in Phuket, where almost all of the business is related to tourism, their lives went from fabulous to horrifying in a single morning of terror. The streets are practically deserted, with very little traffic, even at rush hour because so many workers in the hotel business are without jobs, and the *tuk-tuks* usually filled with tourists are empty. There are simply no tourists here anymore; they are either dead or have returned home.

Our hotel in Phuket City is filled with embassy staffers: The first floor ballroom is the Japanese embassy, the second floor is temporary home to the U.S. and British embassies, third floor is the Italian and Norwegian, and so it goes through the rest of the structure. Not sure where the Swedish embassy is, but it must be a large presence as over 3,000 Swedes are still missing. There are lists mounted to the walls in the lobby, not single sheets, but pages and pages of people missing, bulletin boards with pictures of loved ones, and embassy bulletins asking for assistance in finding missing persons.

However, as far as we can tell, and contrary to news reports from abroad, there are no food or water shortages, no disease outbreaks, and aside from the disaster areas, all of the municipal activities—trash pickup, fire and police—appear to be operating normally. They are doing an amazing job at recovering here.

It seems as though some were living aboard or perhaps used *Julia* as a place of refuge after the disaster. Things were pretty bad, even in the boatyard, which, while far away from the beaches, sits on a riverbank. Photos of the river right in front of the yard show dozens of fishing boats piled on top of each other and water lapping at the base of the cradle in which *Julia* rode out the terror.

When we went onboard for the first time, we wanted to get back on the plane and head home. Our things are scattered everywhere and the boat is filthy with spilled varnish cans, paintbrushes, food wrappers, dust, and dirt. Ironically, the mess is not from the tsunami but from the workers themselves. We sat down in the hot, sawdust-filled main salon, looked around and we both lost it right there. There were no words, only frustration. We were happy *Julia* survived but faced an enormous cleanup. In some ways, we have never felt more isolated. We have to keep it in perspective; we didn't lose anything—or anybody, and we are fine. I'm also glad *Julia* was able to provide a safe shelter for those in need.

Many of you sent us money to donate to the workers, and you will be very pleased to know the money was presented in such a way that you are being held in high esteem. We wanted to make sure the funds reached the workers directly and made sure they understood our intentions. They were extremely happy, as none of them had received anything from UNICEF or any of the other relief organizations. With the thousands of dollars raised, we were able to present each of the ten workers with a substantial offering. The worker who lost his home with everything in it was overwhelmed. The chief woodworker started to cry, and the rest went silent for what seemed like an eternity as they stared at us. Then, one by one, they put their hands together in the traditional Thai Wai, bowed their heads slightly, and said *"Khorb-khun-Krup*—Thank you," over and over again.

We went to Patong Beach to see what the tsunami had really done. It was a horrific site, with damage beyond our imaginations. "Oh, my God," I mumbled as we sat down to absorb the devastation. The entire street along the beachfront was wiped out and all of the shops were gone…obliterated. It wasn't like a bomb blast, or even an earthquake, where some buildings might have withstood the forces. Here, they were all obliterated.

Restaurants we had eaten in, shops where we had bought our Christmas presents for family back home, and the little cafés on the beach where the native boys used to sit looking for well-pocketed tourists—all vanished.

We did the best thing we thought possible and (spending more money than necessary) shopped at those stores that were open; the ones in the back streets a few blocks from the beach. We ate at the few open restaurants, bought beers from the street vendors, and rounded up, rather than negotiated, when making purchases.

Finally, after putting it off as long as possible, with beer in hand, we turned and stared out at the shallow anchorage where *Julia* would have been had we not changed our plans. In silence, each of us imagined what was so fatefully avoided.

We are grateful for the good luck or fate that steered us clear of this disaster. And we are once again reminded to appreciate what we have in our lives—including life itself.

Email / January 16, 2005 / Sad but Optimistic
Tonight we ate dinner at our favorite restaurant in Phuket City. It's a small establishment run by Oaa and her husband, assisted by their daughter and son. From our first grilled squid at Le Café, we were treated like family, and Oaa has taken care of us like we are her own. We asked her: "What was it like the day of the tsunami?" She looked tired. In fact, she was 45, but the weight of her sadness seemed to have aged her more than a decade. She was a large woman, normally standing tall, but now her shoulders were hunched over; her once smooth skin seemed weathered, and her bright, dark eyes had lost their sparkle.

Luckily, her restaurant is away from the beach area and was spared. While still clean and neat, it was deathly silent except for our quiet conversation. Oaa first showed us the sign she had put in her window, which in English (directed to tourists) said: "If you have nothing to eat, come and eat here for free." Then she said, "I opened my home to anyone who needed a place to sleep, and offered food for three days to anyone who was hungry."

Oaa sat down at our table, and as she continued, tears rolled down her cheeks: "I lost nine friends and two cousins." I didn't really know what to say, so I reached across the table and grasped her hand. We sat there for a long time in silence. I couldn't say, "I know how you feel," because I didn't. Nobody will ever know how she felt.

Yet this amazing woman still smiles and hugs us when we come in for a meal. Sadly, every time we have been to her restaurant since our return, we have been the only people there, and since her business relies on tourism, she is a classic example of the fate of a great many people here in Phuket. Oaa told us tonight she will "just wait," and she is sure good times will return. If Oaa can be optimistic, so can we all.

We were indeed lucky to avoid the tsunami's devastation, but we certainly felt the repercussions. We wanted to get Julia back in the water and move on, but our intent seemed futile as we struggled through finishing jobs without key workers, trying to find parts in shops that were closed, and trying to meet deadlines that were now meaningless to people who's lives had been turned upside down.

All we could do was buckle under and attack the problem head on. We pitched in and spent much more time doing the actual work rather than supervising; we hired new workers, cut short some projects, and finished incomplete projects by ourselves. After recovering from the shock of what Julia looked like inside, we dove in with fervor and worked to ensure our departure by early February. We knew if we missed our departure window, we would be faced with worse weather across the Indian Ocean and in the Red Sea. Then there was that nagging thought of aftershocks, and potentially another tsunami. We were motivated to leave.

Email / January 19, 2005 / Working Hard in Phuket

We are working hard at getting *Julia* shipshape again and should be splashing back into the water in a few days. We've confirmed our friends Rob and Suse Alexander will join us for the Indian Ocean crossing. As it turned out, not all of our friends' boats made it through unscathed, and their boat, *Ain't Misbehavin'*, was heavily damaged in the tsunami. True to their British spirit of adventure, they want to keep sailing. They'll leave their boat in Phuket for repairs and join *Julia* as far as time permits. At home in England, Rob works in banking and Suse in the pharmaceutical industry, but I can't see either of them in suits at business meetings. Then some people can't imagine me dressed in a suit, either. Rob played rugby in England and, while on the shorter side of 6 feet, is built like a tank, and has a natural talent at the helm. He's an easygoing, quiet guy, who occasionally pipes in with a hilarious comment to let you know he's listening, and he's right there when the proverbial crap hits the fan. Suse is tall, at least five-nine. Effervescent and outgoing, she's an assertive problem-solver, first to volunteer for any task, and she's always smiling. We're an upbeat group and are looking forward to sailing together.

Email / January 30, 2005 / The Weakest Link

Still in Thailand. We launched *Julia* back into the water amid much fanfare and the traditional 999 good luck firecrackers, which hang off of the bow and are set off as the boat enters the water. We were too busy handling lines and monitoring *Julia* sliding down the railway tracks towards the water, and had forgotten all about them. Just as I was about to call, "Let go the starboard line," *Kaboom! Pop, Pop, Pop!* "Holy crap, what was that?" I shouted. As I looked forward, Ken had his fingers in his ears and was laughing his head off because he was also taken by surprise.

With *Julia* in the water, I turned the key and our engine started effortlessly. We motored out to anchor at Ko Rang Yai, a nearby island where we planned to spend the night. When we dropped the anchor and the chain ran out, Ken watched in shock as the chain broke. After 90 feet had run out, the chain snapped in a second without any strain. Ken ran back to the cockpit shouting, "Hit the MOB, hit the MOB!" The MOB button marked our exact GPS position, but I didn't yet know why we needed it "The chain broke! We lost our anchor!" Ken shouted in alarm.

"Quick!" I yelled, leaving the wheel, "I'll get the second anchor to the foredeck. Go below and pass the chain back up to me." As we rigged our secondary anchor to the remaining chain and re-anchored *Julia* securely, I asked, "What happened?"

"I don't know, I was running the chain out...and it just broke. There wasn't any pressure on it at all," Ken said.

"Well, looks like we're going diving," I said.

As fast as we could, we donned our scuba gear—not a very fast process. We didn't realize until we got in the water that the visibility was less than 1 foot. The green water looks clean and pretty but is filled with silt, which provides its unique emerald tint. Descending toward the bottom, we lost sight of our depth gauges, which were right in front of us. We then lost sight of each other, and it was even difficult to determine where the surface was. I was beginning to get nervous when, at that moment, Ken grabbed me so we were facing each other's masks a foot away from each other. In dive sign language, he was telling me, "Abort the dive! Surface now!" and I nodded in agreement. We held onto each other as we rose slowly to the surface, frightened out of our wits.

We dinghied ashore to find Patrick, who is also a professional rescue diver. He came right out to the boat and attempted to find the anchor, but he was also defeated by the lack of visibility. That night, we slept uneasily and felt more than a bit sad about losing our $1,000 anchor. "So much for the good luck firecrackers," Ken muttered and then rolled over back to sleep.

The next day we took *Julia* into Boat Lagoon Marina. Sipping a cocktail, Ken said, "We have to be able to find the anchor; we know its exact coordinates."

"Maybe we can drag the bottom with a grappling hook," I suggested.

Patrick interjected, "Why don't you get a sea gypsy?"

"A what?" Ken and I said in chorus.

"They're fisherman from a nearby village, and they're comfortable finding their fish traps in zero visibility water," explained Patrick.

The next day, Daeng showed up, a 17 year old with big brown eyes, smiling in anticipation of earning a healthy reward. I was skeptical, but Patrick, Daeng and I headed out in the dinghy with our GPS position transferred to a handheld unit to guide us to the spot. I didn't really have much hope of finding our treasure, but...*you should believe in the sea gypsies.* After two hours of feeling around on the bottom, surfacing occasionally for directions from me, and heading back down to feel around some more, Daeng popped to the surface and shouted, "Okay!" He had found it.

We are having the chain repaired and re-galvanized and will continue to use it because our alternative is to buy inferior chain made from Chinese steel (there's nothing else available here). It's times like these we appreciate what the western world offers: quality products.

We are late departing, but it seems as though Thailand's grip is hard to break. After the tsunami, it is too easy to get depressed and lose sight of my ambition: continuing on with the circumnavigation. The disaster has taken the wind out of my emotional sails. Even if the voyage now seems more intimidating, I am determined to sail *Julia* back under the Golden Gate Bridge.

Personal Journal / February 4, 2005
Life is a series of events and experiences, and all I can do is try to have as many good ones as possible before my demise. Because, as the saying goes, none of us are going to get out of this alive.

I've never been one to stay down in the dumps for long and have since pulled myself up by the bootstraps, poured a bucket of cold water on my head, and said, "Snap out of it!" I'm ready to continue my journey with an eagerness I haven't seen in myself in some time. Maybe the lows are necessary to see the highs.

I'm looking forward to our new adventures, which will include going up the Red Sea and then into the Mediterranean. Not sure what to expect, but then that's the idea. Right?

The Indian Ocean was the strangest part of this journey to me; I was unfamiliar with the waters, the countries, and cultures. It felt like the other side of the world, which, of course, it was. From our Thailand departure, this feeling continued until we reached the Mediterranean. It wasn't bad; in fact, it was new and exciting, and proved to me I truly was on the adventure of a lifetime. Even so, friends and family were concerned about the territory we were sailing into, and that only put me more on edge....

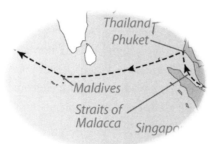

CHAPTER 13

Not Much In the Way of Food, But the Fuel's Terrific!

"The church says the earth is flat, but I know that it is round,
for I have seen the shadow on the moon, and I have more faith
in a shadow than in the church."
FERDINAND MAGELLAN

Email / February 10, 2005
Sometimes I have to pinch myself. We are about to cross the Indian Ocean... I can't believe I'm actually doing this.

We left Langkawi, Malaysia, yesterday morning and are now heading west across the Andaman Sea, south of the Nicobar Islands, south of Sri Lanka, and then northwest to Uligan in the Maldives, a total distance of 1,650 miles. After a rest in the Maldives, we have another 1,500 miles to Djoubiti in the Red Sea, so we have a lot of sailing in the next few weeks.

All is well aboard. That includes the autopilot, which is working like a champ. We are having some issues with our GPS as it keeps losing its position, but we have backups, and those are working fine. Ken is determined to find the cause of the intermittent operation of our main system. Yesterday was very rough and our newly installed microwave oven came loose from its brackets. Since we store our eggs in the microwave, try to imagine the mess when it separated from its mounts—would you like those scrambled? Tonight, we'll sail just north of Bande Aceh in Indonesia where the tsunami hit hardest, but we will be far enough away to not even see land.

Email / February 11, 2005

Ken and Rob are asleep and I've awakened Suse for her turn on watch. Life aboard *Julia* runs 24 hours a day. Ship traffic and the weather don't care if we're tired, so there's no letting down our guard or stopping at night. The boat and we are one. We have become a well-oiled machine that keeps going regardless of conditions.

There are hundreds of ships from all over the world converging in "The Great Channel," just south of India's Nicobar Islands, heading to and from Malaysia and Singapore. Our course takes us 50 miles south of Sri Lanka, and we have heard reports on the SSB radio from boats ahead of us that west of Sri Lanka there are clusters of trees and logs in the water—leftover debris from the tsunami—we'll keep our eyes open in that area.

The propane gas alarm under the floor in our cabin has been giving us some problems. It continues to pick up scents other than gas, including dirty socks, oil, diesel, and spray lubricants. Every other night it wakes us out of a sound sleep, and we get up, look around, see or smell nothing, and go back to sleep (or we simply hide the old socks). Last night, it happened again, and Ken said, "I'll get up and take care of it." I went back to sleep. In the morning, Ken smiled and proudly said, "I fixed the alarm." I looked under the floor to see what he had done...and I saw nothing. Beaming, Ken said, "That's right, I fixed it for good this time," as he nodded toward the open water.

N 06°03.1′ E 091°57.4′

Personal Journal / February 11, 2005

Whirlpools. Overfalls. Are we going to fall off the edge of the earth? Will we get sucked down underwater? This is what must have worried the early trans-oceanic explorers of Magellan's era.

As we approached what looked like harmless waves crashing onto a reef, it was all hands on deck. "Check the chart, Ken. Are you *sure* there's nothing?"

"I don't see anything," he responded, never taking his eyes from the chart plotter. "There's nothing out here, except that it says 'Overfalls.'"

"I agree," added Rob.

"Sure looks like a reef to me," Suse said. "Something besides wind is making these waves."

The rumors are true. These things *do* exist—and we just went through them. While they are marked on the charts as "Overfalls," we called them the "Rings of Fire." We sailed through three huge patches of ocean, miles across, where the waves shot straight up 3 to 5 feet in the air. In addition to the vertical chop, there were whirlpools and crosscurrents, making it look like white water foaming over a shallow reef. We studied the charts over and over again to make sure we weren't missing anything. Finally satisfied there were no charted reefs nearby, we timidly headed into the first patch of turbulence. We watched in amazement as water splashed up all around the boat, and the currents slowed us by 1 knot. Twenty minutes later, we came out the other side into calm water. We all looked at each other in awe, wondering what could possibly be causing this phenomenon. Then we went through two more turbulent patches; each one successfully bigger and with more wild currents and waves, but we came out of those unscathed as well. Just more mysteries of the deep. No wonder early sailors were fearful they'd reach, and eventually fall off, the end of the earth.

To make the whole scene even stranger, in the early morning hours we saw more ships shooting their water cannons down the sides of their hulls to prevent pirates from boarding. With the glow of their bright floodlights, it made for a very eerie, strange night and day.
N 6°16.4 E 94°41.6

✉ **Email** / February 12, 2005 / The Washing Machine
The seas have eased down to 5 feet. The past 24 hours, however, have been a different story. To get the feeling of our living conditions, crawl inside your washing machine, set it on random, erratic, and agitate, and try to live your life. We have rolled left, right, bounced up, down, then

left, then up, then right, then down, and every other combination possible. Now try to go to the bathroom, cook, and repair wiring problems, retie the dinghy, sleep, write emails, study the weather, make popcorn, and watch a movie. I usually get into sync with the motion and rhythm of *Julia* as she rises and falls on the swells. There's no rhythm today—only hanging on. We know we'll make it through, and laugh about food flying, and the difficulties of using the head.

N 05°28.4′ E 087°13.7′

Personal Journal / February 14, 2005

I find myself saying, "I hate the tropics!" So what am I doing here? I will admit I'm having a hard time adjusting back to boat life. The discomforts of sleeping, cooking, eating, using the head—and the ever-present heavy heat—drive me crazy. I'm looking forward to the Mediterranean where hopefully it will be cooler.

Writing this reminds me I am not appreciating enough what I'm experiencing. I am going to endeavor to appreciate the journey more and to complain less. I need to remember to choose happiness, which I know is in my power.

Email / February 15, 2005 / Mid-Way

It's a big day aboard *Julia*. We are currently 375 miles from Uligan in the Maldives, having just passed Sri Lanka down below the southern tip of India. The big news is tonight we will cross the longitude line of East 78°27′. Its significance? If you have a globe, find Zihuatanejo, Mexico, and then draw a line all the way around the earth, and you will discover that at 78°27′, we will have traveled halfway around the world. Wow, three years and 23,061 miles. It's cause for celebration, and the mood is happy and proud aboard *Julia* tonight. We've learned to recognize the little successes and things that make us feel good. Please join us in a toast to making it this far—we'll see you on the other side.

N 05°12.5′ E 079°06.3′

Email / February 16, 2005 / Hold the Champagne

It was a short-lived party. At 0230, I was on watch and started the generator to charge the batteries and run the refrigerator. I flipped the breaker for the refrigerator and heard a familiar sound of a motor attempting to run—but nothing happened. My heart sank as I pictured our freezer full of meat spoiling within hours in the 90°+ heat. Everyone was sleeping soundly and I didn't have the heart to wake them; we couldn't work until daylight anyway. I postponed the news until 0800 this morning.

"Good morning, Ken. As first mate and newly appointed chief engineer, you'll be interested to know the refrigerator motor is stuffed."

"Oh, no," he groaned.

Personal Journal / February 21, 2005

We're at Uligan, northern most of the 26 atolls in the Maldives. We are the only boat here, and it feels isolated, adventurous, and eerie. That's to be expected, though, as the Maldives is a vast expanse of atolls and 1,190 coral islands, which, combined, cover almost 35,000 square miles. The Maldives has the distinctions of being the smallest country in Asia and the lowest country in the world, with an average ground level of less than 5 feet above sea level. This low elevation was the cause of much tsunami damage in the capital city of Male.

With 450 people living on Uligan, we were surprised by the formal visit from four men, each representing customs, immigration, health, and port control. Their visit to *Julia* was welcoming, as long as we obeyed the laws: no scuba diving without permission and escort, no bringing of alcohol ashore, no wearing of tank tops or bathing suits while ashore, and no overnight stays ashore. As usual in the Third World, each department had their share of paperwork and each had their own rubber stamps to make it all official. But wait! I couldn't let the opportunity pass. When I produced *Julia's* brand new official boat stamp, the smiles widened, and our stature increased dramatically.

Our first order of business on land was to find the yacht agent. We didn't have to go far as he was standing on the pier waiting to help pull our sea-weary bodies up to the wooden planks of the dock. He seemed pleased with our order for 350 liters of diesel and promises delivery in jerry jugs to the boat—as long as we have a siphon hose. We've also been shopping for provisions in the store, a small room the size of four phone booths where we found spam, pasta, and canned tomatoes. We are definitely back in the Third World.

✉ Email / February 25, 2005

Uligan is a sleepy community with streets of soft, white sand that squishes between your toes, and houses built with white coral and cement bricks. It's dreamlike. The fully dressed Muslim women of the village sweep away the palm and breadfruit tree leaves each morning, and keep the streets immaculately clean. There are no cars on the bright, sandy lanes, just a few bicycles and the occasional group of kids playing soccer. It's strangely quiet.

While the water is clear, almost all of the coral is covered with thick layers of white sand, a remnant of the tsunami. My flipper exposes the vivid coral waiting for the waves to wash the sand away.

Uligan is a good place for us to rest before continuing on our voyage across the Indian Ocean. Yet it's hard to focus on the natural beauty, as the Arabian Sea and Gulf of Aden loom. Djibouti is still 1,850 miles away, at the mouth of the Red Sea, and the only way to get there is right through the middle of Pirate Alley. Our route will take us well to the north of Socotra, hopefully staying far enough from the coastline to avoid trouble, but rumor has it the pirates are operating farther out to sea these days. We are constantly discussing what to do about pirates: where to hide computers and valuables, will we fight back, under what conditions, and with what weapons? It's all very stressful, we're nervous about it, and the closer we get to the Gulf of Aden, the more the tension builds.

N 08°19.3 E 069°49.8'

📓 Personal Journal / February 26, 2005

Today, I was ready to throw in the towel because of repeated alternator problems. Jury-rigging an alternator to fit and installing it at sea was, to say the least, a challenge. Doing it twice while keeping our cool was well beyond twice as hard. Damn, I wanted to go sailing, not be a mechanic. I suppose I'll recover, but right now... go ahead, make me an offer.

✉ Email / February 27, 2005

I have the sunrise watch from 0500 to 0800, and it's one of those wonderful long, slow sunrises where the pale yellow light keeps growing, gradually washing out the brightness of the nearly full moon. I popped my head up to see the bright red sun peek out from behind the clouds, as it spreads red rays to their undersides, turning the entire eastern sky aflame in deep purple, yellow, and orange. Another day begins; it seems all will be fine when the sun comes up. As the song by The Cyrkle goes: "And I think it's gonna be all right, yes, the worst is over now. The morning sun is shining like a red rubber ball."

Then I received this not so uplifting email from my brother: "I understand you're about to sail into the Gulf of Aden. Are you nuts? With the American flag and the rainbow flag, why don't you just paint a big red bull's eye on your sails?"

I replied: "We're thinking of also raising the Star of David. Do you think that's a good idea?"

Email / February 28, 2005 / Bad Vibes

With little wind, and making almost no headway, we resorted to the engine again. While slipping the gearshift into forward, the boat shuddered and a bad vibration started coming from, according to Rob, "Down there somewhere," meaning outside the boat. After searching through the entire engine room area and still not finding the issue, we concurred with Rob it must be external. We shut the engine down and stopped the boat.

Without even a second thought as to who would go, I donned my mask and fins, and in the middle of the Indian Ocean, I slipped into the deep blue water to have a look. Sure enough, there was a big plastic rice bag wrapped around the propeller. With knife in hand, and an image of Tarzan wrestling a crocodile, I dove underwater a second and third time. *Julia's* 25 tons of fiberglass was bobbing up and down, trying to bonk me on the head, but I managed to hold onto the prop shaft with one hand, and finally cut the bag free with the other.

We were motoring off in no time. It's a strange sensation being underwater in the middle of the ocean. With no silt, it's cobalt blue, incredibly clear, and the visibility seems to go forever. Looking around underwater at our tiny boat (yes, 50 feet becomes very tiny mid-ocean), I'm reminded once again it is *all* about the boat. The boat is the only thing that matters out here. Climbing aboard, I had a renewed appreciation for keeping *Julia* in top working order.

At dusk, we caught a beautiful blue fin tuna. Rob hauled it in and I gaffed it. As we were pulling it aboard, it gave a last gallant effort and wiggled like a hula dancer on steroids. As quickly as we pulled it in, licking our chops in anticipation of sushi for days, it thrashed around so hard the hook and gaff pulled right through its jaw, and in the blink of an eye, it was gone. All we were left with was a huge cleanup, but the rare blue fin tuna survived and I'm glad about that. After all, he beat us at our own game and there's no sense being a sore loser.

Email / March 1, 2005
We're changing course because I'm concerned we may run out of fuel; therefore we are headed to Salalah, Oman. Even between here and the port, we'll still have to watch our supply closely. Running empty is not something we take lightly, because there is no AAA to come to our rescue. "Excuse me, Mr. Supertanker going 20 knots, would you mind stopping and loaning us 100 gallons of diesel?"

Because there is nothing except sky and ocean, when it's very dark, stars appear all the way down to the horizon making it difficult to distinguish them from a boat's lights. It's very tempting to alter our course because of the "There's a boat right in front of us I'm sure of it" factor, which turns out to be a star. Fortunately, the moon has come up and is shedding more light on the subject. And, of course, stars don't show up on radar.

Email From my friend Serbiene:
I am concerned for you with the pirates. Do you have weapons aboard? Remember, shoot to kill, not scare.
Love,
Serb

Personal Journal / March 3, 2005
Hailed by an Iranian fishing boat. Mohammed, the captain, suggested we alter our course from 306° to 350° for five hours in order to avoid his long fishing nets. He said he was our friend and "not to worry." We, of course, were very worried about being steered into a pirate trap. "I don't know, sounds fishy to me," Rob said.

"Even so, he sounds like a nice person on the radio and why would he bother with a small boat like us?" Suse reasoned.

"If we motor into his net, we're toast," Ken said.

I sat for a minute weighing the circumstances, and then with great trepidation, decided we should believe him and alter our course. Turns out he was indeed our friend and helped us to avoid his big fishing nets. I called Mohammed back on the SSB and thanked him. Some say not to trust people, but this is one more reminder that you should try, because most people are good. Well, there was that boat a few months ago headed straight for us when we were in the Straits of Malacca. We never waited around to see if he had good intentions or not. I'm sticking with "People are good." Generally.

N 14°22′ E 58°

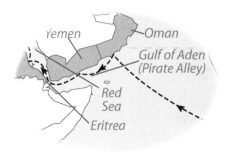

CHAPTER 14

A Whole New (Lonely and Desolate) World, and No Magic Carpets

"The true voyage of discovery consists not of seeking new landscapes, but having new eyes."
MARCEL PROUST

Email / March 5, 2005 / Safe Arrival in Oman

En route to Oman, we observed the engine oil pressure rising over its normal rate. Unable to figure out the cause, we hailed *Northstar*, a passing tanker, and spoke to their chief engineer. He kindly walked us through potential issues, such as a clogged oil filter or possible mixed oil viscosity.

Meanwhile, in the engine room, water was spraying everywhere from a broken fitting on one of the watermaker pumps. Despite our best efforts, the problem continued. Long story short: With Bill Claypool playing 20 questions via email, we determined saltwater from the broken connector had sprayed onto the oil pressure sensor, causing an erroneous reading on the gauge. Cleanliness is next to Godliness and that applies to oil pressure sensors too.

N 16°56.1′ E 054°00.3′

📓 Personal Journal / March 6, 2005

I haven't sold the boat. We are in Salalah, Oman, sitting onboard waiting for customs to come out to the boat and clear us into the country. We've been waiting since our arrival at 1700 yesterday, and it's driving us mad. While killing time, we watched a slaughter of another kind as truckloads of sharks were loaded at the dock. Their fins already had been cut off for soup and the bodies will be discarded. I don't like encountering them while diving, but this is a really sad sight. Are these people oblivious to how important sharks are to the ecosystem?

This is one of the largest seaports on the Arabian Peninsula and we see huge cargo ships unloading containers with modern cranes working at break-neck speed. There are supposedly beautiful green mountains not too far away; from the anchorage, though, all we see is barren desert... miles and miles of desert into the far distance.

✉ Email / March 9, 2005 / The Arabian Sea

A rental car in Salalah provided the opportunity to do some sightseeing. We drove past white sand beaches, on wide boulevards through small towns, and even lay in the sun at a resort hotel. There we saw men and boys in bathing suits, but the women, both young and old, were dressed head to toe in burkas, even while splashing and frolicking in the pool. Camels led by men in white robes walked the streets and herds could be seen grazing on the side of the road.

At the end of the day, though, we used our tiny motorized camel for that one thing we do in every port—food shopping. It's quite a challenge to buy supplies without speaking a word of the language, but it's amazing how much you can get done with pointing, rolling of the eyes, and shrugging.

In a search for mushroom soup, Ken turns to the store clerk and makes like he's holding a bowl in his hands, and then spooning out something.

"How does he know you're scooping out soup?" Suse asks. She makes the same bowl in her hands, but this time says, "Mushroom soup" to the clerk. Nothing.

Another shopper approaches us and asks in perfect English, "Can I help you?"

"Oh, yes, please," Ken says. "We are looking for soups. Mushroom soup in particular."

The man turns and yells something, in Arabic, across about four aisles, waits for a response, and says, "Wait here." Within half a minute, a young boy comes skidding around the corner of the aisle saying something we don't understand, and motions for us to follow him. He's talking all of the way as he leads our little procession, but we have no idea what he's saying. Sure enough, we are soon standing in front of a shelf filled with all kinds of soups, including mushroom, canned and packaged.

During the customs check-in, we'd heard from other cruisers to look for the agent named Mohammed in his white robe. That's a good one, a guy named Mohammed in a white robe in a Muslim country. We didn't have to worry. Sure enough, a tall black man in his flowing white robe hailed us from shore to come and get him. We dinghied ashore and met Mohammed, a dead ringer for Eddie Murphy right down to the big laugh and shining teeth. "Ha, ha, ha, welcome my friends to Oman!" he beamed as he flashed his broad white smile. Once again, our own rubber stamps—the ones we had made for us in Thailand—lightened the moment. I even armed us with two colors of inkpads. Mohammed thought that was the funniest thing he had seen in a while, and we sat there laughing with him while we waited. "Ha, ha, ha, you will out-stamp the customs, ha, ha, ha!"

Our fuel was delivered to the dock in a tanker truck today. After bringing *Julia* to the dock, we paid for the liquid wind in U.S. dollars—cash only—and departed Oman in the afternoon. With great trepidation, we are heading west through the Arabian Sea and Gulf of Aden right up the middle of the most notoriously pirated waters in the world. Our next port of call is Aden, Yemen, a 600-mile passage, and barring any unforeseen excitement, we should be there in four or five days. To hide our position from potential pirates, we will be fairly busy and most likely won't email until our arrival. We will be running silent—no radio transmissions. Yes, we are very, very anxious.

N 16°43′ E 53°52′

Nowadays, there are organized convoys, escort services, and even a "safe corridor" patrolled by many navies of the world to prevent piracy. At the time of our transit, however, the only safety net was to join an informal group traveling together. About a week before our arrival in Salalah, a dozen yachts, including many of our friends, went through this same area together. Because we were too late departing Thailand, we missed the group. We were pretty much on our own.

I was too busy and nervous to write emails during the passage through Pirate Alley. There were so many discussions among us and with the crews of the only other two boats in the harbor, we had practically worked ourselves into a frenzy. For some reason, I turned on the video camera and taped our last crew meeting to discuss the options. It was a tense and heated meeting punctuated by cocktail refills.

"Okay, guys," I said. "What are we going to do if we're attacked? First of all, what if we see a boat heading towards us but no shots are fired? What if we see a boat coming towards us and they're shooting? What if we're being followed? Do we stop? Try to outrun them? I do not want to be surprised; that means two people on watch 24 hours a day and no sleeping while on watch. If we want even half a chance at outrunning pirates, we're going to need that head start of seeing them first." I suspect the crew was waiting for me to breathe.

"Don't let them aboard under any circumstances," Rob said as he puffed up his strong rugby-built body.

"Come on, we have to let them aboard if they're shooting," Suse said, even though she was tall and tough.

"If they shoot warning shots, we have to stop and let them aboard," Ken added. "Let's hide valuables and leave out what we don't mind them taking."

"Stuff that will hopefully satisfy them," I agreed. It never occurred to us we might be held hostage for ransom.

"What about lights and radios?" Ken asked.

"No running lights, no deck lights, and below deck, red lights only. No outgoing radio traffic either," I said firmly.

This went on for hours until I summarized, "Okay, we'll hide things in the safe under the floorboards. As a precaution, I want everyone to leave out some money, a watch, the older computers, a portable GPS, and some other stuff that might satisfy them. And I want weapons ready. That means both flare guns, and move four more fire extinguishers here into the main salon. Everybody knows how to use them and shoot the chemical right into someone's face, right?" The group nodded. "No sweat," Rob added.

"One more thing: We are a big boat; 25 tons is bigger than most pirate boats. Let's use that to our advantage. If a pirate boat is heading for us, be prepared to turn and ram them."

We left Salalah under beautiful conditions, giving us 4 to 5 knots of speed and the promise of fair weather. In the company of only two other boats (hardly a convoy), Edvina *and* Rikili, *we motored to keep our speed up, as we had been cautioned to go as fast as possible through this 600-mile area and not look like a target. Like walking on the wrong side of the tracks at 3 in the morning—walk fast.*

Email / March 13, 2005 / Running "The Gauntlet"
This passage started out with intense anxiety. Every year, some yachts get pirated at gunpoint. It's all anybody talks about in this area.

By Day 3, we started getting more nervous as we were entering the specific area between East 49° 50' and East 46° 50', the 300-mile corridor where most attacks occur. Additionally, we heard on the radio net that only three days ago, a pair of pirate boats with machine guns had attacked two sailboats we know, *Mahdi* and *Gandalf*. Our friend Rod, aboard *Mahdi*, evidently shot and killed two of the pirates, and *Gandalf* rammed one of the attacking boats. Both yachts escaped without injury but everybody was quite shaken up, and now there is fear of retribution from friends and relatives of the attackers. The risk, of course, is not only to the crews of *Mahdi* and *Gandalf*, who defended themselves, but also to any of us who might be their friends. The radio has been crackling away with the news, only amplifying our fear.

They were attacked 25 miles from the coast; too close according to the pilot book, which recommends staying at least 50 miles offshore. Our route kept us 80 miles from Yemen and 100 miles from Somalia. We were fortunate to have 20-knot winds by Day 3, which kicked up big following seas, something we are quite comfortable with. Evidently pirates don't like these rough seas as it makes it more difficult to board a boat. On the other hand, it's not easy to spot a pirate boat in blustery conditions.

We had to dodge a few cargo ships as we were trying to be less visible by running with no lights and weren't able to contact them because of total out-bound radio silence. We had pulled away from *Rikili* and *Edvina,* and since we were alone, had to take all precautionary measures possible. More hours passed discussing different scenarios and how we would react. We readied our amateur weapons—not much of a match for AK-47s, but we felt better having them at hand.

We steered clear of all boats and ships, not knowing if they were friend or foe; we didn't want anybody reporting our position to their "pirate friends." I confess I started rethinking my previous conclusion that it's generally okay to trust people. Then again, the bandits on these waters were a far cry from the helpful captain of an Iranian fishing boat trying to protect a net packed with tuna.

On Day 4, there was a palpable sense of relief aboard *Julia.* At 0630, a prime time for pirate attacks (they like to catch a crew in the sleepy early morning hours), we were 50 miles from Aden when the VHF radio jumped to life. Our nerves were already frayed. Then we heard a voice in a heavy French accent say, "Little boat, little boat, little boat at position N 12° 43' E 45° 38.4', please identify yourself." We knew we were through the worst part: It was a French warship requesting our identification. Needless to say, we were only too happy to oblige.

"C'est le yacht Julia*, des Etats-Unis,"* I replied in my best high school French. I bumbled through their questions: "Where was your last port? When did you leave? How many people onboard? What are their nationalities?" I guess I gave the answers they were looking for because the next call said, *"Okay, bienvenue – vous pouvez poursuivre,"* buzzed back the response, and just like that, we were free to proceed into Aden Harbor.

We are anchored in Aden, not more than 100 yards from where the *USS Cole* was blown up on October 12, in 2000 (exactly two years before the Bali nightclub bombing). I look to the right and see brown desert, rubble, ruins, and what looks like a land that time forgot. Looking left, I see huge oil tankers—what a contrast. It's all a bit overwhelming and unfamiliar.

Every day is a new adventure, and we have to be comfortable with unfamiliarity to make it here. Language, customs, money, *baksheesh* (brib-ery), and understanding the underlying tones of what people say and mean, are all vastly different. For example, the customs officials "don't drink," but certainly a "Gift of two bottles of wine would be a nice gesture, as we welcome you into our country." We have seen this movie before and know enough to give two bottles *and* two packs of Marlboros...and the paperwork is done.

A big milestone happened on this passage: *Julia's* nautical miles log clicked over the 25,000 mark. We have traveled the circumference of the earth but only made it slightly more than halfway around the world.

A toast: To running "The Gauntlet" and not being pirated.

Second sip...to 25,000 miles.

Third sip...to fresh sushi.

Fourth sip...to new adventures for us.

Fifth sip (hic)...to every one of your days being a new adventure.

Sixth sip...zzzzzzzzzzzzzzzzzzzzzz

Personal Journal / March 14, 2005

We have refueled at the dirtiest, most disgusting fuel dock I've ever seen. What an eye-opening experience it is being in Aden. The people are kind and seem happy and keep saying, "We love you Americans. America good; Bush bad." We walked around the town yesterday and bought some fairly fresh vegetables in the market. A striking contrast was to observe women dressed in all black burkas with only slits for their eyes, while the men wore whatever they wanted. The streets have a sweet and sour smell that is by now so familiar in the Third World. It's a combination of fresh foods in the open air, mixed with garbage and sewage in the streets. There are vendors everywhere peddling shoes, belts, toys, and even electron-ics. Food, spices, pirated movies, and cheap, used clothing are stacked in neat piles on the ground. A young boy in a torn Adidas T-shirt sitting on a nearby blanket filled with holes gladly accepts a U.S. dollar for an over-whelming amount of limes.

Long controlled by the British, the architecture is a clear representa-tion of their presence, even though most of the buildings are terribly run-down. We try to find a bag of ice made from purified water and are just about to give up, when a young man who has latched onto us as a sort of guide, suggests the fish store. A few cubes survived by the time we got back to *Julia*.

Email / March 19, 2005 / *Baksheesh*
   We departed Aden today headed for Massawa in Eritrea, 400 miles to the northwest. Sadly, it's only Ken and me, as Rob and Suse had to finally head home. Their boat is still damaged enough that it will remain in Thailand for quite a while. We had a great time together and will miss them.

The forecasts are for very light winds, which normally wouldn't be a problem, but rumor has it there is no diesel available in Eritrea. This means we cannot refuel until Sudan; we really needed that wind. Last night, after checking out with customs and immigration, our last purchase was jerry jugs to hold more liquid wind. For $1 each, we bought six cheap plastic containers of 20 liters each, one of which cracked right away and had to be tossed; the other five are tied onto the foredeck and full of diesel, adding another full day of motoring should we need it.

Fueling in Aden was an unbelievably complicated process. First, we pull *Julia* up to a splintery dock covered in grease and oil. Choose: grease and oil on the boat or on the fenders, on your bare feet, or ruining your shoes. Then go to the main fuel office where the fuel depot manager meets you and explains the procedure:

1. Go upstairs to the fuel calculator's office, tell him how much fuel you want in liters or Imperial gallons, and he calculates that amount into tonnage. He then writes out a receipt of two copies with carbon paper... do you remember carbon paper? Because he is giving me last week's price for fuel, he makes it very clear he is doing me a favor. One pack of Marlboro cigarettes and we're square.

2. Take the receipt and walk about 200 yards to another building to see the cashier and pay for the amount of fuel specified on the receipt, in U.S. dollars, cash only. The cashier's office consists of two women dressed in black burkas. Even their hands are covered, which makes handling the cash and books somewhat awkward, but they seem to manage. The Yemeni women must stay completely covered all the time when outside of the home; supposedly, so no other man can lust after them. The men wear western clothes; T-shirts and jeans. We find it quite contrary to our goals

of equal rights and amazed that religion rules everything, all in the name of Allah…but I digress….

3. After paying the cashier, walk back to the first office and show the fuel calculator the paid receipt. He then calculates the tonnage of fuel back to Imperial Gallons and phones the fuel dock where Achmed is sitting, smoking cigarettes. (Yes, smoking cigarettes at the fuel dock.)

4. Uh oh. In a separate transaction, we paid for 27 Imperial gallons but only took 25 into our jerry jugs.

5. Walk back to the first building and the gentleman there calculates the difference is $4, phones the cashier, and tells me to go back again.

6. Walk back to the cashier's office, and they have my $4 ready and waiting.

7. Return to the dinghy where Ken is waiting with Achmed, who clearly has his hand out: one pack of Marlboro's and we're square.

8. Customs: one pack of Marlboro's and we're square.

9. Immigration: two packs of Marlboro's and we're square.

It's called *baksheesh,* and it's the way of life here in the Middle East. You can't fight it, and if you don't play the game, you wait that much longer for your fuel or your paperwork. We knew this is how it works. We don't even smoke, but smartly loaded up on dozens of cartons of Marlboro cigarettes for just this purpose while in duty-free Langkawi several weeks ago. We're getting good value for them.

N 12°38.2′ E 044°43.5′

CHAPTER 15

Walls of Water…So That's Why Moses Walked Across

"Perseverance and persistence in spite of all obstacles, discouragement, and impossibilities: It is this that in all things distinguishes the strong soul from the weak."
THOMAS CARLYLE

Email / March 21, 2005 / Sea of Diamonds
It's quite a milestone to have made it *into* the Red Sea, and the next big one will be to make it *out* of here.

We have been in radio contact with Harvey and Jean on *Guitar* who have diverted to Djibouti for major engine repairs. Their reports, which we trust, are of a dirty, dangerous city and we are taking their recommendation to avoid it. They expect to be there for weeks, and we empathize with them, having gone through a similar scenario with our transmission in Indonesia.

We experienced a real treat before the wind came up; the phosphorescence in the water was brighter than we have ever seen by 100-fold,

221

and because the wind was light, the calm, glassy water allowed the super bright neon green to cast its glow up and out of the water, much like The Nemo surfacing in *20,000 Leagues Under the Sea*. It was so intensely bright we could almost read by it. As *Julia* moved through the water, a wide green line formed in our wake, which kept shining brighter and brighter. Then it started to rain, creating a spectacular finale. As the rain pelted, each drop struck the phosphorescence, causing that spot to explode with a shimmering white burst. More and more drops fell, the sea flattened out completely and began to light up white, then silver, and finally it became a sea of diamonds glittering for thousands of yards to the horizon. It was absolutely mesmerizing.

Reality woke me from a hypnotic state: "Beep, beep, beep!" A ship had entered our 2-mile safety zone and the radar alarm was screaming to take evasive action. The fairy tale rain dance was nice while it lasted, and the picture is etched into my memory forever.

Still beating against the wind, we took shelter at Dumeria Island. It's a strikingly beautiful red desert composed of rocks and rubble in contrast to very blue, clear, calm water. It was a welcome respite. Our good fortune returned, and by 0700 the following morning, we were sailing north with wind that had come around from behind. We've been riding that 20-knot southeasterly for a day and half now, with a bonus of a 2-knot current going our way. With speeds over 10.5 knots while flying the spinnaker, we've been smiling all day and reminding ourselves how nice it is to have the wind behind us. What a difference it makes in how we feel, with the renewed ability to cook, eat, move around, use the bathroom, or even sit down to write a log entry.

N 14°33.3′ E 41°43.5′

Email / March 24, 2005

We've been pounding to windward for days in our first taste of the notoriously rough Red Sea. The decks are slippery as the cheap jerry jugs from Aden can't take the beating and are beginning to leak diesel fuel.

A Royal Navy helicopter did a fly-by and dipped down close enough for us to see the faces of the servicemen staring out the open doorway. I wonder if they were thinking: "Look at those crazy guys out there in that tiny boat." We waved and they returned the salute, then as quickly as they had arrived, they were gone. Today, over the radio, we heard a U.S. Navy ship calling boats to identify themselves. I certainly don't mind having the good guys out here with us.

I know many of you won't believe this, but I'm sorry to have to tell you the truth: the Red Sea is *blue*…very, very blue.
N 15°32.4′ E 39°59.2′

 Email / March 25, 2005

Ours is the only boat in this extraordinary anchorage at Shumma Island; a real desert isle. The water here is the kind you typically see in post cards, and contrasts dramatically with the umber-toned sand. Not unlike the kind you see in cartoons that depict a man stranded on a desert island.

Under a full moon, the water is pure silver…making the scene surrealistic. What if we weren't here? Would it be this beautiful? The water is completely flat and calm; the reef stark against the clear water, the moon intensely bright, and the absence of other boats make it all quite overwhelming. It feels very alone out here, even though the two of us are together. As we are totally self-sufficient, we are that much more dependent on each other's trust and love. The sights and sounds make us afraid, aware, on edge, alert, yet at the same time relaxed and at peace. I remain in constant wonder about the world around us.

 Email / March 31, 2005 / War-Torn Massawa and the Ruins of Sudan

We are in a different world. Five days ago we entered the harbor at Massawa, Eritrea, to pick up CJ. Massawa is a war-torn city; a seaport that has been fought over and changed hands as far back as the 8th century. The Ottoman Empire architecture must have been stunning in the 1500s, but the bullet holes and bombed-out buildings and mosques overshadow whatever beauty once existed here. More recently, the war with Ethiopia has made the very poor people struggle to make ends meet. There is a distinct lack of young men as most have been conscripted into the military. The government keeps close tabs on the people, doesn't let them leave the country, and our own check-in and out was strict and without smiles. It's a modern-day reminder of war's wastefulness.

After Eritrea, we motor sailed for two full days on water so glassy it looked like a sea of mercury, and with thousands of jellyfish, it seemed one could walk on it.

When we entered Suwakin Harbor between gun emplacements and under the watchful eye of port control, the radio crackled: "White sailboat: Who are you? Where are you coming from? Where are you going? How many people onboard? What are the nationalities of all aboard?" Looking at the big guns pointing our way, I nervously replied, "We're a pleasure craft from the United States, on our way to Suez, and request permission to stop in Suwakin. We have three Americans onboard."

After a five-minute silence, while we motored in circles, the reply came in: "Okay, yes permission granted to enter the harbor." Crossing in front of the armaments, we motored past Old Suakin City, on an island not more than a boat length away from the channel. Old Suakin is a city 3,000 years old and is showing its age. No longer inhabited, its buildings made of whitewashed coral lie mostly in piles of rubble. With only a few structures left standing, it resembles bombed-out Dresden, Germany, after the war. As I nervously kept *Julia* in the narrow channel and away from the rocks of the island, I kept thinking, "What a great set for a war movie."

As in Eritrea, the people in Sudan are friendly, eager to help, but are desperately poor and struggling from day to day. From the boat, we see donkey carts are a popular mode of transportation, and as in many Third World countries, these animals are left to stand in the hot sun and worked incessantly. Camels, on the other hand, are highly valued, and we observe them being led to water by their handlers.

The military is everywhere, training its troops and trying to keep them motivated and fresh because of the constant state of civil war between the north and south that has been going on since 1955. In 2005, a tentative peace treaty was signed, and while the people we met seem hopeful, they are yet guarded about the prospect of real peace. Our agent, who checked us in (yet another gentleman named Mohammed, also in a long flowing white robe), told us Sudan produces plenty of oil but is poor because of the civil war, which is utilizing all resources, including the people themselves, for military purposes. There are signs of bombings, bullets, and poverty in every direction; we didn't even go ashore. Resources of oil and water could be shared, but it seems religion trumps all in this area and prevents a lasting peace. I don't get it. Why does one person care what another person believes about God? Is it really worth fighting over? I know mankind has been fighting wars over territory and religion since day one; nonetheless I'm stupefied by it all.

Trying to forecast the weather in the Red Sea was nearly impossible. The SSB morning radio net focused on the weather, and we listened intently to reports of the barometric pressure in Cairo, which was the best indicator of what would be happening to us mid-Red Sea. We learned not to trust the forecasts we received predicting wind speed and direction. They were plain wrong much of the time.

The Red Sea acts as a narrow funnel sucking the air from north to south and, at this time of year, that's really the only thing predictable. We took advantage of the calm periods, but we learned the hard way that sometimes even the predicted calms ended sooner than expected.

We were forced to scratch our diving plans for the Similan Islands in the Andaman Sea, again because of the late departure from Thailand. Therefore, we were determined not to miss the top-notch diving and unique marine life in the Red Sea. When the weather was calm, rather than making tracks north, we anchored behind a reef and went diving. "Just one more dive in the morning and then we'll go," threw us into a battle with the roughest storm of our lives….

Personal Journal / April 1, 2005
It's terrifying how something so routine can become a life-endangering situation in an instant. After returning from two dives on spectacular Sanganeb Reef, our friends from *True Blue* asked if we would free their anchor buoy, which had tangled in the chain 30 feet down.

The dive gear was still in the dinghy, and there was still 15 minutes of air left in my tank. What harm could there be in a short dive to free a tangled line? Rather than bother re-rigging both of us, we agreed Ken would remain on the surface in the dinghy. What were we thinking?

I slowly followed the anchor chain down in water so clear I could see Ken up on the surface, bobbing in the dinghy. He was looking down and waving; I gave him the "OK" sign. At 35 feet, I reached the buoy and its excess tangles of nylon line floating around the chain like a bed of kelp.

No wonder it was tangled—there was way too much of it, and given any opportunity, line will always do its best to tie itself into a snarl.

As I attempted to unwrap the line from the chain, I noticed I was having a hard time maintaining my depth. I added air to my buoyancy compensator (B.C.) but continued to drop faster and faster, and before I knew it I was on the bottom at 45 feet. A quick scan of the oxygen pressure gauge revealed only 10 remaining minutes. My breathing became short, quick, and panicky—exactly the wrong way to conserve air and stay calm.

What had pulled me down to the bottom? I looked around, turning my head left and right, up and down, reaching my arms over my head to feel the top of the tank, and immediately discovered the problem. The buoy line, which was looped around the anchor chain, had tangled in my air valve. With each surge of the water, the chain straightened, then slackened, and that pumping action along with my weight must have caused the buoy line to slip down the chain, taking me with it to the bottom. No amount of air in my B.C. was going to float me free.

It had all happened very fast. I panicked and thrashed about, reaching up and around trying to get free, but my movements were erratic and not working to untangle the line. Had a shark been nearby, it surely would have attacked with the assumption I was wounded, and therefore easy prey. I was well aware that we had just seen numerous sharks on our dives earlier that day.

My mind was racing but irrational. *Stop and think! You're not the type who panics. You still have 10 minutes and you're trained for this. You know how to take off your equipment and put it back on underwater…you practiced a hundred times!* All I would have had to do was loosen the B.C., slip the tank over my head, and disentangle the mess. Yet I couldn't seem to connect my thoughts to action. My movements had made things worse, causing the line to wrap around one of my flippers, making me view the nylon line as some attacking sea creature out to get me.

Now I was really getting scared and any logic was lost—I'm not one prone to panic, but here I was caught in it—a powerful force new to me. I looked up at Ken on the surface and realized how stupid it was to be down there alone. *I've done three dives today and I could get the bends. Do I abandon my gear and try to make it 45 feet to the surface on one breath? No, that would be foolish and certainly cause serious problems.* I wasn't thinking clearly.

Help! But there was nobody to help me. There were no thoughts about God or prayer, or any other external force—I was on my own. Was it logic or training that finally prevailed over panic? Suddenly, I stopped flailing about to look around for an answer to my dilemma. I glanced down, and there, strapped to my leg, was my shiny 6-inch sharper-than-a-razor titanium dive knife in its quick-release holster. In the time it takes to say, "I've had enough," I popped it out and sliced through the line like butter.

Still panicky, I began a rapid ascent to the surface, leaving the line, buoy, and tangled anchor on the bottom. I came up quickly and rational thinking returned; I made sure not to rise faster than my bubbles. Breaking the surface, I ripped the regulator out of my mouth and gulped in the clean fresh air tasting its sweetness like never before. I was so scared I was shaking.

I had broken almost every rule in the dive book. The only thing I did right was to have a knife on me; without it, I might not be here to write this. Why did I abandon my normally meticulous precautions? Maybe I'm too confident, too sure about my skills, and silly enough to assume they can get me out of any situation. I was severely scolded and warned by the sea: Don't dive alone, don't do a favor if you can't follow the rules, always keep any line you're working on in front of you, and always carry a knife. I'm lucky to have escaped with only light discipline and a severe humbling. I'm only a visitor in these vast waters and was reminded to never lose respect for the sea's immense power.

What more can happen to us here in the Red Sea? This is a lonely, desolate place, and I don't like the feeling I'm getting....

The Red Sea was like a wild dog peacefully asleep, and the next thing you know, it's at your throat. After my dive incident, we figured we still had more than 24 hours before the predicted 30-knot northerly arrived. Away we motored in calm waters, headed north...right into the middle of hell....

Email / April 1, 2005

The wind is supposed to pipe up to 30 knots against us from the north. Tomorrow, after our morning dive at Sanganeb Reef, we will run 100 miles north to Marsa Shinab to be sheltered from the winds and wait it out for a couple of days. *Marsas* are small inlets of water on the coasts of the Red Sea surrounded by dusty, barren land. In this region of the world, they are the safety stops.

N 19°43.9′ E 37°26.8′

✉ **Email** / April 3, 2005 / Beaten Back by the Red Sea

We must be in hell. The last 24 hours revealed the angriest seas I have ever experienced in all my years of sailing. God must hate the Red Sea, as do I at the moment. The Red Sea is trying its best to defeat us.

Thirty miles north of Sanganeb Reef, Ken turned to me and said, "You know it's supposed to be flat calm for another day."

"Yeah, I know what you're thinking," I replied. The wind had increased from zero to 20 knots—right on the nose. The Red Sea is like living in the bottom of a valley: Walking out of your house, no matter where you want to go, it's uphill. Want to go see a friend, go the market, go *anywhere?* It's uphill.

Looking slightly worried, Ken said, "It's coming early, isn't it?"

Then CJ jinxed us. "I've always wanted to be out in a big storm."

We both looked menacingly at him while shouting, "Never say that! The wind gods can hear you!"

"Crap," I mumbled as I realized we were motoring directly into a front. I knew we couldn't go back to the reef, as it didn't offer enough protection, we were too far from shore to get any shield from the land, and we couldn't go through a small channel into a *marsa* in the dark. Our only choices were to keep going, turn and run with the wind, or heave to. At this point, we chose to continue on course.

Just then, CJ, who had been monitoring the wind speed, shouted, "30 knots, it just hit 30 knots!" I knew we were soon going to be using a lot of power running the radar, autopilot, and SSB radio that night, so I started the generator to ensure our batteries were topped up. It's a lot easier to keep an engine running than start one in rough conditions, especially if big seas force water up into the exhaust. Gale force winds of 30 knots can make for a miserable night, but I didn't know they were only the prelude to the big stuff.

In the darkness of 0230, the wind had turned cold, was blowing 40 knots and *still* building. The seas visible from the glow of our lights had come up to 20 feet; they were as high as the first spreaders. We were pounding right into it with engine on, and sails reefed to a size more appropriate for the dinghy.

"Are you happy now? You got your storm, didn't you?" Ken said to CJ, an unmistakable bite in his voice.

I went below and poured over the charts and the "Red Sea Pilot" to find an anchorage closer than our original destination, one not restricted by the Sudan military, and a place that offered more than a reef for protection. We were being bounced around so much, I could barely read the words on the soaked paper. Just reading and operating the chart plotter was a challenge while holding on, but I finally came across a spot, confirmed it as a good anchorage in the pilot book, and then yelled up to Ken and CJ in the cockpit: "I think I found a place for us! Turn port to a course of 272°, and let's ease off the sails."

We had traveled 70 miles in a northeast direction, until at 0430, we turned west for an anchorage that was 40 miles away. As we turned away from our original destination, the wind was still strengthening, the seas were now the size of three-story houses, reaching as high as halfway up the mast, and had big breaking waves on their crests. The tops were being blown off by steady 45-knot winds with gusts to well over 50 knots. These seas were significantly bigger—and steeper—than any I had seen before. I counted, "One thousand one, one thousand two, one thousand three" and *wham!* We were hit with another wave. In addition to their monstrous size, the 30-foot seas were coming every three seconds; the frequency and steepness were alarming.

The noise was deafening. I've heard that people who call to be rescued from their boats in a storm are most frightened by the noise, and now I know why. The wind didn't whistle through the rigging; it screamed and howled like a wounded animal, and it never let up. It made you want to go below and crawl into a bunk, close your eyes and ears, and not look up again until it stopped. It wouldn't stop though, and the increasing noise pressed into my brain like the wind pierced the skin on my face.

We were now beam to the wind. As each huge wave rushed toward us, *Julia* rolled to the portside, dipping the rail in the water, the dinghy strained at its lines, and then she would recover in time for the next big roller. When the water crashed over the bow, *Julia* went airborne as we flew off the tops of these enormous masses of water. The whole boat and rigging shuddered and shook as we landed in the deep trough of the swell with the sound of a cannon blast. I don't know how many times I thanked Stevens, our vessel's maker, for a boat that can handle big seas and is built like a tank. The autopilot would strain and whine as the motor fought to keep up with the fast movements the boat was making. I traded off with the autopilot, giving it a rest every so often to save its reliability, but we didn't have to worry; this autopilot held its own, even in these conditions—and it never got tired.

The sea-state was menacing. Sheets...no, walls of water crashed over *Julia*, drenching the dodger, the cockpit, and us. Every boat leaks and this one is no different. Both the Pullman and forward cabin turned into swimming pools and everything got soaked: towels, sheets, pillows, sweaters, the floors, food, books, computers, CDs, and all became covered with a layer of salt.

While we were all determined, vigilant, and safety conscious, we were also exhausted, overwhelmed, and frightened by the sights, sounds, and motions. We couldn't cook, eat, or use the head because it was so rough, and anytime we moved around, we were attached to the boat by a 3-foot tether on our harness, which further hampered mobility.

At the morning radio net, we checked in with our fellow cruisers for the first time ever as "Priority Emergency Traffic." Anyone listening knew we were badly spooked.

"Priority traffic, this is *Julia*," I said, my voice shaking.

"Go ahead *Julia*," said Ellen, the net controller.

"We are caught right smack in the middle of this storm. We're okay, but I want to give our position and that of the little *marsa* that we're headed for. I also need an hourly radio check until we arrive at our anchorage. We have 30-foot seas, whole gale-force 50-knot winds and are pounding into it. I just need someone to know where we are."

"*Julia*, we suggest you find an island to hide behind if you can," a listening yacht broke in.

I replied, "I'd hide behind a phone booth if I could find one! We are running for the closest anchorage we can find." It was comforting to know others were concerned about our safety, but there wasn't much they could do to for us. You're pretty much on your own out here.

We had to be prepared to change our plans. If we didn't run for the safety of an anchorage, we would have been stuck out in the huge seas and 50-knot winds making almost no headway. Our position was at one of the narrowest points in the Red Sea, only 125 miles wide. This constriction added to the funneling effect, which increases wind speed, and contributes to the steepness and frequency of the waves.

By chance, we got caught in the worst place at the worst time. We continually considered our options of turning to run downwind or heaving to, and kept both possibilities open. We didn't want to lose the ground already gained, nor did we know how long the storm would last; it might have pushed us too close to shore after stopping to heave to. While the conditions were tough, we felt well prepared to handle the situation as long as it didn't get worse. We also now had a new plan and were headed toward a supposedly safe anchorage, a small inlet called Marsa Inkeifal.

Arriving at Inkeifal was a thrill ride. We flew in under power, transitioning from 6-foot waves to the relatively calm waters protected by land. The entrance resembles a river mouth and is only three or four boat lengths wide, with the deep channel only two boat lengths wide. A wooden stake marks the tip of the reef on the south side of the entrance. I knew to come in fast to keep from being blown off course. It was either hit the deep channel the first time or go aground with certain disaster. We had no choice but to trust the charts and our tide calculations for water depth at the entrance: we hoped to have an extra margin of 8 feet under the keel. After 24 hours of no sleep, we checked the numbers again and again until we were as sure as we could be about our math. Without any local knowledge, we didn't know if the storm had shifted the sand at the bar, or if there was a wreck blocking the channel, or if there was some other reason not to enter in these conditions.

"Hold on!" I shouted, fearing a sudden stop as we approached the narrow entrance. Setting *Julia* up for the entrance was like rafting on a whitewater river and threading the needle between two rocks—something I have done hundreds of times—except this boat weighs 25 tons and would be a total loss if I missed my mark. I steered upwind of the entrance and on a slight angle because the waves continued to hammer from starboard, pushing us downwind into the reef. When we were in front of the narrow entrance, I straightened the boat out, gave us a big boost of power, and we dropped perfectly right into the middle of the channel. Suddenly, like a roller coaster coming to its stop, we were motoring in calm waters.

"Good shot!" CJ said, now humbled by the big storm and looking like a drowned rat. Ken looked at me and smiled his approval and relief.

We had made it. At noon today, after 24 hours of anxiety, *Julia* finally dropped anchor on a soft sandy bottom, and I'm betting there was a big sigh of relief in the nearby fleet knowing we reached a safe haven.

As I take a moment to record the events, the wind is still blowing at 35 knots and we are anchored in the middle of a sandstorm. I'm used to having the sting of salt beating against my face, but now that sting is compounded by brown, gritty sand. There still are no clouds in the sky, no rain, just sandy haze blowing from the shore. We are the only boat here, which is unnerving by itself. Why are we the only ones? Is there something we don't know about this place? So far, through the blowing sand, we have seen three camels, a goat, and only one person onshore. It feels like we are in the most desolate place possible at the end of the earth, and while protected from the seas, we still feel uneasy.

This is a small *marsa*, only half a mile long with only a hundred yards of low-lying sand separating the calm waters from the sea. We are hoping our anchor will hold, as we are but two football fields away from solid ground. After the chain breaking in Thailand, we have to once again learn to trust the anchor and ground tackle; there's really no choice and at a certain point you just have to have faith. However, I believe in stacking the deck in our favor by checking the shackles, connections, and bridle, and in this case, adding a second bridle. Stacking the deck *makes* good luck.

The forecast is for the strong winds to remain at least another three days, and we aren't going anywhere until I see 0-10 knots. We are tired, hungry, wet, salty, and gritty. The cabin looks like a bomb went off because books, clothes, food, papers, folders, and other stuff went flying during our steep rolls. We need sleep—we desperately need sleep.

Now we know why Moses took the shortcut through the Red Sea on foot...because it's too damn rough to sail. We are safe, surprised by our strength and endurance, and are certainly stronger from our experience. We learned a few lessons along the way. We couldn't trust the weather forecasts in the Red Sea. We learned the best-laid plans could be shot to pieces, and when they are, you better be ready to modify them and do something differently. Even though this was far worse than what we had experienced, it didn't hurt our chances by being well trained, especially from the storm on our way to Australia and the gales that hit us en route to New Zealand. Most of all, we learned to tough it out, to stick with it, and, in Winston Churchill's words, "Never give in."

N 20°46.9′ E 37°10.3′

Email / April 6, 2005 / Three Days and Counting

The Red Sea gets its name from the color everything turns as it becomes covered in sand. At least that's the way we see it. We've been waiting for three days for the winds to calm down. In the meantime, sand and dust blowing from the desert shore are turning *Julia* a shade of pale, reddish brown. There's dust in the sails and rigging, and to protect the winches, we have them covered with canvas and plastic bags. It's permeated down below on the floor, in our sheets, our clothes, our nostrils and ears, and we haven't left the boat. It's too choppy, even at anchor, to put the dinghy in the water, so there are no shore excursions. We've been watching movies, reading, cleaning up from 24 hours of hell, and cooking, which is getting increasingly creative as the fresh foods are consumed, and we resort to canned and frozen consumables.

When we start to hear consistent forecasts of easing winds, then we'll move. In the meantime, we sit, until the last can of soup is gone—or the wind lets up—whichever comes first.

Email / April 8, 2005 / Working Our Way North

After four days in the relative safety of the coastal *marsa*, we timidly ventured out in a 15-knot wind to continue our journey north. We felt great trepidation as we no longer trust any forecasts. Once the wind dropped, we were surprised to look ashore and see an entire mountain range that had previously been blanketed by the sandstorms.

Distances seem easier to manage if we break them down into shorter passages. We still have 170 miles to go to Port Ghalib, where we will check into Egypt. Then it's 110 more miles to Hurgadah, and another 175 to Suez. From there, it's only two days transiting the Suez Canal, and we'll enter the Mediterranean. From where we are now, though, all of that seems like a long ways to go if it's upwind.

We were continuing to motor hard, but wouldn't you know it—suddenly, the engine shut down. "Oh no, now what?" I groaned. There is no worse sound than losing the power in your engine (well, maybe losing power in an airplane). Ken immediately jumped into action and determined the engine oil pressure switch, which activates the oil alarm and engine kill switch, had broken a lead.

As he handed me the tiny broken piece of metal I asked, "That little thing is shutting us down? We can put a man on the moon but we can't make an oil switch that doesn't break its leads off? Can it be fixed?"

"Nope."

"Well?"

Smiling, Ken said, "Remember when we were home last time and I asked you to order that part from Westerbeke because I said ours was weak...?"

"Yeah, I think so," I replied as my eyes lit up.

"That's the one."

I knew exactly where it was stored and went to the spare parts box. One hour later we were all smiling. And that's how I learned never to argue when Ken wants to buy spare parts. While this is exhausting, all is well aboard, and we know we're having the experience of a lifetime, so we're taking it as it comes. The Red Sea is not going to win this time.

We're not having much luck fishing either, and we've already thrown back a couple of barracuda, as they're not the best eating. More to the point, their teeth are too scary to bring them aboard—we're waiting for kingfish or tuna.

Personal Journal / April 10, 2005

After days of slogging our way into more north winds and avoiding lots of scary ship traffic, we arrived in Port Ghalib, Egypt. Our arrival was frustrating as we were told by three different officials to dock at a variety of places. I finally raised my voice at the harbormaster and that seemed to do the trick. He quickly agreed to the place I selected against the quay wall. Port Ghalib is a pit, with swarms of flies and mosquitoes, lots of construction, and a huge amount of sticky sand that felt like bits of wet cement as it blew onto the boat.

We said goodbye to CJ here as he was headed back to work. It was good to have him aboard, and I think he learned his lesson about the wind gods.

Email / April 20, 2005

Egypt is an exotic mix of the very old combined with a good attempt at modernization. We're on our third day off the boat, returning from an outstanding excursion to the city of Luxor: home to the Temple of Karnak, the Valley of the Kings (home to King Tut's tomb), the Valley of the Queens (where we felt more at home), the Luxor Temple, and Luxor Museum, all along the banks of the green Nile River. There is extraordinary history here wherever you turn. Most of the ancient ruins are more than 3,500 years old and were brought to life by a university-trained guide who even taught us to read hieroglyphics. Ken caught on right away, but it's still alien to me. The contrast between old and new is ever present, especially when we drive in an air-conditioned mini-van to the entrance of a tomb, which was built by hand in this blazing heat thousands of years ago.

Egypt is amazingly inexpensive and our three-star hotel, which was only $40 a night, even boasted a rooftop pool overlooking the Nile. Watching the river traffic, we could only imagine the hustle and bustle of commerce that plied these waters millennia ago. While the study of the people, the culture, and ruins are fascinating, we tired of the incessant fascination with death that seems to prevail in every story we hear about the ancient Egyptians.

The police and military are everywhere—all for tourist protection. In fact, our van was required to join a military procession, which travels three times a day to and from Luxor. The morning of departure, six military vehicles escorted the convoy of some 50 buses and vans—all required to go through various checkpoints along the only travel route allowed. We were not sure if it was such a smart idea though—seems the terrorists would know right where to hit. The Egyptians are friendly, and although they always have their hand out for *baksheesh*, if you play their game, you can get things done.

Nick arrived from Switzerland yesterday and will sail with us as long as time permits. It's great to have him back aboard; his good sense of humor and solid sailing abilities have already provided a much needed lift to the atmosphere onboard *Julia*.

N 26°50′ E 33°57′

Email / April 22, 2005 / Dolphin Encounters

We have made peace with the Red Sea, or at least a truce. It's calm, quiet, and the sea abounds with life. The anchorage was calm, and we went board surfing behind the dinghy, skimming right over the top of the reef. Later in the afternoon, we saw a pod of dolphins swimming 200 yards from the boat. We hopped into the dinghy, motored over to where they were playing and turned off the motor.

I slipped quietly into the water with my mask and snorkel and was immediately face-to-face with a 6-foot bottlenose dolphin. It was 5 feet away when it turned to expose its underbelly, then bounced its head back and forth to get a better look, nodded up and down and started talking to me, "Eeeeiiiii, eeeeiiiii, eeeeiiiii." Incredible. I swam toward the magnificent animal; at first it scooted away but then came right back, and we played around each other for about a few minutes before it finally swam off to join the rest of the pod. If ever there was a moment of bliss in my life, I think this was it. It was the closest encounter I've had with a dolphin in the wild and an absolutely exhilarating experience. I was left with a giddy smile on my face that just won't quit.

N 27°48.5′ E 33°52.1′

Email / April 25, 2005 / There Are No Plumbers at Sea

At sea it's the little things that count. We discovered the little plastic pull-tab from a vinegar jar had fallen into the toilet and stopped it all up. In searching for this culprit, we also discovered the electric motor had corroded. Thanks to Ken's creativity and the inventive use of some dental floss to hold the new motor brushes in place, everything is now flowing properly. Small victories like this keep us motivated.

N 27°56′ E 33°54′

I couldn't help asking myself why we had so many mechanical problems aboard. From engines to toilets to batteries, we seemed to be plagued by breakdowns. Did we buy the wrong equipment? Had I bought a lemon? Nope. It's fairly common for almost all cruisers to experience similar problems. The more systems you have, the more problems will follow.

We had equipped Julia with nearly every system possible, from a deep freezer to watermaker. Everything eventually corrodes in saltwater, from electrical connections to hose clamps, and we were using the boat hard almost daily under intense conditions. Most of the marine equipment available isn't made for such hard sailing but rather for the recreational sailor. Cruisers talk about two things when they get together: the weather and what's broken and how to fix it. It just comes with the territory. While there wasn't much I could do about the failures of equipment, I tried continually to work on my reactions when things broke.

✉ **Email** / May 2, 2005 / Completion of the Red Sea Passage
We made it. We're in Port Suez, top of the Red Sea, and have thus completed the toughest 1,200 miles yet. Even so, late last night the wind came up to 30 knots on the nose in order to give us a last slap in the face before our arrival.

Today, the Suez Canal Authority came aboard to measure *Julia*. It's a complicated system based upon how much wheat your vessel can carry through the canal. I'm not kidding. By determining how much wheat your boat can hold, you are charged accordingly by that volume, even if you're not carrying grain. It goes something like this: Take the interior volume of the main salon minus the toilets, minus the beds, add in the cupboards, minus the engine room, add back in any closets, multiply by some strange factor and presto! You have your volume times a dollar and there's your measurement. Those variables are, of course, greatly influenced by the exchange of Marlboro cigarettes, T-shirts, and anything else the measurer can extract as *baksheesh*.

"Captain, I am liking to take a souvenir from each boat; perhaps a camera or a watch, or new shoes?"

"Excuse me? " I replied under lifted eyebrows.

"You know, it is something to remember you by, perhaps those binoculars or a GPS?"

"Oh, look. I have a brand new camera for your children. It will last for years." (Or as long as 24 pictures will last) Tomorrow, we'll find out how we did when we get the bill for our canal transit.

Once again it's toast time. To striking a truce with the north wind and the Red Sea and the boat measuring agent and our eventual safe passage. In other words, here's to getting our butts bashed for an entire month by the evil north wind and the Red Sea from hell.

Last night on watch, I wore socks for the first time in three years, and tonight we'll sleep with a real blanket over us. Fantastic, we won't be sleeping in wet, sweaty sheets.

N 29°56.8 E 32°34.3

Email / May 5, 2005 / The Suez Canal

We awoke early to join the first yacht convoy of the day heading north into the Suez Canal. For this section, they have changed from the old system of having a pilot aboard each yacht to having all of the yachts go in a procession led by one pilot boat. The 0500 convoy finally got under way at 0830.

The pilot boat set the pace at about 6.5 knots and there was a 2-knot current in our favor, making easy-do of the 45-mile transit to the Ismalia Yacht Club. We motored by Egyptian soldiers stationed up and down the canal on both sides, military bridges poised to swing into action, lots of machine gun stations, military trucks along the roads, all of it looking rather ominous until you look closer. Then you see the smiling soldier sitting back with his cigarette, gun pointed into the air, joking with the other soldiers, and they happily wave to us as we pass. Ruins from the 1967 Six Day War litter the banks of the canal: tanks, trucks, and blown-up buildings, all with "No Photo" signs posted. Do they fear we will pass them on to the enemy?

In addition to the large military presence, there are several Suez Canal Authority stations monitoring every vessel going up the canal, making sure they have paid and are on the day's approved list of transiting boats. The *baksheesh* and camera gift to our measurer worked well, as our total cost for transit was a reasonable $425. As with buying fuel in Yemen, they only take U.S. dollars—in cash. Some cruisers were complaining about the price of the canal transit on the radio net. Ken picked up the microphone and said, "You do have a choice—you could go around Africa."

Huge ships passed no more than three or four boat lengths away, the crews waving and staring in amazement at our small vessel. There were

tankers, car carriers, and container cargo ships of all shapes and sizes. It was fascinating watching the commerce of the world moving along throughout the day. We couldn't help but feel part of a larger global picture as we were making the enormous transition from where we have been for the past three years. Entry into the Mediterranean will close huge chapters: The South Pacific, Oceania, and Asia. And other adventures are going to happen as we head into Western civilization for the first time in 17 months. And we'll pay for it, too. Here we are paying 10 cents a litre (about 40 cents a gallon) for diesel fuel; in the Med it will be at least $1 a litre. Here we pay $9 per night for a marina; there it will be over $100 per night. That's okay. We're ready for a taste of the Western world.
N 30°35′ E 32°16′

Email / May 10, 2005 / The Great Pyramids
I always knew someday I would see The Great Pyramids of Egypt, and that day has arrived. We said our sad farewells to Nick as he left for Switzerland. With Harvey and Jean of *Guitar*, we hired a private car and driver for the 70 miles from Ismalia to Cairo. The car was a 1975 black Mercedes sedan with green window curtains, which must have made us look like dignitaries—or silly tourists who paid too much for their transport.

First stop: the pyramids. In awe, we stood before the three Great Pyramids of Cheops, Khafre, and Menkaure. Upgraded tickets allowed us *inside* the Pyramid of Cheops, the biggest of them all, requiring a climb up a steep, narrow, and claustrophobic stone passageway, 130 feet to the inner tomb. Once we reached the 10-by-10-foot king's chamber in the middle of the pyramid, our imaginations went wild, picturing thousands of people toiling and dying for the sake of these enormous monuments to their kings. The chambers were cool in temperature, but the air was thick and heavy, and smelled over-used. Being in the pyramid's interior was a spooky experience, and we took stock of the fact that we were inside the heart of a 5,000 year-old man-made stone mountain. It was an extraordinary feeling. In contrast to three years in the wide open, I felt cramped and trapped. The throngs of tourists packed into the small spaces only increased my claustrophobia; we stayed just long enough to get the creeps, then made our way back down to the entrance and fresh air.

Next, it was Ken's turn to fulfill his wish as we roamed the ruins of the Great Sphinx of Giza. We bought the usual *tchotchkes* from vendors who seemed to multiply with every purchase we made. We toured more tombs and pyramids at Sakkara, an enormous burial ground 1 mile wide by 4 miles long. By the end of the day, we'd pretty much reached our limit on tombs, sacrifice and the afterlife.

Tired of the focus on death but knowing this was most likely a one-time opportunity, we completed our overdose with a visit to the famous Egyptian Museum in Cairo. It really is amazing to see all of what was taken out of the tombs, especially the intact items from King Tut's tomb, such as bowls, vases, jewelry, statues, and gold...so much gold. The museum has scores of mummies and sarcophagi; they are stacked floor to ceiling in piles—waiting—I presume for a more prominent place to display them.

Cairo is one of the most densely populated cities in the world, and it is the very definition of crowded. Swarms of people jam the sidewalks, donkey carts are oblivious to their motorized counterparts, and vendors line the side streets selling everything from lemons to shoes. We were in need of peppercorns for the boat and found a seller not far from our hotel. One kilo, or 2.2 pounds, was ours for $2. I didn't have the heart to negotiate. The Muslim Salat, or prayer, is blared over loudspeakers through the city five times a day, starting well before sunrise. We've become quite used to it, though, as the singsong recital became part of our day the moment we arrived in Oman two months ago.

We like to explore a city on foot, but in Cairo doing so can be dangerous. It is intensely crowded, and the traffic is endless; you feel like a sardine about to be gobbled up by a much bigger fish. The density of traffic makes the Manhattan rush hour seem like a country drive. The stoplights are merely for decoration, certainly not for controlling traffic. And it seems that to make a car operate, you must press the horn with the accelerator at the same time.

Our walk downtown forced us to cross a ten-lane boulevard; that is, if there had been painted lanes. Crossing that street will rank high on the list of the most dangerous things we have done on the entire trip. The locals easily crossed the street while we darted from space to space, trying to make eye contact with drivers so they would see our plight and slow down for us. It was kind of like playing dodge ball—but with Renaults, Fiats and Volkswagens. We hired a donkey-pulled carriage for our return to the hotel.

For the most part, people here are friendly, and when they find out we are American, they're even friendlier. The local police, of which there are thousands, are determined we have an enjoyable and safe time in their city and country. Access to our hotel is through two layers of police and a metal detector. I wish I could say it made me feel safer, but at least they're making a good showing. The policeman in front, always smoking and leaning on his gun, barrel pointed down at the gritty street, only looks up if the metal detector beeps.

The Egyptians we have spoken with are upset about the country's internal strife, which is hurting tourism, and most don't care about the fundamentalist faction, wishing it would cease. The day before our arrival in Cairo, another bomb went off, and the police tracked down and supposedly shot and killed the terrorists. Or so they reported. I'm skeptical because their view of history is slightly skewed—we have seen several monuments to the 1967 war in which "Egypt won an astounding victory." Hmmm....

The plan is to transit the second half of the "Marlboro Canal" tomorrow. Lately, though, U.S. warships have been coming through the canal and arrive unannounced, for obvious reasons. When they are in the canal, all traffic stops. We'll see if our pilot arrives at the scheduled 0600 tomorrow. I'll set my alarm for 0800.

Ismalia is the last chance for cheap diesel, and every boat headed to the Mediterranean wants to fill their tanks at these prices. However, visiting yachts don't get the cheap rates because of a tax placed on fuel delivered to your boat. Still, the officials underestimated the cruising community's creativity and desire to save a buck.

Between the boats and the streets of Ismalia lies a formidable barrier of guards and customs officials who take their job of checking our passports and papers very seriously—every day—in spite of the fact that they know our names by memory and have enough cigarettes from us to last a year.

We were told each boat was allowed two jerry jugs of fuel from a gas station in town. As 10 gallons is only a drop in the bucket to most cruisers, a bunch of us got together to pool resources. There was Simon, the Englishman from *Ocean Pirate*; Thomas, the Belgian from *Mercator*; Will, the Welshman from *Brandamajio*; Harvey, the Englishman/Floridian from *Guitar*, and Pete, the American from *Sojourner*. We all had one common goal: cheap fuel. With *Julia*, we represented six boats leaving the marina, each with two jugs, which had been pooled from every participating boat. As the guard pocketed a pack of Marlboros from each boat, he didn't question a dozen jerry jugs leaving the marina empty. The next challenge was finding taxis, as not many drivers want to stop and pick up yachties carrying gas cans. Eventually we piled into three of them; jugs and all, and headed to the nearest gas station where we loaded up with clean, cheap diesel for 40 cents a gallon...and another pack of cigarettes as a pumping fee.

Approaching the gate, the guard put up his hand. "You can't bring that fuel in here."

"We talked to the other guard on the way out, and he said it was okay," Harvey said with frustration. Some people didn't like the system of *baksheesh*, but I found it easy, and usually a pack of smokes is cheaper than a cash tip.

"That was a different agent, not me," declared the official.

"These two are only for my boat," Will innocently expressed.

"And these two are mine," Pete said.

"Looks like you're running out of cigarettes," I added while handing over another pack.

With that, the gate swung open and in we walked with 60 gallons of diesel for one of our boats. This process was repeated six times until we were ready to drop from heat exhaustion. It really wasn't worth the savings—it rarely is—but we enjoyed helping each other.

CHAPTER 16

Western Civilization Is So...
Civilized

"Today is life—the only life you are sure of. Make the most of today. Let the winds of enthusiasm sweep through you. Live to-day with gusto."

DALE CARNEGIE

✉ **Email** / May 13, 2005 / Mazel Tov
We've definitely left the Third World behind us. What a contrast from Egypt. Not necessarily better, just different. Israel is a modern First World country with warm and friendly welcoming people, drinkable water, Internet and phones that work, good food, and functioning ATMs, and, of course, higher prices to support those services. Our arrival coincides with Israel's Independence Day and the Star of David is flying from cars, buildings, boats and houses. There are celebrations everywhere; we have sailed right into the middle of a huge party. Strangely, nobody seems very nervous about the fact that rockets shot from the Gaza Strip recently landed a mere 15 kilometers (9 miles) south of here. Maybe I'll get used

to it like the locals have, but for now that seems too close for my comfort.

Thirty miles from the coast, we received our first radio call from the Israeli Navy: "Little white sailboat with blue trim at position 31°39'N 34°03'E, on course 79°, at a speed of 5 knots, who are you? Where did you come from? When did you leave there? How big is your boat? How many people onboard? What is your citizenship? What is your crew's citizenship? Why are you coming to Israel? What is your current position (the one they just told me)? How fast are you going (the speed they just gave me)? And so on. How did they know we were there? How could they see us?

My first response was, "Where are you calling from? How are you reaching us on VHF? How can you see us?" I knew VHF doesn't go beyond line of sight or follow the curve of the earth, so 30 miles is pushing the limit.

Their response was a firm but polite, "We see you. Please answer the questions." So I did. After playing 20 questions, we were required to send an email to the navy with our pertinent information, which we had sent two days earlier, but they supposedly hadn't received it, so we sent it again. Minutes later, we received another call from a different navy radio operator: "Who are you? Where did you come from? When did you leave there?" taking us through the whole process all over again. It was getting tedious, and for some reason reminded me of an elderly uncle at a Jewish wedding repeating the same question, "So...tell me again why a nice Jewish boy like you isn't married?"

Moments later we received a visit from a jet-powered navy gunboat headed towards us at an astonishing speed. "Larry, you want to come topside for a minute?" asked Ken.

"Not now, I'm busy on the radio with the navy," I replied.

"I *really* think you should come up here *now*," Ken said in a tone that was clearly no longer a request.

I climbed the five steps of the ladder in two. "What *is* that?" As we both stared in amazement, the gunboat that had only been a speck on the horizon a minute ago, zoomed straight for us at what we later found out was more than 60 knots. When it got to within 50 yards, it slowed, turned sharply, circled us a couple times, took a good look at us through the sights of its big guns on the foredeck, and when satisfied we were indeed innocent tourists, took off in a flash. It wasn't exactly *aloha,* but at least they didn't blast us out

Relaunching *Julia* after repairs in Phuket. Note the smoke from the 999 good luck firecrackers under the bow.

Camels roaming freely in Salalah, Oman.

Vendors and their vegetable carts at an open-air market in Yemen.

Keeping cool in the shade, a Yemenite smokes apple-flavored tobacco.

Aden, Yemen, a city of fascinating contrasts. Women clothed in traditional burkas and men wearing casual western garb.

Julia, anchored in Aden, Yemen, just 100 yards from where the USS Cole was attacked in 2000.

An unusually mercurial, yet ominous morning in the Red Sea.

Preparing for a dive at Sanganeb Reef in the Red Sea.

Sunrise over the Red Sea.

Sharing the road with the commerce of the world in the Suez Canal.

Strawberries in abundance on a Cairo street.

Heading north past Mt. Sinai, Egypt, in the Red Sea.

Nick, my trustworthy friend and capable sailor.

Cairo's dense traffic borders ancient history.

Egypt's stunning Temple of Karnak at night.

"Please, sir, only $1 to have your photo taken with the camel."

Queen Hatshepsut's palace in Deir el-Bahri, Egypt.

Israeli soldiers in Jerusalem take an ice cream break.

Anchored with *Guitar* at Skopia Lamani, one of our favorite anchorages in Turkey.

The 2,000-year-old Library of Celsus in Ephesus, Turkey.

Dove Bars delivered by the ice cream boat in Turkey.

An abundance of fruits and vegetables greeted us weekly at the open-air market in Turgutreis, Turkey.

Julia, docked at Hasan's restaurant in Turkey, just before frying our electrical system.

The blindingly white-washed walls of the streets of Mykonos. Fun for shopping and easy to get lost in the maze.

Kastelorizon, Greece, as seen from the top of the island during an early morning hike.

Meltemi gale-force winds ripped our mainsail from luff to leech while en route to Amorgos, Greece.

Transiting the Corinth Canal in Greece. It's only 15 feet wider than *Julia* is long!

Twilight on the quaint town of Cefalu, Sicily, as seen from *Julia*.

Skiing in foul-weather gear atop Glacier Paradise, Zermatt, Switzerland.

Provisioning for the Atlantic crossing required much planning and creative stowing.

Julia under sail, headed for the Canary Islands.

Late afternoon downwind sailing across the Atlantic.

We became accustomed to 20-foot seas during the Atlantic crossing.

L to R: Francis, Ken, Larry, and Patrik go tropical on Union Island in the Caribbean.

Plumerias in bloom on Union Island, The Grenadines.

A spotted box fish in the extraordinary Mayreau Gardens, Tobago Cays.

Julia, as seen from the top of mast while checking the rigging—and taking in the view.

A deserted beach in the Los Roques Islands, Venezuela.

Ken and Larry in Guayraca Bay on the north coast of Colombia.

Walking the streets of Cartagena, Colombia, with Ken, Nancy, and Ted.

A Kuna Indian lad selling fresh fish in the San Blas Islands, Panama.

A giant neon arrow points the entrance to the Panama Canal.

Entering the first lock of the Panama Canal at night.

Ken awaits the opening of the last gate of the Panama Canal, returning us to our home ocean, the Pacific.

Heeled over, a 25-ton boat makes an impressive bow wave.

The tiny marina in Golfito, Costa Rica.

Our room with a view: sunset from the aft cabin porthole.

Nearly six years after departure, *Julia* sails back under the Golden Gate Bridge on August 4, 2007.

of the water. Shortly after the boat departed, we received another radio call, stating simply, "*Julia*, you are clear to enter Israeli waters."

Our route from Port Said would take us near Israel's "natural gas platform." Nine miles away from it, the radio crackled to life again: "*Julia*, this is the Israeli Navy. You are too close to the platform; your present course takes you within 4.5 miles, and you must be at least 5 miles from the platform in all directions." Among ourselves, we questioned whether or not this really was a gas facility. We concluded it was an Israeli Defense Forces station used for communications, which sounds much more intriguing anyway.

Being a little insulted they were questioning my navigation skills, I told the radio operator to stand by while I checked our route. Sure enough, our route would have taken us slightly inside the 5-mile perimeter, so we altered course to allow a wider berth. The navy called again to thank us for changing course and advised us we would now be clear of the platform. Who *are* these guys?

Three people from Israeli security greeted us upon arrival at Ashkelon Marina. Wearing T-shirts, and with guns tucked into their jeans, they looked more like street kids than security forces. We recognized their profession from the official badges they wore around their necks. Ken and I were immediately separated to see if we answered their questions the same: "Who has been on the boat recently? When did you leave your last port? What were your last three ports? Why are you coming to Israel?" The questions kept coming and were followed with an inspection below and a chemical swipe test for explosives. We didn't mind, though, as they were only doing their job. They were handsome, too.

The questions began to take a very personal direction—too personal. "Mr. Jacobson, we understand you had to sell your home in Berkeley to go on this trip, and is it true you left your partner of 20 years to run off with your boyfriend, Ken, to go on a sailing trip? Why did you do this? Who would do such a thing?"

I stood dumbfounded. I knew Israeli intelligence was good, but this was over the top. As I was nervously about to answer these extremely personal questions, not able to keep a straight face, the security guys started to laugh. Out of the corner of my eye, I saw Pete from *Sojourner* standing on the dock doubled over with laughter. Pete and Julie, who arrived the day before, had made friends with the security guys, fed them all of this information, and got them to wind us up as a joke. The laughter subsided, and we became friends with the security people, always making sure to say our casual hellos when we saw them in the marina. We have made it to the inside of Israeli borders, and we feel secure.

We're looking forward to setting up some tours and seeing more of Israel, so we'll be here a good week or two. It's frustrating, because there aren't many signs in English, and for the life of me, I can't remember much of my Hebrew school studies. I can say, "Please, thank you, hello, and goodbye," and am working on, "Do you come here often—would you like to have a drink later?"

Staring in amazement at the high rises and freeways, we recognize this port marks quite a milestone. What will our lives be like in a busy, cultured world as opposed to our relaxing under palm trees? We needn't worry. One of the great things about cruising is the ability to move. Now think about that for a minute. If you're driven nuts by the loud rock music from the teenagers who live next door or Mrs. Kravitz's poodle pooping on your lawn, you're stuck with it. If we don't like our neighbors, we pull up the anchor, start the engine, and move.

This ability to change cities, countries, and cultures simply by lifting our anchor and sailing onward gives us an amazing feeling of freedom. I used to not like change—now I embrace and accept it as part of life in general. Cruising is indeed reflective of life; even if you're not on a boat with the ability to shift anchorages, while it may take more effort, you too can change your situation. Just start hauling up the anchor, in whatever form that may be.

Email / May 24, 2005 / Fields of Green
Every Sunday as a boy attending Hebrew school, I brought a dollar to temple that went towards planting a tree in Israel. It wasn't an option—everyone brought a dollar—every Sunday. I often wondered where the money went. Now I have the answer, and it's here in Israel's fields of green. For as far as the eye can see, there are pine forests, orange groves, vineyards, fruit farms, cornfields, and wheat fields that seem to go on forever. Where there was once only desert, rock and swamp, is an absolutely amazing expanse of green growth. These people, like none before them,

have actually adopted the land and made it work for them. Seeing what the Israelis have done with the land is a stark contrast to what we have seen in the countries recently visited, including Oman, Yemen, Eritrea, Sudan and Egypt. While there were lush farms near the Nile River, it was the only green we saw in any of those countries.

The Israelis are fiercely protective of their home, but they don't want to use their might—they want peace. Most of the locals we met are eager to live in peace with the Palestinians and support pulling out of the settlements. Even so, helicopter gun ships fly daily patrols south towards Gaza and until peace comes—if ever—they continue the military exercises.

At the marina we see groups of school children on excursions, singing, dancing, and enjoying themselves. They are happy to be alive, content with what they have, optimistic about the future, and are generally upbeat people. On the other hand, driving while honking and yelling (to no avail in the Cairo traffic), and living with *baksheesh* is the way of life in Egypt. We have seen a lot more hugging than yelling in Israel, and although traffic is heavy, the citizens seem to understand they are all in this together and don't blare their horns out of frustration. Israel is very high-tech, everyone has a cell phone, and calls go through on the first try. The other day, we took our IBM computer in for warranty service and had it back with a new display in an hour. We feel we have been transported back to the First World, and for now, our days of *baksheesh* are over. The contrasts between the Arab countries and Israel are striking, and it seems odd they even occupy the same point on the globe. I'm once again struck with how important it is to see the contrasts in life.

Tel Aviv blew away any notions I had of an ancient city, with a deli on every corner. This cosmopolitan metropolis is clearly a result of European influence; it reminds me of a coastal city in the Western Mediterranean, such as Barcelona or Nice. Much of the city's modern architecture was influenced by French and German refugees who built high-rise hotels along the water, a wonderful beach boardwalk (reminding me of Rio de Janeiro), cafes, restaurants, shops and wide boulevards with green meridians down their center.

To our surprise, we have stumbled into one of the largest gay communities in the Eastern Mediterranean. Yes, it's okay to be gay in Israel;

there are even laws to ensure equal rights, including military service. We went to a gay club the other night, and while we had to go through two security checks before entering, we took it in stride. The upbeat atmosphere and warm welcome more than makes up for this inconvenience, which guarantees our protection in the club. Not to mention that the security guys who frisked us were friendly, touchy feely, and very good looking.

In a rental car with Harvey and Jean, we drove to Jerusalem, which was much as I expected from an ancient walled city. We spent the afternoon wandering through the religious quarters of the city, roaming the tiny back streets, shopping for *tchotchkes*, ate bagels and cream cheese at a cafe, wailed at the wall, and absorbed the enormity of where we are.

From Jerusalem we drove to the Dead Sea for one of those things you just have to do—swim in the saltiest water at the lowest point on earth. You could float as if you were sitting in a chair, but don't put your head under because the heavy salinity of the water burns your lips...I learned the hard way. On to Masada where the Jews made a stand against the Roman Empire, but in the end committed suicide rather than be captured. Up the Zohr valley and back to Ashkelon Marina, we did it all in a day.

Who knew Israel was such a cool place?

Email / June 6, 2005 / Amazing Israel

I sit onboard fair *Julia* writing you in the sunset hour with a glass of Israeli chardonnay in hand. Tel Aviv continues to amaze and astonish us. It's a cross between Santa Monica and Manhattan, with happy families, romantic couples, and hopeful singles cruising the beach boardwalk, going out to cafes, fine restaurants, and the theater.

In spite of the daily military activity, Israelis are curiously happy. They sing, dance, and rejoice in life while living every day to its fullest. At a wedding party held at the yacht club, I asked someone in the midst of celebration and dancing, and as the helicopters flew overhead, "How can you live with the constant fear and danger of war?"

She replied with a lovely but intense smile: "Our army will take care of us—that is their job. Our job is to enjoy life." I looked at her and smiled, and as I walked away, I reflected on how much we are learning over and over again from these people. How important it is to enjoy the life we have now because you never know when it will be over.

We tour with our new friends Iris and Nava, whom we met at the marina when they noticed our rainbow flag. Iris stopped, pointed to the flag and said, "Us too!" See, it pays to advertise.

In particular, we've noticed the children here. From my observations, children are the same all over the world: always looking for fun and mischief; here the kids seem exceptionally happy. We came to Israel with the intentions of refueling and having a quick look around, but now we're rethinking our schedule. We like it here.

Personal Journal / July 3, 2005 / Magnetic Pull of Israel
It seems we can't leave. We came to Israel for fuel and planned to stay a week…and that was six weeks ago. Attended the gay parade, which attracted 100,000 people whose primary objective was to have a good time. It was a bit odd seeing snipers on the rooftop for "our protection," but we're getting used to it. Israel continues to hold us in her clutches.

Personal Journal / July 5, 2005
Every evening at 5, it's cocktail hour aboard *Julia*. Alex, the Ukrainian engineer; Igor, the sea captain; Yonatan, the fierce Israeli soldier; Liran, the hot bartender; Shawn, head of security at the marina; Roy, the marina dockmaster, and others from various countries all join us onboard. Alex, with a degree in engineering, left Ukraine with his wife and baby for the Promised Land and a better life. Shawn, a scrawny kid who looks like he couldn't hurt a flea explained why he was the head of security at the marina: "Because I'm the best shot in the Israeli army." Yonatan, named after the heroic soldier killed in the raid on Entebbe, tells us in no uncertain terms how they should deal with their unruly Arab neighbors. Liran, who was in the army, couldn't wait to get out and is now a bartender and fashion model. He hangs around because he wants us to take him along as crew to Turkey, even though he's never been on a sailboat before. He says he can cook, and he sure is easy on the eyes.

Ukrainian, Israeli, American, no matter; all borders disappear after a couple of vodkas.

Email / July 14, 2005 / The Boy Behind the Gate
The setting: the twilight hour in Tel Aviv and we sit aboard *Julia* listening to a live band playing easy jazz. We are the first boat inside the

locked gated area of Herzliya marina and have the best seats in the house.

I look up and see a boy with dark curly hair and big eyes standing behind the gate, staring at the boats, staring at me, and I see none other than myself so many years ago standing behind a similar gate, imagining a lifestyle I dreamed would someday be mine. I remember deciding then that I would settle for nothing less than being my own captain. I wanted to be the one sitting on the boat. Now I've made that happen. I hope that boy too will turn his dreams into reality and find himself on the inside—rather than outside—of the gate.

The helicopters fly overhead, the violence continues to heat up and another bomb blast recently went off 9 miles north of here; yet the Israelis are listening to French jazz at the marina. They are the experts in appreciating and getting all they can from life.

Enjoy life to it's fullest. Climb your mountain, cross your ocean, get your degree, get your promotion, quit your job, quit your career, marry, divorce, move, do whatever it takes to make you happiest in this life for, as far as I can tell, this is it; this is all we get. Get up, put your climbing boots on and go for it. Don't dream about life, live it!

Email / July 27, 2005

As they say here, "That's it." Meaning, we're through, it's done, move on... so that's what we are doing this morning. All systems willing and cooperating, we are departing Israel and heading to Turkey. That's it. Shalom to all.

Email / July 30, 2005 / Back at Sea

It's good to be back at sea again. After three months in Israel, we have now sailed far enough away from the coast that we won't be turning back. There was a moment when we considered turning around because the brand new refrigeration system stopped working just 100 miles at sea. At first we were depressed but attacked the problem with analytical minds, and lo and behold, we figured out what was wrong. The pump had sucked up a plastic bag into the sea strainer of the refrigeration cooling system. Not only have I learned how to fix things, but also that I *can* fix them.

N 35°34.6 E 30°53.1

CHAPTER 17

Turkey…Unwrapped

"A man who dares to waste one hour of time
has not discovered the value of life."
CHARLES DARWIN

Email / July 31, 2005 / We're Here, but Don't Tell

After a nearly perfect passage, we made landfall near Kekova, Turkey. While you're supposed to go straight to a check-in port upon arriving in a country, we decided to buck the system and sit at anchor for a couple of days first. The scenery is striking: *Julia* sits alone in a small cove 50 yards from the rocky coastline. Ruins of a castle rest atop a nearby craggy point, covered densely in clusters of green bushes. The high mountain peaks in the background are surprisingly steep; it's a classic anchorage for Turkey and we are soaking up all the beauty.

N 36°12.7′ E 29°53.5′

Email / August 4, 2005 / Stronger Than Jolt

Yesterday we dinghied to a tiny inhabited village of ancient stone houses. Above the village, a Roman castle sits on the edge of a surprisingly steep hill. We docked at Hasan's restaurant and were immediately picked up by Hamida, a 65-year-old local guide. She was *schlepping* her box of scarves, beads, and trinkets assuming (correctly) she would make a sale if she guided us to the castle. "I take you castle," she offered, forcing us to postpone our cold beer until later. She stopped a few times along the way to point out the various wild herbs and flowers, but mostly because we could barely keep up with her. We were huffing and puffing our way up the hill while she stood with her hands on her hips as if saying, "You fat old tourists, come on, I don't have all day." Upon reaching the castle, we were rewarded with expansive views, and it was such a beautiful setting we wanted to stay. Racing back to *Julia*, we hauled up the anchor and brought her over to dock in front of Hasan's.

Docking includes electricity and water and is free with dinner at the restaurant; we were excited to be able to run our new air conditioner. When I plugged the power cord into our ship's outlet, my body recoiled from the 220-volt shock making my right arm shake uncontrollably. I tried to shout but no voice came out. I tried to let go, but it was as if my hand were glued to the plug. It was only a couple seconds but long enough to scare the daylights out of me.

Afterwards, I was stunned; smoke poured from the outlet where the cord plugs into *Julia*, and the electrical panel switch melted. Dan Sehnal from *Dakare* came racing over from the anchorage to assist. We had met Dan and Karen, his wife, in Israel where our boats were docked side by side, and we've since become good friends. Dan knew something about electricity and worked on the problem with Ken; obviously I wasn't willing to even touch an electrical plug. It turns out the wires in *Julia's* outlet had been reversed for the Israeli marinas, and we didn't know the plugs are the opposite in Turkey.

Personal Journal / August 15, 2005

Yesterday was Mom's 83rd birthday, and we talked on the phone before her party in Long Beach. I wish I'd been there to give her a big hug. I told her I'd be home for her 85th, and she seemed very happy to hear that news. Sometimes the world seems so big and friends and family so far away. Others say it's a small world, but I don't think those folks ever tried to circumnavigate the globe.

Email / August 18, 2005 / Cruising Again

It's easy to tell when we're cruising again. We lose track of what day, date, and even month it is, and we forget how long we've been anchored somewhere. We're currently at Kastelorizon, a small island in Greece a couple of miles from Kas, Turkey. We're not officially checked into Greece yet, but we took down the Turkish flag, put up the Greek one, and nobody seems to mind that we're here, especially the restaurants and cafes lining the waterfront. We dinghy right up to the restaurant's front door, the waiter takes our line, and we tie up for a delicious cheap meal of seafood, olives, stuffed grape leaves, and wine. Our original purpose in coming to Greece is the "Booze and Bacon Run," where cruisers come to stock up on all of the things that aren't sold in Muslim Turkey—mainly alcohol and pork.

This tiny town must be the inspiration for many children's books, with houses and shops built to three-quarter size, painted in gingerbread colors of yellow, purple, pink, orange, and of course, the famous Greek white-wash, all with fresh geraniums and bougainvillea flowers hanging from the window sills. In contrast to being awakened by the haunting Morning Salat blaring over loudspeakers, we are instead clanged awake by church bells. It's as good a reason as any to wake up, so Dan and I hiked the steep trail to the top of the mountain for the view back at the bay, where *Julia* and *Dakare* lay perfectly still in the early morning calm.

We haven't dived since the Red Sea, so we were eager to get underwater in the Mediterranean. Yesterday, with Dan and Karen, we took the plunge. With 100-foot visibility, we swam through deep rock canyons, over huge boulders that looked like they had only recently tumbled from the mountains, over and around a shipwreck, and witnessed some amazing light refractions and cobalt blue colors I have never seen before. I was hoping the ship was an ancient Greek wreck, but it looked more like a fairly modern-day fishing boat. While there were no coral or other tropical features, it felt like we were diving into the lost city of Atlantis. At least that's where my imagination was going.

N 36°09′ E 029°36.1′

 Email / August 20, 2005 / No More Palm Trees

At this anchorage in Skopia Lamani, we can hear the wind

whistling through the pine and olive trees that line the shore. The hot wind has been howling all day as we sit securely anchored and tied to the shoreline 10 feet from our stern. What a contrast this setting is from the usual complement of palm trees. The anchor rests in 80 feet of water and we're backed up to the shore with two long lines tied to olive trees to hold us in place. It's a new way of anchoring for us, but it's how they do it here. When in Turkey....

The ice cream boat just pulled up on our starboard. Two teenagers in a small wooden boat, with a big outboard motor and a freezer full of Dove Bars, waved and grinned as they held up a picture board of the various flavors. It was clear they were used to this sort of nonverbal sales call and probably knew they already had closed the deal. How could we resist? We love the ice cream boat, and its crew seems to know exactly where we're anchored every day. Additionally, other boats have come by offering fresh vegetables, olive oil, fish, eggs, and pretty much anything else we might want. What a place. When was the last time you had ice cream and bread delivered to you with a smile?

N 36°38.6′ E 28°51.8′

Email / September 10, 2005

We're anchored at Keci Buku in Turkey, a beautiful wide sweeping bay surrounded by tall mountains and pine forests. The water is a deep green, clear, clean, and warm enough to enjoy an evening swim. The hot wind blows gently down the towering cliffs bringing the smell of pine, making it seem as though we are anchored in a large mountain lake rather than the sea.

The best times cruising are because of the company we keep with other sailors. We're enjoying René and Ginette Besson, our new friends from Switzerland who coincidentally are good friends with Nick. I guess it is a small world after all. They're both retired, sailing on a 28-foot boat, and have a big German shepherd named Nuska. How they all live together on that tiny boat is beyond me.

Personal Journal / September 11, 2005

Mike and his son Ben have arrived on their new boat, *Wind Sea'n,* which was recently delivered from the factory in Slovenia. Ben's head has healed from his fall in Vanuatu, and there's hardly even a scar, as kids mend quickly. Mike and I kayak daily together, pushing each other physically and challenging each other mentally with hours of discussions about life and relationships. We talk about my relationship with Ken, and then how Mike would like a partner—female, of course.

As we paddle, we share personal secrets, and we both recognize we're lucky to have this friendship. We push ourselves harder, each trying to pull away from the other, but we're well matched. Mike struggles to catch me, and I yell back at him, "You can't paddle worth a crap!"

"You paddle like a girl," Mike shouts back, now digging in deep.

"We'll see about that!" We stopped talking, and with sweat dripping, sprinted back to where the boats were anchored. I beat him, but he says he let me. He's a good buddy and we laugh a lot.

N 36°45.6 E 28°07.5

Email / September 15, 2005 / Anchoring Fun

Anchoring in the Mediterranean is a challenge. At Kuruka Bucu, we sit in a cove with our bow anchor set in 50 feet of water and our stern backed up to the forested shore where a 150-foot line tied to an olive tree holds us tight. The water is such a clear blue we can see the chain all the way to its end. It's important to drop the anchor in fairly deep water because there is so much grass growing in the shallow depths that it can't always dig in adequately. If we drop it in 50 feet or more, there is less grass and it has a better chance of digging in to sand. Once the anchor is set hard by backing down, one of us takes the long line ashore, either by dinghy or by swimming, and ties it to the nearest sturdy pine or olive tree. This is a process much easier said than done and is mixed with laughter, animated waving, hand signals, and sweat.

The real fun is in watching the charter boaters do the same process. Some of these folks are people who book one week at a time, once every who-knows-how-many years, and have little clue as to what they're doing when it comes to "parking the boat." This evening, we were entertained by several boats as they tried to set their anchors with far too little chain out, then dragged the anchor as they backed towards shore, nearly ran over the person they had swimming their too-short line towards shore, and then started the process over and over again. We poured a fresh cocktail every time we heard someone screams "Hey! Look out!" and we were toasted in no time.

We were the unlikely but obvious entertainers yesterday as we made two failed attempts before successfully setting our own anchor in those long grasses. We have learned to do our share of laughing at ourselves. Hmm, wonder if anyone got toasted watching us because we must have certainly provided the amusement.

N 36°44.8 E 27°53.7

✉ **Email** / September 24, 2005 / Pick a Place

Two days ago, when discussing which direction to sail and where to go next, Ken said, "Let's go somewhere close by, not a long passage."

We agreed, maybe a place 5 or 10 miles away would be good, so we looked at the chart. "Okay, how about this place?" I asked, pointing to a brown, amoeba-shaped spot on the computer. "It looks like a nice island with lots of anchorages." I wasn't wearing my glasses.

"Larry, zoom in on that and put your glasses on. That's 100 miles away," Ken said.

"Oops, well it looked closer on the chart, but hey, look what the island is—it's Mykonos!" One hundred miles is less than 24 hours away, and I had always wanted to go to there. "You do know it's the gay capital of the Mediterranean…think of the nightlife, the beautiful beaches, the hot nude men…."

"Sold," Ken said. "Let's go to Mykonos!" And here we are.

✉ **Email** / September 28, 2005 / Greece Is the Word

Mykonos. The desert-like landscape reminds us of Arizona, and the whitewash houses, all built in the same spare fashion by law, are a vivid contrast to the brown hills and shimmering blue water. We're anchored at Elia Beach and enjoying swimming, lazing around on the beach, and feeling very comfortable on this openly gay island. The town is a beautiful mixture of shops, galleries, and restaurants lining the narrow streets. And this maze-like series of streets is so easy to get lost in, we joke that the only way out is to buy something from a shop and ask for directions. While these walking streets are clean enough to eat off, there are more than enough restaurants to fill the need.

Nightclubs abound and we have even stayed up late to go out with our friend Katerina, the Queen of Mykonos (one of the best professional guides in Greece whom we used to work with in my previous business life). She has taken us under her wing, determined to show us the best of the island. We can't seem to get on the local land schedule of dinner at 11 pm and then dancing at 2 am. For us, 9 pm is late, and it's a major effort to stay up until midnight, so we're happy to enjoy Mykonos by day. The next big move will be to Super Paradise beach, a couple miles away. Then it's a short sail to the island of Delos to see the ancient ruins, a distance of about 5 miles.

 Personal Journal / October 5, 2005

The sun was barely up when we heard, *crunch!*

"What was that? Larry, get up!" Ken shouted as he grabbed his under-wear in one hand and headed towards the forward cabin.

"Sounded like we hit something…or something hit us," I said, heading topside, not bothering with underwear. Ken popped his head out the for-ward cabin hatch as I scrambled onto the foredeck in time for us to both be staring at a 38-foot charter boat banging repeatedly into our anchor roller.

"Hey! Hey! Wake up! Hey! Hello!!!" Ken was screaming at the boat, which had no signs of life onboard.

"Help me fend it off; they must be asleep," I said. There we were in the early morning, Ken with his underwear still in his hand, and me naked as a jaybird, pushing this boat around trying to get it off of *Julia*, and then, as if in slow motion, a young couple, equally naked, stepped into their cockpit rubbing their sleepy eyes and saying, "Huh?"

"You dragged; help us push!" Ken said to them sternly. But they were so flustered, they just stood there looking dumbfounded.

Having no idea if they even spoke English, I shouted: "Start your en-gine!" I guess they heard that. Without uttering a word, they motored off, dragging their anchor along with them. They never said, "Sorry." Never looked back, or came back.

We looked at each other and started to laugh. "Bloody Mary?" Ken asked.

CHAPTER 18

A Bang-Up End of Season

*"We are tied to the ocean. And when we go back to the sea,
whether it is to sail or to watch—we are going back from
whence we came."*
JOHN F. KENNEDY

Email / October 11, 2005

Accidents happen, but I never thought this would happen to us.
We wanted to end the season with a bang; couldn't we have achieved it
some other way?

We were moving from Ornos Bay to a calmer anchorage with a nicer
beach. Checking the chart, we both approved of our route; it was close
to shore between the island and a big rock outcrop. The chart showed
32 feet of water and no underwater rocks. I was at the helm; we had no
sail up, engine in neutral, and were still going 5 knots because of the
strong tailwind. As expected, I saw the depth of 32 feet. One second later,
the reading fell to 16 feet under the keel, then 8 feet, and one second
after that, we hit. And hit *hard*. The sounds were sickening—the heart-
stopping noises of fiberglass when slammed against granite: *Craaaack,*

Crrrunch, Griiiind, and then a big solid thud.

The boat shuddered severely as it stopped. We went flying; me into the wheel and Ken into the companionway. Scraping and grinding, *Julia* rode up the huge rock until a good 3 feet of the hull was out of the water. There was no time to think and not much to say; action was needed.

"Reverse! Reverse!" Ken shouted at me. I threw the engine in reverse and swung the rudder hard over to starboard and, after the longest 10 seconds, we spun off the rock and backed out of the shallows. "Take the helm," I told Ken, but he was already there beside me with his hands on the wheel. I leapt down the five-stair ladder in one jump and began pulling up the floorboards, fully expecting to see a flood of seawater. I was shaking so badly I could hardly find a flashlight, even though it was right where it was supposed to be. Light in hand, I found no leaks anywhere but kept the floors open to keep an eye on the bilges. A quick glance at the electrical panel showed that none of the four automatic bilge pumps were running—a good sign we weren't taking on water. We seemed to be in one piece.

"What do we do if there's a hole?" Ken asked.

Nervously, I said, "Try to plug it, but if we can't, then we'll have to run her up onto the beach. I don't see any water coming in—yet." Strange images began flashing though my head: Like in the movies aboard a sinking ship, there were bells and alarms ringing, and crew scrambling to their stations. Then came images of the life raft, beaching the boat, plugging a gaping hole in the hull, and ultimately, our safety. Except this wasn't a movie.

With Ken at the helm, we motored to Psarou Bay, a mile from where we hit the rock, and quickly dropped anchor on a beautiful soft sandy bottom. Instantly, we were overboard with mask and fins to check the damage.

We didn't sink. I am so relieved! In fact, I'm amazed and impressed with how well we fared. Only the keel is damaged: There's a big chunk taken out of the leading edge of it, 8 inches long, but only half an inch deep. Some fiberglass ripped off the bottom, a big piece of fiberglass is missing on the side, and there are deep scratches along the side. We were lucky to have hit low on the keel, saving us from damaging the integrity of the hull itself.

I'm still beating myself up. "Oh, what an idiot you are for taking the inside route to save a few minutes! Is this where it's all going to end...all this way around the world and then sunk by a rock in Mykonos right in front of a nude beach?"

Personal Journal / October 11, 2005

I should have put the engine in reverse as soon as I saw the depth shallow under 32 feet, which is what the chart shows. I was more frightened than I expected I would be, and as I write, I'm still shaking. The sea reminds me: Be humble, don't take things for granted, and always stay sharp. One more thing; it's usually not the sea that gets you; *it's the hard bits around the edges.*

Personal Journal / October 20, 2005

Back in Turkey having the damaged keel repaired. At least one hull is fairing well.

Personally, I don't feel so great. I'm in shape—if you call "round" a shape. I get out of breath easily and am not sure what that's all about. I go for a walk in town occasionally but get tired easily. What's going on?

Email / October 17, 2005 / Life on the Hard

We're living life on the hard this week. That doesn't mean life itself is hard; rather, *Julia* is hauled out and sitting in the boatyard high off the ground while repairs are done to the keel.

A funny thing about hitting a rock and then sharing the story with fellow sailors. Some will look around, lean in close, and whisper, "I've hit one too," and then smile as if we've joined a secret organization. The price of membership: running aground and not telling anyone.

One of the benefits of being on the hard is sleeping well, knowing we most definitely will not drag an anchor tonight. A drawback, however, is getting up in the middle of the night to do your business; first you must climb down a 15-foot ladder before trudging off to the restroom. And you can't just jump overboard for a morning swim.

As I write this, I hear the sound of sandblasting as the workers prepare the keel for fiberglass work tomorrow. We've checked the humidity of the keel and it's low enough to be repaired, meaning we had no water leakage whatsoever from the accident. Welcome news.

The Turkish workers are great but keep telling us to follow them and "control" while they point to something. We obviously have no control and don't know why they think we should. We finally asked a translator and discovered that "control," not at all spelled like the English word and pronounced somewhat differently, in Turkish means to "look." Now we understood they wanted us to look at the job they were doing and its many steps along the way. Being able to communicate is important.

While we were hauled out of the water in Turkey, we again revisited the engine alignment issue that had plagued us since Australia. In a Hail Mary effort to solve this chronic problem, we decided to install a flexible bearing drive, like a CV joint, which allows the engine to function even slightly out of alignment. Having learned to filter though the clutter told to us by many mechanics before, we could only hope this would be the fix we had needed all along.

Personal Journal / October 30, 2005 / A Heart-Racing Week
With our free time, we raced with Mike on his boat in the five-day Bodrum race week and did famously. With only the three of us sailing his 43-footer, we took first place, trouncing the other boats with crews of six or seven aboard. Clearly there was a problem with just three of us working so hard.

On the third day, I was cranking in the jib and got so out of breath I had to sit down. My heart rate skyrocketed to over 120 and wouldn't come down for over an hour. I was worn-out for the rest of the day. That evening, Ken and Mike expressed their concern about my heart (evidently I turned blue), and they insisted I go to a cardiologist the next day. While usually I would say, "It's nothing," this time even I was a bit scared, and agreed.

I was nervous as we taxied to Bodrum Universal Hospital, which was more like a Hyatt, with a marble floor in the lobby and concierge to greet us. Dr. Nazer took an EKG, then an ultrasound, and hooked me up to other machines, which seemed to be all the latest, greatest equipment.

"Well, Doctor, how's my heart?"

"Your heart is fine. Strong as a horse, I believe is how you Americans say it, but your blood pressure is high. Very, very high."

"How can that be? What causes it?" I said.

Dr. Nazer said, "There are four things which are affecting your blood pressure: "Genetics, which you can't do much about—and there's weight, diet, and age. In other words, you're too fat, you drink too much, and you're more than half a century old."

What? Half a century? Did the doctor have to put it that way? And when did that happen? I try to think back to when I felt or saw myself getting older, and I just don't see it. Hopefully, with the pills the doctor has prescribed, my blood pressure will drop and I'll be able to go on with a normal life.

I thought I was unfit and out of shape, which was painfully true. After speaking to Mom, I found out she also has high blood pressure, as did my grandmother.

Since my hospital visit, I've also stopped drinking hard liquor in an attempt to get my weight down and to ease up on my heart. I am slowly learning I was indulging way too much, and this is my first wake up call.

 It turns out I'm a slow learner. I didn't quit. I reduced the quantity some, but not all, and I should have....

CHAPTER 19

Trains, Planes, and Gondolas

"Happiness is the meaning and the purpose of life, the whole
aim and end of human existence."
Aristotle

Email / December 9, 2005 / Europe by Train

How amazing. I'm sitting on the TGV high-speed train, laptop computer plugged in to the wall, sipping white wine, and watching the French countryside whiz by at 180 mph. While *Julia* sits in the cold boatyard in Turkey, we're on our way to Lausanne, Switzerland, to spend time with Nick, his lovely wife, Jacqueline, and our good friend Catherine Schueler. Plus, we're going skiing, and maybe even soak up a bit of culture. The green fields have turned to snow-covered mountains, and my eyes are watering merely from looking at the incredible beauty here. While walking through Christmas-decorated streets one night, I remarked we must have been dreaming or dropped into a fairytale.

What an eye-opening excursion. Not because of the beautiful environs but rather because this trip is so different for me. There are no drivers waiting at airports or train stations, no fancy hotels, limited taxi use, and we carry our own luggage. Yes, we are those people you see wheeling their suitcases down the streets, backpacks on our backs, map in hand, looking like the tourists we are. More importantly, we are relaxed, with no schedule and all the freedom in the world.

Previously, traveling on an expense account was luxurious, but the shackles were the price I paid. Now, with little money, I've been set free to experience travel on my own terms. What a glorious feeling.

Personal Journal / January 1, 2006

It's New Years Day and we're at Nick and Jacqueline's house overlooking Lake Geneva, nursing a slight hangover. I know I shouldn't be drinking, but I didn't have the willpower to resist champagne while at Catherine's house, high in the hills overlooking the frozen vineyards. The view across the lake included the twinkling lights of Evian, France, but bubbly seemed more appropriate than bottled water. Last night, Ken told me his life was a "crescendo of joy" since we met and how much he appreciated us. Naturally, we had to toast to our good lives together.

The time is flying by and one of the things I'm getting more and more nervous about these days is our ultimate return to San Francisco and how we will (or won't) be able to integrate into life there. While I don't want to be a sea gypsy all of my life, I'm pretty sure I don't want to be in the business world again, at least not at the same intense level. We're spending a lot of money these days, which is also making me nervous.

Well, life is short and I still say do it now, enjoy it now, and live life for now.

Email / January 10, 2006 / When in Rome

We're loving the sightseeing but mostly doing like the Romans… eating very well. We knew we were in Italy the moment we boarded the Italian high-speed train from Switzerland through the Alps to Milan and then Florence. The toilet didn't flush, one of the doors to the train car didn't work, a window was boarded over, the ride was much bumpier than the Swiss trains, and one of the connecting trains was late. But the food… oh my…the food, even on the train, is over the top.

Our game in Switzerland was to try and find a late train (we never did), and now we are trying to find a bad meal in Italy; we don't think it's possible, but our search goes on and so we eat.

Email / May 10, 2006 / The Marina's Buzzing

The marina is abuzz as most of the boats that have wintered here are getting ready for the sailing season. After the 0500 wakeup from the Morning Prayer over the town's loudspeaker, I usually go right back to sleep. But now, a paint compressor, or the hammering of the engineers, keeps me awake. We're part of it: Not wanting to look left out, we put our sails on yesterday and got lots of *oohs* and *aahs* over our rainbow jib. The small yachts (like us) and super yachts (with paid crew) are rigging their boats, cleaning, rebuilding, varnishing, and painting. The smells of fresh paint, fiberglass, and sawdust fill the air.

But once you step out of the boatyard, you're rewarded with spring. The hills are more beautiful than they were in October, with the scent of fresh flowers and herbs hovering just beyond the boatyard…I love the contrasts.

Email / May 15, 2006 / Crazy for Soccer

We anchored in Bodrum, right in front of the medieval Castle of St. Peter, a perfect example of a true knight's castle built in the 1400s. We crawled through narrow passages, imagining the defending knights shooting arrows and pouring hot oil on their attackers, and looked through the sights of a canon aimed right at *Julia*. History comes alive when you're standing at the top of a castle tower. This particular castle also happens to house the museum of underwater archaeology, which beautifully displays ancient shipwrecks and their treasures of pottery and gold.

In search of a relaxed birthday dinner for Ken, we meandered the streets and bazaars, stopping occasionally for a beer in one of the many drinking establishments in this city, which prioritizes the tourists' needs over the demands of religion. The Turks are as crazy for soccer as the rest of Europe…and tonight was their national championship. As we walked along the main street on the waterfront, all we could hear were the screams of fans as crowds gathered around televisions in bars. While dining on the waterfront, we finally heard a loud roar and honking horns. We stood on the side of the main drag while fans ran through the streets shouting; the game was over and the favorite team had won.

We quickly learned the winning team colors were red and gold, and as we walked along one of the main streets, a restaurant manager ran out, grabbed Ken and pulled him aside, frantically pointing at Ken's blue and gold jacket, which apparently represented the colors of the opposing team. "This no good!" he screamed over the crowds' shouting, and intimated that someone might get crazy and want to rip Ken's jacket off of him and beat him to a pulp. "Take off! Take off!" he said as Ken rapidly removed the jacket and tucked it under his arm. "Okay, okay," the restaurant manager said, and we walked quickly back to the dinghy and got the hell out of town. These people are crazy for soccer and equally crazy for red and gold. But I wonder, what about the losing team? What about all those people who were wearing *blue* and gold and were cheering earlier in the evening? Do they get nothing? Do they get the crap kicked out of them on the way home? Where did they suddenly disappear to—or did they change clothing as well?

We're safely aboard *Julia* and tomorrow we're out of here. Crazy for soccer is crazy here.

✉ **Email** / May 16, 2006
The most secret and beautiful anchorage in all of Turkey is Pabuc Koyu, a small circular bay 100 yards wide offering protection from every direction. Here are the coordinates for your trip…someday:
N 36°58.61 E 27°33.972

📓 **Personal Journal** / May 18, 2006
We ran into a visiting family from England, including Paul and Angela Wilkinson, and their 16-year-old son, Kyle. When we met them, we immediately knew Kyle was gay, and he knew we knew. He made his way over to *Julia* and hung out on our boat, asking us all kinds of questions about gay life. "I think I might be gay."

"You think you *might* be gay?" I said.

He blushed and said, "Yeah, I guess I am. Yeah, I'm gay. Oh, my God, I said it. I'm gay."

"How does it feel?" asked Ken.

"Like I've been let go, freed, like you untied me," Kyle said.

"Great," I said. "But please don't go around saying we had you tied up in the first place." Then I asked him if his parents knew.

"No way. They're blind and ignorant about the whole thing."

"I think you might be wrong about that. They probably know more than you think; I mean, you do have painted nails," I said, trying to keep the mood upbeat.

"And face it," Ken said. "You're not the most butch of the boys."

I offered to tell Kyle's parents for him and he was thrilled at the idea. Later, while having cocktails with Paul and Angela, I steered the conversation around to being gay, and not one to beat around the bush, I said, "You know your son is gay, right?" Silence ensued for about half a minute.

"We have wondered sometimes," said Angela. "Are you sure?"

"Are you blind?" I said lightheartedly. "I'm very sure. He's afraid to tell you because he's worried you won't love him after you know." Angela and Paul reaffirmed they would love their son no matter what and thanked me profusely for getting involved. I'm glad because I knew it was a bit risky on my part to be meddling in their affairs. I couldn't help myself. I knew I could do some good here.

I told them Kyle was lucky to have such understanding parents. I explained how every kid gets to this place when confronted with revealing themselves. They get stuck and need something or someone to push them through this point. For most kids, it doesn't go this easily. There are plenty of parents who, when they hear their kid is gay, either pretend they never heard it, or throw him or her out of the house.

"So what do we do now?" asked Angela.

"That's easy," I said. "Go tell him you love him."

Email / May 19, 2006 / Local Knowledge

When a local gulet (a large wooden passenger schooner usually filled with German and English tourists over the age of 70 wearing Speedos and bikinis), dropped its anchor very near ours and started backing toward shore threatening our coveted spot, we protested loudly. "You can't drop your anchor there. You're going to back right into us!"

How wrong we were. This captain put his boat in a perfect position in relation to the shore, to the wind, and to us, all in one try. I felt so humbled and embarrassed by our outburst, I jumped in the dinghy and motored over to offer my apologies. He welcomed me aboard, and as we walked towards his private cabin, I said, "Captain, you are an excellent boat handler; I'm very impressed. Please accept my apologies for doubting your skills."

"*Problem yok*" (no problem), he replied in Turkish.

"Your experience shows. And I imagine these big gulets don't back very well, do they?" I asked.

"Very badly indeed. But the engine is big. I can give more power and usually get boat where I want. What would you like for drink, my fellow captain?" this most friendly Turk asked.

I considered, that as a Muslim and a professional captain, he probably didn't drink alcohol. "I'll have whatever you are having," hoping to be politically correct.

He was a striking man with jet-black hair, weathered skin, and a thick traditional Turkish moustache. When he looked at me, his piercing eyes were hypnotizing. He snapped his fingers, and in an instant, a cabin boy appeared out of nowhere. A few words in Turkish and he was heading back out the door. Only a few minutes had passed before the boy was politely holding a small silver tray in front of us. As I took the glass of familiar-looking clear liquid, the captain said, "You have same as me. Is from my private collection. Only the best from Russia."

I wondered aloud if all captains like vodka on ice. We talked about boats, the responsibilities of being in charge, our trip around the world, how we liked Turkey, and of course, anchoring methods. I learned some good tricks to this challenging art of anchoring and tying to shore so popular in Turkey. All in all, it was interesting, humbling, and I absorbed much from listening and watching rather than talking.

Moments after returning to *Julia*, a small dinghy from one of the local restaurants arrived carrying two young lads asking if we needed any services? "Yes, we do," I responded. "Can you please take our rubbish, bring us four large bottles of coke, six bags of potato chips, four beers, and two ice cream bars?"

"Yes, you please to wait 30 minutes," the boy said, "Please to wait, please. *Problem yok*." Half an hour later, everything we requested was delivered to our starboard side. Now, that's the way to go shopping! You gotta love it.

N 37°00.324 E 027°47.234

 Email / June 13, 2006 / Turkish Delights Part I, The Open Market
The autopilot computer finally processed its last bit of information,

and we have declared it a total loss. While waiting for a replacement, we're making the best of the time and enjoying some of what I call Turkish delights.

In the small town of Turgutreis, the weekly market is on Saturday and we try our best to make it there every week. The market is open-air, but under huge canvas tarps to keep the heat out, and consists of row after row of vendors selling fresh fruits and vegetables straight from the farm. Huge piles of vine ripe tomatoes sit next to stacks of lettuce, squash, beans, strawberries, mushrooms, oranges, lemons, peaches, melons, and on and on. It's like your local supermarket's fresh food department, but on steroids.

We are powerless to resist, as the prices are ridiculously low: A kilo (2.2 pounds) of bright red tomatoes for about $1. Two kilos of juicy peaches for $1, a kilo of mushrooms for 50 cents, and our basket on wheels overflows and gets heavier as we move from one stall to the next. "Hey, watch it, don't squish my strawberries with your watermelon!" Ken says.

I reply, "Well, don't put your potatoes on top of my peaches." We laugh our way through the market, often shopping with Pete and Julie from *Sojourner*. Then we move to the cheese, olive, nut, and cookie counters. Fresh feta and goat cheeses, a dozen types of olives stuffed with almonds, lemon rinds, orange rinds, and garlic, in different sauces and oils. Yogurt so smooth and creamy we use it instead of cream cheese, and every type of nut you can imagine from almonds to pistachios. Then there are the cookies: Oh boy, do I get in trouble here. I just can't resist and they too are only $1 for a kilo. Other areas of the market are filled with live chickens, little ones and big ones; brown and white eggs; baskets; pottery; T-shirts; and underwear.

Email / June 14, 2006 / Turkish Delights Part II, The Haircut
Curiously, it's not all about yogurt. One of the best things to do in Turkey is get a haircut. It all starts with handshakes, greetings, and the offering of apple tea. As you are eased into the chair, the barber wets your hair, and the scissors fly over your head like a bee working a flowerbed. A silver tray appears with apple tea carried by a boy with an ear-to-ear smile. I've noticed it's never a young girl doing these tasks. After the barber cuts your hair, the tidying up starts. This includes the trimming of your nose

hairs (now that's where your trust in the barber has to be solid), your eyebrows, neck shave, and then the best part of all, removing the unwanted ear hairs.

When we get older, hair seems to grow in places we don't want it, and recedes from those places we wish it would remain. In Turkey they take care of those unwanted hairs in your ears by burning them off. Yes, I said burning. Using a burning alcohol-dipped cotton swab, they swiftly flash the flame over the "unwanted hair area," and *whoosh,* the hairs are gone. It's a bit warm on the ears, and never burns, but it makes me wonder what the learning curve is for this skill.

Finish up with lemon-scented oils, more apple tea, a neck massage, neck cracking, an arm massage, hand massage, finger pulling, and finally a deep shoulder massage. You walk out of there feeling like a million bucks...all for $15.

Email / June 28, 2006 / Turkish Delights Part III: Ephesus
The ruins of the Great City of Ephesus are just a three-hour drive from the marina in Turgutreis. The city, which has been under Greek, Roman, and Ottoman rule since the 5th century B.C., has always been on my must-see list, so the other day we rented a car and set out to brave the local roads and drivers.

The ruins are amazingly well preserved and include the partially restored Library of Celsus, and a 25,000-seat outdoor amphitheatre that is still used for performances 15 centuries later. Baths, temples, and houses in surprisingly good condition complete the city. Additionally, there and fountains, aqueducts, cisterns, and streets of fine, solid white marble. We walked down the main street imagining what life was like here more than 2,000 years ago. It gave me chills to think I was walking on the same avenue as Alexander the Great when he conquered the Persians in 334 B.C. If we hadn't lost our autopilot and been forced to stay in the marina and look for Turkish Delights, we might not have ever seen this incredible site. I'm learning to find the silver lining.

CHAPTER 20

Beating Our Heads Against the Med

"And the sea will grant each man new hope...his sleep brings dreams of home."

CHRISTOPHER COLUMBUS

![envelope icon] **Email** / July 5, 2006

As the saying goes, "Sailing around the world is 30 days of pure boredom, followed by 30 minutes of sheer terror," and these last couple of days have proved that expression to be true. When things go badly with severe weather or a massive mechanical breakdown, I have to admit sometimes I have the desire to throw in the towel. I have experienced terror from sea conditions, surprise from breakdowns of critical equipment, frustration from not being able to fix things, depression from being beaten back by the sea, and loneliness when critical decisions need to be made by only the captain.

That describes the last few days; now that we are through the terror stage and safely at anchor, I am euphoric from our victory and accomplishment.

We're back in Mykonos. We had no plans to return here, but as we began our 45-mile sail toward the southwest tip of Amorgos, the wind started to build much stronger than was forecast. Amorgos is a strikingly beautiful island (where *The Deep Blue Sea* was filmed) with 300-foot cliffs that drop straight down into the water.

We were in the lee of those cliffs, in a full-blown gale with winds of 40 knots, when we heard a sickening sound: *"Rrrrrrip."* We looked up to see the mainsail in two pieces, split horizontally on a seam from luff to leech (front to back), about a third of the way down the sail. We hastened to get the sail down and tightly secured, then continued under staysail and a small amount of jib. We still made it to our anchorage in record time, covering the 45 miles in a little over six hours.

However, once the anchor was down, reality dampened our enthusiasm: We no longer had a mainsail, and the next port of call where it could be fixed was not until Sicily, almost 700 miles away, with 400 of those miles upwind. We looked at the sail and tried to fathom sewing it ourselves, but the split was right on a seam where a machine had produced its zigzag-locking stitch. It's just not something possible to render by hand. We decided our best shot would be to get to Mykonos where our friend Katerina could help us find a real sail maker to do the job.

The next day's forecast was for 30 knots with 10-foot seas, while the forecast for the night was only 15 knots with 3-foot seas. Which would you choose?

Hoping the calm night would make for a smoother passage, we left our safe and snug anchorage at night. We were headed north, northwest, and the wind was coming from, you guessed it, north, northwest. ^&*@$#%! Did it follow us from the Red Sea? The wind continued to build, and within a couple of hours, we were slogging our way into 10-foot seas, 40-knot cold winds, green water crashing over the bow, spray flying, and the boat pitching and rolling steeply. So much for forecasts.

As if the conditions weren't bad enough, at 0300, we heard a shrill screeching noise from the engine room. Without the engine, the evening was going to turn into a nightmare rather than merely a bad dream. We quickly shut down the engine, bore off by staysail only, and this time it was Ken's turn to go below to open the floors. We thought it could be the water pump, or hopefully something simple like a broken fan belt. Yeah, right. We weren't very optimistic as Ken opened the floorboards.

Lady Luck was with us. A hose had come loose from its position and its clamp was rubbing on the alternator. As soon as the hose was tied into place, we started the engine and off we were pounding into the huge seas again.

A little later, in the dark morning, the seas were rough and the wind was cold as winter, and I was becoming very tired. That's when I started to hallucinate. Maybe it was sleep deprivation, but we've noticed in the Mediterranean, there is a low mist that covers the horizon when the wind is really blowing, and in my sleepy state, I saw islands and rocks. At one point I shouted, "Ken! Come up here; we're going to hit a wall!"

"There's no wall," he shouted back, now standing beside me and looking out off the port bow as we bashed our way into waves the size of houses.

"There, look there. Don't you see it? It's an island, I'm sure of it."

"The radar doesn't lie. Look, there's no island. And there aren't any walls out here."

"I'm sure of it! I can't believe you don't see it!" I insisted.

"Larry! There's no wall, there's no island, it's only the mist. Now go below and get some sleep!"

Through the night, we encouraged each other by saying things like: "Hey, only six more hours to go of this…" and "Look at the bright side— it's not raining." We've become good at making each other laugh, and so it went as we passed the time through the night.

We slogged on through the chop and finally made it this morning to our familiar anchorage at Ornos Bay, where we found the wind blowing the spray off the tops of the waves. It was difficult to even see where to drop the anchor. As he made his way to the foredeck and anchor, I reminded Ken, "We're only going to get one shot at this." If the anchor didn't set the first time, it was going to be tough to get all the chain back aboard and start over again.

"It's honkin' up here…keep the power up so we don't drift back too fast," he shouted back over the screaming wind.

"Roger, roger." And then we were onto our system of coded hand signals. He signaled with a fist to stop the boat when he saw a good place to drop the anchor. I gave him thumbs down to drop it when the boat was actually stopped, my fingers letting him know how much chain to put out after my calculations. In this case, we put out six times the depth, plus the distance from the surface to the bow roller, plus allowance for the tide to rise. And then I doubled it, giving us more than 250 feet of chain in water only 20 feet deep.

We have other signals for faster, slower, and for bringing the anchor up so we rarely speak at all while anchoring. Fellow cruisers have commented on how impressive it is that we achieve the whole process without shouting. Our experience of anchoring hundreds of times in good and bad conditions has really paid off; we made a textbook job of it today.

Our passage last night lasted 12 very long hours to travel a meager 44 miles—we could have walked faster. The boat is a mess, with books and papers, charts, and other stuff that went flying everywhere. We've since hung clothes, towels, and foul-weather gear out to dry, and even while I sit here, the biting wind is blowing 35-40 knots with a forecast of another *week* of this. The evil north wind is blowing cold, and we have that sense of loneliness and frustration from not quite being in control. But we also have the feeling of accomplishment that we made it through last night by relying on our own skills, teamwork, and determination.

Personal Journal / July 6, 2006
Sitting at Ornos Bay in 35 knots of cold howling wind that has been blowing its tits off for five days now. It's lonely, eerie, and we feel trapped, like the weather will never let go of us.

Today, we removed the mainsail, dragged it ashore where our heroine Katerina greeted us with hugs, and helped get it on a ferry to Akilas, a sail maker on the island of Syros, 20 miles to the west.

Personal Journal / July 8, 2006
The sail is back in less than 24 hours...unbelievable. The repair looks like I sat at a sewing machine for the first time, but at least it is stitched. It takes us two hours to put the mainsail back on in 35-knot winds, but we are happy it's repaired and onboard. See, everything always works out.

Email / July 14, 2006 / Making Tracks West Through the Corinth Canal

For three days, we have been up at 0500 sailing hard into the northwest wind towards anywhere out of the Aegean Sea. The Aegean is famous for its own harsh wind known as the "Meltemi." Now we know it only too well, as it has been beating us up for days. We don't have much choice in the matter, so have risen to the task and sailed about 50 miles each day in absolutely crappy conditions. The seas are rough with short haystack chop of 6 feet, and the wind averages 30 knots on the nose (how does it know which direction we want to go?).

While in Rome, I threw three coins in Trevi Fountain and aimed them precisely at Neptune's calm waters statue, specifically avoiding the rough waters statue. So much for legends—or maybe I had the wrong statue? Our anchorages, though, have indeed been legendary: Kos, Kastelorizon, Kalymnos, Amorgos, Mykonos, Kynthos, Poros, and Aegina. Because of the rough conditions, we haven't really been able to appreciate some of these beautiful places. Too bad, but sometimes that's what happens when you have your eye on a goal; you don't have time to see what's on the path beneath your feet (or keel).

The fastest way out of the Aegean was the Corinth Canal, which saved us going all the way around the Peloponnesian Peninsula. Even though we heard the canal transit was expensive, we were in favor of anything that would speed our exit from the Aegean. Upon arrival at the canal, I hopped onto the dock with papers in hand and said, "Fill 'er up," leaving Ken to direct the refueling while I checked with the transit officials. We paid for the fuel, paid our 216 Euros, (approaching $300), for the 3.2-mile canal transit, and then left the dock with strict instructions not to enter the canal until we were called. Just 65 feet wide, the canal is so narrow that traffic only goes through one direction at a time. Like an airplane in a holding pattern, we waited our turn, motoring in circles until the boats finished coming east. Then we heard the control tower call our name over the radio: "*Julia, Julia, Julia,* you will follow the large motor yacht, *King George.*" As the gate swung open, we got in line a couple hundred yards behind the enormous *King George*, put *Julia* in gear, and opened the throttle.

"Don't get turned sideways," Ken forewarned. "It's barely wider than our length."

As we entered the canal, I increased our speed to the recommended 7.5 knots. We looked straight up at the 250-foot-high vertical walls of limestone and couldn't help but be amazed at this engineering feat.

"For a big ditch, it sure is pretty," I said looking at the nearly white walls contrasting against the glacial blue water. "Did you know they cut this through solid limestone? And did you know it was completed in 1893, and the Roman Emperor Nero actually started the canal in the year 60 A.D.?" There was my history lesson for the day.

"Yeah, that's incredible." Ken was preoccupied. "Just keep us in the center and smile for the camera."

The historical and engineering significance was not lost on us; it was truly exhilarating being on our own motoring through the canal. Too quickly we could see the end of the canal ahead, as our transit took only 20 minutes. We popped out the west end, waved to the spectators ashore, and we're now anchored in the Gulf of Corinth. What a day.

Personal Journal / July 14, 2006
Dolphins in the early morning. A dozen surfing on our bow wave, some were looking up at us. They're always smiling, which always makes me smile.

After transiting the Corinth Canal, we anchored at Naupaktos to change the oil and filters in both engines. It was well past 100 hours per engine, and we had been putting it off too long. Then the generator wouldn't start. I'm sick of the breakdowns, even though by now I recognize they're part of cruising. But the uncertainty of things, which I guess is another way of saying "adventure," is starting to get to me.
N 38°23.4′ E21°49.7′

Personal Journal / July 17, 2006
Last night, when we were sailing into the pitch-black, I was so tired I started hallucinating again. It took both of us to stay awake. "Ken, wake up, you've been asleep for half an hour and I can't stay awake anymore. You have to let me sleep for 10 minutes," I pleaded. Then the generator wouldn't start again and, after taking it apart, Ken found a corroded wire.

We replaced the wire and got it going again. Damn, this is hard.

This morning we headed for the Straits of Messina and by 0730, we were through and on our way to Porto Rosa. The feared straits weren't as scary as they were built up to be by other cruisers. Maybe it's because we have already been through the Malacca and Singapore Straits, the busiest in the world. After five years, I suppose we actually have the experience of how to time things, such as avoiding traffic and adverse current.

Email / July 20, 2006 / Sicily

We made it to Porto Rosa, Sicily, in record time: 400 miles in under 54 hours. The forecast was for calm seas, and we were expecting to motor the entire way...so much for forecasts in the Mediterranean. I'm convinced the weatherman pulls a number out of his ass, posts it on the weather forecast, and if it's wrong, he just gives the double shoulder shrug and says "*Eh?*"

What can you do? A passage is like life: some good and some bad, and once you make it to the other side, you realize the bad wasn't so bad, and the good was better than expected.

Personal Journal / July 20, 2006

While sailing through the Aegean, I came to the conclusion that I was sick of the trip. I was ready to call FedEx and say, "Hello, I have a package...how big? Fifty feet by 25 tons...I'll leave it here in Greece and you can pick it up."

I really want to complete this round-the-world trip and had a good long talk with myself to find the strength and determination to continue. I had better toughen up. The weather in the Mediterranean is lousy for sailing. The winds change direction on a whim and can go from 0 to 40 knots in an instant and always seems to come from where we want to go. Glad to be out of the Aegean and its evil Meltemi winds.

Part of our hurry to get to Sicily is Nick kept his boat there, and we planned to do some buddy boating together. It was a great reunion; we hadn't seen him since the Red Sea, and here he was on his own 50-foot boat. His crew consisted of Nino, an older man of about 70, who, in spite of his many gold teeth, smiled a lot. His weathered skin showed his years in the sun, but it wasn't until you heard his stories (which I have sworn to secrecy) that you saw what an interesting life he had led. It seems a life in the Sicilian Mafia is difficult to get out of, but for reasons unknown to us, the presiding don let Nino go. He is free to fish, sail, and enjoy his remaining years without fear.

Off we went, our two boats ready to cruise the Aeolian Islands, north of Sicily—starkly beautiful volcanic islands that attract so many summer cruisers, you have to almost become Sicilian in your aggression to find an anchorage. Then, once you do, others think nothing of anchoring one boat length away from you. The day is spent fending off collisions, with lots of shouting and hand gestures, followed by smiles and laughter, as a crash is avoided and another glass of wine is poured. On the island of Panarea, I have never seen a more crowded anchorage; I could have walked ashore boat to boat without ever getting my feet wet.

Nick and I hiked to the top of Volcano Island where sulphur is venting and the scene is eerily prehistoric. We were afforded a beautiful view of our boats as they lay at anchor. "Pinch me," I said to Nick. "Is that really my boat down there I'm sailing around the world?"

"It certainly is, young man," Nick said. "You are one of the few. You said you were going to do it, and here you are doing it."

After a week of cruising together, Nick and Nino said farewell, and we waited at Volcano Island for our tried and true crew to return and sail with us; Ralph and Femke from Holland joined us for the sail to Barcelona. It was great to have them aboard again as their upbeat attitude and outlook gave us a much-needed lift.

 Email / July 31, 2006 / Computer Crash and a Sneaky Stop in Sardinia

The onboard computer drive crashed. It happened two days ago while en route to Sardinia, so we took a day of rest at a beautiful anchorage where Ken spent the day attempting to rebuild the computer with what information we had backed up previously.

The decision to stop in Sardinia was out of desperation, caused by continually pounding into the wind that was getting on everybody's nerves. However, Sardinia has a new yacht tax that requires a payment of $650 even if you stop and anchor for only one night. Even so, when I presented the option of stopping, Ralph and Femke jumped up immediately and said,

"We'll pay half, *pleeeese* can we stop?" We found an absolutely beautiful anchorage where Ken could work on the computer and everyone could relax.

We purposely disabled the engine. In case the tax police showed up, we could say we were having mechanical problems and had no choice but to stop. At one point, we saw the *Guardia Financia* going around collecting the taxes and were all prepared with our story, but it must have been our lucky day; they didn't stop at *Julia*.

We also spent yesterday patching another tear in the mainsail, but it's looking okay until we can get it re-sewn in Barcelona, 350 miles away. Next is the upwind sail toward the island of Menorca, Spain. I don't think Ralph and Femke realized what they were getting into with this upwind sailing, and I have to confess I didn't tell them in advance or they might never have come. Oops, I'll try to remember next time.

CHAPTER 21

Good Thing Lightning Doesn't Strike Twice in the Same Place

"You don't stop laughing because you grow older. You grow older because you stop laughing."
MAURICE CHEVALIER

Email / August 6, 2006 / Hello, Barcelona

Julia is docked at Port Ginesta, a short 15 miles from the city center of Barcelona. We pressed on hard to beat the coming Mistral winds that scream out of the Gulf of Lyon, barely making it before a squall and hailstorm of 40 knots blasted the marina. Warned about the Mediterranean conditions by other cruisers, we really didn't believe it, but we do now.

We'll be living in Barcelona for the month of August and possibly some of September while we complete our project list. Our to-do's include re-sewing the mainsail, re-mounting the autopilot, rewiring the starboard side of the boat because of the corroded wires we have found, resealing the foredeck to try and stop the leaks into the forward cabin, replacing our cracked watermaker center block, and repacking the life raft. Plus a "few" other things. Big thanks go to our wonderful friend Javier who has arranged our marina for free and a Smart Car for a mere $65 for the month. We first met Javier Rodrigo when he was crewing on *The Spirit of Ireland* in Vanuatu and have kept in touch ever since. He's tall and lanky, wears his jet-black hair long and messy, sports a 5 o'clock shadow, is animated and enthusiastic. And he always sees the bright side of things. His English is nearly perfect, he knows practically everybody in town, and tries to get us to stay out late with his friends. "Come on, dinner is early tonight, 10 pm, early enough even for Americans." We have become good friends very quickly.

We are trying to learn Spanish with our book, *Spanish in 10 Minutes a Day,* and we've already mastered the two most important phrases in any language: "Where is the bathroom?" and "Two beers, please."

Personal Journal / August 20, 2006

Our talk is always bigger than our bite, and we have managed only a few late nights out in Barcelona, and one in Sitges, the big nearby gay resort town. The dancing was fun and the men are beautiful, but both of us find Spain's late schedule exhausting. Like Greece, dinner is typically at 10 or 11 pm, out to bars and dancing until about 3 or 4 am, home by 5 am, sleep until 2 in the hot afternoon, get up and try to function for a couple of hours, then take a nap, and start it all over again.

I've been taking a walk along the beautiful beach right next to our marina three days a week but still have gained a lot of weight; too much of the good life I guess. While we have been fairly lazy during the month, it felt good to have plenty of days doing nothing, especially after the exhausting sailing from Turkey. It's as if we're stocking up on strength to get ready for the push to Gibraltar and the Canaries.

The emails I write to the *Julia* followers are, generally speaking, upbeat. I try to keep a smile on my face, but lately I've been down...not sure why. I know it sounds crazy. *What's the matter with you?* Maybe too much of a good thing? Actually, it's draining. No wonder so few people actually make it all the way around the world. In fact, according to Jimmy Cornell, only about 60-80 boats complete a circumnavigation each year (twice that number climbs Mt. Everest annually).

Going to new places is exciting but also stressful. Where are we going to anchor? Will it hold properly? Will the weather turn? Can we go to shore and leave the boat safely? We can never really leave the boat for long without worrying about her. Things breaking on the boat are getting out of control, and the money I'm spending on repairs is virtually endless. I know I'm whining, but hey, it's just to myself and I feel better putting my angst to paper. Well, can't quit now. I'm actually looking forward to the Atlantic crossing.

Email / August 25, 2006 / What a Night
The evening was filled with an air of excitement and expectation, as tonight was opening of the Sitges Festival Major, the annual weeklong blowout that turns this party town upside down. We were looking forward to the fireworks spectacular as we gathered with our Spanish friends at a fabulous apartment overlooking the beach. Dinner was a most delicious combination of cured meats, including Spanish cured ham, the world famous delicacy. Tasty local cheeses, Moroccan hash, and excellent Spanish red wines rounded out the meal nicely.

At 11 pm, we heard the first *whoosh, whistle*, and *BANG!* as an explosion lit up the night sky signalling the show was about to begin. Looking around, we could see every balcony filled with eager faces, young and old, waiting in anticipation.

By chance, or jealousy on Mother Nature's part, at 11:01, an enormous lightning bolt illuminated the town cathedral, creating an eerie silhouette. From that point on, we were treated to the most spectacular fireworks *and* lightning show ever. It was as if Mother Nature were countering the fireworks display and said, "Oh yeah? Watch this…" and *"Crack!"*—a blasting display lit up the entire sky. Then the fireworks producers would respond with an almost equal barrage of their own.

The cathedral is the centerpiece over the town square and with each different color of fireworks, it took on a new personality. When red showed through the bell tower, it seemed as if the church was on fire, with sparks pouring out the windows. Then the producers poured on more red, and we commented, "It's as if the devil himself is at work." They fixed that by drawing our eyes skyward again with bursting rockets that showered the beachfront with embers. The cathedral faded into a black silhouette as the show continued and the crowds cheered.

Tonight was one of those nights. When Ken and I looked at each other, I said, "Remember this moment. Here we are in Sitges, with good friends, watching this incredible show, and *this is our life*." Remarkable.

Email / September 2, 2006 / Losing Track of Time

The plan was to spend the month of August in Barcelona, and then move on to the Balearic Islands for September. However, as is often the case with this journey, we have been lost in time...one day it's August first and the next it's September. We are hard pressed to know if it's Monday or Saturday, and as the time seems to slip by, we forget the months, too. Being in Spain for August is like slipping into a time warp, because the entire country shuts down; it's almost as if August doesn't happen. Big corporations, marine hardware stores, and even the laundromat closes; instead of getting things done, we have simply gone with the flow and become lost in time.

Now that it's September, people are returning to work. The propane company has reopened, and today we paid them a visit to fill our gas canisters. As we stood in the office of the huge gas plant with our two empty tanks, the plant manager wagged his finger at us: "Impossible. You will never get *those* filled in Spain." He was indicating the ones with non-European fittings that were bought new in Thailand because our American bottles couldn't be filled there. Now we're faced with changing our propane system yet again to fit the European standard "camping gas" and then will most likely change it back on arrival in the Caribbean. But the work has piled up for the guy who can help us change our system and now that it's September, it's tough to rise to the top of his list.

While checking the rewiring in the forward cabin, we noticed our windlass was looking slightly crusty. Close inspection revealed it had raised its last anchor and was corroded beyond repair. Ouch. We spent the next few days researching which windlass to buy, which one would have enough power, and which one wouldn't cost an arm and a leg. The only thing that really mattered was finding an open distributor with one close to our requirements in stock.

See? It could always be worse; we would really be up the creek if we lost our anchor windlass far away from repair facilities. Note to self: The term "routine check" means more frequent than what we have been doing.

The fiberglass repair guy came to remove the old windlass and start cutting new holes in the foredeck. He's Danish and speaks Spanish, but no English, so communication isn't the easiest. While pointing and nodding, we discovered we both speak French, so now we are chatting in *Franish*, a strange combination of languages. We're discussing things like:

"The bolts are not strong enough."

"*Que*? No long enough?"

"No, *pas forté* enough...."

"*Si*, and not long enough."

"*Si*."

"*Oui*." I hope I'm getting stronger bolts.

In the meantime, we are continuing to love Spain; the people are friendly, the food is superb, and we cruise around Barcelona in the Smart Car (which is actually smaller than our dinghy)...maybe we could take it with us and put it on the foredeck. While small, it is amazing how many groceries fit in that tiny car, and it's fun to drive, just like a go-cart. We park it with ease, and then walk until we drop. We wander down the big broad boulevards and their parks, shop in tiny souvenir stores, and eat at stand-up tapas bars. There's nothing like fresh calamari with a cold beer on a hot afternoon. We take the next beer seated at a seaside café with a view of the boardwalk and the young roller-skaters dressed in nothing more than skates and their Speedos or bikinis. This is a place where beautiful bodies are appreciated, laughter reigns, and food and drink are the catalyst for interaction. History is everywhere, but my favorite sight is the statue of Christopher Columbus at the waterfront. We have the luxury of time on this journey. We don't have to try and cram every sight into a weeklong jaunt, and thus we learn to live like the locals in almost every place we go.

We don't always adapt. Last night, we planned to go out in Sitges; we went to sleep at 10 pm for a disco nap. We slept right through the alarm. When I finally woke up at 2 am, I nudged Ken and said, "Well, do you think it's too late...do you want to go out?" I think I heard him grunt, "No way," and then heard his deep sleep breathing. I laughed and put my head back on the pillow...maybe we'll try again tomorrow night. I have lost track of time; not necessarily a bad thing.

Email / September 13, 2006 / Who Invited Zeus?

We have slipped the dock lines and departed the marina. It's always such an exciting feeling to be on our way again and to be free from the ties of land. At the beautiful island of Mallorca, about 120 miles from Barcelona, the water is clear and clean, the landscape green and mountainous, and there are plenty of beaches and anchorages along the shore to give us a choice of where to stop each day. It's not always this calm and beautiful, though, as this is the dawn after the big party thrown by Zeus and his friends.

It was another incredible storm with *CRAAAACKing* thunder so loud it sounded as if a tree were splitting right over our heads. The lightning slammed the water and was so frequent it looked like a strobe light in a dance club. And the rain fell so hard it flattened the seas like wet asphalt under a steamroller. As the rain hit the sea, it produced a *hisssssssssing* noise that added to the eerie, damp, and heavy atmosphere. At 0400, we woke up to the loudest and closest thunderbolt ever in the history of the world (okay, maybe not *ever*, but it sure scared the crap out of us). So much so, we got up and had cookies and milk to help take the fear away.

Email / September 16, 2006 / Not as Lucky as We Thought

At the end of the day, we weren't as lucky as we thought the night of the huge lightning storm. While we did not actually get struck—there was enough electricity in the air and the near hit from the bolt that had blown us out of our beds—it fried our chart plotting instruments.

We contacted the local Ray Marine dealer, and he said, "After that storm, get in line." Evidently, many boats have had electrical problems, especially with navigation instruments, from what is now being called "the biggest lightning storm in Spain's history."

While expensive, we like it on Mallorca. Aside from Ken's toothache, which we're discovering can be eased with vodka, we don't mind waiting for the dental appointment. It's just another day in the life aboard *Julia*. Lots happening: some good, some bad, but its life as it comes. All we can do is deal with it one step at a time, and try to smile through it all. So smile we do, missing teeth and all, enjoying the good, trying to laugh at the bad, and appreciating all we have.

Email / September 30, 2006 / Sailing Backwards

In most of my emails I try to be upbeat, positive, and happy. I try to show the footloose and fancy-free life of a sailor wandering the oceans of the world without a care. Yet every once in a while, we hit a wall, which makes it seem as if there are invisible forces working against us. While we have a policy of never going backwards (or we would never make it around the world), we have now sailed back to the port of Palma, Mallorca, for repairs beyond our skills. I'll spare you the details, but we need fixes on the watermaker, air conditioning, refrigerator, and generator.

We are in a beautiful marina filled with super yachts and, beside them, little *Julia* looks like the poor refugee that has moved into the rich neighborhood. On one side is a 150-foot yacht, on the other, a 90-foot.

Setting repairs aside, we've recently returned from beautiful Ibiza, where we had a wonderful time with Andre and John from New Zealand, and Patrik, too, who rejoined *Julia* for a couple of weeks. The infusion of new energy from good friends was a big boost for us.

Ibiza has a reputation as a party island and it's well justified, but I realized again my desire to stay out late is waning, and I prefer a good book and a cup of tea.

Personal Journal / September 30, 2006

These last couple of days have been depressing. For the first time, we are wondering aloud if we are indeed losing the battle with *Julia*. Can we make it all the way back to San Francisco and at what cost, financially and emotionally? Ken was so depressed last night he was nearly in tears: "We can't keep up with it. Every time we fix something, another thing breaks. It's too hard, it makes me want to go home."

"C'mon," I responded, earnestly trying to comfort him while being realistic. "It *is* hard. Remember, that's why not very many people sail around the world. We've been in worse places than this with no engineers. Tell you what," I added as I hugged him, "tomorrow I'll make some calls and we'll get a bunch of engineers down here to fix things." I knew exactly how he felt and wanted to break down, too, *but there's never room for both of us to lose it at the same time.*

The short-term answer is to throw money at the problems and get them fixed. We both agreed we want to sail home as fast as we can, which will mean going through the Caribbean this winter. I think we're both over it. Time to move on to the next thing, whatever that may be.

While I have always had a lot of persistence, patience has never been one of my best attributes. I have truly had to relearn what it means to be patient, relaxed, and accepting of what is happening at the moment; a difficult lesson for me.

We first met Simon and his gang from Ocean Pirate *in Ismalia, Egypt, half-way up the Suez Canal. We really enjoyed their company in Egypt and Israel, and kept in touch with them on a regular basis. They continued on to finish their circumnavigation in Spain while we spent the season in the Mediterranean. Simon was a big guy, strong as an ox, tough as nails, had fists the size of a child's head, and being an ex-professional boxer, could crush you with his bare hands. But he is also one of the nicest, sweetest people I have ever met, and wouldn't hurt a flea. We were eager to see them again and made a point of stopping near their home in Spain.*

Then we got an email from Chris Rohan, my protégé with whom I had left my clients upon departure in 2001. He and his wife, Meg, were going to be in Spain on vacation, and he wondered if we were going to be anywhere near there at that time. "Well," I told him, "we're going to be exactly where you are at exactly that time. Come sail with us!" So they joined us for our excursion to see Simon and then sailed with us to Gibraltar.

Email / October 9, 2006 / On the Move Again

We spent two happy days with Simon, Em, and Nadine from *Ocean Pirate* in Calpe. "What's for dinner? Pizza?" I asked. We all cracked up, remembering our dinner while docked in Ismalia. There, wanting to make sure we had enough, Nick had mistakenly ordered 12 assorted pies, providing enough for both boats for days. "Funny, isn't it," I said. "That dinner is one of my fondest memories of Ismalia."

"And what about the boat that tried to run you into the side of the Suez Canal?" Simon asked.

"You saved our butts by taking him on. He was no match for the horse-power you had on *Ocean Pirate*...Ah, the memories...do you miss it?" I asked.

"Of course," said Simon. "But here we are...time to move on," he said.

After two days of reminiscing, Chris and Meg joined us for the 350-mile sail to Gibraltar, and we're sailing downwind in fairly calm seas and following winds...just the way we like it. Today we crossed the Prime Meridian at 0 degrees longitude and are now officially back in the Western Hemisphere. So far, it doesn't feel a whole lot different, but there is an air of excitement knowing we are indeed heading west...heading for home.

Personal Journal / October 18, 2006
We're waiting on the weather. What else is new? While the pilot charts, which illustrate historical weather patterns, show there should be winds behind us all the way to the Canary Islands, the patterns from the last week and next week show nothing but southwest—right on the nose. Weary of beating into the weather, so we're waiting. In the meantime, we're shopping, walking, and are going to take the tram to the top of Gibraltar to see the monkeys. It's fun being a tourist again.

In Gibraltar, we met Brimman Frazer, a college kid from Santa Cruz looking for a crew position across the Atlantic. He's young, energetic, polite, and he sure can cook, so we took him on as far as the Canaries to see how we got along. All was fine aboard and we liked each other, but he was in a hurry to get across the Atlantic and left us in the Canaries, looking for another boat leaving before us.

That's when we ran into Francis Schouler from South Africa. He too was young, energetic, a great cook, and was in the Canary Islands looking for adventure before going back to college. Patrik also wanted to cross the Atlantic so that rounded out our trans-Atlantic crew perfectly. For the first time on an ocean crossing, we had an all-gay crew.

Perhaps it was a coincidence whenever we set out to identify a new crew for some legs of our voyage around the world. Or maybe we had a good sense of who would fit in onboard and who would not. We heard horror stories of others who had picked up crew like we did, from bulletin boards in marinas and word of mouth, only to see the crew panic as soon as they were out of sight of land. Or they couldn't cook like they had professed. Or they didn't want to do their share of standing watches.

We had a system. If someone wanted to crew for us, we always took them for a test sail, made them cook us a meal, and had them spend a day aboard helping to clean and stow provisions, all before we left on passage. We felt this screening process was important because most people who are out there looking for crew positions are in their vagabond stage of life. Our process served us well, as we loved all of our crew.

CHAPTER 22

Blue Water Again

"Luck is what happens when preparation meets opportunity."
Seneca

 Email / October 27, 2006 / Hello Atlantic Ocean

We have finally departed Gibraltar. This morning we sailed out through the famed Straits of Gibraltar, and early this afternoon, entered the Atlantic Ocean. While the weather forecast isn't the greatest, it's the best we've seen in two weeks so here we go, headed for the Canary Islands. As we sailed through the narrow straits with Morocco to port and Spain to starboard, I couldn't help but think about Christopher Columbus who sailed this very route, headed for his first stop at the Canary Islands. I wonder if there is something to my birthday being on Columbus Day?

Now that we're outside the actual straits, we know we are in the ocean again because of the big 12-foot rolling swells. Being back at sea is going to take some adjustment.

 Email / October 29, 2006 / Back in Blue Water

Last night was dark with rainsqualls illuminated by the lights of

Casablanca while sailing down the African coast. As we slipped through the dark, we left a phosphorescence trail behind us, glowing like a giant green sea serpent.

Julia is motor sailing into very light winds, and it looks like we'll be motoring the rest of the way to the Canary Islands, another 300 miles to the southwest. We have an extra guest along too; a small, yellow-breasted bird. We think it might be a canary that's lost and in need of a ride home to the Canary Islands—we're letting him stay—as long as he behaves himself. Maybe we'll even feed him a morsel of our freshly caught tuna and mahi-mahi.

I thought it would take time to get used to being back at sea, but it was an easy transition and I love being out here again. My imagination, which has gone wild with images of Christopher Columbus and lost canaries, proves I've checked out and am at sea again. Or that I've truly lost my senses.

Email / October 31, 2006 / Safely Anchored in the Canaries
We made it to the Canary Islands just four days after departing Gibraltar, having sailed 658 miles at a speed of nearly 7 knots...not too shabby. Our anchorage is at the south side of Isla Graciosa at Playa Francesca, otherwise known as San Francisco Bay (the original one), which gives us cause to smile knowing that in a year, we'll be anchored in that other bay by the same name.

The islands are many shades of brown and black, and volcano cones abound, which clearly establish how these islands were formed. The steep dark cliffs contrast sharply against the Atlantic blue water, which really is a deeper blue than we have seen, giving the whole area a bright but almost prehistoric feeling.

Email / November 1, 2006
Well, we *were* safely anchored...that is until this morning. We awoke to winds of 35 knots and waves breaking over the bow with the shore a close 100 yards behind us. *Yikes.* Two boats dragged, and eventually every boat left the bay. We were the last to go because it's hard to leave when you know your anchor is set well. Still, it's not good seamanship to be anchored in front of a lee shore because if any piece of

equipment, like a shackle or the chain, were to break, there wouldn't be time to react before being blown ashore. It was one thing in the Red Sea *marsa*, where there was no choice, but as long as we can move to safer anchorage, we will.

The North side of Lanzarote Island is a slightly better place. We're set well, but there's a big northerly swell to deal with and the gusts off the mountains are reaching 45 knots on a regular basis. The wind blew furiously while motoring over here; hard enough to snap the fiberglass man overboard pole in half. We also blew out a turning block for the staysail sheet, but other than that, all is okay. The tops being blown off the waves look like snow blowing across the water.

It's times like these that make me want to be anywhere on land. The noise of the wind howls through the rigging, making relaxation nearly impossible. The constant stress of wondering if the anchor, bridle, and chain will hold, wracks the nerves. Onboard, the talk about weather never ceases and has become exhausting, as are the discussions of where to go next for a safer anchorage. We'll see what tomorrow brings.

✉ **Email** / November 11, 2006 / Sahara Sandstorm

After the Red Sea, we thought we were through with sandstorms from Africa, but oh, no. Surprise. We are in day three of a sandstorm with air so thick we can't see the mountains a mile away. *Julia* is once again covered in a layer of red sand, and even breathing is difficult. It's a gift from Morocco, well over 100 miles away and it seems like the Moroccans are sending us the entire Sahara desert. The sand coats the deck and rigging outside, the floor inside, and even our mouths so every meal has a desert grit flavor.

It seems we're constantly on the move. We were at anchor for a gorgeous two days, and we cleaned *Julia's* bottom and propeller to help speed our way across the Atlantic. Now we're back in the marina, and we'll stay here until these 25-30-knot winds have eased. Then we'll head southwest 95 miles to Las Palmas on Grand Canary where we look forward to meeting Patrik for the Atlantic crossing.

 There are countless stories about ill-prepared people and boats attempting to cross oceans. These are the people who get onto television and radio

talk shows. "You made it halfway across the ocean, lost your power because you ran out of diesel, then ran out of water and food because you didn't have enough aboard, didn't have the spare parts to fix your engine, and you survived until the coast guard came to your rescue. Wow, how did you do it? You're a hero!" Or, "You survived a hurricane, that's incredible. Didn't you know it was hurricane season?"

Some of these people are heroes, but many are simply unprepared. We didn't want to be one of them (the media likes a disaster and it makes for good print or air time; it wasn't going to be us though). I was adamant we would not leave until our boat and crew were ready, and I took preparations for a passage very seriously. Preparations are key to a successful passage. Maybe that's why we didn't have any real disasters on long ocean crossings. As Ken says, "The best crossing is a boring one."

 Email / November 21, 2006 / Preparations for the Atlantic Crossing

This marina is the very definition of busy. Thanks to Javier in Spain, we were welcomed in Las Palmas at the private Club Maritimo, and in spite of all marinas being completely full, we have a great berth, and even found a space for our Kiwi friends Dean and Hannah onboard *Risqué Affair*. We have found ourselves smack dab in the middle of a group of 250 boats getting ready to cross the Atlantic in a rally called the ARC. There are name badges, pretty flags everywhere, including all of the boats with their dress flags, a hospitality desk, and people scurrying everywhere trying to complete their last minute preparations.

To join in the fun, we have hoisted the rainbow and it's flying proudly on our mast and causing a good stirring up locally. We overhear comments around the marina like, "There go the gay guys," and "I bet they have more fun at sea than we do!" However, most of the people in this rally are crossing an ocean for the first time, and when they find out we have come nearly all the way around the world, we are barraged with questions, such as "What do you think about our plans as follows...?" and "What's it like out there at sea?" It appears we're now the experts.

In the grocery store, we split up into teams of two, each armed with a list. "Okay, we'll meet in the vegetable section in half an hour. Ready, set, go!" And we're off to buy provisions for three weeks at sea. Thirty breakneck minutes later, we reunite over the green onions. "Uh, guys, how did we end up with six carts and only four people? Does anybody have anything they can put back on the shelves?" I ask.

"No can do, Skipper, but I got all of my list," says Patrik.

"I have to have everything in my carts, if you please," says Francis ever so politely because he's new.

Ken just looked at me with that "Are you kidding?" look of his.

"Right, okay then, shall we get the fresh veggies?" I ask as I push my two carts down the aisle laughing. We must have been quite a sight heading to the checkout counter.

Personal Journal / November 23, 2006

The safety of my crew is paramount. Even though I've done this before, I still ask myself over and over again if I have done everything possible to make the crossing a safe one? I answer yes. Butterflies; tomorrow we go.

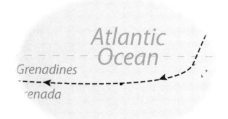

CHAPTER 23

3,000 Miles
to the Next Rest Stop

"Go out on a limb. That's where the fruit is."
WILL ROGERS

✉ **Email** / November 24, 2006 / Bon Voyage to Us
We have left Grand Canary Island and are on our way across the Atlantic Ocean. It's a strange feeling to sail out of the marina alone. Unlike the start for the ARC group in a few days, we have no line to cross; there is no fanfare, except a few waves and horns from our newly found friends.

There is only that final decision of "Let's go now." It's made after lots of preparation: route planning, studying the current and historical weather conditions, updating the spare parts inventory, estimating food consumption, vacuum sealing and stowing the food, and calculating fuel consumption. I tend to err on the conservative side, so we strapped another six jerry jugs of diesel on deck, but unlike the jugs we bought in Yemen, these don't leak. Crackers, pasta, and chips take up half of Francis' double bunk in the forward cabin, and I've stashed away four bottles of champagne for our arrival in the Caribbean. We even bought a new man-overboard pole to replace the one that snapped in high winds. I'd say we're ready.

While I have lots of support from friends and crew in preparation for a passage, there's still that lonely decision made only by one person: the captain. It's a big responsibility to finally decide in favor of leaving the safety of the marina for a crossing such as this. We will be alone at sea for 18 to 20 days while sailing 3,000 miles. We have to be completely self-reliant, and there are plenty of funny feelings in our stomachs as we watch the last of land disappear behind us on the horizon.

We're following the early explorers' directions: "Sail south till the butter melts and then head west." That means heading south toward 20 degrees latitude where we should begin finding the warm trade winds, which will carry us downwind all the way across the Atlantic to the Caribbean.

✉ **Email** / November 28, 2006
The last couple of days have been nothing but rough seas; rollers the size of two-story houses that came marching down from the northwest. The wind came from the northeast and when it met the rollers, we were caught in the middle, making for a rough, rolly ride. Not to complain, as the wind remained behind us and was fairly well behaved. As usual, *Julia* took it all in stride, letting the huge rollers get ever so close and then riding right up over them like they were big bumps in the road.

It's our fourth day at sea, and we are slowly getting into the rhythm of life onboard. I spend countless hours each day planning the route for the best winds, calmest seas, and fastest passage. Other hours are spent trimming sails to that course, which requires attention from any one of us who are on watch. For the first time, I even found myself reading for relaxation as I regain the confidence we are doing things correctly. We are eating as if on a cruise ship, and the "chef of the day" program is working out beautifully with some amazing meals coming out of the galley.

We are definitely headed south. On this morning's sunrise watch, I saw the North Star disappear below the horizon, and then the Southern Cross came into view. We're still waiting for the butter to melt and for those warm trade winds as we follow Columbus' route.

The visuals and emotions on this trip are over the top for me: maybe because it's my last big ocean crossing or maybe because *I've learned to appreciate it more.* I find myself staring endlessly at the horizon in amazement at how vast the ocean is, and how lucky I am to be out here enjoying this incredible experience. The moon is reflecting brightly, the mast is creaking, the water is *whooshing* by and we're flying down silvery waves that foam white as we push tons of water out of our way.

Sometimes it's too hard to believe the experience is genuine...because it's almost too grand to be real. Experiences are sometimes like that; I could almost miss this if I don't stop occasionally and recognize where I am and what I'm doing. If I immerse myself too much in the job at hand, that of getting the boat safely across the ocean, I might not stop, step back, and look at what's happening.

And what I see is incredible. Everyone has amazing experiences every day, but sometimes we are so immersed in what we are doing we don't catch sight of their magnificence. Don't blink for too long; you don't want to miss out on anything.

Personal Journal / December 2, 2006

There were only two boats headed south on our departure day: *Julia* and *Risqué Affair*. We have daily radio schedules with Dean and Hannah to discuss the weather, the weather, and more weather. It's almost all we talk about because it's that important; the weather is everything to us. We also talk about how many fish we have caught and how many dumb errors we have made aboard that day. It's nice to have the company of at least one other boat going the same way we are.

Dean reports they have caught two mahi-mahi, and three flying fish have landed on deck, but it's no match for our three mahi-mahi, two flying fish, and a yellow-fin tuna.

Then comes my weather report: "Giant swells coming from really far north for a few more days, but moderate winds of 20 knots." I was interpreting the weather charts recently received over the SSB radio, but I also had our weather router's input every other day making my forecast well respected. Even though we can't tell who's monitoring our conversation, I'm pretty sure other boats were also listening.

Ken took the microphone and asked how their 1-year-old, George, was doing. I can't even imagine what a challenge he would be to have onboard. I wasn't looking forward to the next segment of the radio call.

"Any dumb errors over there on *Julia*?" Hannah asked.

"Well, now that you mention it," Ken replied. "I think we win in the dumb department, and this one's a doozie. Here's Larry, let him tell you."

I rolled my eyes and sat down at the chart table to confess all. I explained how we went to make a simple jibe, something that should have been really easy. Because the mainsail was triple reefed, the boom was swung outboard further than normal, and the galley hatch was pushed wide open under the boom vang...a rare event. When the boom swung across the cabin top, the boom vang grabbed the hatch and tried to bring it along, twisting the aluminium frame like a pretzel and shattering the hatch glass.

We didn't even notice the destroyed hatch until a minute later when I was re-attaching the preventer. It's amazing how much power was in that small sail as it came across because the hatch was destroyed. Boy, what a stupid mistake that was. All because we didn't check every last detail before jibing.

"Yachting is an expensive sport," Dean said.

I couldn't blame anybody except myself because as captain, the responsibility sits squarely in my lap...you'd think I wouldn't allow mistakes like this anymore, but it reminds me I can never let my guard down; I'm still learning. We should be able to replace the hatch in the Caribbean, but in the meantime, it's holding together with a boater's savior: duct tape.

We're 1,200 miles into the crossing, and I feel good. We have plenty of fuel, water, and the food coming out of the galley is delicious. So far, we are all getting along amazingly well together, and it's already been eight days. In another 12 days we'll arrive in the Caribbean. I'm excited to be getting back to waters closer to home; excited yet sad, because I know by this time next year, we'll be home, and I'll be punching away at the laptop sitting in the cold marina in Emeryville. That's beginning to press on my mind a bit, but I'm not going to let it spoil the Caribbean or the last part of the trip.

Only days before our departure, I received an email from a former client. She told me my friend Stephanie has been diagnosed with pancreatic cancer and will soon be struggling with surgery, chemo, and everything else that goes with putting up the fight of your life. I sent her an email promising I would dedicate the success of our Atlantic crossing to her, and that she, too, will have success when she rids her body of cancer. I wrote, "We're going to have it easy on this passage compared to you, Stephanie. You're the hero about to cross that rough ocean."

Email / December 3, 2006 / Fish Stories
Last night, we had fresh mahi-mahi for dinner...what a feast in the middle of the ocean! We caught three of these beautiful fish and ate them all in one seating. Speaking of fish, there are thousands of flying fish that leap out of the water while being chased by bigger fish or when *Julia* comes screaming through the water towards them. We've been playing a game of finding the fish that stays airborne the longest. As we see one jump out of the water, we start the count: "One thousand one, one thousand two, one thousand three..." Their flights go on easily for 10 to 20 seconds. They really are astonishing aviators. We often find them on the deck in the morning: evidence of their takeoff and flight but with an unexpected landing. It's not unusual to see hundreds of them jumping out of the water at any given time; they entertain us endlessly.

Last night we landed another one of these flying fish. This time, at 0200, the fish flew out of the water, into the cockpit, and right through the small porthole into the aft cabin. Ken and I were asleep, and it landed squarely on Ken's leg, waking us with a start. It started flopping all around which, of course, made Ken jump out of his skin, which made me jump up 3 feet, bumping my head on the low ceiling above the bed. As the fish was squirming around, trying to figure out how he got *in* bed with us, we were trying hard to catch him and get him *out* of our bed. We finally grabbed hold and tossed him overboard...the fish was left with its life and a horrible memory; we were left with fish scales in our bed and a memorable fish story.

Email / December 4, 2006 / Ten Days at Sea
Today, we reached the halfway mark of our Atlantic crossing. We have sailed 1,510 miles out of a predicted total of 3,020 to our landfall in the Grenadine Islands. We are doing really well on the crossing, making better time than expected with winds averaging a solid 20 knots.

We had a bit of drama today though with the yankee. Each day at noon, I bring the crew together to show our plotted position on both the electronic and paper charts, so we can see the real progress we make while we tally our mileage for the previous 24 hours. There we were all down below, when—*BAAM!*—We heard what sounded like a gunshot. Ken and I looked at each other, knowing noises like that are *not* normal.

"Doesn't sound good," Patrik said, heading up the ladder, with the rest of us right behind him. We looked toward the bow where the yankee used to be—nothing.

"We lost the yankee!" Ken yelled.

"No we didn't, there it is," I said, pointing to a big heap of sail dragging along the port side in the water. It was still attached by the sheet and tack but no halyard holding it up to the top of the mast. It was all hands to bring the sail back aboard. While heaving and panting, we looked up to where the halyard should have been at the top of the mast and saw nothing. The halyard had snapped from years of wear over the sheave. "We can rerun what's left of it...but not at sea," I said.

"Sure we can, Skipper," Patrik said.

"Oh really? And who's going to go up there while we're rolling side to side and surfing down waves?" I asked.

"You've got a point there," Patrik said laughing. "Let's wait until we're anchored."

Because the air is so clear out here, the moon shines with an especially bright intensity. As we surf the steep silver waves, with a quick glance back they look white; it's almost as if we are skiing down a hill of foaming snow or on a never-ending sleigh ride. The sensations of surfing a 25-ton boat down a wave at sea are exhilarating. As we take off on the wave, we feel the immense power of the ocean; *Julia's* stern lifts up, the bow hunkers down, and we accelerate to speeds over 12 knots, giving us the feeling of being out of control. At the bottom of the wave, *Julia* slows and rounds up, as if getting ready for the next wave. Sometimes we're glad it's night because then you can't really see how immense and scary the seas are. A two-story wall of water coming at you from behind isn't something you normally encounter in everyday life. It is for us though; we are actually getting quite used to these conditions of constant motion, and now 15-foot seas seem natural to us.

We're getting a fair amount (okay, a lot) of roll from side to side, and everybody is waking up sore from the workout we get while attempting to sleep. And it's not only while in bed. We're getting our workout while walking from one place to another, or trying to keep one's head upright while typing at the computer. It's isometric exercise at its extreme. Try to imagine what it's like cooking or using the toilet. On second thought, don't go there.

Email / December 6, 2006

Many of you have asked us about what life is like onboard. Here it is: I've been on watch since 0500, when the moon eased itself down into the west, and the sun rose in the east. I stare at the stars, and the shimmering sea, think about nothing, think about lots of things, and then nothing again. At 0700, I started the generator to charge our batteries, turned out our night running lights, started the watermaker, connected to email stations in the Canary Islands and Trinidad, tidied up the cockpit, put out the fishing lines, and awakened Francis who goes on watch in an hour. Ken is asleep after having the tough early morning watch, and Patrik is stirring because he knows today he is "chef of the day."

We look forward to what will appear out of the galley, because cooking at sea is like a magic act. Rolling 20 to 30 degrees is not uncommon; imagine what havoc that can cause for the chef. If you set the eggs down on the counter, and look away for even a second, they are guaranteed scrambled. Set a can down and watch it slide across the counter and then go flying to the other side of the boat. The stove is gimballed and swings with the roll, but following its back and forth movement with the frying pan is quite a trick. Do all of this while jamming your body into the galley, so you yourself don't go flying to the other side. It takes practice.

The roll makes not only cooking a challenge. Sitting at the chart table, I literally have to sway my body left to right and back, 20 degrees, to stay upright. When taking a shower, you have to move back and forth to stay under the water; when sleeping, you have to jam pillows next to you so you don't roll around in bed; when reading or relaxing, you have to brace your feet against something to keep from sliding across the cabin; when eating, you have to tilt your plate so your food doesn't fly off; and when going to the foredeck to do sail changes, you have to really hold on. Ken and Patrik have their own challenges trying to keep their tools nearby when repairing things. Imagine trying to crimp a wire or drill a hole while your tool bag slides back and forth across the floor. With respect to using the toilet—as mentioned—you can use your own imagination.

We all have chores that help pass the time: Francis is keeping the boat clean and tidy, Patrik is continually fixing carpenter-type things, such as the refrigerator door hinges, and Ken has electrical responsibilities on his plate, including fixing the bright spotlight and replacing the fan in Patrik's cabin. I will plot our route, monitor our accuracy to it, check the weather several times, connect to email again, and twice daily hold our radio schedule with other boats that left shortly after us and have since joined our radio net. It's fun to have other boats to talk to, and we sit around the radio like a family tuning into a nightly 1940s radio show to catch a hint of gossip, see the other boats' positions, brag about what we are having for dinner, and hear the "fish score."

Because there are four of us aboard, we have enough time to read; each of us has already gone through a couple of books. We also have audio books, and we occasionally watch a movie or *Will & Grace* episode for entertainment.

As you go through your day, perhaps you can imagine doing whatever you are doing in our world. Start by swaying back and forth, imagine warm trade winds at your back, change into your bathing suit (or less), and feel the warm air caress your skin....

Email / December 7, 2006 / Time Goes By

It was a cold, crisp morning on December 7, 2001, five years ago today, when *Julia* sailed out the Golden Gate and headed for the South Pacific. With a great deal of amazement, pride of accomplishment, and awe over how time flies, please celebrate with us the five-year mark of this journey's beginning.

Email / December 11, 2006 / Seventeen Days at Sea

The wind eased in the late morning, and we decided to hoist the spinnaker because it tends to flatten out the roll. We rigged all of the lines, raised the sail, and were right in the middle of pulling the sail out of its "sock" when it happened. The wind gusted and filled the sail, and the spinnaker proceeded to blow up right before our eyes. It ripped horizontally and vertically on seams, and right through the material even where there are no seams. Like the other spinnaker, which ripped to shreds in the Red Sea last year, this one's material was too old to stand even 15 knots, and breathed its last breath as it flew into the Atlantic. We dragged it alongside until we recovered from our shock, and then heaved the worthless piece of material aboard and stowed it away for some future giveaway. With no more spinnakers in our inventory, we're sailing downwind under the big genoa, which is working quite nicely for us.

I'm genuinely proud of the incredible teamwork aboard *Julia*. We're working together like a crack E.R. team, and our skills at improvising are impressive. We've certainly been through the school of hard knocks to get here; there are simply too many jobs at sea you have to learn on the job, or more to the point, on the water.

CHAPTER 24

Hey Mon, Dis Da Caribbean... You Need to Relax!

"How inappropriate to call this planet Earth when it is quite clearly Ocean."
ARTHUR C. CLARKE

Email / December 16, 2006 / Settling in to the Good Life

We made the right decision not to come in here at night, as the charts are far enough off that we would have hit a reef had we followed our determined route. My gut told me to wait for daylight, and I've long ago learned to trust that instinct.

The Grenadines are laid-back, with friendly boat boys who come out to offer everything from tuna to petrol. In their lovely singsong Caribbean accent, we are quickly hit with the sales pitch: *"Ya Mon. You want da tuna? Or haw abat da dasel for ta engin? And I got ta gud ganja for ya."*

"Okay," I reply, "we'll take two tuna filets, 100 gallons of diesel, and let's see a sample of the ganja."

After a 3,000-mile passage, we feel we deserve a bit of rest so we haven't done much in the last couple of days. We're settling in, relaxing, and working on slowing down to "island time." The Caribbean is a wonderful change from the Mediterranean, and although prices here are nearly as high, the pace is certainly slower. I'm reminded once again how I seem to thrive on the change. I loved the Mediterranean, and I love the Caribbean, yet they are so different.

Personal Journal / December 20, 2006

Talked to Mom the other day and it was nice to hear her voice. On the 18th, I remembered it was Dad's birthday and I stopped for a moment to reflect. I really do wish he were here to see what I'm doing, especially to see me fix a diesel engine. He was an aircraft mechanic in World War II and could repair a B-17 bomber engine in his sleep; I think he'd be proud of me now. I wonder if I'm really more mechanical than I thought. Does it run in the genes? I remember getting a new bicycle on my 10th birthday. I ripped open the box and was so disappointed to find it in pieces and in need of assembly. It didn't look much like a bicycle to me, lying there on the floor with the frame, two wheels, and bags of nuts and bolts. Trying to help, I grabbed the instructions and started reading: "Place part A on top of part B, remembering to use bolts C, and nuts D." Dad laughed, took the instructions, and threw them over his shoulder.

"Watch and learn," he said. "It's all logical; you just have to practice putting things together. Let's go get some tools. This adjustable one is a crescent wrench, this is a Philips screwdriver..." and right before my eyes, Abe put that bicycle together in record time without ever looking at the instructions again. By now, I've had the practice he was talking about way back then.

Now that I can see the end of the journey, I'm starting to feel anxious, eager, and even a bit proud, but hoping not to jinx it. I will save the pride for when we cross our outbound track at Zihuatanejo, Mexico. It ain't over 'til it's over.

Personal Journal / January 9, 2007

I can't really let go of the fact that we will be home "this year," something I haven't been able to say until now. What will I do for a living? Where will I live? How will Ken and I get along at home? So many questions. I'm trying hard to enjoy these last months of the trip and not let the influences of city life take over until I get there; what was once only in the back of my mind is pressing toward the front.

Email / January 25, 2007 / *Baksheeshing* Again

After a long week of working on *Julia* while she's out of the water, we're relaxing in our cool, air-conditioned apartment across the street from the boatyard. It's hot here in Prickly Bay, Grenada, and the work is hard. We couldn't bear the thought of living aboard in the dusty, dirty, noisy yard in 100-degree heat. Been there and done that in Turkey, and that facility was luxurious compared to this one. While the reasons for hauling out started small—having an insurance survey and painting the bottom—the list has grown to two pages and we are amazed at how many projects we have completed this week.

It didn't start out that way though. The morning we hauled out of the water, *Julia* just sat in her cradle with no attention from any of the workers. When I asked about the personnel we were promised, I got the usual Caribbean retort: "They're comin' mon." Knowing that meant anywhere from a day to a week, I took matters into my own hands and began what I call the "Ben Franklin two-step." It has worked all over the world, and it worked here as well. First thing I did was give a Ben Franklin to the supervisor while saying, "I'm sure you're going to do a good job, thanks in advance"; same thing to the project supervisor, and then handed an Andrew Jackson to any worker who showed up to work on *Julia*. By lunchtime, we had five people working for us and most of the other boats in the yard had been temporarily abandoned. For a few hundred bucks, we were in and out within one week. It's the same old *baksheesh*, just in a different place.

Tomorrow, we launch *Julia* back into the water and are excited to begin heading west through the Venezuelan Islands.

The talk now is of which agency to use for the Panama Canal transit, what islands we'll visit on the way, as well as planning the long haul up the west coast. We're a little bit melancholy these days, as we realize this is the last haul out before home, and soon we will be trying to integrate back into our American lifestyle. Some hard thinking going on here.

Personal Journal / February 3, 2007

Having already made marina reservations in Ixtapa for mid-May, we are really feeling as if we're approaching the home stretch. Sold some charts to another cruiser the other day, clearly indicating we're not going to need them again. We're both ready to be home. A few minutes ago Ken finished a phone call with his parents. With red eyes and tears streaming down his cheeks, he turned to me and said, "My grandma died, and I wasn't there."

I held him in my arms for the longest time. I knew this was hard for him.

"I want to go home," he said.

"I know you do. We are." I assured him. But just saying the words brought up even more questions for me. I thought *Julia* was my home. If she's not, then what is? What is home: a boat, a house, a port? Or is it where loved ones are?

Email / February 4, 2007 / Grounded in Grenada

While cruising around the town of St. George's looking for parts, we took up a conversation with Jaffa, our taxi driver. "Oh, you are American. Okay, Americans!" he said in pidgin English, giving us the thumbs up.

"Why do you like Americans?" I asked.

"I was on that hill over there when they came," he said. "Hiding from the Cubans." Jaffa went on relating his story about the 1983 U.S. invasion. "I was scared little boy, army gave me food, chocolate, water. I saw the parachutes, and then the soldiers kept coming. Thousands. They took me and protected me. They save me—and my country."

We thought we had completed all of our jobs while hauled out in Grenada. We put *Julia* back in the water with fresh bottom paint and all systems running well. That is, until we discovered our refrigerator control systems had shut down. We spent the day taking apart and working on the digital control systems. *"Ew! Ew! Ew! Ewwwwwww!* Gross!" screamed Ken.

"What? What's the problem?" I asked.

"Eww! I'm not touching this. You do it," Ken said as he walked away from the refrigerator controls.

"What's the big deal?" I said as I walked over and looked at the controls.

"Yuck!" I shouted as I scrambled up on deck to where Ken had already retreated and was still gulping in fresh air. "What are those?"

They were cockroach eggs. We've been battling cockroaches onboard for quite some time and had discovered they lay their eggs where it's warm around circuit boards. The eggs were shorting out the system. We took out the boards, cleaned them with soapy water, and let them dry in the baking sun. By the end of the day, they were re-installed and our refrigerator was humming along nicely.

Proud of our fix and full of smiles, I started the generator, but moments later heard Ken shout, "Shut it down! Shut it down!"

"Now what?" I asked.

"Look at this mess," he said as he started unloading his closet.

The generator was drawing saltwater into the coolant system and overflowing the coolant tank, which happens to be in Ken's closet, so his clothes are now all green and scented with *"Eau de coolant."* It's one thing after another.

I'm becoming worried: "I'm concerned about our ability to reintegrate into society," I said to Ken. "We won't be able to pick up and move on if we don't like a place."

Ken didn't miss a beat: "We'll be able to shop for parts on Sunday, we'll have services that work, we can pop over to the store for fresh vegetables, we won't have to use the radio to connect to the Internet, and my clothes won't smell like coolant. Let's go home."

"I guess what worries me is now I'm not sure if I'm happy or sad about the trip ending. It's very strange," I said.

Email / February 12, 2007 / Margaritaville

After four long days of work on the generator, we are up and running again. We left Grenada on Friday and sailed the 140 miles to our present anchorage at Isla Margarita in Venezuela, with the best sailing conditions we have experienced during our entire world tour. So much for the superstition that you're not supposed to leave on a Friday. The winds were an easy 15 knots from behind, the seas were small, and 2 knots of current in our favor boosted us along our route. We sailed calmly under bright moonlight until our early morning arrival. Oh, please…let the rest of the trip be like this.

On arrival, we contacted the local fuel barge and filled our tanks with diesel: the same volume of diesel we paid $800 for in Europe, cost $52 here. The price: 40 cents a gallon. Makes you wonder.

This is the place Harvey told us about when we first met him in the Marquesas Islands, over five years ago. I remember him telling us about the cheap fuel and liquor over our first vodka together. We have stocked up with enough wine, liquor and prime South American beef to get us home, which means *Julia* is sitting slightly lower in the water tonight. You should have seen how we nearly sunk the dinghy, with the waves splashing over the sides, soaking all of our groceries and liquor as we slowly motored out to where *Julia* was resting at anchor. Hmmm, I wonder if all of this liquor and beef has anything to do with me being overweight?

Our schedule calls for moving fast now, and we only have had two days here. Tomorrow morning, we'll leave for Los Roques Islands and then on to Bonaire for what we've heard will be some great scuba diving. By the middle of March, we will be at the entrance to the Panama Canal. Now we're cooking with gas!

Email / February 13, 2007 / Check the Charts
Sometimes I really feel like an explorer, especially when making landfall at a new anchorage that has little or no information in the guidebooks. Even more so when the charts are off by a third of a mile. There's nothing quite as exciting. If the position of the chart is wrong, then what else is incorrect? Are the depths shown anywhere near true? We have been in plenty of places where the charts are useless, so we've learned to use our eyes, instinct, and experience to find our way. We read the depths of the water by its color: the darker the water, usually the deeper it is. So this morning, as we approached the interior of the reef-strewn lagoon of Cayo de Aqua, and headed toward water that was a pale baby blue, almost white, we knew we had gone the wrong direction.

This small island is at the western end of Los Roques, 80 miles north of Venezuela. We already knew the charts were way off by reading the radar over the chart plotter. After two tries, we made it to the inside and now that we're anchored, our position on the chart actually shows us *out at sea* rather than on the inside of the stunning lagoon. The deserted beaches are pure white sand, covered with swaying palm trees. The quiet is only pierced by the swarming bird life, which includes herons, terns, and pelicans. Picture-perfect.

Email / February 17, 2007 / Clear Waters of Bonaire
Bonaire is one of the great scuba capitals of the world. The water is the clearest we've seen since the Red Sea and we're in heaven. To protect the reefs, anchoring is not allowed, but mooring balls attached to 6 tons of cement are cheap and available, making us feel secure. Today's dive was the most convenient we've ever had; we jumped in right off of *Julia* and were rewarded with tons of fish and a beautiful coral reef directly under the boat. Beautiful or not, I couldn't clear my left ear, so we aborted until I get rid of this sinus cold. How could I get a cold just as we arrive in Bonaire for a week of diving? Grrrrrr.

What else do you do if you can't dive in Bonaire? That's easy; go visit the donkeys. The island is home to the Bonaire Donkey Sanctuary. Yes, there is such a place, and it's home to hundreds of the adopted animals. Donkeys have been on Bonaire since the 17th century, and many have been abused, hit by cars, or left to starve after being worked nearly to death. The Dutch couple that founded the sanctuary showed us around and introduced us to some of the animals they had rescued. There was Frencie, who had been left for dead after being struck by a car; Harry, a 30 year old rescued from owners who tortured him by cutting his ears and nose to pieces; Pancho, an 8-month-old also hit by a car and suffering a fractured leg. There were many more, all surprisingly cute, amazingly friendly, and affectionate. We fed and played with many of them, and, of course, we couldn't resist donating to the preservation fund. Donkeys unite!

Personal Journal / February 22, 2007
Another close call. Guided by the site map from the Bonaire tourism board, we dinghied to a dive buoy located in the channel between Bonaire and its little sister island, Klein Bonaire. The channel is a natural funnel for current, but we were too busy donning our gear and didn't realize how strong it was flowing. Until it was too late.

We jumped in, gave the signal to descend, and deflated our B.C.'s. While descending, we sensed the current pushing us in the direction of open ocean at an alarming rate. When 20 feet down, Ken signaled to abort the dive, so we reversed our direction and headed up. By the time we broke the surface, we were surprised to see we were already at least 100 yards from the dinghy (think football field) and being pushed steadily out to sea. Instinctively, we tried to swim back to the dinghy, but we were struggling against the current. At first, I was out in front giving the encouragement: "C'mon Ken, we're going to have to swim hard to make it. Make sure your B.C. has air. Come on, I know you can do it."

After five minutes, which seemed like much longer, we were only halfway there, but Ken had taken the lead. The gear was slowing us down; as I'm sure were alcohol and our out-of-shape physical condition. In my youth, I could swim 100 yards with one arm behind my back, but that was a long time ago. Now, my arms were moving so slowly I wasn't making any headway.

"You have to keep swimming!" Ken shouted back at me. We swam on and on, but now I was really breathing heavily and going only where the current dictated—out to sea.

"Maybe we should swim for shore," I said weakly while gasping for air. I figured we could swim across the current like I learned when I was a kid surfing in the riptides of Southern California.

"I think I can make it!" Ken shouted from way ahead of me now. I had stopped swimming. Looking ahead, I saw Ken more than halfway to the dinghy and still going strong. *I have to drop my gear,* I thought. *I'll never make it without dropping my gear!* I looked around. There were no boats at which to blow my emergency whistle, I was back to where we had started, and shore was now as far away as the dinghy. I had to drop my gear if I was going to make it, but that would leave me without a B.C, and I didn't like that option very much. *Think! What do I take off first? Weights!* "For God's sakes, make sure you drop your weights first," I said out loud so I would hear myself.

As I was about to unbuckle my weight belt and drop it into the depths, I heard shouting. I looked up and saw Ken waving at me. He had made it and was hanging onto the side of the dinghy, catching his breath. I waved back, and then with a huge sigh of relief, turned over on my back and floated to rest. My side hurt, and I was breathing so hard I was gulping air like I had been swimming for a mile.

Within minutes, Ken came roaring up to my side and cut the motor. "Are you okay?" He was still breathing hard and looked like he had seen a ghost.

I grabbed the side of the dinghy and held on. "Okay," I said. I handed up my weight belt, then my tank and B.C., pulled myself into the dinghy, and flopped on the floor like a dead fish. "You did great! Since when can you swim faster than me?" I asked.

"Since you got old," he answered.

"Well, you mustered some deep strength. Way to go," I panted.

"I don't *ever* want to do *that* again." Ken started the motor and raced us back to *Julia*.

Why didn't we drop our gear? It would have floated with the B.C. inflated, and weight belts are easy to replace. Why didn't we swim for the shore, walk back up current, and then swim out to the dinghy? Why did we panic, struggle, and swim up current? Am I letting my guard down? That's a bad idea out here.

Email / February 25, 2007 / Getting Ready to Sail

There's always a great deal of preparation before any passage, and getting ready for this last push to Panama is no exception. If I stop to think about what we are about to do tomorrow, I get butterflies in my stomach. While going to sea is always exciting, leaving the comfort and safety of the mooring ball here in beautiful Bonaire is not really my number-one choice. Perhaps one more day of diving...or two...or three. The forecast for this passage is not all that great. Nothing major, but it calls for 30 knots, with gusts to 35, and 15-foot seas—not the ideal weather window, but typical for this route.

Nick flew in to sail with us again, and we had a reunion at the airport as we loaded his gear into our rented pickup truck. He'll be aboard as we sail north of Curacao and Aruba, west past Punta Galinas, and along the coast of Colombia. Other than that, we'll keep well enough offshore to avoid drug smugglers and pirates, as this area is well known for both. Our destination is the San Blas, a beautiful chain of islands near the coast of Panama.

Here we go...the last push to the Americas.

Email / February 27, 2007 / Racing Toward Colombia

Screaming down the face of 15-foot waves, while making 12 knots, we're racing our way toward the coast of Colombia. We're sailing in good company with Ted Nobbs and Nancy Knudsen from Australia, on their boat *Blackwattle*. While we chat twice daily on scheduled radio calls, there's not much about the weather to discuss since we're only about 10 miles apart. On this call, though, when I give Ted our exact position, and tell him we are in huge 20-foot seas, he pauses and asks me to stand by.

Then I hear Ted's voice again, "*Julia*, have a closer look at the chart. You should get out of the shallows; your depth there is only 600 feet." An hour later, we're 7 miles farther offshore, the seas are definitely smaller, and I'm back on the radio thanking Ted. Out here, every detail counts.

The wooden shims that help keep the mast in position at the deck have been creaking worse than my bones on a Sunday morning. Taking the advice of our rigging friend in Spain, we poured olive oil on the wood, and guess what? No more creaking. However, some olive oil has worked its way down the mast into the main salon, making the boat smell like an Italian kitchen.

Email / March 1, 2007 / Wind Watching

I never thought I would see wind coming from all directions at once. It's midnight in Guayraca Bay on the north coast of Colombia, and the moon is nearly full, casting a shimmering silver light across the bay. This light allows us to stand on deck and watch the gusting wind come across the water with such force we have to hang on when it hits. Standing naked on the foredeck, we first see, then feel the blowing water sting our skin. It feels like we're being hit with thousands of cactus needles as the wind and water slam into us. *Julia* stretches out on her anchor chain and swings to meet it head-on, so we're in constant motion. The winds hiss loudly as they fly down the steep flanks of the nearby cliffs, from the beach and from out at sea. We're moving around so much, our track on the computer screen looks like a child's finger painting.

Email / March 4, 2007 / Diverting to Cartagena for Emergency Repairs

We have lost control of our steering in 15-foot seas off the coast of Colombia. The 30-knot winds were from behind, and we were sailing along fine, surfing down these walls of water, when we heard a loud *"BANG!"* The gunshot sound got our attention, but it was Nick's comment that summed it all up: "Uh-oh." He was at the helm when, suddenly, the steering went loose and he was left with little control of the rudder. To keep us from broaching sideways to the waves, Nick was turning the wheel wildly, like steering an old Cadillac.

In these rough conditions, it was a challenge to get down close enough to the steering gear to evaluate the situation. We feared a broken steering quadrant, or cable, but a quick check proved otherwise; all seems intact. We know something down there is busted since we can't steer with the wheel. However, we can steer using the autopilot—because it's connected directly to the steering quadrant. The problem is dangerously serious, and we are immediately diverting to Cartagena.

I think it was meant to be we go to Cartagena though. Everybody says it's one of the most beautiful cities in the world, and while we had originally wanted to visit, didn't feel we had the time. Schedule or not, that's where we're headed.

My calculations show we'll arrive at the huge seaport in the middle of the night, which is going to make this landing a real challenge.

Email / March 7, 2007

Our nighttime entrance to Cartagena was textbook. With good moonlight and decent charts, we followed the complex channel one buoy to the next until reaching the anchorage. With no wheel for steering, we navigated our way into the huge harbor past 30 red and green markers using only the push button autopilot. While I "steered," Nick watched for the next buoy, and Ken kept us on course via the radar and chart plotter.

Using our high-powered binoculars, Nick called, "Coming up on port, about 100 yards, I think I can make out a number."

"Roger, there should be a green on port, number seven," Ken confirmed from the chart. Navigation 101, this was not. But tonight, our experience again paid off. With a great sigh of relief, we finally dropped the anchor off of Club Nautico at 0330 in the morning and promptly fell asleep.

At 0800, we were startled awake by a knock on the boat. *"Julia, Julia, buenos dias."* I stumbled up the ladder to find the marina manager and yacht agent. *"Si, buenos dias,"* I mumbled in my French-accented Spanish.

"We have a place for you at the dock," said the marina manager who turned out to be from England. "But you have to go there now, or we have to give it to another boat."

Our SAT phone had sure come in handy, as we had telephoned the club the previous day advising them we were coming in with a serious problem. We maneuvered via push button into the berth and promptly fixed a batch of Bloody Marys.

What happened? The simplified explanation is a pulley broke away from its mount, loosening the cable from the steering quadrant. As Lindsay taught me back in Tonga in 2002, everything can be fixed. A mechanical engineer has already been aboard and taken the guilty parts to the welder. And here we are in Cartagena thoroughly enjoying ourselves.

Last evening began in the Old Town with drinks in the Spanish Plaza de Bolivar…or was it Plaza Santo Domingo…does it really matter? There were acrobats, dancers, musicians, restaurants and bars, and there were, of course, street vendors selling art, shoes, T-shirts, carvings, cigars, and ladies and men of the night. As we took our seats at a plaza dining table, waiters appeared out of nowhere—and so did the street vendors. *"Señor,* have a look at my paintings, *por favor.* I make them on small mirrors and make *especial* for you."

"No gracias," I reply.

"Wow, those are really cool," Ken says. "They would make great gifts."

"Si, señor," as he turns his attention to Ken. "I use my finger, no paintbrush. I make *especial* for you. Which you like, maybe a boat?"

"Oh, now you've done it," Ted says.

"Good going," Nick says with a laugh.

"That's it, you're done for," Nancy adds.

"Well, I like them," Ken says in defiance. "How much for that one?"

"Oh, *señor,* I cannot make *justa* one, but maybe will make for you six."

"How about three?" Ken asks.

"*Señor*, I hava family," as he looks at Ken with sad eyes.

"Fine, I'll take five," Ken gives in.

"*Mui bueno señor!*" the happy artist says. We watched with admiration as the artist created five hand mirrors with paintings of boats and sunsets, done only with the tip of his finger. We all concurred; they are beautiful.

While everybody's attention was focused on Ken and his painted mirror purchase, I was doing a bit of my own negotiating. "*Señor*, I see you have no hat—and the sun—she's very hot," the vendor says.

"But it's nighttime," I protest.

"*Si señor*, is nighttime now, but *mañana* will be daytime and very, very hot."

Nick had turned back to watch my fine art of negotiating. "He's got a point there," Nick said through tears of laughter.

"I've always kind of wanted a Panama hat like this one. How much?" I ask, thinking I am an experienced negotiator.

"I make special for you because is nighttime. For you, only $12," the vendor replies.

"No, no, way too much," I say. "I can only give you $5."

"*Señor*, you have so much. I am only a poor street vendor, and I have a family. I have friends too; maybe you like a girl for the night? Or maybe a boy?"

"No *gracias*, just the hat please." I know he'll win in the end, so I break down early. Here's $10, okay?"

"*Si señor*, it looks good on you. $10 is good, *muchos gracias*," and he walks away happy.

"Oh, aren't you the big negotiator," Nick says. "You got $2 off." We all have a good laugh. "Another round of drinks *señor*," Nick says to the waiter.

I'm happy with my new hat, Ken is happy with his mirrors, and the street vendors are happy with their sales. That's what I call a win-win sale.

We feel welcome like old friends in this most hospitable city. Wandering through the impeccably clean streets, we are impressed by the beautifully preserved Spanish architecture. The brightly colored buildings of blue, orange, yellow, purple, and green reflect the liveliness of the city, and the sound of Latin rhythm fills the sultry evening air. Once again, we are reminded that from lemons, come lemonade. If the steering gear hadn't broken, we wouldn't have stopped in this wonderful city. It takes more effort, but we all need to continually look for lemonade in the lemons that cross our path.

Personal Journal / March 7, 2007

Yesterday was another milestone: We changed *Julia's* shore electrical system back to 110 volt. She's been 220 volts since the converter was installed in New Zealand, and everywhere since there has been 220 volts. Now that we're close to the U.S., electricity is 110 volts, including Colombia.

We have hired Carlos, the boat boy, a handsome brown-skinned 21-year-old who polishes the stainless steel, cleans lockers, and scrubs the deck for $10 a day. He's also glad to provide other services and products: "*Capitán*, do you want to try the local product?" he asked.

"What do you mean," I inquired innocently. "What local product?"

"You know, from Colombia, it is the best. The *cocaínya*."

"Oooh, *that* local product." I figured supporting the local economy would be the right thing to do. "Okay, how much for 1 gram?" It was $10, and Carlos seemed surprised we only asked for such a small amount. "Uh…yeah, that would last us a month since it's really not our thing," I said.

Sure enough, the next day, our boat boy arrived and handed us the strongest, purest cocaine I have ever tried (not that I've tried a lot, but I did live through the 1980s).

"Ew, I don't like it," I said. "It's too strong. Wow."

"Makes me too jittery," Ken said.

"It might be good to reorganize the entire boat's interior," I said with a laugh.

We gave it back to Carlos and he was crushed, thinking he had failed to deliver on his promise. I found myself apologizing, telling him the quality was fine, it wasn't his fault, and he could keep the money.

"Then maybe there is something else you like to have from me, *Capitán*?" the boy asked with a wink and sexy smile.

"Uh-oh, now how are you going to get out of this one?" Ken asked while laughing.

"Hmmm, maybe I don't want to get out of this one," I teased Ken. "That's okay, Carlos, not at the moment, but I'll let you know."

Email / March 11, 2007

Our repairs have been completed quite professionally, and tonight we bid farewell to lovely Cartagena. The friendly and helpful people we met, and the city's physical beauty, tried hard to keep us longer, but it's time to move on, and tonight we set sail for the San Blas Islands and Panama. Nick has been called back to Switzerland for a business meeting, leaving us on our own again. Too bad because he likes rough conditions, and that's exactly what we have. We're heading farther south in hopes of calmer winds and easier seas.

Personal Journal / March 14, 2007

I honestly don't know if Ken and I are going to make it. At the moment, I'll feel lucky if we make it all the way home together, given the current daily arguments. What's particularly sad is the bickering is usually about petty things.

I take some responsibility—in fact, I'll take half—but I have to attribute a fair amount to alcohol. The arguments may not start because we're drinking, but the alcohol certainly exacerbates the situation. If we can make it home intact, then there's hope, because then we'll have other diversions and distractions. To make it back with this amount of arguing, though, is going to be tough. He's ready to head to the nearest airport, and I'm ready to buy his ticket. What a shame; here we are in the San Blas, with beckoning white sand beaches, calm anchorages, and great sailing conditions, yet the alcohol-fueled tension overwhelms the beauty.

Personal Journal / March 15, 2007

We apologized, both promising to stop yelling at each other. I can tell we both really want to make it work. There are days we get along so well, and at night we hug so close we both know our love is genuine.

How do we get past the bickering? I'm hopeful. We're both currently under a lot of pressure to get *Julia* home safely, and that's causing quite a bit of stress.

💡 *We lived a lifetime of lessons in one journey, many of them about relationships. Living together on a boat has its challenges. Space is tight, and it's hard not to feel like you're constantly living on top of each other, which you are. I think it's like dog years. One year equals seven. When people ask, "How long have you two been together?" I reply, "Let's see, six years times seven, that's 42 years on the boat...."*

We know of three couples that, after finishing their cruise or circumnavigation, divorced within a month of returning to their home cities. But we could tell they were sick of each other. We weren't. We were just stressed and drinking too much. Well, maybe we were just a little tired of being together....

✉ **Email** / March 16, 2007 / It's the Basics in Life

Of the hundreds of islands that make up the San Blas group, only a few are populated by the Kuna Indians. The Kuna culture is sacred to the natives, and they're doing everything possible to keep the western influence out, while ironically, still welcoming tourists by yacht. For example, the rules clearly state scuba diving is prohibited, as is water skiing, jet skiing, windsurfing, and bikinis because these things are not natural to their culture.

Our interactions with the locals was always very friendly, but remained all business: They have things to sell, and we have money. Try as the older natives may to keep out the western culture that surrounds them, the attraction of making business deals has long ago taken root. *"Molas,"* are the primary crafts from these islands. They're a type of tapestry woven with brightly colored stitching to create big, bold materials with pictures of parrots or fish, or native Indian designs. They really are beautiful, and we found ourselves falling into *mola* mentality and bought more than we should have. How can you resist? They're beautiful, and the sales tactics are superb. It's the same story all over the world. Whether I'm in Thailand, Indonesia, Colombia, or here, I have no power to resist entrepreneurial effort.

While anchored, a family of five paddles out to *Julia* in their *cayuko*, a one-piece dugout canoe, cut from one single, really big coconut tree, and is in itself an amazing work of art. One of the kids is bailing water, the other, looking longingly with puppy dog eyes at our yacht, asks for candy. His brother grins ear to ear. Then the husband introduces his wife who makes the *molas,* and asks, "Won't you please buy one from us?"

"Well, we already bought from the other canoe," I say.

"Yes, we understand, but that was from them—what about us?" I find it hilarious how entrepreneurs all around the world use this same tactic, and even funnier is that I fall for it every time…maybe because I appreciate a good sales pitch. He presses his case: "They were another family; we aren't as rich as they are. Can we please show you our *molas?* They are different." And so it goes until they are aboard the boat, drinking sodas, laughing, joking, showing us dozens and dozens of *molas,* which aren't really much different from what we've already bought. Yet before we know it, we are the proud owners of a few more of these pieces, which I'm sure my grandmother would call "*schmatas*" (Yiddish for rags). In the end, they're happy, we're happy, and we have had a good time getting to know a few locals and experiencing a small view of their lives.

As I have said before, it's the people that make this trip worthwhile, and the Kuna Indians are another example of how wonderful it is to meet people from different cultures around the world. We all want the same things: to wake up another day, be healthy, love our friends and family, have a good meal, make a few bucks, laugh, be happy, and enjoy life. Seeing the Kuna Indians reminds me it is indeed these basics that make for a happy life. I'm reminding me, and I'm reminding you…stick to the basics.

From the moment we entered Shelter Bay Marina on the Caribbean side of the canal, there was nervous tension in the marina and aboard Julia. *We asked others who had been through: "What's it like? Scary? Exciting? Fun? Nerve-wracking? Dangerous?"*

We received an assortment of answers from a variety of people, so we had to just wait and see for ourselves. The answer is "Yes" to all of the above. Taking Julia *through the canal was incredibly exciting, and quite nerve-wracking, especially in the beginning as we were lifted up in the locks. It's also dangerous, a bit scary, especially eerie at night, lots of fun, and overall, an amazing and rewarding experience. A lot of feelings for just the price of admission!*

CHAPTER 25

Open Up Those Canal Gates, Pacific Ocean Here We Come!

*"Success is not final, failure is not fatal: It is the courage
to continue that counts."*
WINSTON CHURCHILL

Email / March 26, 2007 / The Panama Canal: Gateway to Home
Our agent efficiently arranged for the Panama Canal Authority
(ACP) to measure *Julia* for the fee on a Monday, and we began our transit
on Friday. Unlike the Suez Canal, the Panama Canal Authority doesn't
care how much wheat you can carry but rather the volume of water your
boat will displace in the lock. Bill and Larry from San Francisco arrived
and helped enormously during that week as we prepared *Julia* by strip-
ping her of all equipment that could catch on lines. We removed and
stowed the stern anchor, man overboard equipment, surfboard bag, fuel
cans, dinghy, etc. Then, to protect the hull in case we hit the side of the
rough cement lock, we hung our fenders, plus 10 car tires wrapped in
plastic, down the topsides.

The last protective measure was to cover the solar panels with the thick cockpit cushions to protect the panels from being hit by the "monkey fists" thrown to you upon entering the lock. These heavy knots of rope are as hard as a baseball and are attached to a light line. The handlers fire the fists at the boat with superb pitching skill. Once the "catcher" onboard dodges the knot (so it doesn't knock him out), he then must retrieve it from its landing place on deck before it falls overboard and gets caught in the propeller. (It's a gay boat; did you really expect us to *catch* the ball?) That line is then tied to a heavier one, and the handlers up on the walls of the locks tie us off to the cleats. This procedure holds us in position as the water goes in or out of the lock.

David, our agent from Matchship, had also arranged for the tires and the long thick dock lines needed for the transit, and even provided us with a local cell phone so we could receive his calls. We felt like a super yacht; having an agent ease the bureaucracy of the canal is really the way to successfully slip from one ocean to the next. On Friday morning, we got the call saying we were going that afternoon.

Our crew consisted of Ken, Bill and Larry, Ted and Nancy, and Carlos, a borrowed crew member from the agency. We prepared food, tried to rest, and then motored out in the late afternoon to meet the transit advisor. He came aboard via the pilot boat at 1800 hours, and as darkness fell, we rafted together with another sailboat to go through side by side. This uses less space in the lock, and they can fit more yachts and ships in at a time. Rafting up with the other boat was tricky—by the time our boats were tied together and we headed for the lock—we had to hurry to make our allotted appointment. The advisor had our two boats racing forward in the darkness at a good clip in order to get into the first lock on schedule. That made it quite a challenge to slow, and then stop, at the right spot inside the lock.

While darkness had already settled upon us, we were actually moving toward light—lots of it—as the locks are lit up like broad daylight, with huge floodlights. Additionally, there's an oversized neon arrow—the type more akin to a drive-in diner—pointing to the side in which you are supposed to enter. We motored timidly into the first lock, but the transit advisor kept urging me closer to the stern of the big ship with which we were sharing our lock.

"Move up! You have to move closer to ship!" the advisor urged.

"I'm already too close. Look at the size of that thing," I said as I nervously motored us toward a propeller the size of a garbage truck.

"More close, you have to go more close," the advisor insisted.

The line handlers, who surely play baseball on the side, shot their monkey fists at us with the accuracy expected of major leaguers. Ken and Carlos on the foredeck survived the first pitch, tied off the lines, and we secured ourselves in the center of the lock. Unfortunately, the crew on the boat we were tied to wasn't quite as sharp, and by letting their bowline slip, we were forced to motor hard forward and starboard in order to keep from spinning out of control in the middle of the lock. This happened more than once, and I was glad to be at the wheel of the boat with more horsepower.

Once secure in the lock, loud bells blared like a fire alarm and signaled the closing of the giant gates. As the huge doors swung shut, we debated if we had entered through the gates of hell—or was it heaven? Once they were closed, the lock filled with water from all sides as it boiled, frothed, and flooded 26 million gallons in 10 minutes. That's a lot of water; imagine the strength of the currents that made our 25-ton *Julia* bob around like a cork in a bathtub. We could hear the stress on the lines as they stretched to their maximum and hoped the cleats would hold. You could see the sweat on my brow as I fought to keep the boats straight in line. It was unnerving as the water swirled all around us, bubbling up like a foaming caldron.

With the enormous lock filled (110 feet wide x 1000 feet long), we had been lifted one-third of the 84-foot rise provided by these three locks. Bells rang, the gates opened, lines were eased, and we watched the propeller on the ship in front of us start to turn. I cautiously motored forward into the next lock to do it again. By the third lock, the whole crew was soaked from sweat, stressed out, and tired of handling the heavy lines back and forth. We certainly had improved our skills at handling the boat in locks. Once through the third, we breathed a big sigh of relief and entered the vast manmade Gatun Lake where we happily unrafted from the other boat. Then we motored a couple of miles in pitch blackness to a huge ship's mooring to tie up for the night.

Another boat with friends from Norway had come through in the locks next to us, and they tied to the same mooring. Shortly after, the pilot boat picked up the transit advisor and promised to send another pilot in the morning to guide us the rest of the way. It was a fun party that night while moored in the lake, really having no idea where we were, and wondering what was next.

We were awakened at 0600 by the sounds of the jungle: squealing monkeys, screeching birds, and who knows what else. It might sound cliché, but the bright red sun really did rise over the dark green jungle. We were treated to a spectacular view of the serene lake, while the sky filled with birds of all varieties: pelicans, hawks, parrots, frigates, terns, and seagulls.

There was only time for a quick cup of coffee before we saw the pilot boat on the horizon. Once our new transit advisor was aboard, we cast off to motor 30 miles across the lake toward the Pacific Ocean. Motoring through the "banana cut," a narrow channel only for yachts, was much like going through the Disneyland jungle cruise with monkeys in the trees, parrots overhead, hawks soaring through the sky, and thick green foliage. Wait, that's incorrect. It's Disneyland that's just like this…because this is the real deal.

Once across the lake, we continued through the Guillard Cut, basically a ditch blasted right through the rock and shale mountains. It's the narrowest part of the canal, and there's lots of construction work in progress to significantly widen this section of the canal. Trucks, tractors, backhoes, and every other big machine Caterpillar makes were in heavy use. Our attention then turned skyward as we slipped easily beneath the famous and graceful Bridge of the Americas.

On the other side of the cut, we rafted up with our Norwegian friends (much easier this time) and waited our turn to enter the first of three downward locks, the Pedro Miguel. The first descent was 29 feet, and what a difference it makes going down rather than up. Once in the lock, lines attached, it was a smooth descent as the water drained, and we were lowered to Miraflores Lake. Then, after a 1-mile motor across the man-made lake to the Miraflores Locks, it was only two more steps down to the Pacific.

When the last of the gates opened, Ken and I looked at each other with tears in our eyes upon seeing our first glimpse of the Pacific Ocean in more than five years. We shared a flood of emotions, followed by a flood of champagne with our friends. With one hand on the wheel, and the other holding my glass, I caught Ken's eye; we smiled, knowing this was one of *those* moments. Yes, we have many of these aboard *Julia*.

As it opened, I couldn't help but note the significance of this gate, the last one standing in my way, beckoning me through, and thereby making it possible to complete my dream of circumnavigation.

Being back in our home ocean was a bittersweet experience. We're proud of what we've done, yet sad that it's coming to a close. Even so, we were full of smiles as we motored out of the last lock into the Pacific. Looking back at the tens of thousands of miles sailed to reach this point, I'm amazed at our accomplishment. We have crossed the Pacific, Indian, and Atlantic oceans; the Coral Sea; Arafura Sea; Timor Sea; Savu Sea; Java Sea; Bali Sea; Andaman Sea; Laccadive Sea; Arabian Sea; Gulf of Aden; Red Sea; Aegean Sea; Ionian Sea; Tyrrhenian Sea; Balearic Sea; Mediterranean Sea; and the Caribbean Sea; the Suez; Corinth; and Panama Canals, and now are back in our home ocean, the Pacific. That's a lot of water. *Wow.*

Now we'll head west until we see that corner where we're supposed to turn right, point north, and head homeward. I wonder what would happen if we accidentally missed the turn, and kept on going west....

Email / April 1, 2007

Isla Gamez is the perfect picture of a tropical paradise, and it's begging for us to go exploring ashore. I kayaked to the beach and while wandering aimlessly along the sand, collected some exquisite seashells. Hmmm, what am I going to do with them? I'm pretty relaxed these days in spite of how fast we're moving north.

Hey, what if this trip really did change me, and I really *am* this relaxed? Five years ago today, it wasn't the case. It was on April 1, 2002, *Julia* slipped quietly from her anchor at Puerto Vallarta and headed south to cross the Pacific Ocean. I was excited and nervous while considering what lay ahead on our first ocean crossing. It was the first real test of my navigational skills, of *Julia's* systems, and of being self-reliant. I learned at a certain point you just have to make the decision to go, to do the thing you even fear, to lift the anchor, and head out to sea.

I will never forget Al, Bob's incredible father, and his response when I asked him, "Do you really think I should give up everything to go sailing? It means leaving my home, closing my business, and leaving Bob."

At the time, he was in failing health, and from his hospital bed, he took my hand and squeezed tightly. With tears in his eyes, and holding my hand like a vise, Al looked up at me and shouted, *"Go, man…Go!"* We left exactly one year after he died.

N 8°07.727 W 82°19

Personal Journal / April 18, 2007

Golfito, Costa Rica. I can't believe we're broken down with another big mechanical failure. Oh well, what are you gonna do? It's not really different than all the other times we've repaired things. It's just that we're so close to home. But that doesn't really matter; this isn't horseshoes or hand grenades where close counts.

I'm calmer than other times we have had significant breakdowns. Not sure why; maybe the last five years have taught me it will all eventually work out, and getting upset doesn't really help much. The answer lies in getting the job done, and getting upset only makes that process more frustrating. When there's a problem, now I stop and analyze the situation. What went wrong and what are the potential fixes? Once a repair path is chosen, there has to be a plan, and then the first step in that plan needs to be taken.

Well now, this is sounding vaguely familiar…as if I used this logic before…that's right, this is the same logic used to make this entire journey happen. Why don't we apply this reasoning to our relationship issues?

Email / April 19, 2007 / Working Hard in Costa Rica

"I need a break," Ken said out of the blue. "Let's go do something, and I don't mean work on the generator. Here we are in Costa Rica, and all we're doing is playing mechanic."

I only had to think for a moment. "I've got it. What do most people come to Costa Rica for?"

"I don't know, you're the travel expert," Ken said.

"Hellooo, the rainforest! Let's go stay in the rainforest somewhere."

"Uh-uh. Remember, I didn't sign up to go camping," Ken firmly reminded me.

"Not camping; I'm talking about an ecolodge, a place where we can appreciate the wilderness…from our balcony," I proposed.

Next thing you know, we were skimming across the bay in a zippy water taxi headed to the Oso Peninsula. There, a handsome young man in his four-wheel drive greeted and drove us through the back country to Bosque del Cabo, the fantastic lodge in the middle of the rainforest.

"You *don't* want an ocean view?" asked the surprised front desk clerk.

"No, thank you. We'd like to have a view of the land," I said laughing.

The sounds of the rainforest soothed us as we relaxed in an open-walled garden cabin. Through the night into the early morning, we heard the screeching of howler, squirrel, and white-faced monkeys. The morning birdcalls were a battle for the airwaves as a cacophony of scarlet macaws, toucans, and many others fought to be heard the loudest. One night, a local guide gave us a very *Wild Kingdom*-style tour as he pointed out the poisonous dart frog, venomous snakes, bats, spiders, and all sorts of other scary things that live in the fragile ecosystem of the rainforest.

Three days later, we're back on the boat and tied to the dock at the smallest marina we have ever seen…there's only space for two boats and we are one of them. We're fortunate to be at the dock so we can keep *Julia's* refrigerator, freezer, and air conditioner running, and there's even Internet access so we're temporarily living in luxury.

It's hot and humid in Golfito, but the market is a short walk away, where food is inexpensive, fresh, and readily available. Tim and Katie, the owners of Land and Sea, a marina and yacht services hangout, are taking good care of us. We eat communal meals with them and other yachties; they help us find parts, give tips where to hike, and we drink beer while swapping stories long into the night. We've made more good friends, and they inform us we are the new record holder for beers consumed by one yacht. Is that a good thing?

✉ **Email** / April 28, 2007 / Rain, Rain, Rain

Being this close to the equator and tropical rainforest, we're not surprised but are amazed at the volume of rain. All of those beautiful pictures you see of green Costa Rica tell it just as it is: wet.

BOOM! The first clap of thunder cracks through the forest. The rain follows in about 10 minutes, and when it begins, it really lets loose. The rain doesn't come down in drops but in walls, layers, blankets, bullets....

It only took five years, but we have finally fixed all of *Julia's* deck leaks so we can sit in relative comfort and dryness while the world is pouring down outside. All we need is power that runs consistently. Costa Rica has its share of outages, and by that I mean every day for at least two to three hours the power fails. When power resumes, the Internet and air conditioner come back online and we're in business again. That is until today, when the electrical plug melted, shutting everything down again. Ken jury-rigged a new one out of two old spares, and we've got electricity restored (although I doubt the plug would be UL approved).

The beginning of the rainy season is telling us it's time to get going. Once again, we are the last ones out of an area. Those headed south and across the Pacific have already gone, and those few headed north have already left to beat the hurricane season in Mexico. We were last to leave Thailand to cross the Indian Ocean; we were last to leave Kupang, Indonesia for Bali; we were last to leave Tel Aviv for Turkey; and now we'll be the last boat out of Golfito. We'll try to remember to turn the lights off before we go this time, or maybe they'll do that by themselves.

It hasn't been exactly how we pictured our extended stay in Costa Rica, but overall, in spite of the rain and mechanical issues, we're having a good time. In fact, sometimes we even go for a walk in the rain. After all, we are in the rainforest.

✉ **Email** / May 5, 2007 / It Was a Friday
There are lots of superstitions in the world of sailing, but for the most part we don't buy into any of them, except the occasional advice to "knock on wood." I recognize I've flip-flopped on this subject before, however, I just might begin believing the one that says you should not start a passage on a Friday. Yesterday was Friday. With our new oil pump installed, we left Golfito and motored out into the Gulf de Dulce to continue sailing north. We were only gone two hours, motoring in very light winds, when the engine started sputtering, then made a clicking noise, and then stopped (as did our hearts).

"It has to be electrical," I said to Ken as he hung upside down in the engine room.

"I'm sure it's a broken wire; I know it is," Ken groaned.

"Oh, please let it be a broken wire," I said optimistically.

Ken soon appeared topside and said, "I can't find it. I can't find the problem. I'm sorry."

We turned back to Golfito; however, with barely a breath of wind, it was looking like a long 12 miles to get there. For the first time during this voyage (and what we should have done in Kupang), we figured out how to mount the outboard motor on the transom, with its custom-made bracket, and made our way back using the 25 hp Yamaha. About 50 yards from the dock, we cut the power to the outboard and coasted in for a perfect docking to the applause of the bar patrons who had gathered to watch the impending crash landing.

It took Robert, the latest in a long line of trusted mechanics, a couple of hours to figure out what was wrong, but he eventually found a broken wire *(well, whadda you know?)*.

Do we believe it's bad luck to leave on a Friday? Naaahhh, it's all a bunch of hooey, but just in case, I think we'll stick to departing only on days ending in A-Y.

Email / May 11, 2007 / A Great Passage

The air is warm and soft, tropical, sultry. The moisture adds a heaviness, which, while making your skin feel smooth, also makes breathing difficult. I find myself struggling to get the satisfaction of a deep breath. The night is so dark from cloud cover it's almost pitch black, except every few minutes, a huge lightning bolt momentarily converts the night sky to daylight. Then it's black again; all I can see is our phosphorescence wake behind us, and the radar screen in front of me.

It's the fifth night of this passage and we are crossing into the famed Gulf of Tehuantepec, known to have gale-force winds almost half the days of the year. Well, this time it's our turn and luck is with us. The winds are 5 knots, and we're motoring across the gulf in nearly flat, calm seas. Maybe my coins in Trevi Fountain hit the right statue after all.

When daylight comes, and because it's calm, we're able to more easily see the marine life; scores of dolphins play around the boat, surfing our bow wave daily, and we have seen dozens of big sea turtles, each about 3 feet in length, basking on the surface. And thousands of jellyfish float on the surface as far as the eye can see.

The days are very hot and showers are with hot water (because the engine room temperature heats up the tanks), so we never really cool down until nightfall. Even then, the nights are still warm. This might sound enticing to those in cold climates, but for me, I'm ready to get out of the tropics and back into that cold San Francisco fog.

With just two of us, the nights seem longer, and I'm quite enjoying these long dark watches. It provides time to think, to reflect on the trip we are about to complete, to wonder about the future, and to solidify meandering thoughts. And it gives me time to absorb how beautiful it is out here...how absolutely beautiful.

I can see we are indeed headed home. I suppose that's because we're headed in a northwest direction, and our boat position is on the same chart plotter screen as San Francisco. We're definitely close to the U.S. as we had a fly-by from a U.S. Navy AWACS reconnaissance plane. We waved, and they waggled their wings back at us. We encounter three to four ships in a day and night, and stand a vigilant watch 24 hours a day, but it all seems so easy in these near perfect conditions.

The engine is running continuously, and we're trying to stretch our fuel all the way to Huatulco. I don't mind the engine noise anymore. In fact, it's music to my ears to hear it running well. Never mind that we discovered a leak in our transmission cooler—as long as the hole doesn't get any larger we'll be fine. But just in case, I'm preparing to plug the leak by chewing bubble gum. And never mind that because we're running the engine constantly, we haven't needed the generator we spent the last three weeks repairing. Nothing seems to bother me anymore.

This morning, I've checked our route and the charts, and have read the *Mexico Boating Guide* for more information about the marina. I played with dozens of dolphins surfing the bow wave, changed the courtesy flag from Costa Rica to Mexico, cleaned up the cockpit, rigged fenders and dock lines for arrival, made coffee, had a shower in the cockpit, and then I smelled land. We will dock in Huatulco before 0900 with plenty of fuel, and with the memories of an almost perfect passage. I think I might miss this when it's all done.

Email / May 15, 2007 / Margaritas and Montezuma's Revenge
We're en route to Zihuatanejo, motoring in light winds, and enjoying the calm conditions. Patrik is aboard again for this momentous leg of the trip. He didn't want to miss our arrival in Z-town, where we'll cross our outbound track first made five and a half years ago.

We are enjoying being back in Mexico. Within a day of our arrival, we knew we were here: We were hung over from celebrating Ken's birthday with margaritas…and we had the runs.

Personal Journal / May 16, 2007
We're 75 miles from Zihuatanejo and I have a lot of conflicting emotions. I write emails to the group saying we are having a good time, and for the most part that's true. I tell myself nothing bothers me anymore but there's one thing I can't seem to beat—the heat.

We see lots of dolphins, turtles, and other marine life, which would normally spark my enthusiasm, but maybe I'm done. Hurricane season officially starts June 1, and we probably won't reach San Diego until early July. Hope we're not tempting fate.

Email / May 17, 2007 / Circumnavigation Complete
This morning at 0900, *Julia* sailed into Zihuatanejo Bay, crossing our outbound track and thereby completing the circumnavigation. That's 1,880 days, and 38,388 miles. *Incredible.*

So many thoughts are racing through my head. Since age 13, I've wanted to sail around the world. I was lost in that dream for such a long time, and wanted my name to be on the short list of circumnavigators, which includes Drake, Cook, Chichester, and Robin Lee Graham. In particular, I remember reading Graham's story about his own five-year journey, and wondering, "Why can't I be like him and sail around the world, too?"

I've joined that small club of global sailors, and I'm filled with emotion and thought. I am grateful that we made it around the world in one piece. Planning, skill, and good luck all played their role in our success. I'm also aware that any conclusions, thoughts, or feelings about having completed this odyssey are no longer speculation but are instead accurate observations based on real experience. They are, in fact, ocean-tested.

We all have a degree of motivation and tenacity, which give us the strength to do things we didn't think possible. And we have the will to carry on—in any endeavor—if we choose to use that power. I'm not the kind of guy who swims under polar icecaps. I'm not Shackleton, Perry, or Sir Edmund Hillary. I'm not someone who seeks fame by setting records for being the fastest, youngest, or the most daring. I see myself simply as a regular guy who wanted to go sailing.

The obstacles that stood in the way of sailing around the world are much the same as those blocking the realization of almost any goal. I didn't possess the knowledge necessary to circumnavigate but learned it along the way. I thought I had tenacity but didn't know how much was necessary to make it the full 360°. We all have the ability to adapt, change, and learn; to not tap into these resources is to miss one's own true potential for greatness.

Figuratively speaking, I passed through my own gate, which had previously limited me, but now I know what great things one can achieve. Everybody has hurdles that bar progress, but if you stay focused on the goal and never let go, you will eventually open and pass those barriers.

From a jury-rigged part, to an afternoon of fun with just coconuts and friends, I learned to make do with less. So can we all. I also learned to listen better to others; listening has taught me more than talking ever could. I have more appreciation for—and have been humbled by—the sea and the magnificence of the world around us.

I have reached a level of contentment I didn't know I was seeking—or even possible. In my previous life, I was always searching, on the move, looking for the next thing that would bring me happiness. Yes, I still seek adventure, but the desired result isn't in possessions. It's not material things that provide contentment.

Maybe I've saved you the trip. You don't have to sail all the way around the world to find the happiness already inside of you. Do seek your highest goals. Chances are, the joy you seek from their achievement is closer than you think.

Email / May 27, 2007

To congratulate us in person, Ken's parents and sister came to Ixtapa. We ate, drank, and basked in the sun and our glory. They joined us for a day sail and watched in wonder as we rigged, maneuvered, and sailed the boat like a well-oiled machine. Ken's father said, "Hey, you guys actually know what you're doing."

"Well, of course they do, Paul, how do you think they made it around the world?" his mom, Gail, said. Ken was beaming the entire day.

Upon our return to the marina, while having cocktails, all of a sudden Ken's sister Jernee jumped up shouting, "Oh, my God, look!" There, floating in the water right beside the boat was a 12-foot crocodile.

"Oh yeah, I forgot to tell you, they live in the marina," Ken said laughing. "They're looking for pets, small children, and food scraps. Be extra careful walking back to the boat at night, especially after having a few too many." After being chased by komodo dragons, a little old crocodile doesn't scare us.

We received many congratulations on our circumnavigation. From non-sailors, such as my friend John McBirney, many were amazed we could pull off such a feat: "What an accomplishment to have sailed around the world. How few people have the resolve, patience, and talent to do that? You guys are amazing."

It was recognition from veteran sailors who knew what we had gone through, like Clark from Final Straw *that truly gave us a lift: "You've done an incredible job overcoming adversity, beating the odds, and attaining an achievement that will last a lifetime. That says nothing of how much you now know about sailing, navigating, forecasting weather, fixing things, etc. Good on ya guys!"*

To jerk us back to reality, we received this email from our weather router, Bob Cook: "Possible tropical storm. Nasty squalls headed your way. Sail north fast, young man!"

Email / May 28, 2007 / Better Than Sea World

"Hey Ken, is that a dorsal fin? Seems awfully big," I said.

"It's a killer whale!" Ken said while reaching for the binoculars. "There's two of them, no, wait, four, and they're heading right this way."

"Good thing the engine is running so they know we're here. I'd rather not be sunk by killer whales as our last hurrah." As I spoke, two more surfaced only 50 yards from the boat, and moments later, we were in the middle of the herd of Orca. I kept our course, which they seemed to like, as they swam with us for a few minutes. We couldn't have got closer if we had tried.

We continued motoring along in calm waters, and dozens of dolphins came to surf our bow wave. They are such amazing animals; we never tire of watching as they effortlessly swim back and forth, surfing, jumping, and looking up at us. They like our cheering; their antics clearly display more showing off when we shout louder and applaud their performance.

We stopped counting at over a hundred sea turtles lying lazily on the surface. Next were two schools of jumping tuna and hundreds of sea birds circling overhead as flying fish were leaping into the cockpit. By accident, we even caught a blue marlin on our fishing line. When we reeled it in close to the boat, though, it was so big we wondered "Now what do we do?" The fish was 8 feet long, with a sharp bill an additional 2 feet. It was too beautiful to keep, and our only concern was how to release it without harm. We happily let it go and watched it swim away. We only keep what we can eat, and that's good for our ocean karma.

What was this amazing display of marine life today? Was it good-bye? I don't think I'm ready yet.

It was unnerving being so far south during what was the beginning of the hurricane season. The ocean was unusually calm, and the pale blue sky was filled with enormous billowing cumulonimbus clouds, reflecting a tropical depression forming 600 miles to the southwest. The calm before the storm kept us on our toes as we were peppered with a series of intense rainsqualls and impressive lightning shows. We were motivated to get north as fast as we could.

Email / May 30, 2007 / Hurricanes
Nothing instills fear in the hearts of sailors more than the word "hurricane," and we are certainly no exception. You may have noticed Hurricane Alvin is off the coast of Mexico; we sailed right through its present location less than three weeks ago. Talk about good timing! Additionally, there's another tropical depression off the coast but further out to sea. Both storm systems are 600 miles south of our current position, and by tomorrow, they'll be 700 miles away as we are rapidly moving

north. Three weeks and 700 miles *is* a close call in my book.

Personal Journal / June 7, 2007 / Wake-Up Call in Mazatlan
We're not going into the Sea of Cortez. While we were hoping the storm season would be starting late this year, those hopes have been dashed, and we feel it best to get the hell out of Dodge.

We *were* going to leave for Cabo a few days ago but got a big scare, which is keeping us here. I woke up with a funny feeling in my chest like something was quite irregular. "Ken, something's wrong."

"What are you talking about?" Ken asked.

"I don't feel right. My heart doesn't feel normal. The beating isn't regular," I said.

"How do you know; you can't feel that," Ken said.

"Yes, I can. I really think something is wrong," I replied with a worried look.

I guess that look was genuine because all of a sudden, Ken jumped up: "Come on then, let's go. There's a doctor's office right here in the marina."

"Nah, maybe I'll go later; I don't feel like it right now," I said. Ken shot back a look that changed my mind. It said, "I'm not asking you, I'm telling you; we're going now."

"Okay, okay, I'll go," I said.

It was a five-minute walk to the doctor's office and by the time we arrived, I was out of breath and had to sit down. The doctor listened to my heart and breathing, and then took my blood pressure. He looked intently at me as he stood up and began packing some files into his briefcase. "Do you drink?" he asked.

"Yeah, and last night I had a few," I replied, punctuating my sentence with laughter.

The doctor wasn't laughing. "You must go to hospital," he said. "Your blood pressure is very high and your heart is irregular. Very much irregular."

"Okay, when should I go? How about tomorrow?" I was resigned I had to go for a checkup but didn't think there was any real hurry.

The doctor thought differently: "You are going to hospital. NOW. I am driving you *ahora*…right now!" I could tell he meant business. If that didn't scare me enough, then the wild ride to the hospital certainly did. With one hand on the wheel and a cell phone to his ear, the doctor raced through traffic as fast as an ambulance. Ken reached forward and held my hand. Another doctor and three nurses met us at the emergency room, and as I was lifted onto the gurney, I remember looking up and marveling at the brand new neon sign that said, "Hospital Sharp Mazatlan—*Emergencias.*" That's when it hit me. I *was* an emergency.

Without delay, I was given a shot to thin my blood and prevent a clot, which could have caused a stroke. Then an I.V. drip with potassium and more pills to further lower my blood pressure. After a couple of hours in the E.R., they checked me into a room and said I was staying the night.

Later, I looked at Ken struggling to sleep on the uncomfortable couch. He insisted on staying in the room with me all night, and I was touched by his love and loyalty. I was scared and barely slept that night. What if this had been a stroke? What if I had been alone? What if I didn't have him? Suddenly, I appreciated my partner even more.

The cardiologist ran an EKG and an echocardiogram. As the doctor in Turkey determined, they found nothing wrong with my heart. However, I do have arrhythmia, caused by high blood pressure, too much alcohol, not enough exercise, and I'm overweight and have high cholesterol. In other words, I have a really bad case of the cruising lifestyle.

I have a new complement of blood pressure pills, cholesterol-lowering pills, and anti-arrhythmia pills, and we are staying in Mazatlan until the doctor releases me. I have my orders: "Stop drinking hard liquor; you can have a glass of red wine a day, and I don't mean a 7-Eleven Big Gulp. And start exercising. Do you think you're still a kid?" I've heard this before, but sometimes I'm a slow learner.

Personal Journal / June 10, 2007 / Fear

Many people have asked if I ever felt fear during the journey around the world. The answer is a resounding yes, but I never sent that in an email. You would have to lack any respect for the sea not to be afraid in some of the situations we have been in during this voyage.

Fear was certainly present when we lost the autopilot trying to go from Tonga to Fiji in 15-foot seas and 40-knot winds, and ended up turning back, sailing upwind and then approaching the narrow entrance to the inner harbor in a rainstorm using only radar for the approach. Or when the autopilot failed 36 hours from Australia, and in gale conditions, the forestay parted from the mast. Losing the anchor in Thailand was scary. Being chased by a "fishing boat" in the Malacca Straits didn't exactly put me at ease because in my heart, I knew they weren't fishermen. Sailing through Pirate Alley, the 300-mile stretch between Somalia and Yemen, was terrifying. We were lucky not to be attacked, but our senses were tingling and were certainly heightened by the fear. It was unnerving sailing the Red Sea day after day and not seeing anybody but a few Saudi fishing boats. During the 24-hour storm in the Red Sea with 50-knot winds and 30-foot seas, our hearts were in our throats.

Being trapped by a line 40 feet underwater and running out of air...I could have bottled the fear and sold it. I was frightened when we ripped our mainsail in Greece and then had to motor upwind in a gale to find repairs in Mykonos. One of the scariest moments was hitting a rock in Mykonos, and for a minute, I truly thought we were going to sink. I was scared again when we lost our steering off the north coast of Colombia in 15-foot seas. I was afraid when we entered the Panama Canal, and *Julia* was tossed around like a spinning cork as 26 million gallons of water filled the lock, and I fought to hold the boat in position. I have learned, though, that fear is all relative to experience and expectations, and it's not so bad when you're ready for it.

Perhaps one of the most fearful times of all was when we untied our lines from the dock in Emeryville and sailed out underneath the Golden Gate Bridge. We were headed for the unknown, the untried, the untested, not knowing where the journey would take me or what was to become of us.

Soon comes another scary chapter: when I will have completed the circumnavigation and sailed back through the gate; my boyhood dream of sailing around the world will be fulfilled. What is left? I no longer have that dream to drive me, to show me the way, to keep me pushing, keep me pursuing...but I've learned not to worry or be afraid of what is next.

Personal Journal / June 23, 2007

After 36 hours of motor sailing up wind, we're almost to Cabo. We'll pick up Patrik here, and he'll help us sail to San Diego. Good thing, too, because Ken and I are exhausted making this last passage. In truth, I think we might be running out of steam….

We're happy and enjoying each other's company. It's as if a big weight has been lifted from us, and some of the pressure has boiled off; we both know we're entering uncharted waters when we get back to San Francisco, and we need each other's unwavering love and support.

Email / June 26, 2007

We are motor sailing north along the Baja coast 600 miles south of San Diego. For the first time in a *long* time, we're sleeping under blankets, wearing shoes and socks, and long pants. We couldn't even remember where we had stored those clothes and had to dig deep to find them. I know I was complaining about the heat before, but we didn't expect it to get cold this soon. Well, that just shows you...be careful what you ask for; you just might get it.

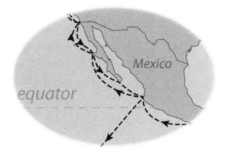

CHAPTER 26

By The Rockets' Red Glare...
Your Passports Please

"I am the master of my fate: I am the captain of my soul."
WILLIAM ERNEST HENLEY

Email / June 29, 2007

We stopped yesterday at Turtle Bay where Ernesto, whom we first met in 2002, still brings the fuel to the anchorage in his *panga*, the same small motorboat with a huge plastic tank on it. I doubt he remembered us after all the boats he's supplied in the last five and a half years. Things have changed, even here in Turtle Bay: Rather than hand pumping, Ernesto asks, *"Señor,* okay to plug in?" as he holds up an electrical plug.

Email / June 30, 2007

A rattling noise was coming from the engine room. We quickly shut the engine down and found the alternator was wobbly and vibrating. The upper mounting bracket had broken, and a large mounting bolt on the bottom had long since worn its hole bigger than the bolt itself. "Skipper, you want to take a look at this?" Patrik said.

"It's just being held on by the belt," I said inspecting the situation closely. Ken jumped right in, and together with Patrik, we all worked on a temporary solution.

"The bolt's too loose. We either need a bigger bolt or a smaller hole," Ken said.

"Who wants a beer?" I asked.

"At 2 in the morning?" Ken shot me a surprised look.

"Ah, I know where you're going with this," Patrik said, as his eyes lit up. "I'll sacrifice and drink the beer."

"Now hand me the can and I'll start cutting," I said, as I got out the scissors and began shaping a shim just large enough to make the lower bolt tight. "Remember when Biagio taught us this trick back in Tonga? We had to tighten the shaft on our steering wheel and make one from a beer can. Of course, that was a Heineken; top quality. I hope it works as well with a Budweiser." I laughed. There we were in the middle of the night making engine repairs and I was laughing; what a difference 40,000 miles makes!

This morning we sighted a huge humpback whale 50 yards from the boat. We were motoring and I was glad it heard us coming and got out of our way, or we simply lucked out and missed it. In Tonga, we learned they are actually attracted to the sound of diesel engines but are also smart enough to avoid hitting the boat. It was a beautiful sight and reminded me how incredible the ocean is and how fortunate I am to be out here amidst its beauty.

✉ Email / July 2, 2007 / Back in the U.S.A.

We're in San Diego earlier than expected. I think *Julia* is the horse running for the barn; she smelled home and took off faster than ever. We cleared customs in San Diego with a few simple questions: "How long have you been out of the country?" asked the customs agent.

"A long time," I answered. "A really long time."

"And the purpose of your trip?" the agent queried.

"Um, well, I'm not really sure. I kind of wanted to make sure the world is round," I said through a tired smile.

"You being a smart-ass?" the agent said lifting his eyebrows.

"Oh no, I really did want to make sure," I said, signing the entry documents.

"What are you talking about?" The agent didn't get it.

"We just finished sailing around the world. And yes, the world really *is* round," I added with a smile.

"Are you serious? Well now, that's something you don't see every day. Welcome home gentlemen." The customs agent shook our hands, turned and stepped off the boat shaking his head mumbling, "All the way around the world...hmmm...."

Email / July 6, 2007 / *Julia* Reunited With Julia

There were tears of joy when *Julia* docked at the Long Beach Yacht Club. It wasn't long before Mommy Julia came walking down the dock and was hugging her wayward son.

I have watched how Mom lives her life, and through the years have learned from her about strength and determination. She taught me tenacity is a trait—and a skill—which is best developed from practice. She taught me you don't finish sometimes; you finish *every* time. Long after you think you can't go on, you keep going. If the will is there, the strength will follow.

Mom's upbeat attitude and encouragement kept me going. When I whined via long distance telephone calls about the conditions at sea or breakdowns, she would say, "Well honey, you have to keep going. You wanted to do this, now you have to finish." Even though on occasion she would say, "Why don't you turn that ship around and come home?" I always knew she was cheering me on to go all the way around the world. I carried her spirit with me and standing on the dock, was filled with pride and gratitude to be hugging her again.

I have completed a full circle in my life. Long Beach is where I learned to sail as a kid and where my dream to sail around the world took root. The gate? *Julia* is made fast at the end of the dock—on the inside of the very one that boy stood behind, 40 short years ago. And the boy? Let's just say he will never be behind the gate again.

Now that we're here, we are mesmerized by how sprawling the cities are. Is it me, or is this society more fast paced than I remember? Nor do I recall there being so many people. Spending time in the Third World has a way of changing your size perception. It's definitely going to take a while to assimilate back into this society. Will I ever again adapt to the environment here? Not a chance, and that's okay. *Because while the world may not have changed much, I have.* I am calmer and more aware of what is truly important in life. At heart, I'm not a citizen of any particular country but rather of the world.

Personal Journal / July 24, 2007

In Long Beach, we helped Mom get ready for our welcome home party, which was really a party to show us off to relatives and friends, and that was just fine. She has been planning this party for a long time (I think since we left), and we easily got caught up in the excitement. Because most people get bored watching slide shows, or most slide shows are boring, we prepared, "Around the world in 30 minutes," and it was a hit. The champagne flowed freely as did the questions. We could barely keep up as they were fired at us from all directions. The questions reminded me the things I now take for granted are completely foreign to most people:

Q: "Where did you stop at night?"

A: "We didn't. At sea, shipboard life runs 24 hours a day." As that sunk in, I could see some of the more elderly folks shaking their heads with perplexed looks, and heard, "Ohhh, Ahhh…"

Q: "How long were you at sea?"

A: "Our longest passage was 21 days to cross the Pacific Ocean."

Q: "What?! 21 days! At sea? But you couldn't see land?"

A: I smiled as I answered, "That was the best part, not seeing land."

Q: "*Mashugana* [Yiddish for crazy person]! You know you're *mashugana*?"

A: "Yes, I know."

Q: "Where did you buy food?"

A: "That's an interesting question, and I was worried about that when we left. But people eat in other countries too. And they have stores." The questions kept coming and we had a lot of fun with the crowd, remaining patient with the perfectly understandable questions I better get used to from non-sailors.

"How did you keep your food from spoiling?"

"Where did you buy gas?"

"Did you have any breakdowns?"

"How did you know how to fix things that broke?"

"Did you run into any storms?"

"How did you know which way to go?"

"What about pirates?"

"Did you carry guns?"

"What was your favorite country?"

"Were you ever afraid?"

"Would you do it again?" The last question stumped me, but Ken jumped right in with the perfect answer: "Absolutely...if I hadn't already done it."

Seeing Mom beaming was a highlight of the trip. I guess even as an adult, this son wants his mother to be proud of him.

I can't really believe the voyage is over... a few hundred miles to go and then it will be complete. I've known this has been coming, but it's all happening so fast...maybe a little too fast.

Email / July 26, 2007 / It Isn't Over 'Til...

We are anchored at Cojo, a small bay amidst huge kelp beds tucked under Pt. Conception, the "knee" of California. We're awaiting darkness and hopefully the calm winds that come with the night. At midnight, we'll head out around the point and turn north up the coast. After a few days in Monterey, there will be one last night trip to Half Moon Bay, where we'll await the morning of August 4 to enter San Francisco Bay. We're hoping all goes according to plan, even though the winds are still blowing pretty hard against us. As we have learned many times over, we wait....

Email / July 27, 2007 / Cold, Beat Up, but Pressing On

It seems Neptune and Poseidon want to make sure we remember their powers before they'll let us get home. Surprise. As soon as we got out from under the lee of land, we were slammed with 30 knots on the nose and 8-foot seas. That brought us back to the reality of the rigors of sailing we had hoped were behind us. It doesn't matter; the weather is nothing compared to my overriding feelings of wholeness and satisfaction. I have never felt so complete in my life.

The first 9 miles took three hours, and we got the crap beat out of us. After Point Arguello, the wind and seas eased and we're already to San Luis Obispo. We were treated to a close-up view of another whale, and there are seals and dolphins escorting us as well. Have I spent too much time in the sun? Because I swear I just heard a dolphin say, "Welcome home; we're glad you're back."

All those years in the tropics have thinned our blood; we're wrapped up in foul-weather gear, boots, sweaters, ski hats, and ski gloves, and we're still cold. We're so close we can almost taste the sweetness of sailing through the Golden Gate, so we're pushing on and praying: "Bless our diesel engine."

Email / July 29, 2007

Is there a buzz and excitement in the air, or is it just me? I don't know how to precisely describe it, but there are those butterflies again.

CHAPTER 27

Home Again—Like a Ship Without a Compass

"We shall not cease from exploration and the end of all our exploring will be to arrive where we started...and know the place for the first time."
T.S. ELIOT

Email / August 8, 2007 / Home
We departed Half Moon Bay in the early morning pea-soup fog; I looked around at the group aboard: Patrik, Ken, and I were sailing, while my brother Jeff, Ken's sister Jernee, and her husband, Rob, hung on for dear life as we pounded out through exceptionally steep 6-foot seas.

"Is this normal?" Jeff asked.

"I don't feel so good," Jernee said.

"Here, take this," Ken said to his sister as he offered her a seasick pill.

"Just hang on a little bit longer, and then we'll be out to sea where it's calm," I said in my most reassuring captain's voice.

"Out to sea where *it's calm*?" Jernee questioned. Maybe my perception of things has changed somewhat over the years.

We were not only on schedule but were early to the outer channel marker. We heaved to, and waited for the right time to head for the bridge. "Champagne?" Ken offered.

While waiting, we popped the first bottle of champagne and passed it around. Everybody joined in celebrating, and we not only finished that bottle but also proceeded to pound down five more as the wind and seas turned in our favor and we headed for the Golden Gate. Our timing with the tide was perfect, and by the time we reached the bridge at noon, we were screaming along in 25 knots of "Welcome back to San Francisco" winds. Two boatloads of friends greeted us, and we saw many other friends standing on the Marin headlands and on the bridge itself.

"*Julia! Julia!* Ya-hoo!" came the shouts from the bridge as we passed underneath it.

"Skipper, you okay?" Patrik asked as he looked at me staring up at the bridge.

"Yeah, I'm okay, why?" I asked.

"Because you're crying," Patrik said.

"Do you realize the last time we sailed under this bridge was almost six years ago?" I babbled. "Oh my God, we did it. We actually did it. *Ya-hoooooooooo!*" I screamed. "We did it!" and I let the tears stream openly down my face. At that moment, I looked at Ken. He was looking at me—his eyes were red, too.

I snapped us out of it with a call for, "Ease the jib sheet!"

Even tough guy Ken couldn't let the moment go by. He threw his arms around me, and said, "We're home. We're home."

Julia was all dressed up with a long string of 40 international courtesy flags as well as a big rainbow flag that we have flown over the past six years. As we tacked back and forth across the bay and sailed by the St. Francis Yacht Club, we cut right through a massive regatta, sailed around an outrigger canoe race, and dodged a windsurfer regatta. After a breather in the lee of Angel Island, we headed toward our home at Emery Cove Marina.

As we motored slowly towards the dock, we were greeted by friends standing on the jetty, on the pier, and then dozens on the dock cheering for us. I struggled to see through tears of joy, and my share of bubbly, I managed to barely avoid hitting the dock.

I turned off the engine and prepared to make my big speech, which is here in its entirety: "Thank you all for coming. I have jush two thimgs to shay: Firsht, the world is, yes indeedy, round. And shecond, everyshing is for shale. More champagne!" I then stepped off of *Julia*, and as is customary, knelt down and kissed the dock. Applause exploded, followed by hugs to spare, and that afternoon the party swelled in size to a blowout bash.

By the next day, the space aboard seemed a lot smaller than it had on the trip, and we immediately went apartment hunting. Sailing is one thing but living aboard in the marina suddenly wasn't so appealing. We signed a lease on a two-bedroom apartment within walking distance of the boat. It has two things we have wanted for years: walk-in closets and a huge refrigerator/freezer with an icemaker in the door.

Personal Journal / August 9, 2007 / Thank You

Two days ashore, and I'm reflecting on my friends, family, and new acquaintances around the world, and what they meant to this voyage. To Ken, Patrik, and every other crew member who sailed with us, I am endlessly grateful. And to all those who assisted us, including the mechanics, riggers and yard workers, you, too, have helped make this adventure such an amazing experience. I couldn't have done this without Bob so thoroughly handling my personal affairs, and Bill for his tireless advice and expertise. To our friends and families who sent encouragement and support through your emails and calls, I thank you from the bottom of my heart. Last but by no means least, my love and eternal gratitude to my mother, Julia. We're home, and we're glad to be here.

Email / August 20, 2007

After sailing a total of 40,455 nautical miles and visiting 40 countries, we have settled back in the Bay Area. Our apartment overlooks a courtyard with no ocean view and that suits us just fine. Yesterday, we had cable TV installed and I was amazed: How does anyone get anything done if they watch all of those channels? The phone company hooked up our landline telephone (now *that* sounds strange to me), and we are moving in furniture like college kids. For the first time in six years, I even have a keychain with car, house, mailbox, and marina keys—amazing. Yesterday I honked at my first person for driving too slowly. Ha. Maybe my worries about re-entering were unwarranted?

Aboard *Julia*, all of the instruments are off, the watermaker is pickled, and all is very, very quiet. The silence is eerie as I sit aboard in the captain's chair and think of all of the excitement that took place here over the great voyage. I must admit I'm sad it's over, but it is. Time to move on to another new chapter in my life. I've learned a lot on this trip, including the fact that all passages, good and bad, come to an end. *It's true. The journey is the destination.*

Personal Journal / September 24, 2007

Today I was sitting by the pool at our apartment building, having swum a measly 400 yards and panting out of breath like an old man. Then I looked down at my stomach and wondered, "Who is this person"? I watched a plane fly overhead and was transported to my life a long time ago, when I was dressed in a suit traveling to business appointments. I was working hard, smart, and had big goals, which kept me going. Those 20 years were an entire lifetime.

Then I achieved my lifetime goal: sailing all the way around the world...wow. And those six years were an entire lifetime.

Now I'm a bit lost. I don't have a goal, don't have any dreams, and like succumbing to some form of post-voyage depression, I'm wondering, what am I doing? I've been burying myself in trying to clean stuff off the boat to get it ready for sale, but that's incidental. Ken goes to work each day at the I.T. job he landed within a few days of our return. While I'm busy doing things like house cleaning, shopping, attempting to write, and getting our apartment set up, I'm not really accomplishing anything because I don't really have a goal yet.

I wonder how many other people go through their lives each day having a dream but not living it.

Email / September 27, 2007 / I Don't See the Night Anymore

Many people have asked, "Aren't you sad to be home? Don't you miss those far away places? How does it feel to be stuck here again?" I like being home. While traveling around the world, we did look for other places to settle and a few were seriously considered: Auckland, Sydney, Tel Aviv, Lausanne, Amsterdam, and Barcelona. We rented apartments in London, Paris, and Amsterdam and had lots of fun living in those cities as if they were our homes. On our way around the world, we happen to now have landed in San Francisco, a place that ranks high on the list.

The other night, I awoke at 2 am and got up to raid the refrigerator. On my short walk to the kitchen, I noticed a big bright light coming into the apartment, and looked out to see the full moon shining in a clear warm sky. I stopped in my tracks and was reminded of the many moonlit nights I saw when we were very aware of the night. At sea, and even at anchor, I awoke several times a night, got up to check on things, and saw the night—moonlit or dark—but I saw the night. Living in our apartment, I go to sleep in the evening, awake in the daylight, and I don't see the night anymore. It's one of the things I've noticed in the transition from sea to land…it's a *big* adjustment.

The last six years have been about change. My life changed daily with events, locations, cultures, and experiences, and I've learned to better deal with it all. I like to think I'm more adaptable to new situations, and to accept what comes my way. Whether moving anchorages or revamping your career, you shouldn't be afraid of variety—it's just a new twist on the same old thing—life.

✉ **Email** / December 7, 2007 / One Last Anniversary

The milestones have long since been passed by…. A year since we did this, two years since we did that, and they tend to become meaningless and less important as time marches on. I'll just share one last anniversary with you: This one has a lot of meaning because it doesn't seem possible it's been this long and that it's over. Today marks the six-year anniversary of the day *Julia* sailed out the Golden Gate. I remember motoring out under the bridge in the cold early morning hours. We were dressed in foul-weather gear and racing to get south between storm fronts. I remember being afraid of what I didn't know, filled with trepidation, trying as captain, to show such confidence that what we were doing was right, and that everything was going to be fine. That day was happy, sad, scary, yet so exhilarating. I will never forget it.

Reviewing the trip, I'm starting to appreciate what we did is amazing in so many ways. We experienced storms, lightning, darkness, huge seas, arriving in strange lands, learned new customs, assimilated new cultures, lived through bruises (to our bodies and to our egos), were humbled by the sea, learned how to stay safe at sea, how to fix things, overcame countless equipment failures, and most of all, we learned to *overcome the fear of those things.* Somehow, I still found the strength to keep going.

There are many reasons people don't follow through and make their dreams reality. Fear of change is probably the most significant. You have to want more than *good.* You have to want *great.*

Then there are those with my problem: the fear that once your dream is fulfilled, it will all be over, and then what? What are we without our dreams? What guides us? What keeps us going? I find myself asking, "What's next for me; what will keep me going?"

Email / June 30, 2008 / Farewell, *Julia*
They say the happiest days in a sailor's life is the day you buy and the day you sell your boat. I understand the part about being happy buying *Julia,* but I don't agree about the moment when I sold her. Yesterday was a sad day as I signed over the papers to Tim and Ruth, *Julia's* new owners. They renamed her *Kamaya,* after their children, and are headed to the South Pacific. I walked away from her with sadness, appreciation, and relief, knowing this was the closing of an era. "Do you promise to take good care of her," I asked the buyers? "Otherwise you can't have her." They could tell I was pretty worked up about letting go of *Julia.*

"We promise," Tim said.

I didn't look back as I walked up the gangway.

Julia was much more to me than a boat. She was my home for six years, in other words, more than one-eighth of my life. She was my oasis in foreign lands, she was my purpose, direction, dream-fulfiller, and she carried my crew and me safely all the way around the world.

I'm also relieved I can pay off the boat mortgage, and now when something breaks, it will be the new owner's problem.

For now, my ocean sailing days are done, and *Julia* will no longer be part of my life. I remember the day she showed up on the delivery truck, looking up thinking, "Oh, my God, what have I gotten into now?!"

I also sweetly remember the naming ceremony and how my mother,

Julia, was bowled over when she saw her name painted on the side of the boat. I remember staring at this boat that had just carried me across the Pacific Ocean, as she lay at anchor in the serene waters of a South Pacific lagoon, and thinking, *she is so beautiful*. And I recall when we were pounding through the gale in the Red Sea, thanking her for being so well built. I reflect on that instant when we struck a rock in Mykonos and worrying we were going to lose her. I remember what a wonderful home she was. I have lost a good friend. Farewell, *Julia*. You will live in my heart forever.

Final Notes / August 2010

It's been three years since *Julia* sailed back under the Golden Gate Bridge, and I'm amazed at how time flies. I am also a bit confused by my reintegration into U.S. society, as I still don't quite feel like I'm back, or at ease. Sometimes, I get the feeling it's time to haul anchor and move to the next port.

I have my California license to sell yachts and the first boat I sold was, indeed, *Julia*.

Julia, my mom, is 88 years young and doing very well. While she is proud of what I achieved, I know she's glad I'm home again.

Ken has seamlessly slipped back into life as a computer engineer and is working on furthering his education in the world of high-tech. We are getting along great and enjoying our lives together. Our shared experience has created an incredibly strong bond.

Bob is one of my best friends and we are closer than ever.

My blood pressure and arrhythmia are under complete control with medicines, and my heart scan shows zero cholesterol buildup. I ride my bike, practice yoga, eat well, drink little, and have lost over 25 pounds since our return.

Stephanie, my friend and former client, stricken with cancer, didn't make it. She passed away and I was honored to speak at her funeral about the journey of life. I know a little bit more about that now....

Ken and I returned as changed men, both as a couple and as individuals. We tested the strength of our relationship and are better people for it. Nothing is the same, as our perspective has also changed. We had to discover for ourselves that the truly important things in life are not sold in stores. We don't quite fit in like before and are learning to accept that.

We continue to work on our reintegration process, and ask forgiveness for perhaps too much storytelling and living in past anchorages.

Recently, I walked over to the marina and bid farewell to some good friends going cruising. It was Biagio, the guy who taught me how to use a beer can as a shim so many years ago in Tonga. He returned from cruising and is heading out again. I couldn't hold my tears as I watched his boat disappear toward the horizon. I was excited for him but sad, too. Were my tears because he was leaving…or because I'm staying? Both, I think. Maybe one of these days, I'll chuck it all and head back out to sea… because sometimes I wonder if that's where I truly belong.

Afterword

Nobody died onboard *Julia* during her journey around the world. Nor did anyone lose a limb or get seriously injured. We watched the weather, learned to read weather charts, and while sometimes caught in surprise storms, were never trapped in a hurricane. We studied navigational charts carefully, and while we made errors, we were meticulous in plotting our course. We were never attacked by pirates, robbed, or even boarded by any coast guard or military from any country.

Our fresh water supply was always full, the spare parts bin for anticipated repairs at sea overflowed, the spare oil and fuel were always abundant, food supplies were in every spare nook and cranny, and we always maintained our radios, engines, and other systems in the best working order possible. There still were a large number of breakdowns but learning to manage them was a daily part of cruising, as well as a valuable learning experience.

Recently, a friend asked me, "Nobody died? Didn't you mess up and have anything really bad happen to you or to the boat? Tell me something *horrible*." He was hoping for some kind of heart-stopping disaster.

"Sorry, nothing that bad happened to us...except maybe having to return," I said.

Were we frightened? Absolutely. Was there danger? Yes, often. Even so, we were willing to take the risks and made it all the way around the world unscathed, returning as better people for having made the journey. Does headline news have to be only about disasters? Or can it be about tenacity, motivation, and bettering lives?

With good planning and grace, we did it right. This is a book about good times, surviving rough times, coming out stronger from the test of our strength, and finding what is truly important in life. What I hope you glean from our experience is that you can do it too. That goes for anything you want to do. You can make your dream come true, drama free. Plan ahead, untie your lines—whatever they may be—and get out of here. *"Go, man! Go!"*

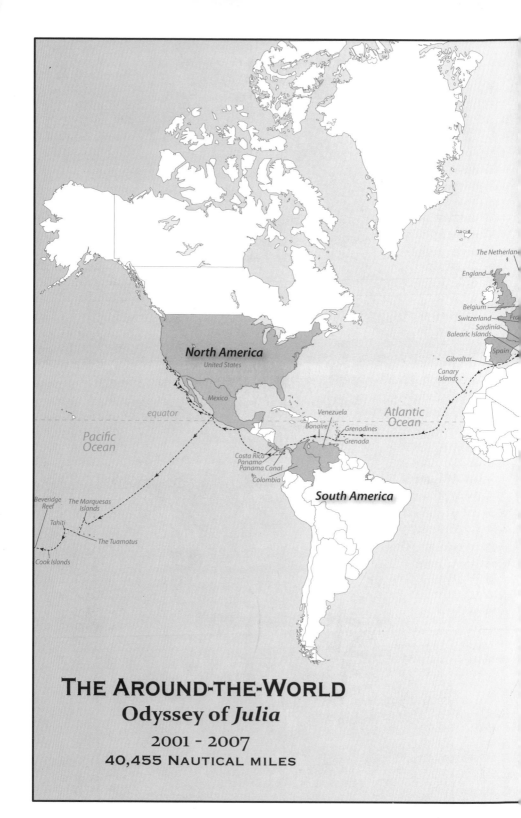

THE AROUND-THE-WORLD
Odyssey of *Julia*
2001 - 2007
40,455 NAUTICAL MILES